**Gift of
Richard Hathaway**

MAJESTIC
FAILURE

MAJESTIC FAILURE

The Fall of the Shah

Marvin Zonis

The University of Chicago Press

Chicago and London

Marvin Zonis is professor in the Graduate School of Business and the
Department of Psychology at the University of Chicago.

The University of Chicago Press, Chicago 60637
The University of Chicago Press, Ltd., London
© 1991 by The University of Chicago
All rights reserved. Published 1991
Printed in the United States of America

00 99 98 97 96 95 94 93 92 91   5 4 3 2 1

Library of Congress Cataloging in Publication Data
Zonis, Marvin, 1936–
    Majestic failure : the fall of the Shah / Marvin Zonis.
        p.   cm.
    Includes bibliographical references and index.
    ISBN 0-226-98928-3 (acid-free paper).
    1. Mohammed Reza Pahlavi, Shah of Iran, 1919–   . 2. Iran—Kings
and rulers—Biography. 3. Iran—Politics and government—1941–
1979. I. Title.
DS318.M593Z66   1991
955.05′3′092—dc20
[B]   90-46355
                                                          CIP

⊗ The paper used in this publication meets the minimum requirements
of the American National Standard for Information Sciences—Permanence of Paper for Printed Library Materials, ANSI Z39.48-1984.

And yet, in spite of all the advantages of time, place and circumstance that a revolutionary movement may enjoy, in our day, because of our huge standing armies and pecuniary resources and the instruments of warfare that only constituted powers are in a position to procure, no government can be overthrown by force unless the men who are in charge of it are themselves irresolute or lose their heads, or at least unless they are paralyzed by dread of assuming responsibility for a repression involving bloodshed. Eleventh-hour concessions, last-minute orders and counterorders, the falterings of those who hold legal power and are morally bound to use it—these are the real and most effective factors in the success of a revolution.

—Gaetano Mosca, *The Ruling Class*

Contents

	Acknowledgments	ix
	Introduction	1
1	Flying Fantasies and Narcissistic Grandiosity	7
2	Childhood and Youth	23
3	Imperial Grandeur: Pahlavi Grandiosity	61
4	Cracking the Shah's Authority	84
5	The Strength of Others	115
6	Cancer: The Failure of Divine Protection	150
7	Xenophobia and Emulation: The Iranian People, the Shah, and the West	166
8	Dependence on the United States	207
9	Revolution and Collapse	240
10	Lessons for U.S. Foreign Policy	258
	Notes	273
	Bibliography	335
	Index	343

Acknowledgments

Many significant obligations were incurred in completing the lengthy project which resulted in this book. More than one hundred individuals—Iranians as well as foreigners—were interviewed as the principal sources of data for the interpretations made here. They were offered the promise of confidentiality, a pledge I respect at the expense of being unable personally to thank them here for the knowledge and insight they so generously shared with me.

Many others made major contributions to this work as well. Bert Cohler, professor of human development at the University of Chicago, proposed important theoretical formulations early in the formation of my ideas. Sol Altschul, M.D., of the Institute for Psychoanalysis, Chicago, has been an important source of support. Jerrold Post, M.D., professor of psychiatry at George Washington University, has been a major intellectual and emotional contributor as well.

Prof. Michael Fischer of the Department of Anthropology at Rice University has been a long-time intellectual compatriot and provided many stimulating ideas about Iran. So has Said Arjomand, professor of Sociology at the State University of New York at Stonybrook. Both made useful and generous comments on this manuscript. Prof. Jerrold Green of the Political Science Department of the University of Arizona has been a stimulus to my thinking as have Karim Pakravan, Ph.D., of the First National Bank of Chicago and Steve Heydemann, Ph.D., of the Social Science Research Council. Daniel Brumberg of the Department of Political Science at Chicago has been a major source of inspiration and an impeccable ally in the struggle to make this manuscript work.

Jill Swenson of the School of Communications at the University of Georgia, Athens, has provided major assistance. So did Spencer Downing, who provided generous service in the arduous task of clarifying the references. Stephen L. Gessner was a wise counselor and a careful reader. David Murrell, thankfully, prepared the index. Over the years, many others to whom I am most grateful have helped as well.

Financial assistance for the manuscript was provided by the Joint Committee on the Near and Middle East of the American Council of Learned Societies and the Social Science Research Council. I greatly respect and admire its former staff director, Rowland L. Mitchell, Ph.D.

The other key actors in the completion of this book have been those whose emotional support and usual tolerance for my absorptions have been a source of strength as well as comfort. To my wife and my children, my deepest appreciation.

Introduction

The fall of the Shah of Iran must be counted as one of the major political events of modern history. The most powerful of the world's reigning monarchs, the major voice in the crucial Organization of Petroleum Exporting Countries, and a staunch political and military ally of the United States and the West lost his throne and his dynasty when he left his country in January of 1979. Throughout the preceding year, the Iranian people had become ever more unified and ever more strident in their demands for fundamental political change and, in the fall of 1978, ever more insistent in their demand that the Shah be overthrown. Simultaneously, they ever more vociferously called for the return to Iran of an aged, exiled religious leader, Ayatollah Rouhollah al-Mousavi al-Khomeini, and the establishment of a republic with the cleric as its spiritual head.

The demonstrations against the Shah culminated in massive opposition parades on December 10 and 11, 1978, the most holy days of the Islamic Shi'ite calendar. Over one million Iranians took to the streets each day to chant their insistence on the ouster, if not the death, of the Shah.

Within weeks their demands were met as the Shah, joined by his wife, Empress Farah Pahlavi, and a few key officials, boarded a plane for what he hoped might be but a brief stay abroad. But his departure was followed by the rapid unraveling of the system he had constructed over his thirty-seven years as Shahanshah, the King of Kings.

In short order, Ayatollah Khomeini returned to Iran after more than fourteen years in exile. The Imperial Guards, the elite military corps so carefully selected and trained to protect the Shah, fought briefly to save his throne, but quickly gave up the fight and returned to their barracks. And the Shah's last prime minister, Shahpour Bakhtiar, whom he had drawn from the ranks of his secular opposition desperately late in the revolution,

1

went into hiding. By the end of February 1979, the Pahlavi dynasty was finished as Ayatollah Khomeini authorized the establishment of a new government under the direction of Mehdi Bazargan, a longtime opposition leader with strong ties to the Islamic clergy.

Watching, from his exile, the disintegration of the political order he had so arduously created, the Shah sank deeper into despondency. His cancer, which had been diagnosed years before but kept a tightly guarded secret of state, became virulent. In August of 1980 he died, universally shunned, in the words of Henry Kissinger, "a flying Dutchman looking for a port."[1]

Events in Iran since then have become nearly standard media fare throughout the world. The captured U.S. diplomats and the failed attempt to rescue them, what appeared an endless war with Iraq, the Iran-Contra arms deals and hearings, the U.S. naval patrols of the Persian Gulf and the military engagements with the Iranian navy, the assassination and executions of government officials and opposition figures within Iran, and Iranian links to terrorism—and to the Western hostages held captive in Lebanon by terrorist groups linked to Iran—have kept Iran and the now late Ayatollah Khomeini and his successors in the news.

This book does not deal with those more recent events, however significant they may be. It looks, instead, at their precursors—the Iranian Revolution and the fall of the Shah. It focuses its attention on the Shah himself. For this book is based on a central premise—that the people of Iran, who by the end of 1978 had become virtually united in their opposition to the Shah, did not so much "win" the revolution as the Shah "lost" it. That is, the Shah's failures to deal effectively with his mounting opposition before and throughout 1978 resulted, not long thereafter, in his overthrow. There was nothing inevitable about the revolution. Neither its timing nor its outcome was ordained.

It is possible to imagine many other histories for Iran. The Shah might have met the objections of key sectors of his opposition by instituting meaningful democratic reform long before 1978. Once demonstrations did occur, he might have met their demands and headed off, at least temporarily, his dire fate. Later in 1978, as the demonstrations became a revolution, he might have kept himself in power through a major military crackdown. But he did none of these. More accurately, he did each of them, but only halfheartedly and ineffectively. He never took significant steps to broaden the base of his regime, nor did he mobilize his impressive security forces to quash the mounting opposition. All these failures—to act and to act decisively—can be explained through an examination of the character of the Shah himself. Moreover, this book argues that the character of the Shah and his style of rule which was based on that character were responsible, to begin with, for the opposition to him. Throughout his tenure as monarch, he had faced both domestic and foreign political enemies. But the revolution of 1978, in which the entire Iranian people had become his enemy, was entirely unprecedented. It occurred because throughout the 1970s and much of the decade preceding, the Shah had acted in ways which convinced ever-increasing numbers of his own people that he was unsuitable to be their ruler, that his claim to the throne had become illegitimate.

In short, what he did do and what he failed to do brought about his downfall. And what he did and did not do can be understood through an examination of his character, the kind of person he was, the goals he set for himself, and the life course he pursued.

These matters are understood in this work through a psychological framework. There is a long tradition of psychological studies of great men,[2] of leaders,[3] of historical processes,[4] and of political events.[5] This book stands squarely in that tradition. But to acknowledge its intellectual roots is neither to celebrate the theoretical or methodological foundations of its precursors nor to share their occasionally unbridled enthusiasm for that genre which has come to be labeled, grossly, as "psychohistory." To acknowledge a common heritage and a resulting "family resemblance" is done here in the service of speaking to the frequently all-too-obvious shortcomings of the genre. The literature critical of psychohistory is nearly as voluminous as that which it criticizes.[6] This work attempts to respond to those criticisms, while seeking to demonstrate that there is utility in this way of approaching a wide array of historical and political phenomena. But this work attempts one additional task. It seeks to assess the lessons of the "Iranian debacle" for U.S. foreign policy.[7]

The United States was a key actor in domestic Iranian politics. The stairs of the former U.S. embassy in Tehran, which the present regime has branded "the nest of spies" and appropriated for the use of the "students in the line of the Imam," had a series of framed photographs on the wall. They showed the Shah meeting with each U.S. president who served while the Shah did his kingly business. Franklin Delano Roosevelt, Harry S. Truman, Dwight D. Eisenhower, John F. Kennedy, Lyndon B. Johnson, Richard M. Nixon, Gerald Ford, and Jimmy Carter each posed for a portrait with the Shah. Collectively, they forged a relationship that brought Iran into an ever closer link with American policy and that resulted in the

United States becoming central to the political process of Iran. Over those years, the United States became not only Iran's principal arms supplier and trade partner and the cultural ideal by which the Shah and his political elite sought to reorient their society, but the United States—through its presidents, ambassadors, other key officials, businessmen, and even its intellectuals—became a central player in the game of Iranian politics.

Through its intense involvement with the Shah and his system, the United States carried significant responsibility for the fate of his regime. But as the revolution engulfed his country and then his throne, the United States did not act as if it were responsible for the regime or as if it understood the nature of that responsibility. And with his collapse, the United States suffered a major foreign policy defeat whose consequences for Iran, for the region, for the so-called Islamic world, and, indeed, for the global balance of power are still unfolding. Yet the lessons of that defeat have still not been properly assessed. What the Iranian Revolution has to tell the United States about the goals it seeks abroad and the ways it seeks to reach those goals has not yet been sufficiently noted, interpreted, and translated into a foreign policy. To do so would alter the ways in which the United States conducts its foreign policy, for such analysis would alter the goals sought and the means by which the United States' foreign interests are advanced.

In short, there is much value in understanding the Iranian Revolution. The nearly breathtaking rapidity with which it unfolded and the shattering consequences of its major events have earned for it a central place in the history of this century, in the history of revolutions, and, if properly interpreted, in the history of U.S. foreign policy.

Before that understanding can be reached, an analysis of the revolution itself is needed. To do so here, a psychological model of the political process in Iran under the Shah has been constructed. The model reduces the complexities of Iranian politics to the Shah, the people of Iran, and to their relationships, while appreciating the violations of history which such reduction entails. The Shah was, unquestionably, the key figure in Iran for many years before the revolution, but he was not the only important political actor. A variety of others played significant roles over time, their importance increasing or diminishing with the vagaries of the Shah's moods and the larger realities of Iranian politics. His third wife, Empress Farah, became a more important player over time. His twin sister, Princess Ashraf, was gradually removed from domestic politics, serving instead as Iran's representative to a variety of United Nations agencies and conferences. But she left behind an important network of supporters in a variety of government bureaucracies through whom she tried to work her will. Two civilian politicians were especially important. Amir Abbas Hoveyda served as prime minister during 1965–78, longer than any other in Iranian history. During those years, the crucial precursors of the revolution, the Shah increasingly withdrew from day-to-day control of Iranian politics, leaving his prime minister with greater power. Assadollah Alam, Hoveyda's predecessor as prime minister and then minister of court during 1965–77, was, more than any other figure, personally closer to the Shah, having been a boyhood friend. They remained close until Alam's death from leukemia in the year before the outbreak of the revolution.

Others were important as well, not so much because of who they were but because of the roles they played. The directors of SAVAK, the State Security and Intelligence Organization, changed periodically. Each was crucial to the Shah. So it was with other key Iranian figures. And so it was with various U.S. ambassadors, dispatched by those eight U.S. presidents. They not only served as key intermediaries, but became, if not exactly confidants of the Shah, then at least important sounding boards. He would frequently try out his latest scheme during the regular audiences he granted them. And he listened very closely to their comments in reaching decisions about his policies.

Besides these figures there were others who were significant before and during the revolution. Secular opposition leaders kept alive the Mossadegh legacy of an independent democratic Iran. Religious leaders in Iran and Iraq—Ayatollah Khomeini, certainly, but other senior clerics such as Ayatollah Kazem Shari'at-madari of Qom—continued to propound visions other than a Pahlavi autocracy and to train students to enter the clerical ranks and maintain a variety of Islamic organizations which were to play crucial organizational roles during the revolution. During the 1970s, a radically politicized cadre of young people formed guerrilla organizations which sought to mobilize the Iranian people and overthrow the regime by force. A much larger segment of Iran's youth became committed participants—some more, some less—within the Pahlavi system itself. They came to occupy increasingly powerful positions in the burgeoning state bureaucracies. Other sat out public life in favor of Iran's vibrant economy, working in what had previously been the less prestigious private sector newly energized by the staggering boost in Iran's oil revenues. And there were, of course, the millions of Iranians, especially in Tehran, but in other major cities as well, who raised their families and kept their jobs to do so, whose mobilization to action during the revolution was to prove the decisive factor in bringing down the Shah.

While appreciating, in short, the complexity of Iran's politics and the vast numbers whose actions and inactions eventually brought about the collapse of the regime, this study focuses on the Shah. For, ultimately, he was the Shah. How he went about being Shah and doing Shah was by far the most important factor in the creation of his regime and in its unraveling.

Attention is also paid to the effects of his rule on different sectors of the Iranian people. But except on infrequent occasions, it will suffice, for the purposes of this work, to treat the Shah and the Iranian people as an undifferentiated pair, linked in a dialectic of initiative and response, response and initiative. Such an approach fails to respect the richness with which Iranians evaluated the Shah and his system or the diversity of their responses, but it does capture the reality of Iran as the revolution accelerated to its conclusion. By then, the people of Iran were virtually united in seeking drastic changes.

Never at a loss for humor, Iranians circulated a joke during the most violent and uncertain phase of the revolution. The chairman of the Communist party of the Peoples Republic of China, Hua Kuo-feng, had recently paid an official state visit to Iran—what was to be the Shah's last visit from a chief of state. The joke had it that in their private meetings, the Shah asked an unusual question of his visitor.

"Tell me," the Shah inquired, "is there any opposition to your rule in China?"

"Why yes, there is," Chairman Hua replied.

"Tell me," the Shah continued, "how large is the opposition?"

"Well," Hua responded, "I suppose there might be thirty-five million or so who object to the rule of the Communist party."

"Fascinating, just fascinating," mused the Shah, "that's precisely the size of the opposition to my rule."

The joke, of course, was that thirty-five million was also the size of the entire population of Iran. The joke captured the truth that as its end approached, the revolution had swept up the entire population of Iran as opposition, or, at best, as sullen and confused bystanders. The Shah was alone. He once had had all the cards—the power, the money, the foreign support—that ensure the rule of even the least popular of rulers. But in the 1970s he lost them all. How that came to be is what this book is about.

1

Flying Fantasies and
Narcissistic Grandiosity

In May of 1972, President Richard Nixon and his secretary of state, Henry Kissinger, made official visits to the Soviet Union and Poland. In between, they flew to Tehran. During that visit they promised the Shah he could buy any U.S. non-nuclear weapons system. The Shah moved quickly to take advantage of the possibility for expanding his armed forces without having to face the rigors of investigation by either the Defense Department or congressional committees. His orders for billions of dollars of arms were not long in coming. Iran became the United States' best customer for military hardware. It has even been suggested that the Shah's role in the OPEC oil price increases of late 1973 and early 1974 was motivated primarily by his need for more revenues to pay for what had by then become his startlingly high arms bills.

While the Shah moved rapidly to raise his oil revenues and expand all the branches of his armed forces, it was the air force that received his special attention and the lion's share of Iran's funds. In the typically measured, understated language of a U.S. Senate committee:

The Iranian Air Force is said to be the pride and joy of the Shah. Of the three services, the Air Force has received the bulk of the funds available for modernization in recent years and is the most technologically advanced. In fact, the IIAF [Imperial Iranian Air Force] inventory will be one of the most modern in the world, including the F-14A with the Phoenix missile system, F-4E, F-4D, RF-4, F-5E, P-3F, and C-130H aircraft.[1]

The Senate report made it clear that the future of the Iranian Air Force was to be even more bright, for the Shah had still more ambitious plans.

The Iranian Government is considering the purchase of additional fighter, attack, and special purpose aircraft. Although no decisions have been made, the Iranian Government is reported to be considering a buy of 250 to 300 of either the F-16 or F-18 fighter aircraft, from 2 to 6 AWACs, additional 747 aircraft, between 4 and 10 E-2C "Hawkeye" electronically equipped aircraft and 12 HH-53 long range search and rescue helicopters.[2]

The Senate report acknowledged that to attribute Iran's aviation purchases to the Iranian government is a misstatement of the facts. It was the Shah who decided what and how much had to be bought.

The defense decision making process in Iran is relatively simple. The Shah decides on all major purchases; his Vice Minister of War, Air Force General Hassan Toufanian, implements these decisions. The Shah is very knowledgeable about modern weapons technology: it has been said that he reads *Aviation Week* before he reads the Iranian press. He possesses enough expertise which if combined with his power as supreme ruler of Iran is sufficient to dampen even the most professional opposition to his procurement plans.[3]

The massive expansion of Iran's armed forces in general and its air force in particular was not the result of deliberations by military or strategic planning bodies within or without the armed forces. The decisions were by royal prerogatives—made solely by the Shah.[4] To those who knew his personal history, it was not surprising that the air force should become his special favorite among the armed forces. For during his entire life he was fascinated by everything that related to the air force and, more generally, to everything that related or stood for airplanes and flying.

Flying, in fact, was a passion for the Shah. Two days before his twenty-seventh birthday, on October 17, 1946, he acquired his "wings" after "18 hours, 19 minutes flying time and 271 landings."[5] Immediately the Shah set about re-creating the Iranian air force. It had been established originally by his father in 1922 as the "Air Office" in army headquarters. By the time of the British-Russian invasion of Iran in 1941, Reza Shah had built his Air Office into the Imperial Iranian Air Force and established four air regiments based in Tehran, Tabriz, Meshed, and Ahwaz. The allied invasion and occupation, however, led to the diversion of Iran's limited resources from its armed forces and the partial dismemberment of Iran's fledgling air arm.

With the withdrawal of British and American occupying troops in 1945, the Shah immediately took "an active interest in the development of the IIAF, which between 1945 and 1947 acquired 34 Hurricane IIC fighter bombers and two-seat trainers."[6] This "active interest" was, as we have seen, to last the rest of the Shah's life. Moreover, his active interest in the

IIAF was only one aspect of a broader passion which manifested itself in diverse ways in a variety of areas of his life.

While the British and Americans withdrew from Iran after World War II, within the time limits specified in the occupying agreements with Iran, the Soviets stayed on. Soviet troops supported the creation of two "autonomous republics" within their zone of occupation. Iranian politicians launched aggressive negotiations with the Soviets, and with strong American support they brought the Azerbaijan case to the U.N. Security Council—its first dispute. Their efforts succeeded. On May 9, 1946, the Soviets evacuated Iranian territory, leaving their political protectorates to fend for themselves.

After it became clear that the Soviets would not reinvade Iran to salvage those protectorates, the Shah led Iranian troops to Azerbaijan to rout the separatists and reassert central control.[7] Of significance here is that the Shah led his troops to Azerbaijan in December of 1946, two months after he received his "wings," his authorization to fly. It would be both grossly simplistic and psychologistic to make too much of this single sequence, to argue that the Shah's "wings" gave him the personal strength and courage to lead his troops to "victory" (although virtually no shots were ever fired). The Shah's victory depended, of course, on the results of months of negotiations and U.S. signals and messages to the Soviet Union.[8] But while objectively an Iranian victory was palpable, its realization required the Shah's leadership. His exercise of that leadership was eased by the strength and courage which his mastery of flying had given him. This early connection between flying and courage and strength—the Shah was still in his twenties—was to be repeated both literally and figuratively for the next three decades of his reign.

Students of Iran rarely allude to the year 1948 as significant for either the country or the Shah. Yet 1948 appears to be a year in which the connection between his courage and personal strength and flying was consolidated. A variety of events during that retrospectively fateful year suggests such a consolidation. Of major significance was an airplane crash which occurred with the Shah at the controls of a single-engine plane. Accompanied by the general in charge of the armed forces in Isfahan, the Shah took off to inspect the site of a new irrigation dam. Some ten minutes after takeoff, the engine went dead. In his autobiography, *Mission for My Country,* the Shah describes what happened:

We had to make a forced landing on a mountainous region in a ravine full of rocks and boulders. . . . With the engine gone I had no throttle, nor could I manoeuver within the narrow confines of the ravine, the only thing was to maintain my speed by going down then and there. Just before we struck, I pulled on the stick to raise the plane's nose and avert a head-on collision with a barrier of rock lying directly in front of us. The plane had barely enough speed left to clear the barriers, and could not surmount a big stone lying just beyond. When we collided with it the undercarriage was completely torn off. . . . The plane started to slide on its belly over the rock strewn ground. A moment later the propeller hit a large boulder, and the plane turned a slow and deliberate somersault, coming to a halt with the fuselage upside down. There we were, hanging by our seat belts in the open cockpit. Neither of us had suffered so much as a scratch. I remember that scene amused me so much that I burst out laughing, but my upside down companion didn't think it was funny.[9]

It seems plausible that the Shah did not think it funny either but "burst out laughing" from the relief of an "unscratched" survival. The Shah, in fact, recounts the tale to explain how his childhood belief that he was protected by God was buttressed by events of his adult life.[10] The Shah noted that, in his childhood, "God saved me from dangers and perils."[11] The Shah's survival of the crash showed him that God's protection was still forthcoming, and this protection would strengthen the Shah through much of his rule. Of more immediate relevance here is the effect of the crash in consolidating for the Shah the link between flying and strength and courage. While flying had already begun to assume significant personal meanings for the Shah—meanings beyond flying as a means of transportation or airplanes as a source of armed security—the crash appears to have enshrined those meanings for him. For the rest of his life, flying and its diverse representations would remain the principal manifestations of his grandiosity.

Another event in 1948 demonstrates that link between flying and the Shah's psychic makeup. In that year the Shah saw his first World War II B-17. It was parked at the Tehran airport and used by Trans World Airlines to transport cargo. Apparently it was love at first sight, and TWA offered him the services of one of their senior pilots to teach him how to fly the four-engine machine. At the very first lesson,

the Shah took the controls. The takeoff was rather bumpy—normal for a first attempt—but as they reached cruising speed the Shah began to fly the B-17 as if it were a fighter. He would dive toward the mountains and pull out just in the nick of time, then weave back and forth through the valleys. Hoping to teach the Shah a lesson, the pilot remarked that he might have even more fun with one of the engines cut. He cut the outside left engine but, undeterred, the Shah continued his tricks on three engines. The pilot said nothing. Finally, they headed back to Tehran. The Shah fouled up his landing approach and had to pull back up. The pilot inquired how he proposed to make his approach this time. The Shah replied, laughing, that he had no idea; he had never landed a B-17 before.

The next try was successful. The Shah bought the B-17, but the pilot emphatically refused to give him another lesson.[12]

Other events in 1948 demonstrated both the Shah's newly won courage and his deepening commitment to the air force. In 1948 the Shah formally took action on his dismal marriage with Princess Fawzia, sister of King Farouk of Egypt. That marriage had been arranged by Reza Shah for the Crown Prince in 1938, a decision made without the participation of the young—not yet twenty—groom to be.[13] From all accounts, the marriage was unhappy from the start. Fawzia, after all, was an outsider, an Arab who spoke no Persian. She, in turn, apparently viewed Iranians as quasi-barbarians, no match for the cosmopolitan sophistication of the Egyptians, and she saw the Iranian royal family as, at best, upstarts.[14] Fawzia was despondent in primitive occupied Tehran, and neither the Shah's mother nor his sisters made life easy for the new female of the court. As the Shah puts it, "Perhaps the happiest point in that marriage was the birth in 1940 of my beloved daughter, the Princess Shahnaz."[15] Certainly there is no indication that any happiness was forthcoming directly from the marriage itself. Yet it was not until 1948, the year of personal consolidation, that the Shah was able to bring himself to divorce Fawzia.

Two other events of 1948 are examples of the growing significance for the Shah of the air force. In May of that year he dispatched the first group of air force personnel to the United States for training, thus linking Iran to the powerful United States. Then in July of 1948 the Shah made his first foreign visit since assuming the throne in 1941. He traveled to England to attend the 1948 summer Olympics. The *Times of London* reported that the Shah arrived "in the uniform of Marshal of the Iranian Air Force."[16] Considering the ragtag collection of dated planes which then made up the Imperial Iranian Air Force, that uniform spoke not to its military power but rather to the power which the air force symbolized for the Shah personally and, as a result, to his future intentions to create an air force whose actual capabilities matched its symbolic power. As we have seen above, the Shah had achieved this goal by the time of his flight from Iran in 1979.

As would be expected, following the Shah's 1948 mental consolidation of the connection between flying and earthly success and divine protection, the air force and its symbolic representations came to play an increasingly significant role for him. An amazing variety of examples could be cited to demonstrate the connection. A few will provide additional flavor for the nature of this lifelong relationship.

After his 1948 divorce from Princess Fawzia, the Shah played eligible bachelor, even maintaining apartments in Tehran so that he might privately entertain young women. Airline stewardesses were reportedly his favorites.[17] Yet from a variety of sources within and without the court, the pressure was on the Shah to remarry. His first marriage had produced no male child, and succession to the throne was in doubt. Accordingly, the Shah's sisters undertook the responsibility of finding a suitable match. His older sister, Princess Shams, discovered Soraya Bakhtiar in Europe, the daughter of an Iranian tribal chieftain and a German mother.

After extensive screening of Soraya, Princess Shams received the go-ahead and was told to bring Soraya to Tehran to meet the Shah. Soraya relates in her memoirs how she arrived in Tehran with Shams on October 7, 1950, to be rushed to dinner that same evening with the Queen Mother and all the Shah's brothers and sisters. After a good deal of family small talk, the Shah finally entered the room, "wearing his favorite uniform of the Iranian air force."[18] In those memoirs Queen Soraya mentions more than once how the Shah "loved" airplanes and flying, and how, through flying and driving sports cars, he would "portray himself as more brave and reckless than actually was true."[19]

Later, when Kim Roosevelt was setting up Operation Ajax, the 1953 U.S.-U.K. effort to overthrow Prime Minister Mossadegh, one of the most difficult parts of mounting the royal coup was recruiting the Shah himself to the plot. The Shah, "depressed and fearing betrayal, perhaps even from the Americans if things went wrong, refused to discharge Mossadegh."[20] It was only after the United States was able to assure the Shah that he and the coup plot had the full backing of the Imperial Iranian Air Force that he was willing (and I claim, was able) to join the ultimately successful coup.

His lifelong interest in flying is demonstrated in other ways. When the Shah's firstborn son reached thirteen, the Shah taught him to fly. Despite Empress Farah's concerns, the Shah "loved" to see Crown Prince Reza fly, assuring her that flying would "give the boy self-confidence and a chance to prove himself."[21] In the summer of 1978, in the midst of the revolution, the Shah sent his son for advanced jet pilot training to Lubbock Air Force Base in Texas.

The Shah's fascination with the air force, then, was manifest in a variety of areas—in his personal flying, in the expansion of Iran's military air force, but also in commercial aviation. He supported the dramatic expansion of Iran's civil air service from a local carrier to one with extensive international routes and a fleet of new jets.

When Iran's oil revenues exploded in 1974, the first foreign company the Shah tried to buy was Pan American Airways. After considerable negotiations, the Shah was rebuffed. His response was unusually candid and unusually revealing. He said he felt that he was treated "as a microbe invading some beautiful, immaculate thing."[22] The Shah's sensitivity to slights is demonstrated by how personally he took the failure of his efforts and the intensity of his hurt. To equate himself with a microbe, a germ, reflected a punishing lack of self-esteem. And to equate Pan American with "some beautiful immaculate thing" is further testimony to how important airplanes and flying had become for him.

The Shah demonstrated that point with other phrases as well. In his book written in exile from Khomeini's Iran, the Shah twice accused the West of wanting to "clip my wings."[23] This metaphor was apparently a favorite, especially in the last years of his life,[24] not surprising given his embrace of flying and his failures to hold the throne.

The Shah's fascination with flying is matched by a fascination with height. In his autobiography, the Shah tells of his earliest memories, the first of which is of Iran's highest mountain:

From my early years I do recall the beauty of the mountains of the mighty Elburz range which loomed above the city and have always inspired me. Looking out to the northeast on any clear day, I could see the majestic cone of Mount Demavand. That mountain, in the upper reaches eternally snow-clad, enraptured me; but of course I did not learn until some years later that Demavand, at some 18,600 feet, towers above any of the mountains of Europe (Mont Blanc included), and is about half as high again as Japan's famous Mount Fujiyama.[25]

The Shah then is not only "inspired" and "enraptured" by Iran's highest mountain, but he comes to see it as superior, because of its height, to the best that Europe and Japan can offer.

The Shah then goes on to the second of his earliest memories:

Another early memory is of the large and imposing figure of my father, who was then Minister of War, as he was driven to and from work each day in his carriage. Playing on words one could say that while the mountain moved me, my father, who at that time was about to become Prime Minister and then Shah, was in the process of moving mountains.[26]

Here the Shah links the size of his father with the impression that size helped make on the young boy. Undoubtedly Reza Shah was as towering a figure for the boy as was Mount Demavand. That concern for size, especially his own size, was to follow the Shah his whole life. A member of court circles in Iran recalled her first meeting with the Shah in 1951 or 1952, when the Shah was thirty-two or thirty-three years old. After she was presented and curtsied, the Shah blurted out, "Why, you're very tall." He then got up from his chair, told the young girl to turn around, and stood back to back with her to see whether she was taller than he was. Since then, stories of the Shah's own concern about his stature, and especially height, have become legion.

He is known to have worn elevator shoes and shoes with relatively high heels. One can also look in vain for a picture of the Shah standing side by side with Empress Farah, for that would show all too clearly that she was taller than he was. Instead, in formal picture after official pose, one or the other of them would be seated or the Shah would be standing on something to give him added height. Few couples have had more photographs taken standing on staircases—with the Shah, not surprisingly, on the upper step.

These lifelong fascinations with height, stature, and flying are clear. The personal meanings they had for the Shah need be inferred. But there is little doubt that all these concerns were of great personal significance to him. There are simply too many instances in too many periods of the Shah's life to attribute these fascinations, for example, to the beauty of Mount Demavand or to Iran's strategic defense needs. Mount Demavand, in fact, is beautiful, and Iran of course does have strategic defense needs. But there are clearly deeply held personal meanings, manifested over the Shah's entire life, surrounding his fascinations as well.

Psychoanalysts and psychologists have, in fact, frequently observed the combination of these very qualities. Freud first noted them; he was especially struck by flying dreams and assumed that they originated in the excitement the young child felt at being swung in the arms of adults.[27] Surprisingly, however, Freud himself did no direct psychoanalytic work on flying dreams, inasmuch as his own patients brought him no instances of such dreams.[28]

Substantial work on the personal meanings of flying fantasies and dreams began with the research of the American psychologist Henry Murray and has been continued by a number of psychoanalysts working in different theoretical paradigms. Through a careful study of one Harvard undergraduate, "Grope," Murray identified what he labeled an "American Icarus" and an "Icarus complex."[29] According to Jerome Weinberger and

James Muller, "Icarus was the son of Daedalus, the fabulous artificer who fashioned wings of wax and feathers to escape the island of the tyrant Minos. Elated by the thrill of flying, Icarus ignored his father's cautions and soared so high that the sun melted his wings and plunged him to death in the sea."[30] The experiences of the mythical Icarus, his needs to fly, to excel, to be the subject of admiration, captured, albeit in dramatic imagery, the more mundane experiences of Grope. Murray defined the three principal characteristics of Grope as "cynosural narcism" [sic], "ascensionism," and "the prospection [sic] of falling."

Murray defined "cynosural narcism" as "a craving for unsolicited attention and admiration, a desire to attract and enchant all eyes, like a star in the firmament."[31] Ascensionism referred to the "wish to overcome gravity, to stand erect, to grow tall, to dance on tiptoe, to walk on water, to leap or swing in the air, to climb, to rise, to fly, or to float down gradually from on high and land without injury."[32] The "prospection of falling" "denotes an undesired or accidental descension of something (usually a human body or the status . . . of a person, but it may be . . . any cathected object)."[33]

Murray shows how these three qualities are associated in the "imaginary activities" of Grope, his young Icarus, and how much they characterize his college days. In fact, most of his days were spent in apathy and withdrawal from college activities. Weeks and months passed with "Icarus" absorbed in daydreams and fantasies, existing at the margins of student life. Murray notes briefly, however, that Grope occasionally found settings that served as an "admirable channel" for his narcissism. Then Grope became "an enthusiastic, self-involved, hard-working, and cooperative fellow."[34]

While different settings clearly provide different opportunities for individuals to "work out" their internal psychic states, they provide but temporary relief. As the narcissistic gratifications lose their power to sustain the grandiosity necessary for personal functioning, periods of apathy and withdrawal frequently follow. In turn, there are periods of renewed, even frenetic, activities to locate additional sources of psychic supplies which might again provide, however temporarily, a renewed sense of well-being.

Given that the needs underlying these patterns originate in childhood experiences, it is not surprising that adult activities prove unsatisfying. For those activities can provide but symbolic representations for the adult of what the child failed to receive or at least wished to receive but did not to some sufficient degree.

Murray, with great insight, recognizes that linkage between Grope's college years and his childhood. He observes that Grope had failed to reach the emotional stage of "object attachment" or "oedipal love." The cause for that failure, he suggests briefly, was the result of Grope's earliest childhood experiences with a mother, who "scrupulously followed her day's dicta; (*a*) that children should be fed by the clock and (*b*) that maternal nurturance should be minimal . . . let the child cry, with his oral and affectional needs unsatisfied."[35] Murray, in short, concluded that Grope's problem as a young adult stemmed from a character structure that originated in inadequate parenting.

While Murray identified the psychodynamics and genesis of the "Icarus complex," he did little to elaborate them. Many years were to pass before Murray's work was taken up by others, but that work has confirmed the basic elements of his original analysis. More to the point here, the subsequent research illuminates the character of the Shah. The components of the character structure which have been associated with flying fantasies can be productively used to identify other characteristics of the Shah. In addition, theoretical accounts for the genesis of these characteristics can be used to understand their origins in the Shah. Finally, the consequences for the individual of these character traits can be used to understand the behavior of the Shah during his entire adult life and especially during the revolution.

In short, the introduction of psychoanalytic theories here is not in the service of obfuscation (from the use of technical language) or mystification (from the use of ethereal concepts). But psychoanalytic theories can point to other components of the Shah's character which are significant—to be sure, in the light of the psychoanalytic theory that specifies such significance—and help account for why he took or failed to take certain actions. His actions and inactions led, ultimately, to his fleeing Iran in the midst of revolution, losing his throne, and dying a tragic and pathetic figure.[36]

The Shah's fascination with flying and with height and size, like Grope's "cynosural narcism," "ascensionism," and "prospection of falling," is among the central components of what psychoanalysts have come, since Murray's work, to identify as a frequently cohering collection of ideational materials which they have labeled "narcissistic grandiosity." Heinz Kohut made a crucial contribution to the development of these ideas through his work on narcissism and through his fascination with the flying fantasies both of his patients and of the reports of such fantasies by others—

Winston Churchill, for example.[37] Kohut came to see flying fantasies as a feature of unmodified infantile grandiosity and exhibitionism.[38]

A crucial aspect of all Kohut's work is its relevance to the investigation of nonpathological individuals. He frequently claimed that the presence of grandiosity and exhibitionism, for example, was by itself no indication of either illness or health. What was crucial for the individual was the extent to which he was successful in integrating such characteristics with the opportunities presented by his life circumstances.

Such integration depends on two factors: first, the ability of the individual to "deinstinctualize," that is, gain some control over his grandiosity and exhibitionism so that he can, to some reasonable extent, determine the timing and modes of their expression; and second, the life circumstances of the individual which determine the range of possibilities available for expressing those characteristics. To the extent that the individual can control the timing and mode by which he expresses characterological grandiosity and exhibitionism, he is much more likely to do so in ways which are not self-destructive and which may have positive personal and social consequences. And to the extent that the individual's life circumstances provide him with opportunities for their expression, he is much more likely to fulfill his social roles appropriately and productively. In short, the presence of grandiosity and exhibitionism or any other psychological characteristic cannot be equated with pathology.

Nothing about the Shah's mental health should be read into this analysis, only about how his mind worked. In fact, it was the good fortune of the Shah to be presented with life circumstances which allowed him virtually unique opportunities for the socially sanctioned expression of his psychological needs. The tragedy was that those same opportunities provided little constraint to the aggrandizement of those needs. To the contrary, being Shah was, for Mohammad Reza Pahlavi, narcissistically gratifying. Over the years of his rule there was a steady and continuous amplification of that narcissism and, as Iran's resources increased from oil sales, their ever-increasing realization. The development of Iran became a tangible fulfillment of certain of the fantasies of its ruler.[39]

Indeed, the need for opportunities to express the grandiose or exhibitionistic components of one's narcissism can serve as an important impetus to alter one's life circumstances. Rather than a source of pathology, these and other personal attributes can be important sources of motivation for productive activities and, perhaps, for altering one's environment to provide more suitable circumstances for the realization of one's fantasies. Where the individual has political power, where he is the Shah, the personal motivations for social change may be crucial determinants of the ways in which he exercises that power.

The Shah suggested on numerous occasions, before oil revenues facilitated Iran's transformation, that he sought to develop and "modernize" his country. On more infrequent occasions he hinted that he sought to do so because a backward Iran was unsuitable for him—Iran was not a fit country for him to rule. In 1962, for example, in an address to the National Press Club in Washington, the Shah said: "This king business has given me personally nothing but headaches. During the whole of these 20 years of my reign, I have lived under the strain of my duties."[40] The Shah's expression of pain came in the middle of a speech in which he made a plea for greater economic and military aid for his poor but promising country.

At least at this point in history, Iran was not satisfactory for the Shah. The Shah's response to that observation was not to change himself; it was to change Iran. His needs, given his position as Shah, made it possible for him to alter his country to fit his own fantasies more closely. Whatever else that says about the relationship of the Shah to the Iranian people, it suggests that to discuss the fantasies which are part of his character structure and which helped motivate him to action is not to imply that the Shah was "sick" or in any way "mentally imbalanced." What is being claimed here is that the Shah manifested qualities identified as central components of one particular psychoanalytically based character structure. The psychodynamics identified as central to that character structure, in turn, can help us understand why the Shah acted as he did and, ultimately, how he came to lose his throne.

Kohut sought to develop a psychoanalytic theory which, while based on the study of patients, could be used to study nonpatients. In the process, he elaborated the ideational content of what he referred to as the "nonpathological grandiose, exhibitionistic self." Following Kohut, there has been considerable attention to elaborating the psychological constellation of which flying fantasies are a part and which Kohut understood as one type of narcissistic personality.[41]

That psychological constellation is now generally understood as characterizing an individual who has two basic "faces," one of which is presented to the public and consciously, of course, to oneself. The other face is the private one, kept secret, to whatever extent possible, from oneself as well as from others. The public face, which this type of narcissist struggles to make convincing, is one of an exaggerated or pseudomasculinity. That pseudomasculinity can be manifested in whatever ways the culture defines as the embodiment of manliness. The most common expressions in the West are extreme attention to adorning the body with clothes, uniforms, and insignia and developing the body through physical conditioning. This narcissist is also an avid, even ruthless, competitor and risk taker. Feats of daring—reckless automobile driving and flying as well as a variety of athletic activities—are favored arenas for competition.[42]

These and the additional opportunities which his life circumstances make available are used exhibitionistically to win the approval and admiration of others. Above all, this narcissist seeks to be admired, to be the "apple of the other's eye." And the more others there are, the more gratified the individual becomes.

While the admiration of others is the basic goal, his relations to those others are frequently characterized by contempt. One observer put it, "arrogance, above all, is a feature of . . . narcissism."[43] The arrogance may be fortified by a "sense of omnipotence and a feeling of invulnerability" which allows such individuals to take the risks they do, believing that some divine protection or charmed fate will constantly guard their safety and well-being.[44]

These qualities of arrogance and contempt, the belief in extrahuman protection, and the constant search to be seen in the eyes of others as special, and specially masculine, mask—as one would expect from psychoanalytic theory where almost everything is also its opposite—a profound sense of inferiority or inadequacy. That sense of inadequacy is reflected in "the passivity, the softness, the need for tenderness and dependency, the wish to trust, and the fear of helplessness, and, therefore, distrust."[45]

What emerges from the descriptions of this narcissistic character is a person beset by contrary tendencies. The public person is a "man's man" with the courage and strength to dazzle and the competitive drive to be a formidable opponent to any who would challenge his claims to uniqueness. Yet those who appreciate his specialness and even uniqueness—the absolutely necessary admiring audience—are rarely themselves treated with appreciation. They are more likely to be the subject of contempt. And from time to time, the entire sense of the self which has been communicated to others (and to the individual himself) unravels. The individual becomes passive and dependent.

This cluster of characteristics provides a psychological description of the

Shah of Iran. The utility of that psychoanalytically derived cluster is immense. It provides a description of the Shah's character which clarifies two crucial aspects of his life—his successes and his failures. It helps clarify his style of rule and the drive to "modernize" Iran during the 1960s and 1970s. During those decades, he sought to refashion Iran not in his own image but rather in an image of power and international significance which would mirror his own grandiosity. With that grandiosity went contempt and arrogance. Those were the characteristics of the Shah which his closest associates and the Iranian people tended to see. They knew him for his least admirable personal qualities.

The other side of his character—the passivity and the tenderness—qualities which might have helped endear the Shah to his people, were buried under the paraphernalia of Pahlavi imperial rule. There were so many medals, tunics, flags, bugles, and all the other trappings of the Shah's authority that only the most astute could discover that the Shah had qualities other than grandiosity and contempt.

What remains to be understood are the factors which sustained the Shah's grandiosity through the more than three and a half decades of his rule. Certainly the imperial trappings were more in evidence, especially as the vastly enhanced oil revenues contributed to the conspicuous consumption of royal paraphernalia. But virtually all of the trappings of the rule of the Shah, including the regalia and the ceremonies and the symbols of power, were in the service of winning the admiration of the Iranian people. The admiration he received from others, and particularly from his primary audience, the people of Iran, was crucial to him. That was one of the bases which the Shah relied upon to provide him the courage and strength necessary for him to rule. He lived as ruler sustained by the belief that he was loved and respected by his people. The cheers, the ubiquitous displays of photographs—his alone as well as those of the imperial family—the pomp, the drama of the imperial show all contributed to the Shah's belief in his own press.

He received psychic support from a second source: he was sustained by his ties to a very small number of close personal associates, and those ties were so close that they assumed the quality of psychic "twinships."[46] Three individuals fulfilled this function for the Shah. His relationship with Ernest Perron, the son of the gardener at the Le Rosey secondary school in Switzerland to which the Shah had been sent by his father to receive an education suitable for a future ruler, was by far the most mysterious. He returned to Iran with the Shah from Switzerland in 1936 and lived in one or another of the royal palaces until the mid-1950s. Another psychic twin of the Shah's was Assadollah Alam, his childhood friend, later prime minister and minister of court. The Shah's third and other psychic twin was his actual twin, Princess Ashraf Pahlavi. At different times in their lives, a psychic merger between the two of them allowed her strength to bolster his own.

The Shah counted on a third source of psychological strength to bolster his masculine, assertive qualities—those he needed to do Shah and not just be Shah. He maintained a near lifelong belief in a watchful and protecting God who had decreed his success in carrying out a divine mission. Ever since he had had visions of Shi'ite Imams descended from the line of the Prophet Muhammad and subsequently had recovered from a series of life-threatening childhood illnesses, the Shah believed he had been specially selected to fulfill a divine mission.

Finally, the Shah relied for psychic strength on his important diplomatic and personal psychological ties with the United States. The Shah had met and dealt with those eight U.S. presidents, from Franklin Delano Roosevelt to Jimmy Carter. They served as objects of identification for the Shah, and he came to believe that he was the agent not only of the Lord, but also of the world's most powerful state.

These four mechanisms—the admiration of others, twinships with other persons, divine protection, and the unflagging support of the United States—provided the Shah with the psychic supplies he needed to split off the devalued, passive, dependent aspects of his self, project them onto others, and, thus, maintain his positive masculine identification. These psychic devices for maintaining his psychic strength were not the only mechanisms which contributed to that purpose. But the argument here is that they were the principal means by which the Shah marshaled the psychological capacity he needed to function as ruler. Other devices helped as well. His identifications with his mother and his father—to be dealt with later—were significant. So were his ties with other countries, Israel, for example.

The Israelis knew how to speak to the Shah's narcissism. Isser Harel was the head of Mossad, Israel's intelligence agency, when the links between the two countries were forged. Harel has explained how the Israelis compared the Shah with Cyrus the Great, the Achaemenid of Iran who freed the Jews from their Babylonian captivity and allowed them to return to Jerusalem or settle in Iran. The Shah was flattered. "The connection was very romantic," Harel recalled, "and I would say of great importance at the time. . . . He wanted to play the part."[47]

But when the Shah most needed his four principal sources of strength—when he had to confront the revolution and surmount the most powerful challenge to his rule—each of these sources of strength failed him. He enjoyed the support and admiration of the Iranian people to an ever-diminishing extent during the 1970s, until, during the revolution of 1978, it became shockingly obvious that almost as a whole, the Iranian people had turned against their monarch to the extent that they sought to oust him and the whole system which ruled in his name.

By 1978, the individuals with whom he had psychically merged were unavailable for counsel and strength. Ernest Perron had long since died in Switzerland. Assadollah Alam had died of leukemia in the final months of 1977. Princess Ashraf had proven to be a major source for popular hatred of the regime because of her constant interference in the government. The Shah had cut his ties to the princess and banished her to the United Nations. With the removal of those three individuals, there were no others who could serve as psychic "twins" for the ruler.

The Shah's belief in his divine protection evaporated as well. After the Shah learned he had cancer in the early 1970s, it became more and more difficult to sustain his belief in both his divine mission and divine protection. When Assadollah Alam died from leukemia, thus removing the last of the Shah's "twins," and as the Iranian people deserted him, his commitment to his otherworldly protection disappeared completely.

The support of the United States failed him as well. Early in the 1976 election campaign and in the first year of his presidency, Jimmy Carter repeated time and time again that the twin pillars of his foreign policy were to internationalize human rights while restricting U.S. foreign arms sales. The Shah understood that he was the principal target of those new goals. He came to believe that the United States had abandoned him just as he needed his psychic relationship with the United States more than ever.

As the four sources from which the Shah derived his psychic strength failed him, he found it ever more difficult to maintain his lifelong psychic patterns and his psychic equilibrium. The Shah began to lose his carefully crafted psychic balance. And as the pressures on him increased, to a torrent with the unleashing of revolutionary fervor in the violence of 1978, the challenges became overwhelming. The Shah regressed to the patterns of his earliest childhood. He could no longer sustain the pattern of splitting and projection. His core character traits became dominant. His passivity and dependence triumphed. When he most needed his father's capacity for fearless courage, he was trapped in his more feminine attributes. He was a man paralyzed. He could not act.

2

Childhood and Youth

Mohammad Reza Pahlavi, the Shahanshah, was a man profoundly dependent on others for his narcissistic supplies. How he came to be that man is worth telling on two accounts. His story strengthens the conviction that he depended on four external sources for his psychic strength, each of which failed him during the revolution of 1978. More, the story explains how he came to be that man. The telling of that story recounts the Shah's personal history.

The basic facts of the Shah's childhood and youth are well known, having been told and retold by the Shah himself,[1] by a host of biographers,[2] and by the government of Iran.[3] While his youth was no princely dream, it had many of the usual elements of a royal upbringing.

He and his twin sister, Ashraf, were born on October 26, 1919. The twins already had an older sister, Shams, three years their senior, and three years after their birth a younger brother, Ali Reza, was born. He was the last of the children born of Reza Khan's marriage to the young Mohammad Reza's mother, who later came to be called Taj ol-Moluk, the "Crown of Kings."

At the time of the future Shah's birth, his father was a senior Iranian officer in the Cossack Brigade, a small military force which was, nonetheless, the most potent military force in the country.[4] Not long before, the British had prevailed upon Ahmad Shah, the weak and widely depreciated Qajar monarch, to oust the Russian officers commanding the brigade, leaving Reza Khan one of the senior officers.[5]

Ahmad Shah proved incapable of organizing the politics of Iran to provide even a modicum of effective government. The Majles, or Parliament, and the cabinet, institutions provided by the 1905 Constitution, had become equally ineffective, subverted by nearly everyone—the Shah, the

British, the Russians, and the many Persian allies of the foreign powers. The British response to the waning power of the Iranian center was to negotiate, in 1919, a treaty with the Iranian government to install British advisers throughout the Iranian system (at Persian expense), a step which, it was generally believed, would lead to eventual colonial status for Iran.[6]

The new Bolshevik regime to Persia's north responded quickly to the announcement of the 1919 accord. It unilaterally abrogated all czarist treaties and concessions with Iran, promising a new relationship. Nonetheless, in the summer of 1920, Bolshevik troops landed in northern Iran where they destroyed a White Russian force and supported an independence movement led by Muhammad Khiabani, a former Shi'ite cleric.

After some fighting and much politicking, including the formation of a strongly nationalist government in Tehran and the discussion of the problem in the newly formed League of Nations, the Soviets offered to withdraw if Iran signed a treaty with them. Iranian nationalist officials delayed on that request while refusing to submit the Anglo-Iranian treaty to the Majles for ratification, effectively nullifying that earlier agreement. Then the Iranian government announced that no treaty could be signed with the USSR while its troops occupied Iranian soil.

At this precarious moment in Persian history, with Iran poised between British disappointment and Soviet betrayal, "on the 21st February 1921, three thousand Persian Cossacks led by a ranking officer of whom no one had heard and accompanied by a well-known newspaper editor, marched into Tehran and without firing a shot, overthrew the government."[7] Much was to be heard of that "ranking officer," Reza Khan, in the future. But in its immediate aftermath, the coup's origins were shrouded in mystery, and, as has always been the case in Iran, mystery bred rumors. Rumor had it that since Reza Khan had risen to senior rank in the Cossack Brigade after the ouster of the Russian officers and since the British had since that time been paying for the brigades and since British troops were stationed in the city of Qazvin where the brigades were headquartered, the coup was a British plot. At least, the coup must have been staged with British permission.[8]

Since the British had concluded, by 1921, that their 1919 treaty was a dead letter and that they were going to withdraw their remaining troops from Iran, treaty or not, that Iran was dangerously vulnerable to Bolshevik penetration. What better solution for the British than to identify a powerful Iranian who could seize control of the central administration and reassert the power of Tehran over the entire realm, in the process keeping at

bay the new regime to the north. Whatever the validity of these speculations, Reza Khan emerged from the coup as the strong man of the new
government, the *sardar-e sepah* as he was called, literally, "general of the
army." Reza Khan officially became minister of war. The "well-known
newspaper editor" Seyyed Zia ed Din Tabataba'i became prime minister.
But in short order, Reza Khan engineered the ouster of Seyyed Zia and in
May of 1921 assumed the premiership. By then he was the unchallengeable
power of the land. Within four years, he deposed Ahmad Shah, the last
ruler of the Qajar dynasty, and on December 12, 1925, was acclaimed Shah
by the Majles, the first ruler of the new Pahlavi dynasty.

Not longer after, on April 25, 1926, the official coronation was held and
the six-and-one-half-year-old Mohammad Reza had a central part in the
ceremonies. After Reza Khan placed the crown of kingship on his own
head, he turned to his young son and placed a small crown on the head of
the boy. With that act, Mohammad Reza Pahlavi was officially designated
Crown Prince.

With the formalization of his future kingly responsibilities, the education of the boy began in earnest. A special primary school was established
on the palace grounds, where the Crown Prince was given his basic education, with a few other specially selected children to serve as classmates. In
May of 1931 the Shah completed his primary studies. That fall he was sent
off to Switzerland, with a few other young Persian companions as well as a
personal physician and a Persian tutor. After a year of special tutoring, he
entered Le Rosey school, where he remained to complete secondary school
in June of 1936. Mohammad Reza immediately returned to Iran and the
next spring, in May of 1937, enrolled in the Iranian Military College. For a
year he received officer training and instruction in military theory, strategy,
and tactics and graduated, appropriately enough, at the head of his class, in
June of 1938.

On March 15, 1939, the Crown Prince married Princess Fawzia, the sister of King Farouk of Egypt. The marriage itself took place in Cairo, but the
major celebrations occurred in Tehran when the young twenty-year-old
groom returned with his bride. Princess Fawzia busied herself with establishing a new royal household and learning the Persian language. Meanwhile, the newlyweds conversed in French.

Whatever joy the Shah experienced from his new, foreign, and previously unknown bride must have been tempered by his new responsibilities and by menacing developments in international politics. Reza Shah

decided that his son, having graduated from the military college and been appropriately married, was ready for serious kingly socialization. The Crown Prince began to spend increasing hours with his father, learning his future role as Shah by observing his father in action and discussing the affairs of the day.

Much of their discussion turned on the outbreak of war in Europe and Iran's deepening involvement in the Middle Eastern politics of both the European and Asian belligerents. Reza Shah had, of necessity, been concerned about the foreign relations of Iran since his 1921 coup, for Iran was then still occupied by Soviet and British troops. He had already made his first trip outside of Iran's borders to Turkey and had devoted considerable resources to strengthening Iran's foreign service. In the 1930s, as he succeeded in creating the instruments of state power, he became even more concerned with Iran's international connections.

In 1937 he negotiated a treaty meant to ensure peaceful relations and increased trade with Turkey, Iraq, and Afghanistan. Called the Saadabad Pact after the palace in Tehran in which it was signed, the agreement marked a new expansiveness in Iran's foreign relations. Reza Shah then concluded a treaty of friendship with Japan and a trade treaty with the Soviet Union. In 1940 he signed a Treaty of Trade and Commerce with Germany.

The allies were, by then, clearly concerned. German agents appeared to be operating freely in Iran and trying to make the most of Iran's Aryan heritage. A pro-Nazi coup in Iraq in 1941 seems to have sealed Iran's fate. Great Britain and the Soviet Union became convinced that Iran would be the next Middle Eastern state to fall to Nazi Germany, an outcome impossible for them to countenance, given the dependence of the British fleet on Iranian oil and the common border Iran shares with the Soviet Union.

On August 25, 1941, Soviet and British troops invaded Iran from the north and south. After sporadic and brief resistance, the Iranian military collapsed and Reza Shah agreed to leave Iran for exile. On September 16, 1941, Mohammad Reza went before the Majles and officially became Shahanshah, the King of Kings.

That, of course, is the publicized and factual narrative of the Shah's childhood and youth, a narrative that highlights the well-known events which were the markers of his growth on his path to the throne. But while the narrative is accurate, it is devoid of psychological significance as long as it remains uninterpreted. The character of the Shah was established by the significance to the growing boy of the events of his childhood. Interpretations of those events recounting these psychological meanings are necessary. To establish those, other types of narratives are necessary. Those other narratives stress his relations with his parents, his siblings, and other adults; the events which occurred in the course of those relations with significant others; and the early signs of the effects produced on the boy.

Those narratives suggest how the Shah emerged from his childhood as a man of poorly integrated contradictions. The bedrock of the man was a character of diffidence, rooted in a lack of confidence in his own worth and ability, a certain shyness and passivity, a softness. Overlaying that narcissistically depleted bedrock were the concomitants of his flying fantasies—a pseudomasculine toughness and bravery, a demeanor which communicated stern, formal, imperious arrogance.

For the Shah, the experiences of childhood that proved psychologically significant began with his father, Reza Khan. Reza was the semiliterate son of an officer in the military service of the Qajar kings. According to the Shah, his father's father, Abbas Ali Khan, had "distinguished himself by his gallantry" during his military career but had died only forty days after the birth of his son Reza in 1878.[9] Reza Khan was notorious among his contemporaries for his quick temper, his ruthlessness, and his refusal to tolerate challenges to his authority. He was, especially in the Iran of his day, a huge man, over six-feet tall with broad shoulders and rugged features.

Clues to Reza Shah's significance for his son can be found in *Mission for My Country,* the Shah's autobiography and the first of the books he wrote.[10] In that book the Shah refers, not surprisingly, to his father as the founder of the Pahlavi dynasty, the great modernizer of Iran, and even the savior of his country. But what is most striking is not how he refers to his father, but how often he does so and how glowing in adoration he is. In his book of 336 pages, the Shah refers to his father on no less than 784 distinct occasions, an average of more than twice per page.[11] He refers to "my father" 286 times. He writes of "he," "him," and "his," in clear reference to his father, 447 times. He remembers "Reza Shah" 39 times, and he refers to his father in other ways a total of 12 times.

Reza Shah clearly was a pervasive figure for the Shah, larger than life. The Shah tells us this not only by referring to his father so often but by referring to him in unabashedly positive and laudatory terms. Some positive mention of Reza Shah would be expected on political grounds alone, of course. For the Iranian people's memory of his father was an important factor in the rule of the Shah himself. Reza Shah, as the first of the Pahlavis, bore a symbolic significance for the legitimacy of the entire dynasty. When the Iranian Majles awarded Reza Shah the posthumous title of Kabir or "the Great," it was not as important for the dead king as it was for the halo effect of greatness it cast on his son. But the argument here is that there are ample grounds for understanding the Shah's references as far more than politically inspired.

The encomiums in *Mission for My Country* are not only similar in character and tone to those the Shah used his entire life when referring to his father, but they are similar to those he used in his most unguarded, spontaneous, and private moments. Most telling, these written references to his father are so thoroughly positive that they seem to refer not to any historic founder of a ruling dynasty or even to a father, but more to an idealization which has assumed mythic proportions for its idolater.

The Shah describes this mythic father in awesome dimensions:

Strength . . . determination . . . a man of actions . . . a towering figure (p. 12)

Imagination . . . caught the spirit of the new age of science and industry (p. 27)

Exceptional (p. 30)

Burned with anger and sadness at the pass to which our great nation had come (p. 35)

Habit of study (p. 36)

A force of character . . . a dominant personality . . . intense feeling of patriotism and nationalism . . . regal bearing (p. 37)

The right man (p. 38)

Cool care and detachment (p. 40)

A seasoned campaigner (p. 42)

Led us . . . into a new age . . . wrought a revolution (p. 44)

A most amazing personality (p. 45)

Simplicity of taste and personal conduct (p. 46)

The observance of order and care in everything that he did . . . sober and hardworking (p. 47)

No man ever believed more in his country . . . more than intelligent . . . easily could grasp the essentials of any problem . . . confidence in himself . . . amazing self-control . . . marvelous sense of political timing . . . energy and endurance . . . selfless (p. 48)

Struck blows at slothfulness and procrastination (p. 49)

Achieved phenomenal results . . . one of the greatest mind readers . . . a scorn of pretense (p. 50)

Manliness and perseverance . . . truth and courage . . . confront difficulties fearlessly and overcome them . . . realize the shamefulness of idle habits . . . regard work as his highest goal (p. 51)[12]

This praise serves at least two purposes. It certainly serves to convey legitimacy to the rule of its author. By elevating the stature of his father, the Shah manages to enjoy enhanced legitimacy for himself and his dynasty.

But the praise serves to fulfill a less political and more personal purpose as well. The overweening, fulsomeness of the praise was not meant as an accurate appraisal of the father's quality as person and ruler but rather as the idealized representation of his father which the Shah had created for himself during his formative years and into his adulthood. (The book was published when the Shah himself was thirty-nine years old.) The treatment of Reza Shah in the son's autobiography helped the son maintain the idealization of his father which he had created and struggled to maintain throughout his life. The idealization, in turn, served to strengthen his own sense of self-esteem. His own worth was enhanced by his sharing in the idealized qualities of his father.

Considerable evidence suggests, however, that this idealization is only a partial representation of the psychological significance of Reza Shah for his son and successor. As a youth, the future Shah experienced his father not only as the idealized figure of the public narrative, but also as a fearsome tyrant, as the Iranian people were to experience Reza Shah as a ruler. For the Crown Prince, Reza Shah was a belittling and humiliating role model. And for Mohammad Reza as Shah, the memory of his dead father was a constant basis for invidious comparison. His memory of his dead father was suffused with jealousy as he always sought to outshine his father's reputation. This pattern of a competitive and envious relation with his father and even with his father's memory became the template for the Shah's dealing with others. Those he perceived as powerful authority figures—on the basis of their characters or their formal positions—were subjected to the same hostility, resentment, and jealousy as was his father.

The nature of the Shah's significant childhood experiences, those which contributed so much to the formation of his character, gives evidence to support the idea that the idealized view in *Mission for My Country* is insufficiently comprehensive—that the father was a far more complicated figure for the son than the idealized picture suggests.

In the midst of the catalog of Reza Shah's impressive qualities detailed in *Mission for My Country,* Mohammad Reza mentions other of his father's qualities:

Reza Shah . . . could be one of the pleasantest men in the world, yet he could be one of the most frightening . . . strong men often trembled just to look at him. He had an almost devastating ability to assess human nature. As though he possessed some secret electronic ray, he could almost instantly size up a man's strengths or weaknesses, his integrity or his slipperiness.[13]

Another of his father's qualities remembered often by the Shah was Reza Shah's eyes. The Shah described his father physically: "Broad shouldered and tall, he had prominent and rugged features, but it was his piercing eyes that arrested anybody who met him. . . . Those eyes could make a strong man shrivel up inside."[14]

Later in the same work the Shah comments, "no wonder many men feared to look him in the eye."[15] Years later the Shah repeated the idea: "His piercing eyes, which dominated his personality, could make a strong man quake."[16] And even after he had lost the throne, in his last volume of memoirs the Shah noted that "those eyes could make a strong man shrivel up inside."[17] Mohammad Reza carried the representations of the terror of his father with him throughout his life, to death.

While the Shah talks about the powerful effect Reza Shah had on others, it was the young Mohammad Reza himself who was most terrorized by his father. If even a "strong man" would "quake" before the Shah, how much more likely that a young, uncertain, diffident boy would be so affected. As if to anticipate this conclusion, the Shah assures us that while Reza Shah terrorized others, he acted differently with his family, and especially with him.

Yet contrary to what many believed, my father was kind and tender hearted especially toward his family. His forbidding sternness seemed to melt into love, kindness, and easy familiarity when he was with us. Especially with me, his acknowledged successor to the throne, he would play lightheartedly. When we were alone together, he would sing me little songs.[18]

Whether or not Reza Shah ever sang "little songs" to his son, a considerable body of evidence refutes the Shah's claim that Reza Shah was "kind" or "tender hearted" to his family. The Shah's twin sister, Princess Ashraf Pahlavi, had a very different view.

Reza Shah was [after the 1921 coup] the most powerful man in Persia. The same qualities that made him a formidable soldier—piercing eyes that could wither a subordinate, intolerance for error and imperfection, insistence on strict military discipline—also made him an awesome and frightening father. Whenever I saw a trouser leg with a red stripe approaching, I would run, on the theory that the best way to avoid my father's displeasure was to stay out of his way.

Looking back, I can't think of a single instance when my father punished any of us, but his physical presence to us as children was so intimidating, the sound of his voice raised in anger so terrifying, that even years later as a grown woman, I can't remember a time I wasn't afraid of him.[19]

It may, of course, be that as the Shah claimed, Reza Shah treated the young Crown Prince differently. Perhaps because he was to be Reza Shah's successor or perhaps because he was a male child and therefore differently valued in the Iranian patriarchal culture than was his female twin Ashraf, the boy was treated by Reza Shah with uncharacteristic gentleness. But at least two of Mohammad Reza Shah's wives offer direct evidence that such was not the case. His second wife, Queen Soraya, described their frequent horseback rides together at a palace north of Tehran:

When riding at Saadabad, he frequently spoke of his youth. He must have been very unhappy, for his father kept him down from childhood. "Reza Shah was a very great character," he said, "but we were all frightened of him. He only needed to fix his piercing eyes upon us and we went rigid with fear and respect. At the family table, we never dared express our own views. Indeed, we were only allowed to speak when asked a question."[20]

The Shah's third wife, Empress Farah, related an incident which confirms the terror the young Mohammad Reza felt toward his father.[21] She tells of a meeting in the 1960s between the Shah and a foreign ambassador which was interrupted when their eldest son, the young Crown Prince, bounded into the Shah's office. The Shah turned from the ambassador to attend to the boy. When the Crown Prince left the room, the Shah apologized to his visitor and told him, "I never want him to feel the awe, the terror, I felt for my father."[22]

What seems clear, despite the Shah's declarations of his father's gentleness and tenderness at home, so different from Reza Shah's awesome public presence, is that the private Reza Shah appears to be much like the accounts of the public version. The result must have been that he generated the same terror in his family that he generated among his subjects. The one person who appears not to have been intimidated by him was his wife, Taj ol-Moluk, the mother of the Crown Prince.

Interestingly, while the Shah refers to his father many times in *Mission for My Country,* he has almost nothing to say of his mother. He refers to her on only twelve occasions: she is "my mother" seven times, "she" or "her" four times, and the "Queen," once. Yet the Shah does wonder over the fact that "it was amazing that my mother's influence so often prevailed in our family life."[23] Princess Ashraf remembers her mother in more detail.

A small, delicate woman with blond hair and beautiful green eyes, she barely reached to the top row of military decorations on my father's uniform. Yet in her own way, she was as forceful as he was. At a time when Iranian women were veiled and "hidden," when they had virtually no rights, when they were expected to submit totally to male authority, my mother wasn't afraid to argue with my father or to challenge his decisions.[24]

Taj ol-Moluk's fearlessness may have originated, at least partially, with her father, known as Bagher Khan Mir Panj, reputed to be a courageous military officer from the Caucasus who, in turn, was descended from generations of military men. Like her husband, Taj ol-Moluk demonstrated the toughness, the hardness, of a child of the military, and she employed that toughness to challenge her husband's authority. Those challenges resulted in frequent confrontations marked by shouting and defiance.

The culmination of the feuding appears to have taken place when the twins, Ashraf and the future Shah, were less than three years old. Their mother was then pregnant for the third—and last—time. Reza Shah had already carried out his successful coup and was the most powerful man in Persia when he announced he had taken another wife, a much younger woman. To take a second wife was not an uncommon practice in Iran of the early 1920s. The first wife was expected to accept her new rival as yet another manifestation of the powerlessness and low status attendant on the female condition. Yet the Shah's mother did not do so. She reacted with fury. She announced her refusal not only to accept the reality of the other wife but even to speak with her husband ever again.

Taj ol-Moluk apparently relented from that threat, but she never again lived with Reza Shah. "For a long time she refused to see my father," Princess Ashraf recalls. "In the face of this unheard of challenge to his authority, the Shah would literally hide when he saw my mother coming."[25]

Characteristically, Mohammad Reza Shah's memories are considerably more bland. In none of his writings does he acknowledge that his father ever had more than one wife. (In fact, over the entire course of his life, Reza Shah married five women, the Shah's mother being the second of his spouses. Apparently the first marriage ended in divorce, although after the birth of a daughter, before Reza married the Shah's mother.) In only one of his many volumes of memoirs does he mention any difficulties between his parents. As the Shah puts it, "My mother, certainly, was a woman with a lot of character. All did not go smoothly between my father and her. She was not a yielding person but maintained her independence. Maybe this was one of the reasons they did not live together. My mother lived separately in another house."[26] Reza Shah never shared Taj ol-Moluk's home (or bed) again. He moved into separate quarters and returned to her household on infrequent occasions only to visit his children, who by then numbered four, with the birth of Ali Reza, the last of Mohammad Reza's full brothers and sisters.

It appears, then, that the Shah's earliest years were spent in a house filled with tension where arguments between his strong-willed mother and powerful father were frequent.

Previous to this actual physical withdrawal, it is reasonable to imagine that Reza, the strong man of Persia, had little time to spend in the company of his family. When his son was born, he had recently been designated commander of the Cossack Brigade. When the boy was but sixteen months of age, his father staged the coup that made him minister of war and opened the path toward the prime ministership and eventually the throne itself. Not long after the coup, marital discord had become so unpleasant that Reza physically moved out, returning for only occasional visits with his children.

In his early years, then, the future Shah was largely raised in a household of women. His powerful mother was clearly the dominant figure. His older sister, Shams, had been born three years earlier. She was reportedly the mother's favorite—a special and intense bond having grown between mother and older daughter. His twin sister Ashraf, who had actually been born before him and who herself developed a powerful character, was the third of the older women in the future Shah's early home.

On the one hand the Shah was clearly the outsider in the midst of these females. Even his status as firstborn son gave him little special status at that young age because his father was still years from the throne and no question of succession could arise for the son of a coup maker, war minister, or prime minister, all positions Reza Shah held before being crowned. On the other hand, it is likely that in that house of women, he received special attention merely for being a male. In fact, the power of his mother and the nearly completely feminized atmosphere of his early home life must have combined to make his mother, and women in general, the most appealing object for his earliest psychological identifications. For it was from women, and apparently from women alone, that the Shah received whatever psychological nourishment he was able to get as a child. (And further I am suggesting that given the qualities of the young boy's mother—her toughness, her special ties to Shams, and her fiery quarrels with her husband culminating in the marital separation—it is difficult to think of her as a loving, caring, nurturing mother.)

Thus it is perhaps understandable that in his later life the Shah appeared to have such ambivalent feelings for her. He claimed in his autobiography that "I personally owe an incalculable debt to my mother."[27] But it is striking that she is mentioned only a few times in his autobiography and that he communicates an inadequate sense of her as a person, especially in comparison to his father. Throughout his life he seemed reluctant to concede her any special place, even in the influences which made him the person he had become. In the 1950s he was asked if his allegedly "mystical" qualities were due to his mother. The Shah responded that "it was part of my environment . . . and my environment . . . was more with her than anyone else—but maybe it was just a gift."[28]

Years later, in the majesty of his power, the Shah was asked whether he had derived any characteristics, other than his religious background, from his mother. "Well, I don't know," he replied, "I believe I am too stubborn; but so was my father. I really don't know."[29] Then he was asked about women in general—whether he remembered any women who were important to him. "Maybe, many. But that is not to say that they had any influence on my life; in fact, they had none at all."[30]

The Shah's most vitriolic outburst on the subject of women was provoked by that astute interviewer Oriana Fallaci. Clearly she had riled him with her provocative questions. When she asked him about women, immediately after asking him if the rumors were true that he had secretly taken another wife while still married to Empress Farah, the Shah elaborated his hostility. While some of the disdain was undoubtedly directed at the interviewer herself, the Shah's words were "of a piece" with his lifelong views on women. After denying that he married again—"a stupid, vile, disgusting libel," in his words—he went on to explain to Fallaci about women:

Q. How strange, Your Majesty. If there is a monarch whose name has always been associated with women, it's you. And now I'm beginning to suspect that women have counted for nothing in your life.

A. I fear your suspicion is justified. Women, you know . . . Look, let's put it this way. I don't underestimate them, as shown by the fact that they derived more advantages than anyone else from my White Revolution. I have fought strenuously to obtain equal rights and responsibilities for them. . . .

But I wouldn't be sincere if I asserted I'd been influenced by a single one of them. Nobody can influence me, nobody at all. And a woman still less. In a man's life, women count only if they're beautiful and graceful and know how to stay feminine and . . . This Women's Lib business, for instance. What do these feminists want? What do you want? Equality, you say? Indeed! I don't want to seem rude, but . . . You may be equal in the eyes of the law, but not, I beg your pardon for saying so, in ability.

Q. Aren't we?

A. No. You've never produced a Michelangelo or a Bach. You've never even produced a great cook. And don't talk of opportunities. Are you joking? Have you lacked the opportunity to give history a great cook? You have produced nothing great, nothing! Tell me, how many women capable of governing have you met in the course of interviews such as this?

Q. At least two, Your Majesty. Golda Meir and Indira Gandhi.

A. Hm . . . All I can say is that women, when they are in power, are much harsher than men. Much more cruel. Much more bloodthirsty. I'm quoting facts, not opinions. You're heartless when you're rulers. . . . You're schemers, you're evil. Every one of you.[31]

That women counted for nothing with the Shah rings hollow given the passion of his outburst and those earliest years of his childhood surrounded by females. Indeed, we might wonder how women could elicit such anger and vitriol from the Shah if their influence on him was as slight as he so frequently claimed. To the contrary, the claim is made here that women—especially his mother—were supremely important to the Shah in his early childhood and in his adulthood.

The importance of his mother is demonstrated by his behavior to her throughout his rule. The Shah would visit Taj ol-Moluk almost daily, even during the early 1970s. They would dine together, usually in the company of other family members and friends, a minimum of four times per week.[32] By the middle of the decade, the Queen Mother had become senile. She was moved from Tehran to the home of her older daughter, Princess Shams, in southern California. There she lived, shielded from the news of the traumatic events of the revolution, of her son's ouster from power, of his wandering exile, and of his pathetic death in Cairo. Her other children sent her a stream of messages, flowers, and gifts, all allegedly from her son, the Shah. She died, after all those events, supremely unaware of the shattered fortunes of the Pahlavi dynasty.[33]

Thus, his mother was of crucial significance to him. She was the parent he knew and lived with for those early years, the parent who provided whatever nurturance he enjoyed, the parent, who, it will be suggested, enmeshed him in her own psychological system in order to take revenge on her betraying husband.

While his mother and his two sisters provided whatever nurturing the

Shah received, his father was the source of terror and anguish. His presence produced fear in his children, and somewhat later his stormy visits were the occasion for bitter arguments with his estranged wife and, thus, the occasion for more fear and terror.

In such circumstances it is difficult to imagine that Reza Shah could have served as an unambivalent idealized adult model for the young boy. It is difficult to imagine the boy fully identifying as a male with his fearsome father. It is much more likely that young Mohammad Reza was able to identify initially with his mother and that over the years of his early childhood managed to establish her characteristics as the ideals he would seek to adopt, however unconsciously, as he grew older. (This argument about the young man's identifications is based on a separation between his identifications as a person and as a monarch. There appears to be little doubt that his role model as monarch was overwhelmingly his father. It is precisely because the Shah as ruler tried to realize the role model of shah derived from Reza Shah that his behavior in that role was so unsatisfactory. For Reza Shah had created a model of monarch which was clearly appropriate for his own character structure and, thus, was comfortable for him as a person. But to Mohammad Reza Shah, the disjunction was palpable. There was, in short, a poor fit between the man and his construal of the political role he was called upon to fulfill.)

In fact, it would appear that Reza Shah sensed he was losing his son to the world of females. For not long after the boy's sixth birthday, his father took drastic action.

On April 25, 1926, Reza Khan was formally crowned Reza Shah Pahlavi. During that ceremony, young Mohammad Reza was officially designated Crown Prince. With that designation, a fateful transformation came over his life. His father ordered that he immediately be removed from the care of his mother and the attentions of his sisters, to be raised in a separate palace so that he might be suitably prepared for his future role as a monarch.[34]

From that time on, the Shah would never again live with his mother or sisters. Another home was found for him. The young boy was installed in a palace supervised by a French governess, one Mme Arfa, who was married to a Persian.[35] Otherwise, the palace was staffed entirely by men. Servants and attendants, tutors and instructors, equerries and adjutants were all sent to provide young Mohammad Reza with the manly environment Reza Shah believed so essential for his princely upbringing.

Ostensibly Reza Shah wanted to remove the Crown Prince "from the skirts of women" so that he could receive an education in the manly qualities requisite for kingship.[36] The feminine milieu of his mother's household was, in Reza Shah's eyes, no proper training ground for his son. But of course one must wonder about the extent to which Reza Shah wished revenge on his wife for her unwillingness to accept his new bride and her persistent "insubordination" in confronting him with her dissatisfaction. What more fitting way to punish her than by eliminating her control and authority over her son, the future king.

For the new Crown Prince it must have seemed extraordinary punishment, a devastating emotional blow. He was abruptly removed from the home in which he had spent his entire childhood. Yet more painful, he was taken from his mother and his sisters, from the company of "his" females and their comforting presence. What he got in their place was "a manly education."[37] Reza Shah established an elementary military school. The Shah recalled that "we wore uniforms and the curriculum was a fairly rigorous one. My life at that tender age was centered in my studies and military drilling."[38]

Being forced from his mother and sisters into a life of emotional solitude and quasi-military rigor must have extracted a very high toll from young Mohammad Reza. His presumed early identification with his mother was rewarded by an abrupt and permanent separation. His elevation to the status of Crown Prince brought loneliness and isolation. Psychologically, the most likely outcome of this early relocation must have been trauma of the deepest sort. To meet the demands of his new position, the Shah, in all likelihood, strove to adopt the masculine qualities of his father while longing to return to his earlier identifications, to what must have appeared to have been bliss: that world of women in which he was the treasured, firstborn son.

The extent to which this abrupt separation from his private world of females and immediate forced subjection to a "manly education" were traumatic for the Crown Prince is revealed by two sets of events which rapidly befell the young boy. He was stricken by a series of life-threatening illnesses, and he had a series of religious "visions."

Shortly after his investment as Crown Prince and his separation from his mother, Mohammad Reza was stricken by typhoid fever. Within the next eighteen months, the boy also contracted whooping cough, diphtheria, and malaria. In the mid-1920s there were, of course, no "wonder drugs," and the state of medical care in Iran was far from advanced. The Crown Prince was near to death from each of these illnesses, bringing panic to his family and terror to the boy.[39]

During his illness from typhoid fever, the Crown Prince "hovered between life and death" for several weeks.[40] His recovery, he later claimed, was precipitated by heavenly, mystical intervention. One night the boy dreamed of Ali, the son-in-law of the Prophet Muhammad and the foremost figure in Shi'ite Islam.[41]

In my dream, Ali had with him his famous two-pronged sword, which is often seen in paintings of him. He was sitting on his heels on the floor, and in his hands he held a bowl containing a liquid. He told me to drink, which I did. The next day, the crisis of my fever was over, and I was on the road to rapid recovery.[42]

Within the next year, the Shah had two further visions. He describes the second vision, which occurred while horseback riding in the mountains.

One had to follow a steep trail in foot or on horseback; and since I was so young, a relative who was an army officer placed me in front of him on the saddle of his horse. Some way up the trail, the horse slipped, and I was plunged head first onto a jagged rock. I fainted. When I regained consciousness, the members of the party were expressing astonishment that I had not even a scratch. I told them that as I fell, I had clearly seen one of our saints, named Abbas, and that I had felt him holding me and preventing me from crushing my head against the rock.[43]

The Shah relates that when his father later heard the boy's story he "scoffed" at the tale.[44] This may account for why the Crown Prince never told his father of his third vision, which occurred that same summer. While walking with his guardian near his palace the Shah "clearly saw before me as a man with a halo around his head—much as in some of the great paintings, by Western masters, of Jesus. As we passed one another, I knew him at once. He was the Imam or descendant of Mohammad who, according to our faith, disappeared but is expected to come again to save the world."[45]

Having been chastised once by his father for his "fanciful" visions, the Shah relates how he failed to speak of this last vision even to his guardian, much less to his father. Nonetheless, the Shah himself believed in the reality of his visions. This belief was to remain with the Shah for his entire life. In fact, in later years he was even to magnify the incidence of those childhood visions. As an adult he remembered "6 or 7 apparitions."[46] But more importantly, the belief in the reality of the visions served as the foundation of an ultimately more powerful and significant belief. The Shah developed the conviction that he was divinely inspired, protected by God.

The Shah first mentioned such protection while contemplating the successful coup against Mohammad Mossadegh in August of 1953. The Shah claimed that the overthrow of Mossadegh "reinforced my faith that a force stronger than mere mankind was helping to shape our destiny. I concluded that my destiny had already been designed and ordered by God."[47]

Over the years, the Shah's claim of divine inspiration and protection became bolder. In 1966 he would say:

I will frankly confess that I was convinced that God had ordained me to do certain things for the service of my nation, things that perhaps could not be done by anyone else. In whatever I have done and whatever I do in the future, I consider myself as an agent of the will of God.[48]

In 1973 the Shah repeated his claim:

A king who doesn't need to account to anyone for what he says and does is unavoidably doomed to loneliness. however, I am not entirely alone, because a force other's can't perceive accompanies me. My mystical force. Moreover I receive messages. I have lived with God beside me since I was 5 years old. Since, that is, God sent me those visions.[49]

At the peak of his power, the Shah reasserted the significance of that "mystical power to which I owe my career and its direction. It is this divine intelligence that directs my actions, as also the timing of them, and assures their success."[50]

As long as the Shah continued to consolidate and enhance his powers, he would speak of his divine protection and inspiration. But after he became ill and lost the throne, he never again spoke or wrote of that heavenly force which had clearly failed him. That is one indication he truly believed otherworldly powers had been with him. There are many other indications that these claims were far more than a political device from which he sought greater authority and legitimacy. For example, his second wife, Queen Soraya, recounts how the Shah often spoke to her of his mystical dreams, of his vision of Ali, and of his belief in surrendering to his divine fate.[51] His claims, then, were no public relations gimmick, but a deeply held belief.

Mohammad Reza's official designation as Crown Prince and his forced removal from the home of his mother and sisters were profound traumas. The typhoid fever followed by his first religious visions and subsequent serious illnesses and yet other visions were the surest clues to the emotional power of the abrupt change in the young boy's life. For those who seek secular explanations, the visions and illnesses indicate his youthful desperation. Finding solace in the protection of a heavenly father can be understood as both a rebuke to his this-worldly father—as revenge for that father's failures—and an indication of how desperately he felt the need for a protecting parent who would bring comfort and safety to his troubled life.

Those traumas would also result in a lifelong psychic configuration for the Shah: a conflict of competing identifications. First the Shah had internalized, had made part of his psychic structure, his early experiences with his mother and sisters. Then the Shah was abruptly forced out of that female world to be made into a "man." By that late age—the transition had occurred at six—it was no longer possible for the boy to consolidate an exclusively "manly education." Instead, he added certain qualities of activity, forthrightness, and aggression to his more passive and indulgent self. He was to manifest both poles of his character throughout his life, leading to divergent opinions about what the Shah was "really like." The Shahanshah, for those who only saw his public role, was a forceful, determined activist. But Mohammad Reza Pahlavi, for those who saw him outside his royal stature, was a different person—a more gentle, shy, withdrawn, even passive man. These dual aspects of the adult Shah were the source of frequently conflicting accounts of the monarch.

The alternate visions of the Shah are reflected in the appraisals Iranians made of him. In reviewing the scores of interviews I conducted to learn more of the man, I was struck by the contradictory adjectives used to describe him—even by the same informant. Not surprising for the last ruling King of Kings of the Empire of Iran, the Shah was described as arrogant, despotic, pitiless, rude, inhumane, stiff, cruel, vulgar, ruthless, pompous, impulsive, determined, and physically brave.

But the Shah was described, as well, in contrary terms: almost painfully shy, remote, withdrawn, indecisive, timid, sensitive, fearful, gentle, vulnerable, insecure, weak, constantly seeking confirmation, and constantly seeking approval. These latter adjectives were used far more often by those with the closes personal relationships with the Shah. The better the Shah was known, the less his imperious nature was seen as dominant.

All the more surprising, then, that as late as 1977, the United States, which by then had had at least twenty-five years of deep immersion in Iranian politics, still understood the Shah in terms of that first set of adjectives. No one has captured those different "personae" of the Shah more acutely than William H. Sullivan, the "last" U.S. ambassador to Iran. He relates his surprise at learning of his appointment to Iran after a diplomatic career in the Far East. The ambassador notes that "the nearest I had ever served to Tehran was in Calcutta nearly thirty years before. I had never lived in the Islamic world and knew little about its culture or its ethos."[52]

When the ambassador first met with President Carter's newly sworn secretary of state, his puzzlement was clarified. Secretary Vance told him that despite his inexperience with Iran or the Middle East, "it had been decided to send a professional who had considerable experience in dealing with authoritarian governments and with leaders who were forceful personalities."[53]

Ambassador Sullivan concluded not long after his arrival in Tehran that to understand the Shah as a "forceful personality" was to miss that entire other dimension of the Shah's character—the side which was to play such a significant role in his last years. The ambassador recounts a particularly poignant story which reveals something of the personal struggle the Shah underwent in order to present himself as he believed he must to fulfill his role as the Shahanshah. Sullivan, invited to witness joint U.S.-Iranian aircraft maneuvers, flew to a remote, desert airstrip to watch the exercises.[54] Once at the site, the Shah invited the ambassador to await the beginning of the air show in an air-conditioned trailer. When the two men entered the trailer, the Shah

unhitched his tunic, relaxed, and talked in his usual easy, gracious way about a number of things. Eventually there was a knock on the door, and an adjutant indicated that the airplanes were approaching and the air show was ready to begin.

With a sign, the Shah straightened his tunic, stood up, and performed a small act that embedded itself in my memory. From the gracious, easy, smiling host with whom I had been talking, he transformed himself suddenly to a steely, ramrod straight autocrat. This involved not only adjusting his uniform and donning dark glasses but also throwing out his chest, raising his chin, and fixing his lips in a grim line. When he had achieved this change to his own satisfaction, he thrust open the door of the trailer and stalked out across the few remaining steps to the reviewing stand.[55]

This slight vignette captures Mohammad Reza in the agony of the complexities being illuminated here—as the person and as the Shah he was. It was not easy for him to be Shah, as he had come to understand what it meant to be Shah, a challenge for which he had to mobilize all his resources to counter the softness and passivity which characterized him and which emanated from those early years amid that harem of females. To do so—to counter his personal inclinations in order to do what he believed he had to do to be Shah—Mohammad Reza Pahlavi paid a steep personal price. It proved a heavy burden for him not merely in the last years, but throughout his rule. On his early visit to the United States when he charmed the National Press Club, few realized that he meant being king was a personal burden for him.

To do what the Shah believed had to be done in order for him to be Shah was an extraordinary burden for two sets of reasons. On the one hand, he had to fight a constant pull toward passivity, toward a retreat to the inner world of his earliest female caretakers rather than to the outer world of males and public affairs. On the other hand, the personal challenge to Mohammad Reza of being Shah was greatly enhanced because his role model was his formidable father. Mohammad Reza not only had to be Shah, he had to be Shah on the model he set for himself, that of his father, Reza Shah.

There can be little doubt that Reza Shah was a significant figure of identification for his son. The many occasions on which the son evoked the father had political purposes—to benefit from any halo effect attendant on Reza Shah. References to his father dominate not only the pages of the Shah's autobiography but his earliest memories as well. As revealed earlier, his first recollections were of the Elburz Mountains and "the large and imposing figure of my father."[56] For the young boy, his father must have been as towering a figure as the mountains overshadowing Tehran.

In an interview given after the publication of his autobiography, the Shah suggested that the following childhood event remained his most noteworthy childhood memory. Significantly, it was also about his father.

The most powerful memory that Mohammad Reza holds of his father is his father's coronation ceremony in the course of which Mohammad Reza was designated crown prince. It was a fantastic celebration with all the famous dignitaries, the military music, unending speeches and applause. Then the most sacred moment, the coronation with the crown of precious gems and the robe of gold. . . . "Judge for yourself," the Shah remarked, "how much fear and reverence all of that could inspire in a child of six."[57]

There exist other indications of the personal significance of Reza Shah for his son. Clearly as the founder and first Shah of the Pahlavi dynasty, Reza Shah was politically significant for his son. Especially in the first years of Mohammad Reza Shah's rule, the legacy of his father affected the receptivity of the Iranian people to the son. Insofar as Reza Shah was remembered as a powerful and just ruler, both the dynasty and his son would be more readily accepted as the legitimate ruling institution of Iran. There was, therefore, always a political motive to the Shah's evoking his father's memory, especially in the early years of his own rule. But in such evocations there was also much more at work than mere politics, and especially so in his later years of kingship. Deeply seated personal motives were at work as well. Basically, the Shah remembered his father more for reasons central to his own character structure than for reasons relevant to the legitimacy of his rule. This appears true especially because of those countless occasions when the Shah mentioned his father in seemingly irrelevant circumstances— where the context did not suggest any particularly appropriate justification for introducing the memory of his father. What made such mentions appropriate was the Shah's inner psychic configuration and not the political circumstances of the moment.

An example of this "out of the blue" evocation of Reza Shah occurred in the Shah's interview with Oriana Fallaci. In the midst of his discussion of women and their effect on him, the Shah blurted out, "No one should forget that I'm the son of the man who removed women's veils in Iran."[58] In the midst of his depreciation of women this remark has a political connotation. But more, it seems to have a personal connotation as well. It is almost as if the Shah were reminding himself of his father's political acts in an effort to control the articulation of his own enmity toward women.

Not all of the Shah's remembrances of his father are positive. In a few rare instances, the Shah allowed himself to criticize his father, and two of those instances from his autobiography have been mentioned above. In a concluding summary of his father's rule, the Shah attempted to respond to criticisms of that rule by showing how Reza Shah's actions were useful for the conditions of Iran at that time. Thus the Shah justifies Reza Shah's failure to advance democracy by citing Iran's low levels of literacy and lack of a sophisticated electorate. Reza Shah's failure to devote resources to the development of agriculture is justified by Iran's primitive level of industrialization and the more pressing need to build factories. The Shah concludes:

It must be remembered, too, that my father possessed a very different personality from mine. His nature admirably qualified him for the tasks he had to perform, but it would have been ill-suited to the conditions of today.
. . . My father's inborn characteristics served his country better then but notwithstanding my admiration for him, I think mine are of greater service to it now. Were he alive to day, I believe he would agree.[59]

That the Shah apparently felt the need to suggest that his father was the best ruler for his day, but not necessarily for the present, is obviously self-serving. It is also a veiled criticism as well as an acknowledgment of the criticisms of Reza Shah current in Iran of the 1950s.

The longer his own rule, the more privately critical of his father the Shah became. In his later years, he was even unwilling to countenance praise for Reza Shah. In the perversion of values which characterized those years in Iran, it was virtually impossible to offer public criticism of any aspect of the rule of the Shah. One way to offer a criticism or at least register a dissent to the existing political order was to praise someone other than the Shah in an even more fulsome manner than the praise conventionally accorded him.[60] Thus the Shah and many Iranians would understand the celebrity status accorded a poet or weight lifter or wrestler as a political act expressing, through that celebration, a depreciation of the Shah. This was, of course, not always the case. But partly in fear that it was true and partly on account of the amplification of his own grandiosity, the Shah became ever less tolerant of criticism of himself and praise of others. Thus it came to be that the Shah was in the extraordinary position of understanding praise for his father as signifying depreciation of himself.

A one-time insider at the imperial court related how during the 1970s the Shah became ever more jealous of Reza Shah and ever more inclined to compare himself with Reza Shah in inappropriate circumstances. At one private audience with the Shah, this official was discussing a program he had drawn up for the large ministry over which he had responsibility. The Shah interrupted him and asked his subject what he thought of Reza Shah. The minister assured the Shah that he thought his father was a great man. The following conversation then occurred:

"Yes, my father was a very great man. But I have done much more for my country than did he."

"Well, Your Majesty, when Reza Shah came to power, the condition of Iran was far different than at the start of your reign. When Reza Shah became Shahanshah, there was complete feudalism and illiteracy. There were no state organizations. . . ."

"Yes, you are right. But I have done much more."

"Yes, Your Majesty, that is true. You have done much more. But you have had over twenty-five years of rule while Reza Shah had only fifteen years."[61]

That last comment so angered the Shah that he rose and ended the audience. That exchange and the other evidence presented about the Shah's memories of his father demonstrate both the immensity and intensity of the complications involved in the relation between the son, Mohammad Reza, and his father, Reza. Reza Shah was a figure of immense positive as well as negative consequence for his son.

Reza Shah was also a "larger than life figure" for his heir.[62] He was, to begin with, a huge man, both unusually tall, well over six feet, and physically large. After his death, the Shah had the title of Kabir, or "the Great," officially bestowed on Reza Shah. While that title ostensibly referred to the contributions his father made to the development of Iran, it also captures how formidable was the man in the eyes of his son as a young boy and as an adult.

In one of the Shah's earliest memories, his father was in the "process of moving mountains." That metaphor represents the awesome dimensions Reza Shah represented for his son. There was much opportunity for the young boy to identify with the strength his father clearly possessed. In some ways, that seems to have happened. Mohammad Reza was able to find strength through a partial identification with his father.

One tangible example of his finding strength in his father occurred as his crisis with Prime Minister Mohammad Mossadegh reached its height. The United States and Britain had recruited the reluctant Shah to participate in the "royal coup," which was to be initiated by the Shah's issuing an imperial rescript, dismissing Mossadegh as prime minister, a prerogative the Shah enjoyed according to the Iranian Constitution.

The Shah, at what must have been his most anxious moment, chose to issue his dismissal notice from a hunting lodge he occasionally used as a retreat in the Caspian village of Kelardasht.[63] As the Shah himself described those anxious days, he had gone to the north with Queen Soraya and "stayed alternately at the villa my father had built on the shores of the Caspian near Ramsar and at the hunting lodge he had constructed at Kelardasht."[64] Not only had Reza Shah built the two residences in which the Shah sought physical as well as psychological shelter, but Kelardasht was doubly significant in that it was the village in which Reza Shah had spent his earliest years.

It was as if the Shah, in order to muster the courage necessary to take the fateful step of dismissing his prime minister—in a scenario largely formulated by British and U.S. intelligence services—surrounded himself, at least symbolically, with the presence of his powerful father. On occasion, the Shah could gain strength by bolstering his identification with his father through being among the remnants of his father's physical presence.

The manliness Reza Shah sought to instill in his young son by raising him in a palace away from the feminizing world of his mother and sisters produced uncertainty, vulnerability, and hurt more than the possibility of courage and strength. Reza Shah's awesome strength, towering presence, and fearsome rages were more a source of terror than strength for young Mohammad Reza.

At least two other instances from the Shah's early years indicate how the young Crown Prince must have suffered under the tutelage of his awesome Shah. Both center on the training the Crown Prince received to prepare him for assuming the throne—the formal education he received under the close supervision of his father and the informal training he received through the "discussions" with his father, general "discussions" over the years and one "discussion" in particular.

The Shah acquired his earliest formal education in the palace elementary school established for him and a few other favored children, and he reported on how rigorous this early elementary school had been, with its military regimen and training. But it was far less rigorous than the subsequent chapter of his formal education.

The Shah graduated from his palace elementary school in May of 1931 at the age of eleven years and seven months. With that graduation came another emotional blow: Reza Shah had decided to send his son abroad for further studies. To avoid the political involvements which would result were the Crown Prince to study in a school of one of the major powers, Reza Shah selected the Le Rosey secondary school outside Geneva in neutral Switzerland. Thus in September of 1931, not yet twelve years of age, the Shah was to experience another traumatic separation. In that month he was packed off with two Persian friends, Hussein Fardoust and Mehrpour Teymourtash, the son of the minister of court; a Persian physician to attend to the still sickly lad; and a Persian tutor to ensure that he did not forget his native tongue. After a year of special preparatory work, the boys entered the Le Rosey school, where the Shah remained until the spring of 1936, when he returned to Iran.[65]

His years in Switzerland were an extraordinarily unhappy period for the Crown Prince. In his entire autobiography, the Shah makes but one mistake in recounting the chronology of his life, and that mistake concerns the length of his stay outside of Iran at his secondary school. "I was to stay in Switzerland about four years," the Shah remembers.[66] Only two pages later he refers to "my first two years abroad" and "my last three years," a total of five, not four years.[67] He did, in fact, remain in Switzerland for what, by all reckoning, were five miserable academic years.

He remembered the total number of years incorrectly, it seems plausible to suppose, because those were years of such sadness for him. Every memory of his years at school in Switzerland—every public memory, at least—was one of great sadness. The Shah recalls his "isolation" at the school and how his Iranian physician, acting as his guardian, refused to allow the boy to leave the school grounds except in his company. The Shah remembers that he could not join his "comrades" at "parties and balls" held in town. "My friends," he notes sadly some twenty years after the fact, "were having fun, laughing and dancing while I was sitting alone in my room. . . . I had a radio and gramophone to keep me company, but what fun were they compared with the festivities my friends enjoyed."[68]

The Shah told an interviewer late in his rule that his guardian was so frightened of Reza Shah that he imposed other restrictions as well. Dr. Nafici "would not even let me swim or ride a bicycle, but some accident should occur and he should be held responsible."[69] Not only was he subject to frustrating restraints on his freedom, but he was subject to close academic scrutiny as well. He was required by his father to send weekly Persian lessons to Tehran so that Reza Shah could witness his progress in Persian under his Persian tutor.[70] To make it clear that Reza Shah paid attention to this aspect of his training, the Shah recalls that "once the mail was delayed and my father was so annoyed that he immediately cabled my unfortunate tutor and censured him."[71]

The Shah's years in Switzerland then were, in his own mind, years of asceticism and hardship. His removal to Switzerland was the second crucial rejection he had experienced. Reasons of state, as they were defined in the mind of his father, had dictated that he be separated from his mother and sisters. Now he was completely denied their presence as well as that of his father and his familiar surroundings in order to acquire more such education. And it seems clear that Reza Shah's instructions and intervention ensured that the Switzerland years were truly "manly."[72]

Reza Shah explained his decision to send his son abroad to one of the members of the court: "It is very hard for me to part with my beloved son, but one must think of the country. Iran needs educated and enlightened rulers, we, the old and the ignorant, must go."[73] However much of a personal sacrifice it may have been for Reza Shah to send away his son, he clearly was willing to make it for his country. It is difficult to see, however, how a not-yet-twelve-year-old could possibly understand it in that way. It is far more likely that young Mohammad Reza experienced being sent to Switzerland as yet another personal rejection—as further proof of his father's lack of care and concern for him, for his well-being, and for his childhood wants and needs.

Reza Shah may have had some sense of how lonely his son had become at Le Rosey. In 1933 he sent Taj ol-Moluk and the Princesses Shams and Ashraf to Switzerland to visit the boy. The royal party left Tehran by car and drove to Bandar Pahlavi on the Caspian Sea. There they embarked on a boat to Baku in the Soviet Union, where they boarded a train through Moscow to Geneva. After an eight-day journey they reached the Crown Prince during his summer vacation. But Reza Shah himself did not visit his son.

An indication of how pained the Crown Prince was by the separation from his father is revealed in a letter written by Reza Shah in 1934, shortly after his return from his sole trip outside the borders of Iran, to visit Ataturk in June of that year:

On my return, I read your answering letter. I was touched and moved by your delicate sentiments, complaining that I had come as far as Istanbul and still failed to meet you. To express the depth of my suffering from being away from you would indeed be difficult. However, because of my greater purpose, I must tolerate it.[74]

The Crown Prince had, apparently, complained of the difficulty of the separation and his father's failure to extend his trip from Turkey to Switzerland.[75]

When the future ruler finally returned to Iran in 1936, after his foreign studies, he at least made a favorable impression on his twin. Princess Ashraf remembers that "my brother looked happy and healthy, stronger and more fit than he had in Tehran."[76] The Crown Prince undoubtedly had benefited from his years in Switzerland, but his happiness at returning to Tehran probably was more a comment on his misery at Le Rosey. His only source of comfort appears to have been the company of a friend he had made at the school, Ernest Perron.

Their relation had become so close that the Crown Prince returned from his years abroad with his Swiss friend. Reza Shah was apparently horrified. In the company of his ministers, he referred to the Crown Prince as a "playboy" and scorned him for his close ties to Perron. The ruler berated the boy and announced that he considered his son's stay abroad a complete loss.[77] Finally he apparently decided to heighten the pressures on his son in hopes of yet toughening him in anticipation of his eventual kingly responsibilities. When Mohammad Reza enrolled at Iran's military academy, the Shah insisted that his son be treated with greater severity and discipline than his classmates.[78]

Another part of his regimen for toughening the future ruler was Reza Shah's practice of lunching with his son. The Shah told one biographer that his father had begun the practice before he left for Switzerland. As the Shah has made clear, those earlier lunches took the form of Reza Shah's lecturing his son on such subjects as the appropriate fashion in which a monarch should live and rule, the character of a monarch, and other subjects meant to prepare the youth for the throne.[79] The Shah does not tell his readers how he responded to these lectures on sobriety and asceticism, but from his remembrances of his lonely stay at Le Rosey it is reasonable to conclude that he rejected them outright. Later, when the Crown Prince had graduated from the Iranian officers school, when the boy had not yet reached nineteen years of age, Reza Shah began more regular training for his son.

They met daily and lunched together for "discussions" of the pressing problems Iran faced. But there was, in fact, little actual "discussion," as the Shah was later to acknowledge: "I and all the officials of my father's government had such respect for him and were so much in awe of him that 'discussion' with him had none of the give-and-take the word implies. I advanced my views and made hints and suggestions, but discussion in any usual sense was out of the question."[80]

Just how intimidated the Shah was by his father's austere and formidable presence throughout his father's rule is conveyed by other events. Apparently convinced that he had to check his son's burgeoning friendship with Ernest Perron and seeking to ensure the perpetuation of the dynasty, Reza Shah decided to find a suitable bride for his son. In 1938, by the time of Mohammad Reza's graduation from the military academy, Reza Shah had succeeded. The Crown Prince described how he came to be engaged without so much as having ever seen his bride-to-be.

My father had evidently seen pictures of the lovely Princess Fawzia of Egypt. With his characteristic forthrightness—perhaps better adapted to engineering than to affairs of the heart—he started an investigation. First, he had the girl's pedigree checked. Then he had his legation in Cairo contact the Egyptian Government who, in turn, got in touch with Egypt's royal family. My father officially inquired whether the Princess would be available as a wife for his son. Negotiations rapidly progressed, and the first thing I knew, I was betrothed.[81]

The Shah was married in Cairo soon after, apparently never having protested that he had never been consulted about his marriage, much less participating in the process by which his bride was selected.

The Crown Prince had already been asked by his twin sister to intervene in a similar affair, but he had refused. Some two years earlier, when Princess Ashraf was seventeen, Reza Shah had decided it was time for her and her older sister, Princess Shams, to marry. He selected two eligible young men. Ali Qavam, the son of a prominent family from Shiraz, was to marry Shams. Fereidoun Jam, a young army officer, was engaged to wed Ashraf.

Ashraf, at seventeen, "shrank from the idea of marriage, let alone marriage to a man I had never seen . . . so I asked my brother to intercede, to ask Reza Shah to change his mind."[82] But the Crown Prince would have none of it: "My brother listened sympathetically, but when I had finished, he held out little hope. 'Trying to change our father's mind on this matter would be a waste of time,' he said. 'He believes a girl should marry at a certain age, and opposing him is useless. I think you must do as he says.' "[83]

In fact, Reza Shah's mind was changed, but not by his son. When the prospective brides first saw their prospective bridegrooms, Shams decided to try to change the whole scheme. She was more attracted to Jam than to her own fiancé, Qavam. She went to Reza Shah urging him to switch the partners. Reza Shah agreed, and shortly thereafter Princess Shams married Fereidoun Jam while Princess Ashraf married Ali Qavam.

Another indication of the relation between father and son was provided by Queen Soraya. She recalls a conversation with her husband about his youth in which he regretted the great distance between Reza Shah and his children. He spoke again of the fear with which they all viewed their father and added, "We never had the right to say anything in family gatherings and our opinions were voiced only in reply to specific questions asked of us."[84]

It is unlikely there was ever much in the way of a genuine exchange between Reza Shah and his designated successor.[85] More to the point here is the extent to which the relation between father and son, Reza Shah and Mohammad Reza, proved fateful in shaping the character of the future monarch. Certainly the father was not the only key actor in the drama of Mohammad Reza's childhood. That powerful and stubborn mother was the other key figure. The sisters and even a younger brother were not without consequence. But it was the father and more particularly the circumstances of his son's childhood which were structured by the father which proved so significant.

It was no wonder Mohammad Reza could not challenge his awesome father. His sense of awe was produced by both the compelling reality of Reza Shah and the character of the Crown Prince, which made him personally all the less able to cope with a powerful and overweening father. The inability of the boy to cope with that father—if nothing more, merely to have been able to have engaged in discussions with him—was taken by the young boy as further proof of his own inadequacies, testimony to his failings, his weakness, and his vulnerabilities.

A particularly poignant instance of the boy's propensity for reaching such conclusions on the basis of his interactions with his father occurred in 1938 or 1939 while the Crown Prince was accompanying Reza Shah on an inspection tour. Reza Shah had initiated such "field trips" as yet another way to prepare the boy for his future duties. Reza Shah was fond of frequent, personal inspections of the countryside, where he could learn firsthand of the fate of the ambitious projects he had launched from the capital. It was on one such visit that there occurred what can be usefully understood as the central metaphor of the Shah's youth.

Reza Shah and his son were spending the night in a tent pitched at Kelardasht, some one hundred miles northwest of Tehran, near the Caspian Sea, the same village in which Reza Shah had spent his earliest years and to which the Shah was to repair when he issued his imperial rescript dismissing Mossadegh. The Shah later reported what happened between the Pahlavi father and son:

> My father said he wanted to improve the Government's administrative machinery to such a degree that if he should die, the day-to-day process of administration would operate almost automatically without the need of continuous supervision from the top.
>
> I was still rather young and perhaps not very mature, and I took his remark as an insult. "What does he mean?" I thought. "Does he think that if he were gone I couldn't take over and continue his work?" Although naturally I didn't say anything, his remark really nettled me. Yet only a short time later, when he was obliged to abdicate and the government and the country were plunged into chaos, I remembered his foresight and regretted his wish for a self-operating administrative system had not been fulfilled.[86]

This seemingly minor incident of the Shah's youth should be understood as an exemplar of the relation the Shah had with his father. Not that this single conversation alone necessarily had a lasting effect on the Shah, but rather that it exemplifies the link between father and son, and as a result, as is suggested below, the memory of it returned to the Shah on numerous occasions when he felt threatened. Reza Shah, characteristically, manifested no empathy for the boy and his sensitivities, seeking instead to control the son in ways the father judged most likely to produce the results necessary to guarantee a successful heir to the throne. The Crown Prince, characteristically, heard his father as belittling the son's capacities and humiliating him in the process. The key this incident provides to the character of the Crown Prince is its demonstration of his propensity for psychological injury.

The injury from his father at Kelardasht cut so deeply that time and again he returned to that conversation. He told his one-time adviser E. A. Bayne of the conversation.[87] He mentioned the story in his second book, *The White Revolution*.[88] He also told the story in an interview he gave at the peak of his political power.[89] But the memory of that conversation was not reserved for his "public" interviews. The Shah remembered the hurt and humiliation at threatening moments in his life. At the funeral of his assassinated prime minister, Hassan Ali Mansur, in early 1965, the Shah turned to one of the mourners, a high government official, and whispered the story of his Kelardasht conversation with his father.[90]

Kelardasht itself—the physical place—took on great significance from this event. Little wonder that when the Shah sought a refuge from the challenge of Prime Minister Mohammad Mossadegh and a safe haven to wait out the results of the joint American-British "countercoup" meant to oust the prime minister, he and Queen Soraya stayed in that same valley, in the hunting lodge Reza Shah had subsequently built. It was almost as if the Shah had retreated to the site of his past narcissistic injury in the face of the persisting and growing threats to his rule, represented by Prime Minister Mossadegh. Perhaps he felt that, having survived the past injury at Kelardasht and, as symbolized by that conversation, all the injuries he had suffered from his powerful father, he could gain the strength he so desperately needed to deal with this new threat from the powerful (and older) Mossadegh. If there was any psychological transference at work in the relation of the Shah to Mossadegh, any predilection by the Shah to relate to his prime minister in some of the ways he had related to his own father, then a retreat to Kelardasht would be a psychologically reasonable course.

But more important here than the relationship of the Shah to Mossadegh is what the conversation at Kelardasht reveals of the relation of that other Shah and the future Shah. It reveals Reza Shah's capacity for blunt talk uttered with little or no concern for the hurt it might inflict on his listener. For surely Reza Shah would have understood his son's sensitivities and the effects his remarks would have on his son. The incident also tells us how Mohammad Reza Pahlavi had emerged from his childhood into young manhood: he was ridden with self-doubts and fearful of his powerful father whom he nonetheless idealized as the embodiment of all the virtues of kingship which in the depths of his own self he believed he lacked. Reza Shah undoubtedly shared those beliefs. His remarks at Kelardasht suggest that he was, in fact, concerned for the capacities his son would be able to exercise as monarch.

The very last exchanges between Reza Shah and his son demonstrate how keenly he understood his son and how troubled he was for the future of the dynasty, then in his son's care. Reza Shah was removed from the throne in August 1941 by the British and Soviets, whose armies, invading from the south and the north, had routed the armed forces of Iran which Reza Shah had so laboriously and expensively built in the previous two decades. The two powers then decided that not only would he be removed from the throne but, to ensure the safety of their occupation, he would be exiled. He was informed that only Mohammed Reza, his bride Fawzia, and their daughter Shahnaz would be allowed to remain in Iran. The rest of the Pahlavis, Reza Shah and his three wives and all their children, were to be sent abroad. Reza Shah pleaded with the British and ultimately received permission for Princess Ashraf to remain in Tehran with her twin brother. For he knew his son needed the strength and courage which his daughter possessed but which he understood his son to lack.

Eventually Ashraf made the long and arduous journey under wartime stringencies and dangers to visit her father in his South African exile. But on the very day after she arrived, he urged her to return to Iran as soon as travel plans could be arranged. As she prepared to leave, Reza Shah told her, "in a voice that shook with emotion, . . . 'I know you can be strong, but I want you always to be strong for your brother. Stay close to him and tell him to stand firm in the face of dangers of any kind.'"[91]

Reza Shah communicated those sentiments directly to his son as well. In his letters from exile, Reza Shah offered his son the constant advice, "Never be afraid of anything in the world."[92] And in his final writings from his own exile, the Shah remained mindful of his own father, communicating from his African exile: "The very last message I received from him in his exile," the Shah recalled, "was on a phonograph record. 'My son,' he said to me, 'fear nothing.'"[93]

It appears reasonable, then, to understand Reza Shah's remarks at Kelardasht as not merely a reflection of his own insensitivity, but as a reflection of his assessment of the qualities his son would bring to the monarchy. Reza Shah understood full well that the young Mohammad Reza lacked the toughness and courage which a king, an Iranian king in particular, would need.

Whether or not Reza Shah possessed, as his son remembered, "a devastating ability to assess human nature," it appears that his son believed he did.[94] And it appears that both father and son shared, at least in their hearts, a common assessment of the future king. For the Shah had grown into a young adult with what psychoanalysts would now characterize as severe narcissistic imbalances. He was a young man of low self-esteem who masked his lack of self-confidence, his indecisiveness, his passivity, his dependency, and his shyness with masculine bravado, impulsiveness, and arrogance. He was, in short, a man of acute personal contradictions.

Depending on the relative strength of his psychic imbalances, he would manifest one or the other aspects of his character. Thus he could be an entirely "different" person from one occasion to another or an entirely "different" person to the same individual over time. He was both gentle and cruel, withdrawn and active, dependent and assertive, weak and powerful.

These contradictions resulted from his personal struggles to compensate for his inadequate psychic supplies, his severe narcissistic imbalances. Those, in turn, were the product of the childhood experiences described here. There are, of course, a number of ways in which these childhood experiences can be understood within a psychoanalytic framework. The one obvious interpretation appears to be the most useful. It accounts for the largest number of psychological facts from the Shah's childhood and adulthood. That interpretation is rooted in the conflicts produced by the Shah's identifications with his mother and with his father. In his early infancy, the Shah must have been a most welcome and loved child. He was the first son of his parents, an especially favored child among Iranians.

In his autobiography, the Shah includes a number of photographs from his childhood, the first of which shows the massive figure of Reza Shah seated on a bench. Perched on his right knee is the young Mohammad Reza, steadied by the embrace of Reza Shah's powerful arm and huge hand over the boy's small body and arm. In between Reza Shah's knees stands his elder daughter Shams, clutching her father's other hand. Considerably off to the side at the edge of the picture stands the lonely and troubled-looking twin, Ashraf.[95] Shams and Mohammad Reza, in all likelihood, were the most favored of all the children—Shams because she was the first child and had two years of attention from her parents before the birth of the twins, and the future Crown Prince because he was the firstborn son.

The Shah's low self-esteem was produced by the disruptions of his childhood. When Mohammad Reza was less than seventeen months old, his father carried out the military coup that would make him the central figure in Iranian politics and, undoubtedly, a far less available father to his son. In the following year, his parents' marriage collapsed.

In the four remaining years that Mohammad Reza lived in his mother's house—before he was installed, upon the orders of Reza Shah, in his own palace—he must have been subjected to powerful psychological pressures. As the oldest male, he remained the favored child and must have been especially indulged. But as the son of her husband, he was also, perhaps, differently treated. His mother's toughness suggests that she may have used the boy against the husband she perceived as having betrayed her. What better way than to estrange the boy from his father by fostering his psychological immersion in that house of females. The indulgences due the firstborn male were intensified by the mother's seeking to enmesh the boy in her own self and, in the process, to distance him from his betraying father. Mohammad Reza became, in the process, a passive, dependent, or in psychoanalytic terminology, feminized, lad.

It was undoubtedly in response to his perception of his son's increasing passivity and dependence on Taj ol-Moluk—and perhaps in the service of taking revenge on his withholding wife—that Reza Shah decided to take action. He forced his wife to relinquish the boy. He installed his son, now the Crown Prince, in a separate palace. The extent of the psychological trauma of that separation is indicated by Mohammad Reza's subsequent illnesses and visions. The enmeshment between mother and son had become so intense that his response to its loss endangered his life.

No physical separation could eliminate the psychological attachments, however. Throughout his life the son retained an identification with his mother. She was the source of his most gratifying and life-sustaining indulgences. He may have been torn from her constant attentions but he would never lose his longing for that lost, blessed paradise, nor renounce what appears to have been a lifelong struggle to re-create the joys of those earlier passive, dependent indulgences.[96]

The origins of the alternative dimension of the Shah's character—his "masculine" self—also need to be explained. Their roots lie in his early identifications with the toughness of his mother as well as his father and in that special palace constructed exclusively for the Crown Prince. There he was scrutinized by his father and surrounded by male attendants. There, in association with Reza Shah, the Crown Prince "learned" what it meant to be a male. He "learned" that females are, in effect, to be scorned, for to come in contact with them would result in the loss of one's masculine toughness. He was to learn that a man must break his ties with the females of his life in order to become the man he was meant to be. In that masculine milieu of his palace, the son came to idealize his imposing, powerful father. That idealization was another dimension of his character, one that served as the basis for his masculine attributes, and was to remain part of his psychic structure, along with his passive, dependent self, for his entire life.

The Shah emerged from his childhood full of contradictions and complexities. As an adult, he would again and again echo the experiences—the indulgences, threats, and rejections—of his childhood. On one occasion, for example, he reflected on the proper role of parents in Iran, in the process offering an insight into his own childhood.

The parents, especially the mother, have a tremendously constructive role to play. Every Persian child should feel that he can count upon the love of his mother and find shelter and refuge in her arms. The young child must feel that his mother, along with at least a few other people in his small world, care intensely about him and his welfare. He must be sure that he can always go to his mother and that he is never cut off from her. If misfortune has taken his mother away, then somebody else must surround him in love.[97]

Not only did he frequently reveal truths about his early years through his words, but he revealed the effect of those years in other ways. With his first child, Princess Shahnaz, he repeated the separations and rejections he had experienced. When she was six years old, he sent her to boarding school in Switzerland. She remained there for five years without a visit from her father; only her mother, Queen Fawzia, visited her. In 1951, when she was eleven, after having spent exactly the same number of years abroad as he had as a youth, she was allowed to return to Tehran for her summer vacation. For those months she lived in a small house on the grounds of the Shah's palace. She was not allowed to stay in the palace the Shah shared with his second wife. As Queen Soraya was to put it, "It was obvious that the poor child had grown up without the love of her parents."[98]

When the Shah's third wife delivered a male heir, Reza II, the Shah repeated with this son and heir the childhood rejections to which he had been subjected by Reza Shah. The Shah established a separate palace for Reza II when the boy was six years old, the same age at which the Shah had been removed from his mother's attentions. The Shah had moved to a new palace north of Tehran at Niavaran, and so he installed his son in a refurbished small residence, originally built by the Qajars, on the grounds of that palace. There the Crown Prince would be raised under the supervision of a French governess. Simultaneously, several of the Shah's own adjutants were appointed to the service of the Crown Prince.

Furthermore, as Reza Shah had not effectively prepared him for king-ship, so did the Shah fail in his son's training. In the summer of 1978 the Shah was asked whether the Crown Prince was ready to assume the throne. "His training period has not really begun officially," the Shah answered. "He is almost 18 years old and is just taking his final school exams. After that, he will go to the United States for one year of aviation training and when he returns, we will begin his initiation."[99]

Later, Reza II was to regret how little time his father had spent with him: "I calculated the amount of time I spent with my father during my entire life. . . . the total amount of time I had with him, if you were to add up the hours, was about two months. My father was a very busy man . . . we had very few opportunities to really sit down and talk as father and son."[100]

These reenactments of childhood events with his own offspring reveal their power for him. They reveal the extent to which his own parents had failed him. The Shah was to struggle with the consequences of those failures for his entire life. He developed two psychological mechanisms—splitting and projection—which facilitated his struggles to do what he be-lieved he had to do in order to be the Shah. He split off from himself those devalued parts of his psychological makeup which he understood to be in-appropriate—the passive, dependent, and feminine qualities at his core. He then projected these outward, onto others. He especially identified his enemies by such feminine attributes. The Shah described Mohammad Mossadegh and his followers, for example, as people who "cried like women and indulged in hysterical tirades."[101] Of Ayatollah Khomeini the Shah wrote, "it mattered little that he should speak . . . since he was no more than a puppet in the hands of the outsiders who condemned my regime."[102]

It was not only onto his enemies that he projected those qualities he sought to renounce. The Iranian people as a whole were feminized, and women in general were especially devalued. The Shah constructed a re-gime in which only he was allowed to be a "man." His senior ministers and advisers and the remainder of the Iranian people were not allowed to be "men." "The Shah," as one of his ministers put it, "would allow no other Iranian to retain a shred of dignity. Even as he treasured the greatness of Persian culture and its contributions to the achievements of world civiliza-tion, he debased the worth of the Persians."[103] According to one U.S. official with long service in Iran and access to the ruler, the Shah viewed the Iranian people as weak, lazy, and venal. In order for him to fulfill his "mission"—to restore the greatness of Iran—he believed he had to do something about his people's negative qualities.[104] The Iranian people knew, even if few were able to articulate their knowledge, that the Shah held them in contempt. They did not understand, nor is it likely that it would have made a significant difference had they known, that his contempt was the externalization of his own sense of himself; that his contempt for them represented his desperate struggle to maintain his psychic balance by splitting off from himself the parts he most despised and projecting them outward, onto others.

The signs of his contempt for his people were everywhere. One such indication was the practice he encouraged whereby his subjects indicated their fealty by kissing his hand. During formal court ceremonies held on every major holiday, his ministers along with leading members of Iranian society would be received by the Shah. They would stand in rows in the mirrored and chandeliered reception room, waiting in their formal morning suits. The Shah would pass from individual to individual, exchanging words of greeting and good wishes. In response, they would bow and kiss his hand.

The Shah's last prime minister, Dr. Shahpour Bakhtiar, lost much of his rapidly ebbing support during the final days of the revolution through just such an act. As the Shah prepared to leave Iran on January 16, 1979, for what proved to be the last time, his senior officials gathered at Mehrabad Airport. In the midst of a newly constituted Regency Council, ranking military officers, and cabinet ministers, Dr. Bakhtiar bent toward the Shah, grasped the monarch's hand, and kissed it. At the very moment when the ruler was fleeing his country, in the midst of its overwhelming rejection of his rule, Shahpour Bakhtiar communicated—in a highly charged and symbolic way—his immersion in the hated system.

As another consequence of the Shah's projection, women were especially devalued. Here, as in so many other areas, the Shah presented contradictions. Under his rule, women were granted rights and freedoms previously unimaginable in Iran (and regrettably, at least as unimaginable, subsequently, under the sacred fascism which came to characterize the reign of Ayatollah Khomeini). The rights and freedoms he extended to Iranian women were nearly unique in the Islamic world as well. In 1963, women were given the right to vote. In 1975, the Family Protection Act was passed. In the words of Princess Ashraf, its principal architect, the act "gave Iran's women the most sweeping civil rights in the Middle East."[105]

With individual women, the Shah was courteous, even gallant. But he was, as well, a notorious womanizer. It is said that Queen Fawzia was incensed by his constant affairs[106] and that Queen Soraya threatened him frequently with divorce if he did not cease his philandering in his private chambers.[107] All indications suggest that the Shah never did cease his extramarital adventures.[108]

This disdain for women was also the result of his splitting and projection, the psychic mechanisms he used to deny his own unwanted characteristics, in this instance his unwanted feminine characteristics. The Shah's depreciation of women was revealed only infrequently and, except on rare occasions, only indirectly. His ambivalence toward his mother is one example. His uncharacteristic vitriol delivered publicly to Oriana Fallaci is another. The Shah's projection, however veiled and infrequently expressed, targeted women just as it targeted his personal and political enemies and even the people of Iran.

Several consequences followed from the Shah's use of splitting and projection to enhance his own esteem. He was deprived of the capacity to empathize fully with his own people. He was not so totally dominated by his propensity for projection, of course, that he had no emotional capacity to deal with the Iranian people directly and on their terms rather than his own. But insofar as he did project, his capacity for any "objective" appraisal of his people was diminished. He was limited in his capacity to understand their desires and goals and the means they sought to fulfill their own psychic needs. As a result, his task of building the "Great Civilization," as he called his vision for Iran, was made more difficult. For his impaired capacity for empathy hindered his ability to see the Iranian people as they were. He was thus in the increasingly untenable position of attempting to mobilize and lead a people whose own aspirations he misunderstood or, at best, inaccurately grasped.

Yet another consequence of his splitting off his depreciated qualities and projecting them outward was the relative enhancement of his own valued "masculine" qualities. To the extent that he was able to believe they were his dominant qualities, his identification with his idealized father was strengthened and it enhanced his sense of comfort and strength. Furthermore, the valued masculine qualities crowded out the devalued feminine parts of his character structure. Thus he constantly struggled to emphasize his masculine attributes, those he associated with his awesome father. The Shah piloted his jet aircraft, drove his fast cars, wore his medal- and braid-festooned uniforms, regularly played cards with his (male) cronies, and acted in countless other ways to maintain his sense of a valued masculine self. It was always a struggle, however.

Countering the Shah's masculine strivings were his feminine longings. The Shah had constantly to ward off his identification with his mother and his wishes to return to that state of pristine bliss when he was surrounded only by females, protected from his fearsome father by their almost magical presence. When the Shah had external sources of psychic support, the intensity of the struggle was reduced. The Shah was able to "split" and "project" and act as Shah.

Throughout his life the Shah relied on four principal sources of psychic support to maintain his capacity to act as Shah. The admiration he received from others, and particularly from his primary audience, the people of Iran, was crucial to him. So was the psychic strength he received through a very small number of close personal associates. His ties with them were so close that these relationships assumed the qualities of psychic "twinships." The Shah also maintained a near lifelong belief in a watchful and protecting God who had decreed his success in carrying out a divine mission. Finally, the Shah relied for psychic strength on his important diplomatic and personal psychological ties with the United States. These four mechanisms provided the Shah with the psychic supplies he needed to split off the devalued, passive, dependent aspects of his self, project them onto others, and thus maintain his positive masculine identification. But when his sources of strength were dissipated in the 1970s, he could not maintain his masculine assertiveness to cope with challenges of the Revolution.

The Crown Prince surrounded by a cadre of youth recruited to serve as members of an honorary guard corps. June 2, 1926. Bettmann Archive.

The young ruler, following his father's deposition, at about the time he ascended the throne in 1941. Bettmann Archive.

The royal family—the Shah, his wife Queen Fawzia, and their daughter Princess Shahnaz, born in 1940. AP/Wide World Photos.

(Above left) President Harry S. Truman welcomed the Shah on his first visit to the United States in November 1949. AP/Wide World Photos.

(Below left) The Shah with Queen Soraya, his second wife, February 13, 1951. AP/Wide World Photos.

(Above right) Assuming an imperial pose, the Shah, in full regalia, projects an image of power, while his actual power was draining steadily toward Prime Minister Mossadegh. October 26, 1952. Bettmann Archive.

Surrounded by journalists in his Rome hotel, the Shah holds up wire service copy announcing that Mossadegh has been overthrown. August 19, 1953. AP/Wide World Photos.

The Shah is greeted by members of the diplomatic corps as he returns to Tehran from his brief exile in Baghdad and Rome. He is wearing his Iranian Air Force uniform. General Zahedi, the Coup-maker, stands, in profile, in the upper left corner. August 22, 1953. AP/Wide World Photos.

On the day after his return from exile to reclaim his throne, the pleased monarch poses on the grounds of the royal palace. August 23, 1953. AP/Wide World Photos.

Vice-president Richard Nixon and wife Pat greet the Shah and Queen Soraya upon their arrival to Washington. December 14, 1954. AP/Wide World Photos.

Queen Elizabeth II, the Duke of Edinburgh, Prince Charles, and Princess Anne pose with the Shah (in his air force uniform) and Queen Soraya on an official visit to the United Kingdom. February 18, 1955. Bettmann Archive.

3

Imperial Grandeur:
Pahlavi Grandiosity

By the 1970s the world had come to see the Shah in mythical dimensions. One pulp novel at the time was entitled *A Bullet for the Shah: All They Had to Do Was Kill the World's Most Powerful Man.*[1] The popular author Paul Erdman had a cover story in *New York* magazine entitled "The Oil War of 1976: How the Shah Won the World." The article was subheaded, "The World as We Knew It Came to an End When the Shah of Iran Decided to Restore the Glory of Ancient Persia with Western Arms."[2] This belief in the mythical dimensions of the ruler and his power came to be shared by the Shah himself and was propagated by him, his family and court, the apparatchiks of the government of Iran, and the country's mass media.

It seems ironic that the highwater mark of the grandiosity of the Pahlavi system was reached only three years before the Shah's fall. The imperial light of Pahlavi rule never shown more brightly than shortly before it was extinguished. Yet it is the central argument of this book that the grandiosity and the fall are linked. For when the external sources which provided the Shah with narcissism were functioning, and the Shah could "do" and not just "be" Shah, his narcissism was far from modulated. Rather his narcissism was expansive to the point of grandiosity.

That grandiosity led to a host of imperial policies deeply offensive to the Iranian people. The Shah's policies, enacted in the fullness of his grandiosity, violated many of the most deeply held tenets of Iranian culture. That many Iranians participated with the Shah in the enactment of those policies, benefited personally from their realization, and therefore were fully immersed in the Pahlavi system did not allow them to escape the sense of having been demeaned by Pahlavi rule. For those Iranians less directly rewarded from participation in the system, the grandiosity of the Shah was no less demeaning. The sense of having been diminished and depreciated by the rule of the Shah, primarily through the policies he enacted in his narcissistic grandiosity, became nearly universal by the mid-1970s. The rage which that sense of depreciation produced was not long in coming.

In the midyears of the decade, however, that rage was no where in evidence. The Shah was firmly entrenched in power. His Empress Farah played an active role in the areas of Iranian life to which she was committed—culture and the arts, education, the family, women, and children. A flood of oil dollars had emerged, and no end was in sight to the seemingly unquenchable demand of the industrial world for the Middle East's most valuable resource. The entire state apparatus shared the new sense of power with the imperial couple. Each bureaucrat mimicked the Shah, but writ small, so as not to incite his ire. But each official seemed to demand, in his own bureaucratic milieu, the same prerogatives which the Shah claimed from the entire system. And each official in the flush of wealth and power strove to expand his domain and importance.

But no one matched the Shah and Farah. In those years, the official imperial symbol of Iran—reproduced on Iran's currency, its stamps, and its flag—seemed to have come to life. It portrayed a lion clutching a sword while partially blocking the still bedazzling light of a full, radiant sun. The Shah and Farah were bedazzling indeed.

The Shah, of course, was prepared for the possibilities the oil wealth presented him. His narcissistic imbalance had inclined him to grandiosity and its handmaidens, arrogance and contemptuousness. Now would be his moment for their realization. In 1973, for the first time, he began to refer to his rule as *tamaddon-e bozorg*, the "Great Civilization."[3] He told the *New York Times* in early 1974, "In Iran . . . what counts is 'the magic word,' and the magic word is 'king.'"[4] That message was to be conveyed to the Iranian people in countless ways.

SAVAK, the State Security and Intelligence Organization, was responsible, among other things, for seeing that the newspapers of Iran celebrated the Shah and his White Revolution. Its officials had long since made the publishers aware that each day's front page was to headline the activities of the royal couple and feature at least one photograph of their doings. Thus the papers had to print the Shah's words and news of his activities, irrespective of any news value. And as the Shah manifested more grandiosity, the newspapers trumpeted that grandiosity and arrogance to the people of Iran.

Two weeks of lead headlines for one of Tehran's newspapers are representative of the grandiosity of the Shah, the sycophancy of the press, and the nearly daily dosage of royal celebration to which the Iranian people were subject:[5]

Shahanshah Points Way to Equal Opportunity—Women's Equality Essential (January 5, 1975)

Shahanshah Orders Full Aid for Disabled (January 6, 1975)

I Wish We Were Neighbors—Shahanshah to Jordan Monarch Pledge: Iran Will Aid You (January 6, 1975)

Sadat Lauds Monarch—Shahanshah Visit—None More Worthy of Such a Welcome (January 8, 1975)

Empress: "Hard to Find Words for All This Beauty"—Egypt's Royal Sightseers (January 11, 1975)

Monarch, Sadat Accord on Mideast (January 12, 1975)

Monarch's Visit a Turning Point in Mideast—Sadat (January 13, 1975)

We Won't Embargo Oil: Monarch (January 15, 1975)

Confrontation Won't Help West—Monarch (January 16, 1975)[6]

Throughout the years of the blossoming of the Shah's grandiosity, the press continued to mirror his style, reflecting it to the people and, as he came to believe, reflecting their gratefulness back to him. And as the grandeur of the Shah increased, the empress came to share, despite her earlier protestations, in the magnificence of the Pahlavi system.

A front page of *Kayhan International* for March 15, 1976, indicates the kind of treatment Empress Farah had begun to receive, treatment which by then matched that of the Shah. The lead story featured a visit of the empress to Iran's Melli University at which she talked of academic standards, the need to raise Iran's intellectual level, and the value of research.[7] A large picture showed the empress in academic robes, unveiling a bust of Reza Shah on the occasion of the anniversary of his birth. The remainder of the front page was filled with comparable stories. One article described the new imperial calendar adopted by the Iranian Majles. The final story on the front page related a ceremony at the tomb of Reza Shah where Court Minister Alam remembered the birthday of the Pahlavi dynasty's founder. A photograph showed the court minister placing a bouquet on the tomb.

That issue of *Kayhan International* illustrated the extent to which the people of Iran were subject to massive doses of imperial panegyric—smothering enough to bring despair to any thoughtful reader. The quintessential example of such panegyrics, however, could be found in the January 31, 1976, edition of *Kayhan Weekly International Edition*. The entire front page was taken up by three articles and a photograph. The picture showed the Shah presenting shares of industrial stock to a representative of that firm's workers as part of the Shah's campaign to broaden the base of industrial ownership. The banner headline across the entire front page proclaimed, "Man's Exploitation by Man 'Abolished.'" The three individual articles were titled: "Shahanshah Launches New Industrial Era," "Workers 'Undying Gratitude' for Monarch's Great Reform," and "Prime Minister Pledges to Battle Corruption."

The Shah never did manage to eliminate such exploitation and thus accomplish what political philosophers had struggled with for centuries. Nor, obviously, did the workers maintain their "undying gratitude." Two years later they would demonstrate the depths of that gratitude in the revolution. And the prime minister may have "battled" corruption, but it is nearly universally believed that it was a battle he, and the Pahlavi system, lost. The newspapers of Iran in the 1970s, then, did not so much mirror Iranian realities as much as they reflected the Shah's personal grandiosity and that of the imperial system which he had created to reflect his grandiosity.

More than newspaper headlines reflected his grandiosity. The Shah's words and actions were even more telling indicators. Shortly after the beginning of the oil price run-up following the October 1973 war between Israel and the Arab states, and soon after the Shah learned he had cancer, Oriana Fallaci caught the Shah in his grandiosity:

Halfway measures, compromises, are unfeasible. In other words, either one is a revolutionary or one demands law and order. One can't be a revolutionary with law and order. And even less with tolerance . . . when Castro came to power, he killed at least 10,000 people . . . in a sense, he was really capable, because he's still in power. So am I, however. And I intend to stay there and to demonstrate that one can achieve a great many things by the use of force, show even that your old socialism is finished. Old, obsolete, finished. . . . I achieve more than the Swedes . . . Huh! Swedish socialism! It didn't even nationalize forests and water. But I have . . . my White Revolution . . . is a new, original kind of socialism and . . . believe me, in Iran we're far more advanced than you and really have nothing to learn from you.[8]

Later the Shah took to denigrating Europe and the United States for their "moral degeneration," the chaos of their "so-called" democratic societies, and the general decline which he perceived in their power and world standing. He warned that "even the great countries could undergo fundamental transformations through internal collapse . . . while other countries such as China, Brazil, and Iran will surge ahead."⁹

Again and again, in virtually every interview with foreign journalists and every speech to Iranian audiences, the Shah repeated that boast. He was utterly serious about the glorious future which he both intended and predicted for Iran. In 1974, he described the Iran of 1984:

In the cities, electric cars would replace the gas engines and mass transportation systems would be switched to electricity, monorail over the ground, or electric buses. And, furthermore, in the great era of civilization that lies ahead of our people, there will be at least two or three holidays a week. . . .
Q: Two or three holidays a week?
A: Yes.
Q: You plan a three-day work week?
A: It must come, with the automation of industry and increasing population, it must come.¹⁰

As the years passed, the Shah always kept his target date for Iran's grand future a decade away, but he continually enhanced the glory that would be that future. In 1976, for example, he told Egyptian journalist Mohamed Heikal, "I want the standard of living in Iran in ten years' time to be exactly on a level with that in Europe today. In twenty years' time we shall be ahead of the United States."¹¹

Not only were these predictions of a glorious economic future hopelessly out of touch with the economic realities of Iran even during the heyday of its oil bonanza, but they also revealed a powerful truth about the Shah. What he was able to offer the Iranian people was a materialist version of their future. The Shah rarely was able to offer a sense of Iran which promised more than financial well-being. He could not articulate a future of spiritual or emotional fulfillment or intellectual or artistic accomplishments. His vision for Iran did not boast of social equality or harmony, justice or liberty. Those qualities might be mentioned by him but only insofar as they contributed to economic progress.

Everything for the Shah seemed to be reduced to its material base. It was from that base that he understood others and their motives. An early and telling example of the Shah's inability to understand the concerns of the Iranian clergy provides a brilliant example of his materialist thinking. The preeminent Iranian cleric of the 1950s was Ayatollah Borujerdi. Recognized by the entire Shi'ite clergy as the most learned of their number, he was designated as *marja-e 'taqlid*, the "source of imitation," from whom Shi'ites could seek the most definitive judgments on proper conduct.

This revered theologian had criticized the Shah's tentative steps toward land reform. True to character, the Shah understood Borujerdi's opposition as a financial matter. "I know the others have been paid for their opposition," the Shah told an American adviser, E. A. Bayne, "but I cannot understand Borujerdi. He has plenty—more than he wants now. He should be above this."[12]

The Shah's limited vision—whereby he understood both his supporters and enemies to be motivated primarily by their material concerns—proved to be not only too narrow but, ultimately, offensive to a deeper moral sensibility at the bedrock of Iranian culture. Dr. Ali Shari'ati, an Islamic thinker of great influence in the 1960s and early 1970s, especially among Iranian young people, repeatedly argued that "a society without a moral dimension, which is separate from and beyond the material structure, inevitably degenerates into dictatorial and fraudulent practices."[13] It was a message widely understood to be directed against the Shah and to have captured the moral degeneracy of the Pahlavi system.

The factors the Shah understood to motivate his own people were also, he had concluded, the prime movers of other states and of international relations as well. Thus, when Iran's oil revenues burgeoned and European economies suffered, the Shah was quick to offer financial assistance—in the same haughty and grandiose fashion in which he addressed his own people: "I have known the most dark hours when our country was obliged to pass under the tutelage of foreign powers, among them England. Now I find that England has not only become our friend, our equal, but also the nation to which, should we be able, we will render assistance with pleasure."[14] The Shah assured the West that since he—no mention was ever made of Iran—"belonged" to "this world," he had no desire to see it collapse and would advance credits to bolster Europe's faltering economy. Ultimately, he advanced credits totaling over one billion dollars to both England and France.[15]

It was not, finally, the sycophantish newspapers of Iran or the Shah's speeches but his actions that captured his grandiosity. What the Shah did, especially during the 1970s, was produce a cascade of events which were seen by the Iranian people as tangible manifestations of his grandiosity—of his increasing distance from their concerns and realities, of his ever more lofty, removed, majestic being.

The decade began with the fabulous celebration of monarchy at Persepolis. The Shah sought to win international recognition for himself, cement the legitimacy of the Pahlavi dynasty established by his father in

1925, and bring renewed international attention to Iran. True to form, the Shah sought these goals by appealing to leaders of foreign states rather than by appealing directly to the Iranian people. The Shah referred to the Persepolis celebration as "the greatest gathering of Heads of State in history."[16] Thoughtful Iranians had long since noted that the Shah sought popularity with foreign rulers—especially U.S. presidents—far more often than he seemed to seek their approval. They understood that his tactic was to convince his own people of his worthiness through the support accorded him by foreign leaders. But there was always a concern that those foreign leaders were in fact more important to him than his own people and that he was more comfortable dealing with foreign chiefs of state than with Iranians.

Whatever the Shah's motives might have been, the Iranian people had become ever more sensitive to his pursuit of foreign support. The announcement of the 1971 Persepolis celebrations fell on jaded and somewhat negative sensibilities. The Shah intended to commemorate the twenty-five hundredth anniversary of the founding of the first Iranian royal dynasty, the Achaemenids. The ceremonies would mark the institution of monarchy in Iran and stress the continuity of that institution with the Shah's own rule, some twenty-five centuries later.

For the Iranian people, however, the institution of monarchy in Iran was not significant. That anniversary had never before been noted, let alone celebrated. But worse, the Shah intended to orient the celebrations not to the Iranian people but rather to the heads of state of all the world's countries. They would be the guests of the Shah. The people of Iran were not invited to the party.

Moreover, virtually all the preparations for the festivities would be the responsibility of foreigners. The gowns, costumes, and uniforms to adorn Iranian royalty, the ceremonial guards, the servants, and the thousands of participants in the staged dramas of Iranian history were prepared in the couture houses of France. Foodstuffs—with the sole exception of Iranian caviar—and wine befitting foreign dignitaries were prepared in French kitchens and flown to Iran. Silk tents to house the foreign visitors in the shadows of the ruins of Persepolis were woven and sewn in France.

When the event finally occurred, the Shah was disgruntled. Too many heads of state had refused his invitations. President Nixon, for example, declined. Instead, he sent his vice president, Spiro Agnew, to represent the United States. Nonetheless, the festivities were held in splendor and opulence. The wife of Ambassador Helms described them.

It was in 1971, 2510 years after Cyrus the Great captured Babylon on October 12, 539 B.C., that the Shah held his famous two-week celebration near the ruins of Persepolis. One hundred and sixty desert acres were covered with some seventy tents, sumptuously decorated by Jansen's of Paris with French crystal, china, and linens, and hung with red silk and velvet and glittering chandeliers. Five hundred guests from sixty-nine countries, including nine kings, five queens, sixteen presidents, and three premiers, attended three days of royal festivities. . . . The royal court had new uniforms designed by Lanvin, and stitched with nearly one mile of gold thread. Chefs from Maxim's prepared a grand dinner of crayfish mousse, roast peacock stuffed with fois gras, champagne sherbet, and expensive French wine. Only the caviar used to stuff the quail eggs was Iranian.[17]

The Iranian people reacted characteristically—with sullen anger. The rumor networks of Tehran buzzed with disdain over the extravagances. The celebrations reportedly cost over $100 million. Iranians resented the audience for the Shah's munificence—all those sheikhs, emirs, and monarchs. They especially bristled at the exclusion of anything Iranian—all those foreign goods and workmen who had been brought from Europe. Thus not only were the Iranians excluded from the celebration of their own monarchy, but they were demeaned in the process. It was as if the Shah counted them inadequate by the standards of the foreign aristocracy, who seemed so significant to him but certainly not to the people of Iran.

There was an added element to the widespread dissatisfaction. In order to guarantee the safety of the scores of foreign dignitaries, heavy security was imposed throughout Iran, but especially around Persepolis and the neighboring city of Shiraz. Tens of thousands of troops were mobilized to form concentric security rings and roadblocks. Potential troublemakers throughout the country were rounded up and held in preventive detention. Extraordinary security measures seemed essential. Only months before the great event, the first instances of guerrilla terrorism had struck the kingdom.

In February of 1971, a band of armed men had attacked a police outpost in Siakhal, near the Caspian Sea. While they were eventually beaten off by the police defenders, there was loss of life on both sides. SAVAK responded with vigor. Most of the attackers who had escaped into the Caspian forests were tracked down and captured. Many of their associates in Tehran were arrested. Some were executed and others jailed. The regime believed it had eliminated a minor irritant. Not long after, however, two men on a motorcycle gunned down the chief military prosecutor of Iran as he was leaving his home in Tehran. They escaped, leaving no clues behind.

It seemed clear that the twenty-five hundredth anniversary celebration would present magnificent opportunities for the terrorists to strike again and embarrass the regime while it was the focus of international attention. So when the Shah ordered security, he got it. The Iranian people were subject to extraordinary measures. They were not only passive witnesses to the spectacle of Persepolis, its foreign orientation, and its staggering costs, but in the process their lives were disrupted to guarantee the safety of foreign dignitaries.

Popular dismay was so widespread that it reached the attention of the royal couple. The empress noted that "even before the celebrations began, criticism, needless to say, was not spared us."[18] But as with so many other aspects of Pahlavi rule in Iran during the 1970s, criticism from the Iranian people did not divert the royal couple. Instead, the ceremonies at Persepolis were carried off with a tone of imperial grandiosity which would characterize the remainder of the Shah's rule.

For all the internal criticism and foreign cynicism about the Pahlavi's *nouveau arrivé* strivings, Persepolis did enhance the international stature of the Shah. That stature was sealed by the visit to Tehran of President Richard Nixon and Secretary of State Kissinger in May 1972. The president approved the Shah's wish to buy advanced American jet fighters and, further, ordered that any future non-nuclear weapons systems the Shah wishes to buy should be approved without "second-guessing his requests."[19] This carte blanche was an extraordinary demonstration of the "Nixon Doctrine" in action, a response to the strategic weakness of the United States in the waning years of South Vietnam. The United States designated foreign states as regional superpowers and supported their efforts to act as proxies for the United States, which could not act itself. Iran's designation came with its guaranteed access to U.S. weapons not available to any other country, even NATO allies and Israel.

By designating the Shah as official U.S. proxy, the president and his secretary of state demonstrated their concern for the two traditional interests in Iran—oil and the Soviet Union. On March 1, 1971, Great Britain had announced its intention of formally withdrawing its military forces from the Persian Gulf. On November 30, Iran seized three strategic islands, possessions of Arab sheikhdoms across the Gulf, which guarded the approaches to the Strait of Hormuz.

Iraq feared and resented the Shah's attempts to dominate the Persian Gulf and on December 1, 1971, broke diplomatic relations. Border clashes between the two states began with the New Year. But what had been a localized conflict became global when on April 9, 1972, Iraq signed a treaty of peace and friendship with the USSR, calling for substantial military assistance.

The Nixon-Kissinger pledge to the Shah was a response to two American fears—the encroachment of the Soviet Union toward the oil fields of the Gulf as well as the possibilities of oil-supply disruptions, given conflicts among Gulf states following the British withdrawal.

In addition to weapons sales, the American visitors concluded another arrangement with the Shah. Iran was to serve as the base for an operation to disrupt and weaken the Iraqi state. Using Israeli and American supplies and advisers, the Kurds would be mobilized to back their demands for autonomy from Baghdad with military action. For the next three years, a major campaign was carried out in which the United States and Israel advanced their strategic interests over the bodies of the Kurds. When the Shah signed the Algiers accords with Iraq in June 1975, restoring peace and settling their major outstanding disagreements, all aid to the Kurds was ended. Then after a short period in which Iran left its border open to Kurds fleeing Iraqi repression, the border was closed. Thousands of Kurds were then killed by the Iraqis.

But the visit of the leader of the "free world" provided the Shah with the explicit international acceptance and recognition that had previously been measured only indirectly, for example, through a tally of the responses to his invitations to the Persepolis celebrations. Now, however, the president of the United States and his secretary of state had designated the Shah guardian of Western interests in the crucial Persian Gulf. Their designation provided the Shah not merely with assurances that the United States had important tasks in mind for him, but, more importantly, it reinforced the Shah's sense of self-esteem based on his psychological relationship to the United States.

If the Shah's self-esteem was reinforced by his psychological relationship with the United States, it was consolidated by the massive wealth which oil exports generated as royalties. For the income which flowed directly to the imperial coffers from the sale of oil not only allowed the Shah to assume a significant international role but also provided the financial means for the material realization of his grandiosity. It was the wealth he derived from the rapidly rising oil prices of the 1970s, for example, which allowed the Shah to take advantage of the opportunity President Nixon and Secretary Kissinger had offered him—to buy any non-nuclear U.S. weapons system he deemed appropriate for the Imperial Iranian Armed Forces. The oil revenues allowed him to pay for the weapons system they were willing to sell. Thus, in the 1970s, Iran became the best customer for U.S. military exports.

The Shah understood the significance of oil revenues to his rule. He had seen how Prime Minister Mossadegh had lost his supporters as Iran's oil output plunged following the Iranian nationalization and the British-imposed boycott on Iranian oil exports. Whereas Iranian oil output had been above 650,000 barrels per day in 1950, it had plunged to 30,000 barrels per day in 1953. With that plunge had gone Iran's oil income, and with that, many of Mossadegh's supporters.

Restored to power, the Shah set about restoring Iran's oil income. He succeeded brilliantly. In the first year after the formation of the new oil consortium, replacing the British monopoly over Iranian oil industry and rewarding the United States for having restored the Shah to his throne, Iran's oil revenues were $34 million.[20] By 1970, Iran's oil revenues had risen to $1 billion, and by the middle of the decade they had exploded to over $20 billion per year.[21]

Not only did the Shah succeed in earning substantially increased revenues for Iran, but he managed to position himself at the center of OPEC and at the center of the international obsession with oil prices which followed the 1973 Ramadan/Yom Kippur War. It was King Fahd and his oil minister Sheikh Ahmad Zaki Yamani who had engineered the oil embargo after the war and unleashed the "oil weapon" against the West. It was the Arab oil producers who abided by the embargo and reduced the international trade in crude oil by close to 15 percent. But it was the Shah who took advantage of the panic which followed to earn new revenues for Iran. He refused to join the embargo but actually increased Iran's output to benefit from panic buying by foreign companies fearful of being shut out of oil markets as the embargo diminished supply.

The Shah was to play his decisive role at the December 22–23, 1973, OPEC meeting held in Tehran. As host of the meeting, the Shah became its spokesman. He was to announce to the world that OPEC had voted to lift its embargo while establishing a dramatically increased posted or official price for oil—$11.65 per barrel. While the new price was considerably less than buyers had been willing to pay in the midst of the embargo panic, it was some five time higher than the former official price. A massive transfer of wealth from oil consumers to oil producers had begun.[22]

The Shah established an international role for himself as the OPEC statesman who came to the support of the West by refusing to join the Arab oil embargo, but a friend of the West who nonetheless demanded a steep price for the oil he was willing to supply. That steep price provided Iran with the revenues to finance the imperial grandiosity. Oil revenues paid for the Persepolis festivities. And they would pay for the weapons systems the Shah so quickly ordered.

The new oil wealth and the ever more significant international recognition the Shah was receiving resulted in a new consolidation of the monarch's self-esteem. On the basis of the strength he derived from that consolidation, the Shah began to act with even greater vigor and determination. He turned his attention to the further transformation of Iran.

In the early 1960s the Shah had launched his White Revolution, promising social change and economic improvement for the Iranian people. In the mid-1970s the Shah initiated a series of "reforms" which would prove more disruptive of established Iranian practices and which, ultimately, would generate far more hostility from the Iranian people than had the White Revolution. The reforms of the 1970s struck more deeply at Iranian custom and at the social and material interests of virtually every segment of Iranian society. Ultimately, the decrees of the 1970s proved more disruptive than had those in the previous decade because the issuer of those decrees had changed. In the intervening twelve years, the Shah had been able to consolidate his precarious self-esteem into grandiosity. With his grandiosity came arrogance. It was the combination of those two qualities that ultimately proved fatal to the Pahlavi system. The people of Iran could undoubtedly have tolerated the Shah's efforts to "reform" Iranian society, however oppressive those efforts were. But what might have been perceived as mere oppression came to be experienced as humiliatingly insufferable. The Shah's grandiosity and arrogance, manifested in his words and deeds, proved demeaning to the Iranian people. His fate was sealed. The rage he engendered in his own people would, ultimately, come to be turned against him and the system he had created.

It was not only the Shah who was seen as demeaning. The empress as well came to be perceived as distant and haughty. In earlier years she was the most beloved of the Pahlavis, but in the fullness of the Shah's grandiosity she was seen as ever more patronizing. She had once been "the best thing that ever happened to the Pahlavi dynasty."[23] By the mid-1970s, however, she too was seen as having succumbed to the powerful attraction of the Court.[24]

As the Shah and his empress had succumbed to the international recognition and the validation of the president of the United States and the phenomenal new oil revenues, so did the entire political system. The regime created by the Shah mirrored his own grandiose, arrogant style. Whatever the personal psychological characteristics of the Shah's ministers, secretaries, directors-general, or chiefs, they all came to mimic his style of rule. All too often, in fact, they outdid him, adding layers of grandiosity and arrogance between the Shah and the Iranian people. By the middle of the decade, the rule of the Shah had been transformed into an imperial and imperious system.

The result of the creation of the Pahlavi system was to multiply the injustices the Iranian people came to perceive as emanating from the Shah. By the middle of the decade, none of that seemed obvious. Yet the Persepolis celebrations, the Nixon-Kissinger visit, and the oil price rises had set the stage for a series of unprecedented government interventions into the lives of Iranians.

The year 1975 began with the passage of the Family Protection Act. Princess Ashraf, then director of the High Council of Women's Organizations, referred to the law as "one of our proudest achievements" which "gave Iran's women the most sweeping civil rights in the Islamic Middle East."[25] In particular, the law

recognized a wife as an equal partner in marriage. . . . It limited a man to one wife (indirectly, since the Koran permits as many as four) by laying down strict conditions which virtually made it impossible for him to marry a second time: the prospective polygamist had to have his first wife agree; had to have the financial means to support equal households; had to prove that his first wife was sterile or incurably ill. The act provided that a woman could seek divorce on the same grounds open to a man . . . and it created a machinery where she could seek, and collect, alimony and child support. In the event of her husband's death, the guardianship of children would be awarded to the wife. Previously all her male in-laws would have been given precedence.[26]

While the law was certainly welcomed by many, especially by many middle- and upper-class women, it was also seen as an intolerable intrusion by religious leaders and others who sought to perpetuate the primacy of Shi'ism in Iranian life. The Family Protection Act was, however, only the first of a series of laws. Four "campaigns" in particular offended entrepreneurs, businessmen, and bazaar merchants, virtually the entire industrial-commercial bourgeoisie.

Early in the year the government passed another law which was to offend many, the Anti–Land Speculation Bill. The law specified that vacant land in urban areas could be sold but once. After that transaction, the land had to be developed or the government was entitled to buy the land at current prices. The law was a response to the frantic real estate speculation which had gripped all Iranian cities, but especially Tehran, since the oil price spike had driven a construction boom. Prices for undeveloped land had been doubling month after month, with no respite in sight. The government feared the consequences of a sudden burst of the speculative bubble and hoped to reduce escalating housing costs by slowing the increase in land prices.

But Tehran's investors saw it differently. Bazaar merchants, industrialists and businessmen, even risk-taking civil servants, were making profits in land and from interest payments on money loaned to speculate in land.[27] As there appeared to be very little risk involved, land speculation had become almost a pastime of the middle class. Now the government was seen as depriving them of opportunities to benefit from Iran's oil prosperity. Worse, it appeared to many that government officials and members of the royal family were trying to monopolize the profits to be made from land speculation.

Tehran's middle class explained the passage of the Anti–Land Speculation Bill by circulating vast numbers of stories of the corruption of government officials and members of the royal family. One story whose truth I have been able to substantiate illustrates the genre. A family of high social standing, with little wealth but social ties to both the Qajar and Pahlavi families, had owned undeveloped land in northern Tehran for decades. Its value had burgeoned when it became clear it was located immediately opposite the western boundary of an entire new city, Shahestan-e Pahlavi, which the government was planning to build on the site of a huge army base. Not long after serious planning for the development of the new city had begun, the family received a letter from the Tehran courts informing them that the government intended to acquire the land by right of eminent domain. After lengthy negotiations with the courts, a selling price was established—a price far less than could have been realized through a commercial sale. Within months, the family learned that two foreign governments had purchased portions of what had been their land as sites for new embassies. The seller had been the Pahlavi Foundation, definitely not the government of Iran. The foreign governments had paid the Pahlavi Foundation ten times the selling price the family had been able to negotiate through the courts. Such stories were both a reflection and a confirmation of Tehran's sense that the Anti–Land Speculation Bill was designed not to eliminate speculative profits on land, but to funnel them away from the middle classes and to the Pahlavis and senior government officials.[28]

In March of 1975, with no forewarning, the Shah decreed the establishment of a single-party political system. All existing parties were banned while a new all-encompassing grouping, the Rastakhiz, or Resurrection, party was established. Years before, the Shah had declared, "If I were a dictator rather than a constitutional monarch, then I might be tempted to sponsor a single dominant party such as Hitler organized or such as you find today in Communist countries. But as constitutional monarch I can afford to encourage large scale party activity free from the straitjacket of one-party rule or the one-party state."[29] The Shah's decision to establish the one-party system convinced many Iranians that he had indeed turned his back on constitutional rule and now saw himself as a dictator.

That interpretation seemed especially plausible inasmuch as the Shah did not merely establish Rastakhiz. He also made it clear that all Iranians were to demonstrate their support for the system, that is, for him, by joining.

A person who does not enter the new political party . . . is either an individual who belongs to an illegal organization, or is related to the outlaw Tudeh Party, or in other words is a traitor. Such an individual belongs in an Iranian prison, or if he desires, he can leave the country tomorrow . . . because he is not an Iranian, he has no nation, and his activities are illegal and punishable according to law.[30]

The politically active were dumbstruck. The Shah, once again, had changed the rules of the game and then attempted to impose those seemingly gratuitous rules in a characteristically heavy-handed manner. That his dire threats were never carried out only served to make the Shah appear more grandiosely arbitrary and foolish.

Other legislation in 1975 was to offend industrialists. In April the Shah issued a decree setting forth the principal of public ownership of industries and mines. Within three years, 90 percent ownership in all state industries and mines and 49 percent of all private industrial and mining corporations were to be sold to the public. Initially, shares were to be offered to workers in those corporations, then to farmers, with all unsold shares finally being offered to the public. The state would establish a loan program so that would-be purchasers could borrow the funds to buy their shares.

The Shah's announcement stirred a deep sense of chaos. Corporate owners believed that their assets were being forcibly distributed. The workers sensed that they would be forced to incur heavy debts to buy paper assets. The foreign partners of joint ventures did not know whether the decree applied as well to their shares of Iranian industry. In the absence of accepted accounting methods, no one was sure of a valid means for establishing the value of the shares to be sold. In fact, the selling price was established by "'a high powered committee of ministers and representatives of the private sector' who determined the value of a given company's stock on the basis of profits and prospects."[31]

The immediate effect of the decree was to panic virtually everyone. "What did the Shah's decree mean? Business fell off heavily while everyone tried to decide."[32] But as time passed and the decree began to be enforced, everyone believed they were worse off. Businessmen saw the government creating yet another mechanism for interfering in their corporations. They sensed that their new co-owners would also demand greater access to company management and records. Most importantly, they felt deprived of their rightful rewards based on their own efforts, investment, and risk taking.

The workers felt no more satisfied. Either they were forced to postpone any immediate improvement in their standard of living by foregoing the purchase of consumer goods in order to buy corporate shares or they were made to incur real debt to buy paper assets. And they had little doubt that they were buying just that. Government corporations that were being sold off were universally perceived to be unprofitable. Their buyers were being forced to buy shares of money-losing enterprises. Profitable private corporations were widely believed to be printing new shares to cover that proportion of their enterprises they were forced to sell. Very few of either the disgruntled sellers or buyers had the sense that the Shah had, in fact, opened new possibilities for prosperity. They saw expropriation instead. The more cynical among them sensed a move similar to the earlier land reform—a public relations gimmick whose ultimate effect would be to reduce the political power of the owners of capital. Not that more power would accrue to the new owners, but that the government would be less fettered and beholden to the bourgeoisie.[33] In short, the Shah was seen as flaunting his power and grandiosity in the interests of magnifying both.

Those suspicions were confirmed when the government, seeking to bring down the rate of inflation, announced yet another major initiative during the summer of 1975, the Antiprofiteering Campaign. Inflation, the Shah proclaimed, was a product of rapacious middlemen who made exorbitant profits. Prices could be brought down by forcing those wholesalers and any others who sought high profits to lower their sales prices to reasonable levels.

Professional economists and Iran's economic planners understood its inflation differently. In the summer of 1974, oil revenues were heading toward $24 billion for the year—up from only $1 billion four years earlier. The Shah had brought his economic and financial officials together for a conference. His instincts and the opinions of his minister of finance, Hushang Ansary, known as "the high priest of economic growth," carried the day. Orders were given to double the government's budget and to plan a minimal twofold increase in the ongoing five-year plan. In fact, government expenditures increased so rapidly that when oil revenues fell slightly in 1975, the government produced a deficit, dismissed by the prime minister as a "miserable few billion dollars."[34] It was that deficit, the sudden massive increase in government expenditures, and the almost frantic economic activity undertaken by individual entrepreneurs which drove the inflation.

Yet the Shah saw the cause in "profiteering." He gave instructions to the leaders of his new single party, Rastakhiz, to mobilize an antiprofiteering campaign. The results were testimony to the pent-up tensions of the Pahlavi system. A mini-class war was unleashed. Civil servants, party members, and especially students and young people, mobilized by Rastakhiz into "anti-profiteering brigades," went into action. Shopkeepers, industrialists, wholesalers—from shoe polish producers to Mercedes Benz dealers—found their businesses invaded. Their selling prices were checked against government-established "appropriate" selling prices. When the prices were out of line, the "guilty" businessman was arrested and his shop padlocked.

The vigor with which the campaign was pursued and the vehemence of the student brigades reminded some of the excesses of China's Cultural Revolution. While the results in Iran were certainly less profound, they were still substantial. In Tabriz, in the first forty-five days of the campaign, 44 shopkeepers were sent to jail and 981 were fined. Over twelve billion rials in profiteering fines were collected. In Bushehr, one of the most prosperous merchants was sentenced to internal exile, to the remote city of Meshkin Shahr, for a minimum of six months.[35] In Tehran the owner of the city's largest brick factory was sentenced to jail for sixty-five days—for selling defective bricks—while the manager of a popular nightclub also went to jail—for serving "overpriced" drinks.[36] The Shah boasted that "8,000 people were tried for price control violations."[37]

The campaign took an even more menacing tone when it seemed to focus on the non-Muslim business communities. The most prominent Jewish and Baha'i merchants were arrested and sent to jail. The members of those communities had benefited from the special protection of the Shah. They had long since begun to play prominent roles in the commercial life of Iran and, in the case of the Baha'is, in government as well. Public resentment against them was clearly strong and deeply felt. With the antiprofiteering campaign, that resentment took an ugly turn.

By the fall of 1975 it was clear that the campaign had been a disaster. It failed to stem Iran's burgeoning inflation. It alienated businessmen and entrepreneurs and led to a reassessment of their plans to invest in expanding Iran's productive capacity. The masses whom it was supposed to aid felt manipulated. But perhaps most seriously of all, it began the political mobilization of Iran's youth. The regime-sponsored mobilization of 1975 contributed to the opposition-sponsored mobilization of the youth of Iran during the revolution. The euphoria and catharsis which stemmed from the antiprofiteering campaign contributed importantly to the proclivity for revolutionary action in 1978. The youth became a significant political force which was not spent until the Shah had died in Cairo, the Islamic Republic had begun the transformation of Iran, and their activism was crushed in mid-1981 on orders from the ruling jurist, Ayatollah Khomeini.

The antiprofiteering campaign had only trivial consequences on consumer prices. It was undoubtedly true that the monopolistic position of certain producers and sellers contributed to the rate of inflation, but it was equally certain that other factors were more significant components of Iran's inflation. And there was an even more fundamental issue—the absorption of the regime with the question of inflation. Few economists believed that inflation was so high as to threaten its economic expansion. Official government statistics claimed that Iran's inflation rate was close to 25 percent in 1975.[38] But during 1975, Iran's economic officials acknowledged that they were basing their calculations on a rate of inflation closer to 50 percent. Even at that higher rate, however, the planners believed inflation was manageable and would not interfere with economic growth.

In the absence of economic factors necessitating the antiprofiteering campaign, thoughtful Iranians understood it as essentially political. They believed the Shah sought to "tighten the screws" against Iran's middle classes while enhancing his popularity with the masses. In that effort, as with his other politically inspired moves in 1975, he failed. The campaign alienated the bazaar merchants and larger commercial and industrial entrepreneurs who saw the campaign as a means to restrict their economic freedoms and further centralize Iran's commercial opportunities among the members of the royal family and their court favorites. But Iran's consumers viewed the campaign no more favorably. They understood the campaign as yet another public relations gimmick, a trumped-up squabble among the wealthy which would do little to alleviate their burdens.

In his memoirs the Shah acknowledged little personal responsibility for the loss of his throne. He did, however, admit errors in this area, although he blamed those errors largely on the zealousness of the antiprofiteering brigades: "We made a major mistake—we asked student volunteers to work as price controllers. Their excessive zeal, their occasional threats, and their ignorance of commercial realities, alienated many retailers. Some of these young controllers were probably simply set on sabotaging our government."[39]

The mid-1970s were marked by a large number of other regime decrees, announcements, and activities. Each new proclamation seemed more grandiose. They all appeared to the Iranian people as largely irrelevant to their daily lives—more eruptions from the Shah, grandiose fantasies which originated with him and increasingly with the empress, and were reflected and amplified by his ministers. They related to the most astoundingly diverse array of subjects and indicated the expansion of the entire Pahlavi system concurrently with its appropriation of control in ever wider spheres, penetrating both more broadly and more deeply in Iranian life.

For example, early in 1975 the Shah announced that the joint U.S.-Iran Commission, chaired by Secretary of State Kissinger and Finance Minister Hushang Ansary, had signed a trade package calling for $15 billion in purchases by Iran from the United States, "the largest agreement of its kind ever signed by two countries."[40]

During 1974 and 1975, the Shah began to boast of Iran's plans for the development of nuclear energy. While it made sense to many that Iran would seek alternatives to petroleum in order to preserve what appeared then to be its dwindling oil reserves, nuclear energy was not the obvious choice. On the basis of availability and cost, natural gas was Iran's most efficient alternative to oil for power generation. In fact, Iran boasted the world's second largest reserves of natural gas. Some of these reserves were by then being sold to the Soviet Union, shipped through IGAT-1, a lengthy pipeline from Iran's southwestern oil reserves to Soviet Azerbaijan. Other natural gas stocks were being reinjected into the ground, both to store for the future as well as to maintain pressure in Iran's oil fields. Those fields were being depleted at near maximum levels to generate the revenues needed by the expanding Pahlavi system. But Iran's production of natural gas was immense, a by-product of its six million barrels per day of oil production. As a result, vast amounts of gas were being flared at the wells, permanently lost as a source of either energy or income.[41]

Despite the abundance of natural gas as a fuel for the generation of power, the Shah insisted that his dream for the technological and scientific advance of Iran necessitated an ambitious program for the peaceful development of atomic energy. The core of that program was to be the construction of nuclear power plants throughout the country. An experimental nuclear reactor was built in Tehran. The Iran Nuclear Energy Commission was established. Iranian students were sent to the United States to obtain degrees in nuclear engineering and related fields.

On countless occasions the Shah announced that the country would adhere to the provisions of all international treaties on nuclear nonproliferation and that Iran had no intention of developing nuclear weapons. But in the face of Iran's rapid military buildup, many questioned the Shah's ultimate intentions in his commitment to developing nuclear technology, especially because of the obvious availability of natural gas as the most efficient fuel for Iran's power needs.

But as Iran's oil revenues grew, so did the Shah's commitment to nuclear technology. In 1969, Iran's Ministry of Power announced its intention of constructing a five-hundred megawatt reactor by 1980.[42] In 1972 the government stated that it would acquire nuclear power plants by 1982.[43] By 1974 the Shah boasted that within two decades Iran would build twenty-one nuclear plants generating twenty-three thousand megawatts of electricity.[44] The costs for the nuclear program were admittedly astronomical, but few specific figures were given. Yet when pressed, huge sums were suggested. In fact, estimates for the capital costs of plant construction, infrastructure, nuclear fuel, and training programs approached $100 billion.[45]

To most Iranians struggling to cope with poverty or economic hardship, inflation, growing political repression, and general economic frenzy, not to mention horrendous air pollution and even more frustrating traffic jams, the notion of nuclear reactors seemed outlandish. For many, the Shah's nuclear ambitions seemed a reflection of fantasy, and grandiose fantasy at that.

There were, of course, scores of other regime-sponsored activities which contributed to the image of an increasingly grandiose and removed imperial system. One was the proclivity of the regime to hold widely publicized conferences that brought hundreds, and occasionally thousands, of foreign visitors to Iran, usually at Iran's expense. While often useful for advancing knowledge or seeking solutions to pressing social problems, the conferences were seen by most Iranians as irrelevant public relations–oriented ventures meant to enhance the status of the regime at the expense of the Iranian people.

The fall of 1975 witnessed the zenith of international conferencing. One issue of *Kayhan* boasted the presence of three simultaneous conferences: an International Congress of Philosophy was meeting in Mashhad, while the International Congress of Mithraic Studies convened in Tehran and the International Literacy Symposium met at Persepolis.[46] While most viewed these international congresses and symposia as regime media events, others in Iran saw a more sinister design. Banner headlines announced: "Under the Patronage of Empress Farah One of the Largest Contemporary Iranology Conferences Will Be Opened in Tehran Today with Empress Farah's Message. Historical Summary Regarding the Cult of Mithra."[47] Thoughtful Iranians knew that the Cult of Mithra was an early Aryan sect that preceded the Zoroastrian religion. They also understood that it was an indigenous Iranian cult that preceded the conversion of Iran to Islam by the conquering Arabs. The conference was seen as yet another indication of the regime's attempts to reduce the role of Islam in Iranian society while drawing its legitimacy from Iran's pre-Islamic past.

But the most astounding manifestation of the Shah's grandiosity was yet to come—an even more egregious confounding of the Shah's grandiosity with his depreciation of Islam. On March 19, 1976, the fiftieth anniversary of the establishment of the Pahlavi dynasty, the Shah issued another imperial decree: he officially changed the Iranian calendar.[48] The year had been 1355, marking the flight of the Prophet Muhammad from Mecca to Medina, a crucial event in the history of Islam. Since then, the entire Islamic world had marked the years in an identical fashion, establishing their sense of being through an Islamic perspective. Now the Shah decreed that Iran would break with the Islamic world. To the surprise of many, he did not propose the adoption of the Gregorian calendar of the West. Rather, Iran would institute the Sal-e Shahanshahi, the "Imperial Year" or the "Year of the King of Kings," based on the putative founding of the first Iranian kingdom, the same event earlier celebrated at Persepolis.[49] The year was no longer 1355. It abruptly became 2535. Orders were issued outlawing the use of 1355. All correspondence, newspapers, and documents had to display the new year. Calendars and diaries which marked time on the basis of the old year were to be replaced.

Prime Minister Hoveyda congratulated the Majles for approving legislation to change the calendar. "Your decision," he assured them, "is indeed a reflection of the historic fact that during this long period, there has been only one Iran and one monarchic system and that these two are so closely interwoven that they represent one concept."[50] That, at least, was the line the Shah and his regime fostered—the comingling of the principles of Iranian nationalism and monarchy to the point where they were indistinguishable or, at the least, to where the former was inconceivable without the latter. Conspicuously absent from this mix, of course, was Islam.

The Shah made the exclusion of Islam from Iran's official or public life clear at the formal ceremonies marking the fiftieth anniversary of the birth of his dynasty: "I declare that we, the Pahlavi dynasty, nurse no love but that for Iran, and no zeal but that for the dignity of Iranians; recognize no duty but that of serving our state and our nation."[51] No mention was made of Islam. The Shah uttered no pledge to advance its interests or to adhere to its law.

Thus, while the Shah declared his commitment to the dignity of the Iranian people, he did not believe that their religion ought to be a concomitant of that dignity. He publicly and consistently ignored the religion to which almost all were committed and which the Iranian Constitution specified he was to foster. But staggeringly, the Shah believed it appropriate to move beyond acts of omission.

He created and imposed an entirely new calendar. The act was breathtaking in its grandiosity. Not only did the Shah elevate himself to the few near-mythic figures whose lives and deeds the peoples of the world have used for centuries to mark their days. In the process, to mark the recording of time he substituted the establishment of the Iranian monarchy for the hegira of the Prophet Muhammad. But by decreeing the year to be 2535, he also managed to disrupt the order of everyday life and the sense of coherence which that order gave the Iranian people. The massive infusion of oil wealth which had followed the price spike of 1973 had already done much to alter irrevocably long-established patterns of Iranian life. The new calendar contributed to breaking the conceptual mold by which the Iranian people had come to conceive of the order of their universe. The revolutionary implications were stunning. If the year could be altered from 1355 to 2535, then no established component of the Iranian order was fixed. If the calendar were not sacrosanct, then even the institution of monarchy was not immune to reconsideration. At the very least, changing the calendar seemed to virtually all Iranians to be the ultimate in gratuitous meddling.[52]

During this same burst of Pahlavi grandeur, the Shah began referring to his regime in a new way—by the Persian term *farmandehi*. His spokesmen translated the term as "command and leadership," but a more accurate rendering would be "commandership." Not surprisingly, the Shah referred to himself as the commander: "As the Commander of this eternal monarchy, I make a covenant with Iran's history that this golden epic of modern Iran will be carried on to complete victory and that no power on earth shall be able to stand against the bond of steel between the Shah and the nation."[53]

The Shah had created yet another innovative political concept for his system, one in which he issued commands and his officials and people obeyed.[54] That was apparently what the "bond of steel" was about for the Shah. But from the point of view of the Iranian people, it was about the Shah's grandiosity—his distance and pomposity. Whatever the nature of that bond, it proved to be amazingly fragile.

4

Cracking the Shah's Authority

The collapse from the heights of the grandeur of the Pahlavi system and the grandiosity of the principal Pahlavi was rapid and decisive. No one contributed more significantly to that collapse than the Shah himself. Both his acts of commission and omission weakened the legitimacy of the Pahlavi system, and four sets of those acts were major factors in undermining the legitimacy of the system. He failed to fulfill Iranian cultural expectations about the nature of the proper ruler. He withdrew from the Pahlavi system. He fostered the "liberalization" of the system. And he took to communicating mixed if not absolutely contradictory messages.

The effects of these steps were mutually reinforcing. They all contributed to a process of cracking his authority. They contributed, in short, to the weakening and, ultimately, to the destruction of the legitimacy of his rule. That, in turn, fed into destroying one of the principal bases of the Shah's psychic strength, the strength that made it psychologically possible for him to rule. One of the four bases of that strength—along with his belief in his divine protection, his psychic merger with others, and the support of the United States—was his belief that he was adored by his people.

Yet the Shah was responsible for those four sets of acts in the 1970s which undermined his rule. They were all components of the institutionalization of his grandiosity, yet they proved the most important factors in eliminating the commitment of the Iranian people to his rule and to the Pahlavi system.

Failure to Fulfill Cultural Expectations of Proper Leadership
It is not by chance that the Shah was succeeded as the ruler of Iran by Ayatollah Rouhollah Khomeini, a man utterly committed to the realiza-

tion of his single-minded vision of a newly politicized Islam. For Khomeini's passion, ruthless determination, and absolute refusal to tolerate opposition to his overarching political vision are consonant with the conception of leadership held by the Iranian people.[1]

Iranian authors have long recognized this persistent theme in Iranian culture. Writing in the twelfth century, Farid ud din Attar composed a parable in the form of an ornithological fable to describe Iranian society. One of the birds argued, "we must have a guide to tie and untie the knots. We need a leader who will tell us what to do. . . . We will obey him from our hearts and do what he says, be it pleasant or unpleasant. . . . Now let us draw lots for a leader. He on whom this lot falls shall be our guide; he shall be great among the small."[2] While Attar's work can usefully be understood as a parable of Sufi thought and practice—a highly personal and mystical form of Islam long practiced in Iran—its themes of leadership are both a reflection of and a contributing factor toward Iran's broader cultural vision.[3]

In a twentieth-century satire of Iranian society, Sadeq Chubak constructs another related vision of leadership. In his story, an itinerant beggar and his captive baboon work the streets of Tehran, the baboon performing tricks and then collecting the pennies offered by the generally impoverished onlookers.[4] Despite his dependence on the baboon for his livelihood, the "master" terrorizes the animal, who

was forever anticipating the raps of his master's cane on his head, the cruel pull of the collar around his neck, the kick in the belly. A glance from his master paralyzed him with fright, for he was more afraid of Jahan than of anyone. His life was one continual state of terror and his terror was matched only by the loathing and disgust he felt for all mankind and for his master, in particular.[5]

At the end of the story, Jahan, the master, expires and the baboon works himself free of his chain. Yet, after beginning to flee, he sees some approaching woodsmen and returns to cower at his dead master's side. After all, Chubak concludes, "What was the baboon to do? Without his buffoon, he was not complete."[6]

This predilection, this sense of completeness and wholeness, which is supplied by a relation to a powerful leader, is not restricted to Iranian literature or Sufi mysticism, but found in Shi'a Islam as well, particularly the interpretations of Shi'a thought articulated by Ayatollah Khomeini. There are several principal components to this set of interpretations, of which two are particularly significant here.[7] The Shi'ites championed the cause of Ali to succeed to the leadership of the Islamic community upon the death of the Prophet Muhammad. They argued that the meaning of the Quran could be divined only by those in the Prophet's family. This view challenged the Sunnis, who argued that any man of sufficient quality could claim the caliphate subject to the consensus of the community.

The Shi'ite dilemma was to operationalize this political sensibility following the disappearance—or occultation, as the Shi'ites would have it—of the twelfth Iman in the tenth century. In the middle of the nineteenth century in Iran, this dilemma was resolved by granting the power of interpretation to the mujtahids, the most learned of the ulama or clerics. Whenever one mujtahid, by his superior intellectual and moral qualities, clearly dominated his contemporaries, he was designated the *marja-e taqlid,* or source of imitation. All the faithful had to select a living mujtahid whose interpretations would govern their lives.

Thus "Twelver Shi'ism" established a hierarchical structure of the faithful with the possibility of the domination of the structure by one grand, leading mujtahid whose position strongly paralleled that of the divinely guided Imams. The doctrine of *velayat-e faqih,* or rule of the jurist, conceived by Ayatollah Khomeini and enshrined in the constitution of the Islamic Republic of Iran, is the most elaborate articulation of this elitist view.

The provisions of *velayat-e faqih* realize, in the political system, the culturally dominant notion of authoritarian leadership.[8] Principle 5 of the constitution of the Islamic Republic of Iran specifies that

during the absence of the Glorious Lord of the Age [the missing twelfth Imam of the Shi'ite sect], may God grant him relief, he will be represented in the Islamic Republic of Iran as religious leader and imam of the people by an honest, virtuous, well-informed, courageous, efficient administrator and religious jurist, enjoying the confidence of the majority of the people as a leader.[9]

Principle 110 of the constitution then specifies the immense power of the faqih. Despite the trappings of a Westernized political republic with a parliament, cabinet, prime minister, president, and an ostensibly independent judiciary, the faqih is given unfettered power to rule. He controls the processes of appointments and elections. He can dismiss key officials. In short, he has absolute power over the affairs of the country.

The constitution of the Islamic Republic of Iran realizes the cultural ideal of a powerful, authoritarian leader.[10] Ironically it was the Shah, with all the trappings of authority which he controlled and occasionally flaunted, who failed to realize that ideal. The Shah certainly appreciated the Iranian vision of leadership. He certainly remembered his own father. As the Shah described Reza Shah, "He was a powerful and formidable man and the good heart that beat beneath his rough cavalryman's exterior was not easily reached. Yet even his enemies realized that he was one of those men sent by Providence through the centuries to keep a nation from slipping into oblivion."[11] The Shah here, and as described in chapter 1, seems to have realized the political significance of presenting at least the image of a determined, powerful, strong leader.[12] Certainly those in his midst appreciated this cultural truth. His twin sister, the astute Princess Ashraf, realized that "in a country like Iran, people are drawn to power and strength. They demand a ruler who has a strong image, and not one who has been tainted with the mark of an appeaser."[13] She finally put it most simply by classifying Iran as one of those countries where "an invulnerable father-like image is all important."[14]

The Shah never put his appreciation of the cultural definition of a ruler quite so simply or elegantly. But his speeches and remarks over the years demonstrate he too understood that cultural vision.

There had been widespread criticism of the 1971 festivities in Persepolis where the Shah had so lavishly entertained foreign leaders. In response, the Shah told one of his biographers:

You Westerners simply don't understand the philosophy behind my power. The Iranians think of their sovereign as a father. What you call "my celebration" was to them the celebration of Iran's father. The monarchy is the cement of our unity. In celebrating our 2500th anniversary, all I was doing was celebrating the anniversary of my country of which I am the father. Now, if to you, a father is inevitably a dictator, that is your problem, not mine.[15]

In 1975, during other celebrations—those for the fiftieth anniversary of the Pahlavi dynasty—the Shah assessed the years of Pahlavi rule and boldly declared, "Enormous difficulties would have arisen if the nation had lacked powerful and progressive leadership. To forestall such pitfalls the nation must have a trustworthy and confidence inspiring leader."[16] Less than a year later the Shah sounded an even more forceful tone: "As the commander of this eternal monarchy, I make a covenant with Iran's history that this golden epic of modern Iran will be carried on to complete victory and that no power on earth shall be able to stand against the bond of steel between the Shah and the nation."[17]

There is every reason, then, to believe that the Shah understood not only the general Iranian sensibility but how that sensibility translated into the particular stance which would have been appropriate for him to project. And for many years before the revolution, the Shah made every effort to project himself as the omniscient, omnipotent ruler who fit the cultural bill of particulars. It was at least partially in the service of projecting such an image that the grandiosity of the Shah became so manifest to his people during the 1970s. His uniform, medals, and insignia; his ever-present photographs; the proliferation of magnificent ceremonies; and his frequent, authoritative pronouncements on virtually every aspect of Iranian life were all components of the projection of such an image.

But careful scrutiny of the Pahlavi iconography of the 1970s reveals a definite but subtle shift in the presentation of the Shah. In the early years of the decade, he was portrayed as the stern, almost glowering ruler of his people, frequently in full uniform, festooned with bejeweled ribbons and medals. If anything, he appeared slightly sinister, given the small scar across his upper lip, a legacy from the attempt on his life in 1949.

As the years passed, the Shah was portrayed in a different light. The most characteristic image of the Shah, post-1975, was an almost whimsical fantasy. He was seen standing against a backdrop showing only clouds and sky. To stress his special relation to divinity, perhaps, the Shah was portrayed standing, but not standing on anything in particular—as if he were able to float through the heavens. To suggest a new relation to "his" people, the uniform was replaced by a "sensible" business suit. The Shah was smiling. His arm was raised in a friendly wave. The stern ruler had been replaced by a caring uncle.

Of course given the patterns of leadership which permeate their culture, an uncle is not what the Iranian people are after. Rather it is more the stern and forceful, even sinister, figure portrayed in the Shah's earlier public photographs which more nearly match their expectations. The Iranians seek a powerful and demanding ruler who is also perceived as just, patriotic, and empathic. Yet the grandiosity of the Shah was always a more powerful determinant of his image for the Iranian people than the pictures of him distributed for mandatory display. The grandiosity undermined the basis for legitimate rule within Iranian culture. The Shah was perceived as powerful and demanding, but not for the well-being of the Iranian nation, but rather for his conception of imperial grandeur. He was seen as patriotic, but to his conception of a pre-Islamic Aryan state, and as unjust. He was perceived as distant in his self-glorification and, thus, nonempathic.

In the 1970s the Shah failed to do what Iranian rulers are expected to do in order to fulfill widely shared cultural expectations about appropriate political leadership. His failing set a process in motion whereby he contributed to the reduction and, ultimately, the destruction of his own political legitimacy. The Shah made major contributions to the cracking of his own authority. Ultimately, these contributions became decisive in undermining the legitimacy of his rule. With that erosion of legitimacy, the Iranian people turned against the Pahlavi system, but especially against the Shah. As that became clear to him, and it became inescapably clear in the midst of the Iranian Revolution of 1978, one of the pillars of his psychological strength collapsed. Along with the collapse in the mid-1970s of the three other pillars which provided psychological strength, the Shah lost his capacity to govern and, consequently, his throne.

Withdrawal of Support from the Pahlavi System

The most important person to withdraw support from the Pahlavi system was, ultimately, the Shah himself.[18] There were three ways in which the Shah withdrew that support. He physically withdrew from the day-to-day task of running the system. Second, he began to talk of the day when he would formally retire from the throne in favor of his son. Finally, he tried to preserve his own rule by shifting responsibility for the ills which characterized Iran away from himself as King of Kings and onto the Pahlavi system.

By early 1976, the Shah appears to have withdrawn from direct participation in the day-to-day affairs of the country. During all of 1976 and 1977, the Shah never attended a cabinet meeting.[19] He made it clear that he cared about only three areas—foreign affairs, the Iranian armed forces, and petroleum. He cared about no other area of governance, not even who became the cabinet ministers.[20] Senior government officials quickly sensed the vacuum at the top as the Shah withdrew from area after area of government, leaving responsibility to the relevant officials.

Prime Minister Amir Abbas Hoveyda, who served the Shah in that capacity longer than any other prime minister in Iranian history—from 1965 until his replacement in August of 1977 by Jamshid Amouzegar—masterfully encouraged this process. He attributed all significant discussions and all responsibility for Iran's growing wealth and power to the genius of the Shah. All the while, Hoveyda was able to reserve to himself responsibility for wider and wider areas of decision making. But, in fact, the same processes which characterized the Shah came to characterize his prime minister. As has been noted earlier, the senior officials of the regime tended to assume the style of the Shah. Hoveyda was perhaps the classic example of this phenomenon. Over time, he also withdrew from day-to-day supervision of the bureaucracies. Yet whenever he wished to achieve a particular goal, he would insist on its realization with the explanation, "His Imperial Majesty's orders."[21]

It is important to stress, parenthetically, the extent to which this phenomenon of the missing leader came to characterize the entire system by the outbreak of the revolution. By 1978, it seems, no one was "minding the store." Examples abound throughout the bureaucracies. One of the more colorful, if disastrous, instances of the missing leader occurred in SAVAK. Responsible for the external and internal security of the regime, SAVAK had earned a reputation for being the "eyes and ears of the king"—for knowing all there was to know relevant to matters of state as well as for ruthlessly suppressing all opposition.[22] Yet SAVAK was apparently caught totally unawares by the depth of the opposition to the Shah, the virulence of its expression, and the ability of the opposition to act in a coordinated and organized fashion in the major cities of the country. Its failures were a major factor in the ineptitude of the regime's responses to the revolution and were a major contribution to the demoralization of the Shah and the entire system.

The magnitude of its failures was so great as to be inexplicable. During the revolution, a former director of SAVAK met with the current director:

"General," he asked, "what is going on in the country?"

"General," SAVAK's director replied, "I do not know."

"But general, how could that be the case? What have you and the other generals been doing during all these years?"

"General," the director responded, "we have been doing real estate."[23]

Whether this is an adequate explanation for the failures of the intelligence organization to fulfill its responsibilities, it accurately captures what happened at the top of Iran's bureaucracies during the 1970s. Virtually the entire senior cadre of government administrators became less and less absorbed with the decidedly unglamorous task of supervising the administration of the bureaucracies. This is not to suggest that the senior cabinet officials and bureaucrats spent their days lolling by their swimming pools or "doing" real estate. Iranian officials were frantically busy as the regime took on ever greater responsibilities for assuring economic growth, ameliorating the lot of the people, and bringing greatness to the system, especially to its leaders.

The Shah's coterie of leaders was stretched thin as the organizations for which they bore at least titular responsibility expanded in scope and size. There was ever less time available for the actual administration of the unwieldy behemoth called the government of Iran as more and more time and energy were absorbed by crisis control, meetings, ceremonies, coordination, planning, and ever larger doses of public relations fluff. No one exemplified that better than the Shah. His failure to attend meetings of the cabinet was symptomatic of his withdrawal from the responsibilities of doing what he had to do in order to function as the Shah. Senior government officials still met privately with the Shah at regularly scheduled appointments to inform him of their activities and receive his approval. But by the mid-1970s, they had the clear sense that he was no longer intensely involved with the day-to-day challenges of running the Empire of Iran.[24]

One consequence was a more profound blurring of responsibility. Government ministers, security officials, and the principal bureaucrats—as well as members of the broad political elite—were ever more uncertain in their efforts to understand how the regime worked. It became increasingly difficult to find out how decisions came to be made. The nature of power and authority in the Pahlavi system was more opaque. That, in turn, fed a growing sense of demoralization and a generalized withdrawal from active governance in favor of a retreat to private concerns and the protection of private interests.

Neither Hoveyda nor his successor, Jamshid Amouzegar, were immune. For example, when President Carter made his fateful New Year's visit to Tehran in 1978, Amouzegar spoke with the president and other U.S. officials on only two occasions, both at the airport. When the American dignitaries arrived, Amouzegar was one of a large group of Iranians who welcomed the official guests to Iran. At the end of the visit, he was a member of an equally large group that gathered at the airport to bid the official party farewell. But at no time during their stay in Tehran did Amouzegar participate in a single official meeting with the president or any of the other Americans.[25]

When the prime minister later asked the Shah about the results of his conversations with the U.S. president, the Shah told him not to trouble himself with such matters. The conversations, the Shah stated, were about security, foreign policy, and oil, all of which were the exclusive concern of the Shah. He told Amouzegar to pay attention instead to economic development, which was "his" area.[26]

The prime minister came away from that meeting demoralized. Not only did he feel personally belittled by the Shah, but he was also disheartened by his knowledge that, in fact, with the Shah's withdrawal, no one was in charge. This was especially menacing because the Shah's grandiosity in the earlier years of the decade had been "reproduced," with only a slight lag, by officials throughout the system.

Those officials had expanded the activities of the government bureaucracies for which they were responsible to previously untouched areas of Iranian life. The scope and range of government activities had broadened in an astounding fashion. Welfare benefits, health services, adult literacy and vocational training, the mobilization of women, a national television grid with an "open" television university, and the convening of international conferences and festivals were only some of the new responsibilities sponsored by government bureaucracies.

As oil revenues climbed, with no apparent end in sight, ever more ambitious undertakings were initiated. But there was no comparable increase in adequately trained government personnel. Given the uncertainties generated by the withdrawal of the Shah and his most senior officials and their inadequate coordination, the results were administrative chaos and the increasing immersion of senior officials in the minutiae of crisis control. Few in a position to know had the luxury to stand back and sense the chaos which enveloped the entire system. Those who did were disinclined to be the bearers of that unwelcome news. In the grandiosity and, paradoxically, the demoralization which seemed to characterize the bureaucracies, there was little tolerance for the realities of Iranian political life.

As long as the oil revenues were flowing and there were few challenges confronting the regime, the lack of a clearly demarcated hierarchy of authority and the growing demoralization presented no special problems. But there were challenges—economic challenges which followed from the bottlenecks of the superheated economic expansion and from the fall in oil revenues from their 1974 peak. Political challenges arose as well. Demands for greater civil liberties and especially for less government control of intellectual life were heard in early 1977. To these challenges and demands the system could respond only ineptly.

Even after the beginnings of violent demonstrations in January 1978, the regime failed to construct a coherent and effective strategy for dealing with the periodic crises which were eventually to meld into a full-fledged revolution. There are countless examples of how loose the system had become by the outbreak of revolutionary violence and of how difficult it was for subordinate officials to get clear instructions on dealing with the emergency. One such example concerns the governor of Khorasan, Col. Abdul Azim Valian.[27] He had served for many years as the minister of land reform and had formed unusually widespread and personal contacts with senior officials. But even he was left with no specific instructions on how to deal with demonstrators.

In March of 1978, he had learned through contacts in the bazaar and among religious circles in Mashhad that riots were being planned for the fortieth day following the deaths in the Tabriz riots. Yet he had no idea what policy the government was following and how he was expected to deal with any riots which occurred in the cities under his jurisdiction. He later explained what happened.

I called Tehran, but the minister of the interior was not in his office and never returned my calls. I then called the prime minister and was told he was on vacation in the south of the country and couldn't be reached. I called the chief of the Tehran police. He was too busy to come to the phone or to return my calls. Finally, in desperation, I called His Imperial Majesty directly. He was on vacation at Kish Island, but I was put through to him late at night. He told me to let the demonstrations go on but to control and contain them. But under no circumstances was I to let the troops shoot at the crowds.[28]

Governor Valian could not understand how such instructions could be carried out and certainly not what they were meant to accomplish. Some of this administrative disorganization may be attributed to the Iranian No Ruz, or New Year's festivity, which falls on March 21, during which time Iranians—even senior officials—vacation in the countryside. It is also indicative of more pervasive ills which by 1978 were at the heart of the Pahlavi system—the breakdown, even absence, of a chain of command and the resultant demoralization.

In addition to withdrawing from the responsibilities of what I have referred to as "doing Shah" as distinct from "being Shah," the monarch withdrew from the Pahlavi system in other ways. He made intimations of his own mortality and he began to discuss the time when he would cede power to his son. One of the driving passions in the Shah's adult life was to institutionalize the Pahlavi dynasty. The basic step necessary to do that, of course, was for the Shah to produce a male heir, a direct male descendant who could claim the throne as successor Pahlavi monarch. Neither the Shah's first marriage to Princess Fawzia of Egypt (1941–48) nor his second marriage to Soraya Bakhtiar (1951–58) resulted in a male heir. In fact, only his first marriage produced any offspring at all, a daughter, Shahnaz. After his second divorce, there was much pressure on the Shah to remarry and reproduce. In December 1959 the Shah took his third bride, Farah Diba. As she put it, "Before marriage, I had not thought for one moment about the question of children, yet this is of absolutely funda-

mental importance to the monarchy."[29] Much to the imperial delight, the
queen quickly became pregnant and gave birth to a child, a boy, on October
31, 1960. "The news," she recalls, "was received with an outburst of joy, as
the future of the dynasty was assured."[30] The birth of his heir did, in fact,
play a special role.[31] The possibility of passing on his throne to a son seems
to have moved the Shah to consider the long-range future of the dynasty
and to take steps to institutionalize the Pahlavi system.[32]

The birth of Reza, named for the Shah's father, contributed to the
Shah's decision to proceed with a formal coronation. From his assumption of the throne in August 1941, the Shah had never been crowned.
Such a move would be another step in formalizing his rule as well as
a step by the Shah in embracing, in some symbolic sense, his role as
monarch.

In the past, whenever he was reminded that he sat on the throne without
having been crowned, the Shah would offer a standard answer: he had
taken an oath of office before the Majles in August of 1941, an act which
formalized his ascension to rule. But, he would add, he had postponed a
coronation ceremony until Iran was sufficiently far along the path of development to make such a ceremony appropriate.

He joked, on occasion, as he did before the U.S. Senate, about whether
Iran was sufficiently developed to serve as the country for which he would
be king. There was, undoubtedly, truth in his concern. Given his grandiosity, the Shah must have wondered whether or not Iran was worthy of
him. But it is difficult to imagine that simultaneously he did not also worry
about whether he was worthy of Iran. His failure to press ahead with a coronation ceremony which would formalize and make palpably manifest his
kingship can be understood as one of his responses to both his concerns
about the inadequacy of Iran for his rule and his own inadequacy for ruling,
especially given the legacy of his father.

The first major political action which the Shah took after the birth of his
heir in 1960 was to deal with the political turmoil raging over widespread
allegations of corruption and rigged elections, all set to the background of
an economic crisis.[33] After appointing a prime minister who was the clear
choice of the United States, Dr. Ali Amini, the Shah more or less withdrew from direct involvement in government and gave significant power to
Amini.[34] Amini pushed through a series of reforms, the most basic of
which was a land distribution program. The key force behind that reform
was the minister of agriculture, Dr. Hassan Arsanjani, and it succeeded in
quieting, at least temporarily, the Iranian political scene. After fourteen

months of Amini's reforms, the Shah apparently had enough. Amini was dismissed.[35]

The Shah appointed Assadollah Alam to the prime ministership in July of 1962. From then until Alam's death, in the fall of 1977, a remarkable association grew. Alam had been a boyhood friend of the Shah.[36] He was the individual whom the Shah trusted more than any other—more, in a political sense, than he trusted his wife. Alam was completely committed to the throne and to its occupant as both a ruler and a person. And Alam was tough and ruthless. He was, in that sense, a nearly complete contrast to the Shah. Alam served the Shah as prime minister and court minister until the leukemia from which he ultimately died weakened him to the point where he submitted his resignation.

That fifteen-year period saw the Shah take amazing steps to transform Iran. The first of the major reforms was the so-called White Revolution, a series of six reforms of which over 99 percent of the Iranian people allegedly approved in a national referendum in early 1963. The combination of the birth of the imperial heir, Assadollah Alam's strength, the tangible manifestation of the people's support through the national referendum on the White Revolution, and the pressures from President Kennedy's newly reform-minded U.S. government provided the Shah with the psychic strength to proceed with the institutionalization of his rule.

On October 26, 1967, on the occasion of his forth-eighth birthday, the Shah, having sired an heir to the throne and initiated measures to transform Iran, proceeded with his coronation. Grand ceremonies were held in Tehran. The Shah, "with great solemnity, . . . took the scarlet crown of the Pahlavi, raised it above his head and, as his father had done before him, crowned himself. Who else was there to do so? He reasoned this way: 'I represent the people of Iran. Through my hands, it is they who crown me.' "[37] The Shah then placed a crown on the head of the empress. Next, he crowned young Reza, by then not quite seven, the same age he himself had been at the time he was designated successor to Reza Shah.[38] With that act, the boy was officially proclaimed Crown Prince and heir to his father, Mohammad Reza Shah Pahlavi, King of Kings and Light of the Aryans.

The formal coronation ceremony marked the establishment of the framework for the perpetuation of Pahlavi rule. The Shah was a fit, trim ruler in the prime of his life with a new sense of commitment to reform from the throne. His young son was the officially designated Crown Prince who could assume the throne when he reached majority, at the age of twenty according to Iranian law. And in the interim, if the need should arise, the empress would serve as regent and chair of the formally established Regency Council, the first woman in Iranian history to be so designated.

The stage seemed set for a lengthy period of dynamic Pahlavi leadership. But it was not many years before the Shah confounded the Iranian people by beginning to talk of his own retirement and of handing over the "reins" to his son. More shockingly, he even began to make allusions to his own death. What had produced this transformation was unknown for many years thereafter to all but a tiny circle of court intimates. The Shah had been diagnosed as suffering from a form of cancer which, while not necessarily life-threatening, required perpetual treatment and must have served as a major blow to his psychological well-being. The Shah's cancer is considered at length elsewhere in this work. Suffice it to suggest here that after his learning of his illness the Shah began to refer, for the first time, to a future period when he would no longer be Shah.

The first reference of this sort was indirect and far from dramatic. In an interview in early 1974, in the flush of his grandiosity following OPEC's hike in the price of oil, the Shah discussed the future of Iran.

We now have a program in which the factories are offering 49% of their shares to the workers. So the workers and the small landholders are in the forefront of our revolutionary movement and are with the regime. De Gaulle tried to do the same in France. He could not. I can, because of the very special relationship that exists between the King and the people in this country. I hope that this leadership will continue until everybody is not only literate but has a good life.[39]

The Shah's first public, if indirect, acknowledgment of his foreboding was a reference to his wish for his "leadership" to remain. But the Shah made more frequent as well as more explicit and blunt references to his own death and less menacing but more frequent references to a different form of withdrawal, to the day when he would retire and turn the throne over to the Crown Prince. The Shah first referred to his retirement in a 1974 press conference: "The ground must be prepared for other people assuming responsibilities. I envision eventually retiring at an age when my son will be old enough—and I, not too old, to be here in his shadow."[40] As the 1970s progressed, the Shah referred more frequently to stepping aside in favor of his son.[41] His references came to center on 1990 as the year when he would elevate the Crown Prince to the throne. By then the Crown Prince would be thirty and the Shah himself would have reached seventy-one years of age, insha'allah, God willing.

All this talk of retirement and the more indirect but more powerful references to his death played a role in cracking the Shah's authority. Part of that authority derived from a certain quality of timelessness, if not immortality, which inhered in conceptions of Iranian kingship. There was no fundamental confusion in the minds of Iranians. They understood perfectly well that the Shah was a man and as mortal (and fallible) as any other man. But nonetheless, the institution of monarchy and the symbols of monarchy were associated, in the minds of many, with a certain perpetuity, a series of kings receding in time to the mythical past, a continuity of centuries of sovereigns.[42] The Shah's references to his death or to his retirement and to his withdrawing from the throne—in one fashion or another—interrupted that continuity and helped crack his authority. However cynical or disbelieving the Iranian people were when they heard the message, the repeated mention of Crown Prince Reza becoming monarch and the Shah no longer being Shah contributed to the sense that the Shah need not be the Shah.

Yet another form of the Shah's ultimate withdrawal of support from the Pahlavi system was the Shah's attempt to preserve his own rule by shifting responsibility for the ills of the system away from himself and onto the officials of that system. The Shah was quite prepared to sacrifice others if it saved himself, but that means of self-preservation proved, ultimately, self-destructive. For in the minds of the Iranian people, there was no disjunction between the sovereign and his system. He was completely identified for them with the institutions constituting the Pahlavi regime. Indeed, his efforts in the 1960s to formalize the system can be understood as efforts to differentiate the bureaucracies of the regime from the person of the ruler so that they would remain even if the monarch should change.

But in the face of revolutionary protest the Shah completely altered course. He was now ready, even eager, to see the institutions change, if only the person of the monarch could remain the same and, therefore, he could remain in power.

A key member of the Shah's ruling elite gave one account of the many ways in which the Shah began to abandon the Pahlavi system. In April of 1978, not long after the first demonstrations against the regime in Qom in January and the major disturbances in Tabriz in February, a dozen key officials traveled to the city of Isfahan and then flew to Shiraz, where a four-hour bus ride brought them to the small town of Yassij. In both Isfahan and Yassij the group had days of lengthy meetings with officials and ordinary inhabitants, trying to understand the currents of public opinion which had begun to surface in the violent urban demonstrations. When the group returned to Tehran, the most senior official was received by the Shah. He reported: "Every time religion was mentioned, the entire crowd applauded. Every time Your Majesty's name was mentioned everyone applauded. Every time dissatisfaction or even tacit dissatisfaction with life in Iran was mentioned, everyone applauded."[43] While this report was characteristically Iranian in its ambiguity, the official came away from his audience with the Shah convinced the Shah had understood the report in one particular way. "The Shah," he commented, "understood this to mean that he personally was still widely popular and supported by the Iranian people, but that his system of rule was not. So he separated himself from the system. He torpedoed the system to save himself."[44]

This interpretation of the Shah's actions during the fateful year of the revolution suggests one key to understanding the dramatically rapid unraveling of the entire Pahlavi system. Psychologically, the Shahanshah himself had begun to withdraw his support from the system years before the outbreak of the revolution. And during the revolution, the Shah's abandonment of the system accelerated and contributed to its collapse. The Shah was certainly not the first Iranian to withdraw his support from and commitment to the Pahlavi system. He was, however, the most significant.

His withdrawal of support was a variant of a lifelong pattern of retreat in the face of adversity or challenge. In his early years, some referred to the Shah as "the suitcase monarch" because he always had his bags packed— ready to flee the palace or Iran, if challenged. This nickname, like so many others, captured something true about its bearer. But the nature of that truth must be clarified.

It was not physical courage he lacked, but rather emotional strength. For example, his daring while driving and skiing were legendary. He confronted his would-be assassin on the campus of Tehran University in 1949 while his bodyguards and military commanders stood paralyzed by fear or amazement. Six shots were fired at the Shah, and not until the would-be assassin ran out of ammunition did the Shah's guards manage to take action. The Shah, meanwhile, "bleeding like a young bull whose throat had been slit," faced his assassin and started "shadow dancing" to present a more obscure target.[45]

His bravery was important to him. When he was asked, just before the revolution, at the peak of his powers, about his father, he recalled that Reza Shah had given him only one recommendation, "Don't be afraid of anything." The interviewer, David Frost, asked if that were possible, and the Shah replied:

No. That is not possible. Physically I am not afraid, but mentally you're always constantly afraid of something, either by yourself or something that might go wrong with yourself or with your friends or with your allies that you're counting on. Death doesn't mean anything for me since at least fifteen years I have seen it so many times right in front of my eyes. I know the day will come. When that day comes, nothing will stop it.[46]

The Shah, then, had some understanding of himself. He did not lack for physical courage. What was wanting was a certain quality of emotional or psychological fearlessness. As he put it so simply, "you're always constantly afraid of something." The Shah was a person of deep and pervasive fears. And when those fears became overwhelming, as they did when the bases of his psychic strength failed him, the Shah experienced a regression—a return to his early childhood passive qualities which contributed to his withdrawal. Withdrawal could take many forms—flight, psychic disengagement, and even a contemplation of the ultimate form of withdrawal, suicide. The Shah has been something of a master of all three forms.

In her memoirs, Princess Ashraf relates an incident in which the Shah contemplates suicide. Like many youthful suicides, to be sure, it was to be a suicide of romance and bravura. The possibility followed the deep concern which swept Tehran after the joint Soviet-British invasion of Iran in August 1941. The Crown Prince, Ashraf states,

was concerned not only about the consequences of the war, but also about the threat to the monarchy. . . . He doubted that the Iranian army would be able to hold the palace in the event of an allied attack. Later that afternoon, he brought me a gun and said: "Ashraf, keep this gun with you, and if troops enter Teheran and try to take us, fire a few shots and then take your own life. I'll do the same."[47]

The proposal that he and his twin commit suicide in the face of adversity was, perhaps, the most dramatic form of disengagement in the life of the Shah. Somewhat less dramatic but still in character were the three occasions when he left or was about to leave his country in the face of political reversals. Certainly the most poignant and tragic of these departures, given subsequent events, was his flight from Iran on January 16, 1979, to permanent exile and death.[48] But there had been a previous flight—during the showdown between the Shah and his prime minister, Mohammad Mossadegh, in August of 1953.

In his autobiography, the Shah alludes to that flight only in passing, as if he had been outside Iran for a short state visit or a vacation. "Although I was abroad at the climax of the uprising," the Shah recalls, "I was in constant touch with the situation during those days, and of course lived with it before and after my short absence."[49] In later years the Shah would present a different version of that flight:

After a great deal of thought, we drew up a plan that should the government [of Prime Minister Mossadegh] fail to follow the legal order of Iran's constitutional monarch [i.e., the Shah's dismissal of Mossadegh from office] we should leave the country. We would give the Iranian people the choice of adopting a measure to their liking. There was no other remedy but that.[50]

What the Shah was referring to, of course, was the coup planned by British intelligence and Kermit Roosevelt and his CIA colleagues, with Princess Ashraf, General Zahedi, his son Ardeshir, and the Shah all playing subsidiary roles.[51] The plan called for the Shah to issue an official rescript dismissing Prime Minister Mossadegh, which the Shah had the power to effect according to the Iranian Constitution, and then appoint Gen. Fazlollah Zahedi as prime minister. The danger was that Mossadegh and his allies in the Iranian military might not accept the Shah's legal authority. Perhaps they would also mobilize their allies among the people. In short order, the Shah could lose his principal supporters and, perhaps, even his throne.

This possible outcome was not fanciful. Only months before, in July of 1952, there had been a confrontation between the Shah and the prime minister. Mossadegh had insisted on exercising his constitutional right to appoint the minister of war, a prerogative the Shah had, nonetheless, claimed for himself. The Shah refused to accept the prime minister's nomination, and the prime minister resigned. The Shah with the aid of royalist deputies in the Majles nominated Ahmad Qavam, a former prime minister, to replace Mossadegh.

Riots and strikes in support of Mossadegh immediately swept the major cities. Bazaars were closed. The Shah ordered the army into the streets; deaths were reported all over the country. "After five days of mass demonstration, bloodshed, and signs of dissension in the army, he gave up and asked Mossadegh to form a new government. Mossadegh had won hands down."[52]

Thereafter, Mossadegh had gone from victory to victory. In early August 1953, he won a national referendum legitimizing his decision to abrogate the troublesome Majles—a maneuver which decidedly violated the Iranian constitution—by gaining "over 2,043,300 of the 2,044,600 ballots cast throughout the country and 101,396 of the 101,463 ballots cast in the capital."[53] However fraudulent the voting, Mossadegh had become a formidable competitor to the Shah. An attempt to dismiss him might not succeed.

It was necessary, therefore, to have a plan in the event that the coup failed. Kermit "Kim" Roosevelt, in his account of those dramatic events, makes an effort to put the Shah at the center of planning. But Roosevelt's entire account and those accounts by others make perfectly clear that the Shah was essentially a bystander and even a reluctant participant. Ambassador Loy Henderson recalls how he spent countless hours attempting to reassure the Shah of Western support.

I did have many frank private talks with the Shah during which I tried to encourage him. . . . I can remember, for instance, that at one time, almost despairing at the position in which Mossadegh had pushed him, the Shah had decided to go abroad. I pled with him not to do so, pointing out that his departure might well lead to the loss of Iran's independence. I was greatly relieved when he decided it was his duty to remain in the country regardless of the humiliations that Mossadegh was heaping on him.[54]

Nevertheless, Roosevelt suggests that it was the Shah who first raised the possibility of failure in the 1953 coup and proposed that, as a fallback position, he "withdraw" from Tehran. But to where? The city of Mashhad was suggested, but it was judged too far from Tehran and too close to the USSR. Tabriz was too close to Soviet troops across the Iranian-Soviet border if they should decide on a military attack in support of Mossadegh and his communist supporters. Shiraz, in the south, was too close to the antiroyalist Qashqa'i tribes. There was no place in Iran which would provide the Shah with a safe haven. The Shah then had a different thought.

"This reminds me, as a good Moslem, of Mohamed's [sic] Hegira in 622 A.D. by your calendar, year one by ours. He 'fled' purely to dramatize his situation. I could do the same.

"Really," he concluded, "I think this is what I'll do. Once we've made the final arrangements, and I have signed the firmans [royal decrees] dismissing Mossadegh and appointing Zahedi, I'll fly up to the Caspian. If by any horrible chance things go wrong, the Empress and I"—this was the first mention [Roosevelt notes] either of us had made of Queen Soraya—"will take our plane straight to Baghdad. From there we can look the situation over and decide to what place we should return."[55]

The Shah's account of the Prophet Muhammad's flight from Mecca to Medina is inaccurate. Islamic scholars agree that the Prophet was in serious danger in Mecca. His flight was not an act of "dramatization" but necessary to preserve his life and, even more significant from the point of view of Muslims, to preserve God's words and the nascent community of Islam.[56]

By establishing a parallel between his proposed action and a historically untenable reading of Islamic history, the Shah managed to accomplish several goals. Through an obvious identification with the Prophet, he provided psychic strength for himself. He and the Prophet, at least in a certain psychic realm, were in this whole business, in particular the business of flights, together. And by dint of sharing that with the Prophet, the Shah could also share, psychically, in the strength, successes, and, even the veneration of the Prophet. By making the Prophet's flight into a purely "dramatic" act, the Shah managed to blunt the sting of potential defeat.

But the plan had yet another psychic dimension: like all complex issues, it had many roots. The decision to go to the Caspian was linked to the Shah's childhood and, more importantly, to experiences with his father. For the Shah and Soraya took refuge along the Caspian coast at Kelardasht, the hunting lodge his father had built and which had been so significant a part of his relationship with Reza Shah. It was as if the Shah hoped that the power of his father continued to inhabit those residences long after the man himself had departed.

There was something particularly poignant in the Shah's staying at Kelardasht while the rescript dismissing Mossadegh was delivered to the prime minister who had succeeded in winning so much power away from the Shah. For it was at Kelardasht that the Shah had experienced what was for him the most significant insult from his father, so significant that, as noted previously, he repeated the event to interviewer after interviewer throughout his life. It was at Kelardasht that his father told him that he wanted to build a bureaucracy that would survive him and not require "continuous supervision."[57]

The Shah, as he told so many, had been deeply insulted. But in August of 1953, as in no other time in the previous twelve years of his rule, the Shah hoped that his father (and he) had succeeded in creating such a "process of administration." For if they had, and the Shah's constitutional powers had been appropriately institutionalized, Mossadegh would accept the Shah's authority and give up his premiership and, with it, his challenge to the Shah's efforts at unfettered rule.

But that wish was not—at least temporarily—to be realized. His attempts to link himself with the Prophet of Islam and the founder of the Pahlavi dynasty were not sufficient. Nor were all the plans which Kim Roosevelt and the Shah had formulated. When Col. Nassiri, later Gen. Nassiri and director of SAVAK, delivered the imperial rescript, Mossadegh refused to accept its order.[58] Instead, he had Nassiri placed under arrest. With that simple act the elaborately planned coup collapsed.

Princess Soraya, then the Shah's wife, relates in her autobiography what happened at Kelardasht.

The uncertainty was so nerve racking that we were unable to sleep a wink. Early on the morning of the 16th exhaustion overcame me, but I was awake again by four a.m. The Shah had entered my room and despite his usual self-control, I guessed at once that something unfortunate had occurred.

"Soraya," he said, "Nassiri and his companions have been arrested by Mossadegh's supporters. We have lost. We must get away as quickly as possible." . . .

On the flight [to Baghdad] the men were deeply depressed, and the Shah said: "It's all over."[59]

After remaining in Baghdad only briefly, the Shah and Soraya proceeded on to Rome. The radio broadcast dire news. Demonstrators in Tehran had stormed government buildings and burned photographs of the Shah. Statues of Reza Shah were being toppled throughout Iran. The minister of foreign affairs had delivered a speech haranguing the royal family. Soraya recounts what happened then:

When I heard all this I too gave up hope. The Shah and I discussed what we should do now. He said, "we shall have to economize, Soraya, for I am sorry to say that I haven't much money—enough perhaps to buy us a farm somewhere or other."

"Where would you like to go?" I asked.

"Probably America."[60]

In short, from Soraya's account and from those of others connected to the events of those days, it is clear that in the mind of the Shah at least, the coup had failed.[61] He was prepared for a life of exile in America and played absolutely no role in the events which subsequently restored him to his throne.

Soraya relates how they learned of those events. On August 18, 1953, only three days after the arrest of Nassiri, she writes,

while we were having lunch in the dining room of the Hotel Excelsior [in Rome], a young reporter from the Associated Press came across to our table and triumphantly handed us a slip of paper. We read . . . MOSSADEGH OVERTHROWN—IMPERIAL TROOPS CONTROL TEHRAN—ZEHEDI PREMIER. The news had just come over the teleprinter.[62]

In fact, Kim Roosevelt and his associates in Tehran had refused to accept the failure of their coup and refused to give up their efforts to overthrow Mossadegh. When Roosevelt had notified CIA headquarters of the failure, Allen Dulles cabled back that he was to withdraw from Iran and cease all clandestine activities. So determined was Roosevelt to succeed, however, that he ignored his boss's orders, later to claim, for the record, that he never received that cable ordering the mission canceled, and proceeded to improvise a new set of plans.[63] After two days of feverish activity and hectic preparations, the second coup, based on the mobilization of the "streets" of south Tehran, succeeded. Zahedi was installed as prime minister, Mossadegh was arrested, and the Shah was invited to return to Tehran, "in triumph," which he did on August 22, 1953.[64]

While this account of the coup sheds light on numerous aspects of the Shah's character and his actions as monarch, it is included here because it particularly illuminates one aspect of the Shah's character—his propensity for withdrawal from threatening or challenging situations. There are other examples of that same propensity for withdrawal. Another also occurred during the Mossadegh period.

As chairman of the Majles oil committee, Mossadegh had long championed the nationalization of Iran's oil. After the assassination of the prime minister, Gen. Ali Razmara, on March 7, 1951, Mossadegh and his supporters—a substantial majority of the Majles—passed a bill nationalizing the oil industry, that is, the Anglo-Iranian Oil Company, as it was then called. Driven by the wild enthusiasm of the Iranian people, the Shah had little choice but to sign the bill and appoint Mossadegh prime minister.[65] Mossadegh had been swept to power by the political fervor of a growing tide of Iranian nationalism.

Immediately after Mossadegh was appointed, the Shah's major concerns were to deal with the consequences of the oil nationalization and the chaos and violence unleashed in Iranian politics. Averell Harriman arrived in Tehran to exercise the "good offices" of the United States in the dispute between Iran and the United Kingdom. Harriman failed in the face of Mossadegh's intransigence, bolstered by the enthusiasm of the Iranian people. He left Iran having made no progress. Mossadegh took the offensive. He traveled to the United States in October of 1951, to plead Iran's case before the U.N. Security Council. Mossadegh's supporters and communists had been battling on the streets of Tehran, opposition deputies were collecting signatures for the impeachment of the prime minister, and he was demanding the expulsion of members of the royal family from Iran.

Soraya described what this tumultuous period was like for the Shah.

Mohammad Reza found himself confronted with a dilemma. He wished to fight back, but at that time the masses would have regarded any opposition to Mossadegh as a kind of treason. Also he was himself too much of a patriot to attack his Prime Minister while negotiations with the Western powers were actually going on.

So to start with he did nothing at all. He continued as usual, to go to his office every day, but this was now a mere formality. His Ministers no longer asked him for advice. They regarded him as nothing but a figurehead, for they thought he had let the real power slip from his hands.

He saw very few people, even in private.[66]

In short, Mossadegh, having assumed the premiership, moved rapidly to amass power. The central position, which the Shah had so assiduously cultivated after assuming the throne in 1941, rapidly collapsed, along, apparently, with his morale. Throughout 1952 those two processes accelerated. Mossadegh's power was relentlessly enhanced, especially after his abrupt dismissal by the Shah in July of 1952 and his equally abrupt reinstatement following street demonstrations. And the morale of the Shah proportionally diminished as Mossadegh appeared to be replicating the pattern of the Free Officers in Egypt whose 1952 coup led to the exile of King Farouk. Mossadegh looked ever more like a rival to the throne, not its servant.

A showdown between the monarch and his prime minister occurred in February of 1953. The Shah claims that Mossadegh "suggested that I temporarily leave the country. In order to give him a free hand to try out his policies, and to have a little respite from his intrigues, I agreed."[67] Princess Soraya and other commentators claim that the idea for the Shah's trip came from the Shah himself.[68] In a psychic sense, of course, it does not matter particularly with whom the idea originated. What does matter is that the Shah accepted the idea. In the face of political challenge, the Shah was again ready to withdraw. On this occasion the Shah consented to a physical withdrawal, to leaving the country.[69]

The Shah must have understood what his withdrawal from Iran presaged. There was an abundant history of monarchs leaving the country in advance of their abdication or displacement. The last Shah of the Qajar dynasty was in Europe when he was deposed by Reza Khan. Reza Shah was himself deposed by the British and Russians and went into exile immediately. There was also a more menacing contemporary parallel. King Farouk's recent Egyptian experience was a chilling reminder to the Shah of the frailty of monarchies in the era of national liberation movements. It must have been clear to the Shah what his departure from Iran might precipitate or, at the very least, suggest to the Iranian people. Yet he was ready to leave, even, by one account, proposing his departure. In this case, the physical withdrawal was never realized. After the Shah had agreed to leave and, indeed, after he had packed and dispatched his baggage ahead of the royal party, the political tide turned.

Mossadegh, by then, had alienated a number of his formerly fervent supporters. When those supporters learned of the Shah's intention to leave, they sent him messages of support. They urged him to remain in Tehran for fear that with his departure, the last obstacle to a complete consolidation of power by the prime minister would have been removed. Large crowds were assembled in front of the palace, asking the Shah to remain. With their support, the Shah's resolve was strengthened. He asked for a microphone to address his supporters. "With tears in his eyes," Soraya writes, "he thanked them for their manifestations of loyalty and promised them that he would not leave Teheran."[70]

Other instances when the Shah actually withdrew physically, and more often psychically, or threatened to do so, can be drawn from his rule. Those withdrawals were frequent and consistent enough so that their occurrence constituted a pattern. It was, then, a method the Shah used to deal with situations he perceived as threatening and provided him with comfort and soothing. This passive position toward adversity can be understood to represent a return to the Shah's childhood in that house of females. There he found intense pleasure, as suggested above, in the company of his mother and sisters. There the women retreated, as do all women in Iran, to the *anderun,* the interior, private quarters of the home, withdrawn and protected from the outside world of men. The young Mohammad Reza grew in that home, threatened by the turmoil between his powerful parents and feminized by the company of women, to develop a passive stance to adversity. Again and again in his adult life he repeated that childhood pattern.

If nothing else, his withdrawals allowed him to conform to his father's judgment of his eldest son, the Crown Prince and future Shah, and in the process, to his own judgment of himself. For Reza Shah never made a particular secret of the fact that what most concerned him about the future of the Pahlavis after his death was the ability of his successor to manifest the courage required to be a Shah and to do what a Shah had to do. Reza Shah told people around him that he feared for Mohammad Reza because he was a weak-willed person.[71]

The fact is, of course, that the father understood his son all too well. He knew his son was, as Reza Shah put it, "tender hearted" and feared that such softness would serve his son poorly as Shah. Mohammad Reza Shah's retreats were one manifestation of that fear and softness. And, as his father had predicted, they did serve the Shah poorly. For they resulted in his failure to confront and deal with those individuals or processes which ultimately led to his downfall. Mohammad Reza Shah failed, too often, to exercise leadership and by doing so contributed to the undermining of his own authority.

As suggested above, then, his withdrawal of support from the Pahlavi system was a key factor in its fall. That withdrawal took many forms, of which three have been discussed here—his physical withdrawal from the day-to-day responsibilities of running the system, his talk of some future withdrawal from the throne itself in favor of the Crown Prince, and his withdrawal of support of the Pahlavi system by laying the blame for the ills of Iran on the system which he had created and for which he had total responsibility.[72]

Liberalization of the Pahlavi System and Communication of Mixed Messages

Two other general patterns the Shah followed contributed to the cracking of his authority and loss of support—his efforts to bring about the "liberalization" of the Pahlavi system and his communication of "mixed" messages to his subjects.

Basically, the Shah understood "liberalization" to mean easing the repression which had been imposed on Iranian society by his regime, principally through SAVAK. That repression was, of course, pervasive in political life. But by the late 1970s, no area in the life of an Iranian was immune. The economy, culture, education, and all forms of communication were subjected to vigorous SAVAK scrutiny and, at least intermittently, to rigorous SAVAK control. This repression had been imposed on the people of Iran in an increasingly heavy-handed fashion since the onset of the White Revolution.[73]

In early 1963, when the Shah submitted his six-point reform program to the Iranian people in a national referendum, the regime had reached a fateful juncture.[74] In effect, for the Shah, the years between the arrest of Mossadegh and the dismissal of Amini had been years of groping. He clearly was trying to control the instruments of power through which he could govern Iran. But those instruments were few in number and quite inefficacious in consequence. Moreover, his competitors for the control of the instruments of power were numerous—the landed elite, tribal leaders, clerics, urban merchants and industrialists, and professional politicians. They wanted their share of the rewards. But they wanted more—control over some part of the system.

The Shah tried different methods to accomplish his goals of institutionalizing his rule. He tried shuffling premiers and cabinets, establishing a two-party political system, building a powerful military, establishing SAVAK, and deepening ties with the West, particularly the United States. But the political turmoil of early 1961 indicated that the Shah had failed in his efforts. The rioters were in the streets. Prime Minister Khrushchev was predicting, in a characteristically down-home metaphor, that the Shah would fall like a "ripe apple." President Kennedy, only recently inaugurated, was sounding inspirational messages about democracy and reform in the Third World. The appointment of Dr. Ali Amini to the premiership, at least partly to satisfy U.S. pressures, indicated the extent of the Shah's failure to control the political process.

The White Revolution was the first major salvo in the Shah's campaign to assert his domination. With Assadollah Alam serving as prime minister, the Shah announced six reforms which constituted his so-called revolution—land reform, the right of women to vote, the establishment of the Literacy Corps, the sale of state-owned factories, the nationalization of forests, and a profit-sharing scheme for industry. With those reforms and with over a dozen subsequent measures designed to extend reform to other areas of Iranian life, the Shah sought to achieve some measure of social justice. Social justice, he had always believed, would earn the support of his people.[75] The support of his people, in turn, would earn him the support of the United States. The support of both his people and the United States would guarantee the achievement of his goal of controlling Iranian politics and the tenure of his rule.

But the White Revolution would do more than achieve social justice and win political support for the regime. It would also serve to eliminate the power bases of the other forces competing with the Shah for control of Iranian politics. The land reform, for example, served to eliminate the power base of the landlords. They had been able to rely on "their" peasants both as troops to staff private militias and as voters able to help guarantee the election of the landlords to the Majles. The White Revolution, in short, would serve to establish direct links between the government, and thus the Shah, and the people of Iran. It would greatly enhance the power of the state at the expense of other institutions, including the clergy. With the reduction of the power of those other institutions, there were ever-diminishing impediments to the establishment of an Iranian leviathan, which, by the mid-1970s, is precisely what the Shah had created.

By 1976 the Shah was aware of his subjects' mounting dismay at the power of the Pahlavi state. One response was the Shah's "liberalization" policy. During the Iranian Revolution of 1978, he offered an explanation of that policy: "When we started to liberalize two years ago, it was with the perfect understanding and knowledge that the democratic way will be our way in the future. Everything that was done was to secure our democratic future. And that was *two years ago*" (emphasis in original).[76] The Shah attempted to explain to the Iranian people as well as to the Americans that his program of liberalization, as he referred to it himself, had been initiated by him in early 1976, independent of any pressure from the United States. Jimmy Carter had assumed the presidency in 1977 on a platform of internationalizing human rights and curtailing the spread of weapons to the Third World. It was important to the Shah to demonstrate that his reform program was not merely an attempt to curry favor with President Carter. He had to demonstrate it to the U.S. president as a means of limiting further American intervention in Iranian affairs. But more importantly, he had to demonstrate it to the Iranian people. The Shah had to speak to the common perception that he was an instrument of foreigners, the Americans and British in particular.

In fact, the actions the Shah took to implement what he considered a liberalization program did not become clear until the first months of 1977. But had the Shah launched his liberalization program in 1976, it could still appropriately have been understood as a response to the pressures emanating from the United States. For by 1976, no well-known ruler, with the exception, perhaps, of Leonid Brezhnev, was as unpopular among the American people, at least among a good share of the American intelligentsia, as was the Shah, and no regime in the world was more frequently criticized for human rights abuses than was his.

Despite his claims throughout the revolution that his liberalization program was his own creation, there is abundant evidence—from the Shah himself—that it was a response to foreign pressures.[77] Early in the liberalization campaign the Shah railed to an associate, "They want liberalization! I'll give them liberalization. I'll loosen the screws until the Americans beg me to tighten them again."[78] Much later, in October 1979, after he had lost his throne, fled into exile, and then been admitted to the United States for treatment of his burgeoning cancer, he was an embittered man, seeking rationalizations for his defeat. Visited in the hospital by the former U.S. ambassador Richard Helms and Mrs. Helms, the Shah explained what had happened to his kingdom after the ambassador had left Iran in 1976: "The real difficulty was caused by too precipitate liberalization. . . . The Americans and the British kept pushing me; they wanted a democratic republic. They wanted me to be more liberal with my opponents. The changes were genuine on my part. But Iran is not ready for Western-style democracy."[79] There is no evidence, in fact, that the Americans or British pressured the Shah for any "Western-style democracy." But there is no question that Jimmy Carter's human rights message was received with trepidation by the Shah and suspicious enthusiasm by his opponents.

The year 1977 began precisely in that spirit. Even before the inauguration of President Carter, an official U.S. report criticized Iran's human rights policies.[80] The Shah promptly set out to "loosen the screws," and the results were quickly evident. During May and June the Shah met in Tehran with Martin Ennals of Amnesty International and with William Butler and other representatives of the International Commission of Jurists. Both had been critical, especially Ennals, of the Shah's record on human rights.[81] Members of the International Red Cross were invited to inspect Iran's prisons. In June the Shah announced a series of measures to increase the rights of defendants in political cases, including opening the trials to the press and giving defendants the right to engage civilian attorneys.

Iranian activists believed the Shah was adapting to the deep concerns of the new president, as he had adapted to the concerns of another reforming U.S. president some fifteen years earlier. They were emboldened to press the Shah for greater liberalization than he was prepared to grant. In May 1977 a group of fifty-four lawyers sent the Shah an open letter criticizing the legal system, demanding reforms to protect the rights of defendants, and announcing the formation of a new committee to monitor the Iranian judicial system. Ibrahim Khajenouri, a noted historian, sent an open letter to the leadership of the Rastakhiz party, criticizing them for "failing to encourage meaningful political activity and neglecting to improve ties between the Government and the people."[82] The Writer's Association sent the prime minister an open letter, signed by over forty of Iran's leading intellectuals, demanding the right to publish their works freely. At the end of June, National Front leaders, including Dariush Foruhar, Karim Sanjabi, and Shahpour Bakhtiar, issued an open letter to the Shah, claiming,

The only way to create new faith in ourselves, to restore a sense of individual liberty, and a spirit of national cooperation . . . is to end despotic government, observe the principles of the constitution, and the Universal Declaration of Human Rights, forego the one-party system, allow freedom of the press and of association, release political prisoners . . . and establish a government based on majority representation.[83]

A large number of Tehran's "bazaaris" announced the formation of the Society of Merchants, Traders, and Craftsmen, whose goal was to diminish government interference in the commercial life of Iran. Haj Seyyed Javadi, a noted Iranian literary figure, sent the Shah a two hundred–page blistering critique of Iranian society and politics and then had the document widely circulated in Iran.

In July 1977, Hushang Ansary, one of the Rastakhiz leaders and one of the most powerful of the Shah's minions, gave a speech urging an even greater outpouring. "Every tongue must speak out," he said, "every pen must write as a right under Iranian democracy."[84] During the same month, Prime Minister Hoveyda invited the public to criticize the government. "Criticism," he suggested, "was a sign of progress; lack of it signified stagnation. Self-criticism was an established tradition in Iran that smoothed the path of progress."[85] Throughout the summer, demonstrations were held demanding government adherence to law, petitions were circulated, and additional open letters were sent to the prime minister and the Shah.

While the Shah had appeared to countenance the expressions of protest which had been voiced during the spring and early summer, he began to issue more mixed signals. At a news conference the Shah made explicit his position on human rights: "We are completely in favor of defending human rights as long as this is in accordance with the interests of the majority. But if this carries us towards the law of the jungle and defeat, then it can no longer be called human rights."[86] The actions of his government were less encouraging. During the summer, Ayatollah Mahmoud Taleghani, one of the most popular and certainly one of the most political of Tehran's ayatollahs, was arrested. Charged with subversion, he was secretly tried and sentenced to a ten-year prison term. None of the Shah's judicial reforms was applied to Taleghani.

In late August a government attempt to clear a squatter settlement in Tehran was resisted by recent urban migrants. On the day the bulldozers appeared, some five squatters were killed attempting to protect their homes. The next day, participants in a large demonstration fought with the police. By nightfall, twelve were killed and scores wounded. On the third day, tens of thousands of people attacked local police posts. Order was restored only after the army was brought in. The rapidity with which the demonstrations grew and the participation in them by organized left-wing groups chilled the government. The people were equally chilled by the apparent readiness of the authorities to use deadly force.

In the fall of 1977, the new school year began with disturbances on a number of campuses. Students throughout the country staged demonstrations protesting regime practices. The boldness of the students increased as the regime failed to respond to their challenges. In October, student speakers demanded the return to Iran of Ayatollah Khomeini. In October the Writer's Association sponsored poetry-reading sessions in conjunction with the Goethe Institute, the German cultural association. Poetry is a traditional Iranian medium of communication, and Iranians took full advantage of its potential by reciting poems bitterly, if elliptically, critical of the Pahlavi regime. By the end of the week, spurred by the rapidly spreading news of their political significance, tens of thousands of Iranians gathered nightly to listen to the recitations. In early November an open letter was circulated in which prominent Iranians demanded an end to human rights abuses and the dissolution of SAVAK.

But perhaps no single government act in 1977 demonstrated the mixed messages emanating from the Shah and his regime as did its response to a key meeting that occurred at the end of November. Over a thousand members and sympathizers of the National Front and other opponents of the regime gathered on an important Shi'ite holiday in a garden outside Tehran to discuss the formation of a unified antigovernment coalition. Their deliberations were ended by over two hundred club-wielding Shah supporters who had been especially bussed to the garden to break up the meeting. More than a hundred people were injured, many requiring hospitalization.

Some weeks later, another group of prominent Iranians sent letters to U.N. General Secretary Kurt Waldheim and President Carter seeking their help with the restoration of human rights in Iran. The year ended inauspiciously, with a bomb exploding at the Iran-America Society, the U.S.-sponsored organization that promoted culture as a way of advancing the United States' image in Iran. Along with the regime, the United States had become a target of the violence as Iran slid toward full revolution.

The Shah did much to bring that revolution about. His unbounded grandiosity led to a series of policies deeply offensive to the Iranian people. In addition, the Shah was Shah in ways which violated the Iranian people's conception of proper leadership. Perhaps most importantly, he created a system of rule steeped in grandeur and the symbols of an imperialism emanating from Tehran and directed at the Iranian people. The result was to distance the ruler from the people, a distance which made the Shah appear almost a foreign imposition, something all the more easy to believe because of his attachment to the United States.

To counter his image as a distant and cold ruler, the Shah presided over a change in the Pahlavi iconography. Before the 1970s the ruler's picture was displayed in every public place, whether it be a shop or an office, a private corporation or a school. In the mid-1970s those pictures began to change, at Government order. The Shah was portrayed not so much as the harsh dictator but as a caring uncle. Yet this image of a caring uncle was also a violation of the culturally constituted vision of leadership which informed the Iranian people. They sought neither a removed dictator nor a caring uncle but an empathic, stern, decisive, powerful father. The Shah made every effort to present the appropriate face, but it was not in him to do so.

Far more serious to cracking the Shah's authority were three other processes, all instituted by the Shah. He withdrew support from his own system of rule. To preserve himself, he took to blaming the system he had created. The problems the Iranian people encountered, he told them, were not his fault. The problems could be found in the failings of the prime minister, the cabinet ministers, and, at every level, the officials of the system. But the Iranian people could not accept the idea that the Pahlavi system was independent of the top Pahlavi. To the contrary, it was universally believed that the Pahlavi system was an emanation of the Shah himself. He had spent many years of his rule assuring his ability to govern without interference and making the imperial parliament and bureaucracies into instruments for the execution of his governing will. When he tried to shift gears and blame the system for the failings of his rule, the Iranian people could not absolve him of responsibility. Insofar as the system was defective, the responsibility lay even more with the ruler who had created that system.

The liberalization which he instituted, whether in 1976 or 1977, in response to the concerns of the U.S. Democratic candidate or on his own initiative, proved another factor which contributed to diminishing the authority of the Shah. For the liberalization policy was enacted with no sense of what it was meant to accomplish or of the limits of acceptable political discourse. Furthermore, the liberalization policy was enacted at the time when the institutions which might have productively channeled political demands through the political system were being destroyed by the Shah himself. The Rastakhiz party could have absorbed the political energies of countless Iranians and provided a mechanism for the dissemination of demands from the people to the regime. But precisely when the Shah was legitimating the expression of political demands, he was dismantling the Rastakhiz party. There was no way in which the fruits of the liberalization policy could have been politically efficacious for either the newly enfranchised political dissidents or for the system itself. To the contrary, when it became clear that there were no institutional mechanisms for the channeling of political demands to the system and, ultimately to the Shah himself, the liberalization policy appeared to the Iranian people as a policy designed to please Washington while distracting and, hopefully for the Shah, buying off the Iranian people.

In short, the entire program was based on a mixed message which served initially to confuse and then to infuriate the Iranian people. They had felt demeaned and depreciated. Now they felt manipulated and ever more enraged. That was the rage which would burst into anti-Shah fervor with the revolution in 1978. The Shah came to appreciate the intensity of that rage and the fact that he was its target. Amir Abbas Hoveyda told U.K. ambassador Anthony Parsons that the Shah had experienced the rage of the Iranian people as a "total betrayal." Hoveyda went on to explain that the Shah was "like a man who had lavished everything for years on a beautiful woman only to find that she had been unfaithful to him all along."[87] The realization proved shattering. It destroyed one of the pillars of his psychological strength and contributed to the paralyzing regression which seized him during the revolution.

5

The Strength of Others

Many individuals—Iranians and foreigners, men and women—were crucial to the Shah during his thirty-seven years of rule. At least five were major sources of psychic strength: his father and mother; his twin sister, Ashraf; the friend he made in Switzerland who became a companion in Iran, Ernest Perron; and his last minister of court, Assadollah Alam. During various periods of his rule, these five were sources of inspiration. But they were more as well. By serving as psychologically significant others, objects of identification, they provided the Shah with much needed strength. And with Princess Ashraf, Ernest Perron, and Assadollah Alam, the relation was more powerful. For virtually his entire life, the Shah merged with others and from those mergers was able to take for himself some of their strength. Along with the other sources from which he was able to draw strength, these psychological mergers allowed him to "do" Shah. But this source of the Shah's strength, along with the others—the support of his people, his divine protection, and the support of the United States—had vanished by the outbreak of the revolution.

Different psychoanalytic theorists have argued for the psychological significance of others for adult functioning. But none has made the adult's relationship with other adults such a central part of his work as Heinz Kohut. Kohut uses the term *selfobject* to refer to "that dimension of our experience of another person that relates to this person's functions in shoring up our self."[1] Kohut describes three ways in which adults use selfobjects to bolster their self-esteem to the point where they can function in ways appropriate to the demands upon them. He discusses these in the form of transferences—mirroring transferences, idealizing transferences, and twinship or alter ego transferences. A mirroring transference is a relationship between two persons in which one reflects approval and positive reinforcements on the other. An idealizing transference occurs when an individual is able to merge, or identify with, or even admire the inspiring ideals and achievements of others. Twinship or alter ego transferences are found when an individual merges with another, a selfobject, in order to generate the self-affirmation and self-strengthening which comes from the association with a calm and powerful other.[2]

It is difficult to establish the precise nature of the Shah's self-selfobject relations with the significant others in his life. For example, it is impossible to establish conclusively the extent to which his relationship with Ernest Perron included mirroring or alter ego transferences. Not enough is known of the details of the relationship between the two men. They, of course, are both dead, and it is unlikely they would illuminate that relationship if they were not. (They certainly did nothing to illuminate it in their lifetimes.) The one person who knows most explicitly of their relationship, Queen Soraya, will not discuss it. It is impossible to specify the precise transference relations the Shah had with his selfobjects.

But his use of others to provide strength failed him, as did his other sources of psychological sustenance. One by one, his psychic "twins" fell by the wayside. His father died first, in exile in South Africa during the Second World War. His mother became senile and was moved to California. Ernest Perron was squeezed out by the Americans after the coup against Mossadegh and died in Switzerland in 1961. Princess Ashraf is still alive and living in New York, but she was rebuffed by her brother and effectively forced into exile because of her extraordinary unpopularity in Iran. Assadollah Alam was the stalwart. He remained with the Shah, nearly to the end, dying of leukemia in 1977. Alam served the Shah as minister of court and was able to give him strength nearly to the end. But not close enough to the end. Alam died just before the outbreak of the violence which would become the revolution. When the Shah most needed the strength of others, he had no one. And he had no one just as his other sources of psychological strength were failing him as well.

Ernest Perron

By far the most obscure of the Shah's psychic "twins" was Ernest Perron, son of the handyman at Le Rosey school on Lake Geneva in Switzerland. Reza Shah had determined to educate his son in the ways of the West and had chosen Le Rosey in neutral Switzerland to minimize the political risks which would follow were the young Crown Prince to study in a country more embroiled in Iranian politics. The Shah was miserable and lonely at

Le Rosey, despite the miniretinue despatched with him from Tehran. His closest friend at Le Rosey was drawn not from his fellow Persians or from any of his fellow students, but was Ernest Perron, ten years the Shah's senior and assistant to his father in caring for the buildings and grounds at the fashionable school. One of the Shah's biographers described the birth of their friendship. Perron, he reported,

> was small and skinny . . . many of the students razzed him, his small size encouraging their bullying instincts. One day, Mohammad saw a student kick over the wheelbarrow full of compost Perron was pushing. He gave the culprit a beating and within a few days, the handyman's son and the son of the Shah of Persia had become intimate friends.[3]

That intimate friendship was to last nearly all of Perron's life. When the Shah returned to Iran in 1936, he brought his friend with him.

No one involved can recall Reza Shah's reaction to his son's return from the West with an older man, the son of a gardener and general handyman at Le Rosey, but Reza Shah must have been outraged by their intimate friendship. The son of a grounds keeper was obviously no fit companion for the heir to the new Pahlavi dynasty. But worse, Reza Shah had long feared for his son's masculinity and had committed himself, as a cardinal mission, to its strengthening. His son's return from foreign studies with an older male intimate companion must have seemed to his father the realization of his deepest fears for his son.

Given the ruler's likely reaction, it is all the more astounding that Perron remained in Iran. Reza Shah apparently took no steps to oust his son's intimate. In fact, Perron moved into the Crown Prince's palace, and when Mohammad Reza assumed the throne, Perron joined the new Shah and his wife, Princess Fawzia, in their move to Reza Shah's former palace.

By all accounts, the friendship deepened over the years. One of the many challenges the Shah's second wife, Princess Soraya, had to face was the intimate bond between her husband and his Swiss friend. It was not a bond she accepted easily. In her memoirs, she reports that Perron had no official appointment but lived at the court as a personal friend of the Shah. Despite his humble origins, he was said to be Mohammad Reza's closest adviser. "He visited him each morning in his bedroom for a discussion," Soraya remembered. "No one could say precisely what it was he did."[4]

While Perron's role in the court—and as the innuendo of Queen Soraya would have it, in the bedroom as well—was unclear, Tehran was, not surprisingly, awash with rumors. The most damaging of those rumors hinted at a homosexual relation between the handyman's son and the Shah. The gossip was part of Tehran's political landscape for the remainder of the Shah's rule, years after Perron had returned to Switzerland and died there in 1961. After the Shah's flight from Iran in 1979, a book appeared in Persian entitled *Ernest Perron, the Husband of the Shah of Iran,* which told the story of an alleged passionate, lifelong homosexual affair between the two men.[5] In the frenzy of the immediate success of the revolution and the ouster of the Shah, the book was sold everywhere in Tehran and widely read. But it offered nothing which constituted evidence for its central and dramatic claim, just a long narrative account of the purported love affair and its complications. (It managed, in the process, to introduce what by then was that inevitable note of the Shah's treachery to Iran. Perron, not surprisingly, was described as an agent for the British—most of the scoundrels in twentieth-century Iranian political accounts are depicted as agents for the British, and more recently, the Americans—who used his affair with the Shah to subvert the independence and integrity of Iran.)

Contrary to the allegation that the Shah's relation with Perron was homosexual, testimony has been offered by a number of court intimates who insist that the relation between the Shah and Perron was completely asexual. One man personally close to the Shah, a court insider, and formerly related to the Shah by marriage, remembered Perron as "a warm man, completely devoted to the Shah. He was grateful for the life-style which the Shah provided him and tried to repay his friend with advice and service. But the Shah was never intimate with him nor would he allow Perron to intrigue in court matters."[6]

A woman who was also a member of the Shah's inner circle was similarly certain that while "Perron was used by the Shah to carry his wishes to members of the court, he had no sexual relationship to the Shah whatsoever."[7]

The precise nature of the Shah's ties to Perron remains uncertain. For this analysis, moreover, the precise nature of their relationship is largely irrelevant. Whether or not the Shah had homosexual relations with his companion is beside the point. To the point is the clear evidence that they had an intimate friendship which lasted for many years and spanned two of the Shah's marriages. The relationship was so intimate and so intense that it assumed the form of a psychological merger. Perron remained in Tehran for over twenty years, "intriguing" in court affairs, on occasion, perhaps, to advance the interests of the British or others. But ultimately Ernest Perron never acted independently of the Shah—an agent perhaps, but for the Shah.

Princess Ashraf has given one account of the kind of services Perron performed for the Shah, of the kinds of "wishes" he conveyed for the ruler. She reports that she had become a friend of Mehrpour Teymourtash, the same young man who had earlier been sent to accompany the Crown Prince to Le Rosey. But only a little more than a year after the boys arrived in Switzerland, Mehrpour's father, Gen. Abdul Teymourtash, fell from Reza Shah's favor. Mehrpour was instructed to return to Tehran because the general was dismissed as minister of court and imprisoned. Stripped of his military rank and disgraced, Teymourtash died soon after "of a heart attack" in prison. Tehran's rumor mills suggested that Reza Shah had made the general drink a cup of "Qajar coffee"—that Reza Shah had Teymourtash poisoned—the way the monarchs of the preceding dynasty had disposed of their enemies.

The fate of the general did not preclude Mehrpour and his brother Houshang from remaining court insiders. Nor did his fate dissuade the strong-willed Ashraf from deepening the relationship with Mehrpour. But Princess Ashraf found herself increasingly attracted to Houshang.[8] After Mehrpour died following a car accident, Ashraf determined to marry Houshang. Yet her cautious brother, Mohammad Reza, who had only recently assumed the throne following the ouster of his father, worried over the potential for disgrace and danger in the new love affair. He did not deal with the matter directly, but sent for Perron. Perron, in turn, met with Houshang Teymourtash. Ashraf recounts what happened.

Realizing how attached I was to Houshang, my brother had sent his friend Ernest Perron to see him. "The shah doesn't doubt the sincerity of your feelings for his sister," Perron told Houshang, "but His Majesty knows his sister, and he knows that a marriage to you will cause her suffering and unhappiness. If you really love her, you will not attempt to see her again."[9]

Houshang Teymourtash never did see Princess Ashraf again.[10]

In addition to these services of a decidedly personal and delicate nature, Perron allegedly served the Shah in more political ways. As a European, he maintained close ties to the Tehran representatives of foreign states. In World War II, he was an important liaison with British and American diplomats and, later, during the Mossadegh crisis, is reported to have served as a link between the court and their intelligence services. For example, the British foreign secretary Herbert Morrison dispatched Robin Zaehner to Tehran to contribute to the ouster of Mossadegh. Zaehner was a lecturer in Persian and professor of religion at Oxford. His access to the Shah's court was through Perron.[11]

Following his restoration to the throne after the 1953 coup against Mossadegh, however, the Shah dramatically changed his relationship with Perron. He asked his lifelong friend to move out of the royal palace. Allegedly the U.S. government had come to believe Perron was a major liability for the Shah, a subject of rumors, a court intriguer, and a foreigner. U.S. diplomats related their conclusions to the Shah—Perron had to be dismissed. The Shah complied in late 1953, and Princess Shams invited Perron to live in her palace. The princess had previously converted to Catholicism and is believed to have felt a special sympathy for her coreligionist.[12] As Perron moved away from the Shah, so he became increasingly peripheral, both physically and psychically.

There is now no satisfactory way to reconstruct the relationship between the Shah and Perron. The Shah left us with no clues. In none of his three volumes of memoirs does the name Ernest Perron appear. At the least, then, it seems he was uncomfortable with their association. That discomfort may, indeed, have stemmed from many sources. Perron was after all a Swiss national. The Shah's most intimate male friend, his companion who shared the imperial palace with the Shah and Queen Soraya, was a foreigner. The deep-seated patriotism of the Iranian people, shading into Iranian (or Islamic) chauvinism and even xenophobia, would make the presence of Perron offensive to most Iranians. The possibility of a homosexual relationship was further grounds for offense.

What is certain from all this is that Perron was an intimate adviser to the Shah and was used by him to carry out assignments which the Shah considered private or sensitive. No one who was a member of court circles in the period of Perron's involvement supports the rumors of a homosexual tie between the Shah and his Swiss friend. More to the point made here is that the precise relationship between the two men is not the issue—the allegation of a homosexual relation between the Shah and his Swiss companion is irrelevant. Whether or not manifest sexuality was a part of their relation, there clearly was an extraordinarily close bond between the two. That bond, as measured by its intensity and duration, suggests how significant Perron was for the Shah.

For over two decades Perron and the Shah were deeply enmeshed. The history of the relation, as we know it, and the psychological makeup of the Shah, as it has been constructed here, both strongly suggest that Perron was no mere confidant, but a crucial source of strength and courage—of narcissistic supplies—for the Shah.

Ashraf Pahlavi

If the Shah's relation with Perron is difficult to untangle, so is another of his most important lifelong ties—that with his twin sister, Princess Ashraf Pahlavi. There was such a deep tie between the two that their relation could be described not merely as twins, but as a psychological twinship, a psychic merger. Princess Ashraf is more forthcoming than the Shah in acknowledging this tie.

It was this twinship and this relationship with my brother that would nourish and sustain me throughout my childhood. . . . No matter how I would reach out in the years to come—sometimes even desperately—to find an identity and a purpose of my own, I would remain inextricably tied to my brother. . . . always, the center of my existence was, and is, Mohammad Reza Pahlavi.[13]

The Shah was never as open about his twin. In only one of the three volumes of his memoirs, in fact, does he mention that Ashraf was his twin sister. In the others she is identified, only by dint of her presence in childhood family photos, as one of his sisters.[14] His failure to acknowledge his twinship in his writings must be seen as comparable to his failure to acknowledge his ties to Perron. For all other evidence suggests that Ashraf was of immense personal significance to him—both necessary, especially in his earlier years, and embarrassing throughout his life.

In her own life story, Princess Ashraf refers to her three "exiles," the three periods in her life when she left her beloved country and was separated from her beloved brother. The first exile occurred after her brother had used Ernest Perron to end her "youthful dreams of love" with Houshang Teymourtash.[15] She responded by leaving Iran to visit her deposed father, by then exiled by the British to Johannesburg, South Africa. Princess Ashraf recalled her desire to accompany her father into exile in 1941. She had asked him again and again to take her with him, but he would have none of it. He insisted she remain behind with her twin. "I would love to have you with me" she recalls her father saying, "but your brother needs you more. I want you to stay with him."[16] The British granted permission and she remained in Tehran.

However, when the Shah ended her relationship with Teymourtash, she was angry and hurt. Almost immediately after, she made her way to her father, in exile in South America, only returning to Tehran in 1944. By the time she reached her brother, Ashraf found that the royal marriage had ended. Princess Fawzia had left for Cairo, and the young Shah was completely alone. The princess decided to act. "Since there were few people my brother could trust and rely on, and since I had promised my father I would stand by him, I began my career on the domestic political scene."[17]

She threw herself into building political support for the Shah. One of her first plans was to use a newspaper to build a political base for his rule. She found a willing editor and financial support from the royal court and turned the Tehran daily, *Ettela'at,* into that organ. *Ettela'at* would become Iran's most prestigious and widely read newspaper. But that was only the beginning. "My first priority," she recalls, "was to make political friends for the regime and to neutralize some of the opposition. Every day I met unofficially with individuals and groups representing various points of view. I listened to them and tried to convince them that Iran badly needed a viable central government and a greater national unity."[18]

Ensconced in a palace across the street from the home of the Shah in downtown Tehran, Ashraf became a formidable player in Iranian politics. Her jet-black hair, small stature, and intense physical energy earned her the nickname "the Black Panther." The Egyptian journalist Mohamed Heikal first visited with the Shah in the spring of 1951 at Princess Ashraf's home. "This was an interesting house," he recalls, "because it reflected the Princess's passion for the Emperor Napoleon. There were portraits and busts of Napoleon all over the place, and in her office . . . all the chairs and sofas were in tiger skins. There must have been the skins of at least a hundred tigers."[19] The Iranian politicians whom she called to her office must have found it difficult indeed, surrounded by busts of an earlier emperor and those jungle skins, to resist her entreaties.

Not only the politically active members of Iran's elite felt the force of Ashraf's schemes on behalf of her brother. Apparently the political scheming extended to her sister, Princess Shams, as well. The two women—the Shah's older sister and his twin sister—battled for dominance in the court. Queen Soraya remembers that Shams told her in 1950 that "my sister Ashraf is a self-serving and conspiratorial woman."[20] She warned Soraya to be wary of Ashraf, who jealously guarded her ties to her brother and would resent his new wife as a rival. Shams, in fact, accused Ashraf of breaking up Fawzia's marriage with the Shah. It was Shams, however, who had found Soraya, deemed her a suitable bride, and arranged for her introduction to the Shah. Soraya always believed that Shams hoped that act would ensure her dominance over Ashraf within the court. Heikal reports that Princess Ashraf disapproved of the Shah's marriage to Soraya.

She thought it had been arranged by their half-sister, Princess Shams, and objected to the diminished status it meant for her—since her brother's divorce she had been the first lady of the land, in effect, playing the role of queen. So immediately after the wedding ceremony she made her disapproval plain by going back to her house without attending the celebrations which followed.[21]

The efforts of the princess to mobilize support for her brother and to assure her pride of place in the court were matched by her strenuous diplomatic efforts abroad. She traveled to the Soviet Union where she met privately with Stalin, seeking to convince the Soviet ruler to withdraw his troops still occupying northwestern Iran after the end of World War II and in violation of the Tripartite Agreement specifying the terms for the wartime occupation of Iran signed by the USSR, the United Kingdom, and the United States. Later she traveled to the United States, before the Shah made his first trip to Washington, to hold private talks with President Truman and Secretary of State George Marshall, seeking a firm commitment for U.S. support of her brother's rule and U.S. aid for Iran's economy.

For all her activities on his behalf, there were rumors in Tehran that the Shah did not completely trust his twin sister. She had been successful in June of 1948 in getting him to support Abdul Hossein Hajir as prime minister. Hajir had been a minister of finance and minister of court and was known as a confidant and close ally of the princess. As she put it, "I must say I was to some extent instrumental in his appointment."[22] The Shah reportedly resented his sister's growing power. He feared she was rapidly building coteries of supporters in key positions throughout the government of Iran, supporters more loyal to her than to him. He even suspected she and Hajir were planning a coup which would oust him from the throne.[23]

Whatever the truth to his fears, the rapidly escalating tensions of Iranian politics were soon to sweep aside those worries and his sister and even to threaten the entire dynasty. On February 4, 1949, at a ceremony on the campus of Tehran University, a would-be assassin fired six shots at the Shah. Amazingly, none proved fatal. But his prime ministers were less fortunate. In June 1950, Hajir was stabbed to death as he entered a Tehran mosque. His successor as prime minister, Gen. Ali Razmara, was also assassinated, again in a Tehran mosque, only a year later.

During those years, Dr. Mohammad Mossadegh, as a member of Iran's parliament, was leading the drive to wrest control of Iran's oil industry from its British owners. Ayatollah Kashani, a senior cleric, had mobilized the streets of Tehran against the British and in support of Mossadegh. The Shah accepted the popular will and named Mossadegh prime minister.[24]

His appointment would lead to many significant changes, but none more immediate than the second of Princess Ashraf's three exiles. As she tells the story, "exactly one hour after his appointment as Prime Minister, Mossadegh sent me a message instructing me to leave Iran within 24 hours. My first reaction was to ignore the ultimatum, to challenge Mossadegh's power. But my brother advised me to leave the country."[25]

Abandoned by her brother at this crucial moment and finding the power base she had so assiduously constructed to have effectively evaporated, the princess had no choice. She gathered her children and left the country. In his triumph, Mossadegh also nationalized her palace and converted it to the official office of the prime minister, a use it enjoys to the present. Mossadegh immediately moved in across the street from the palace of the Shah, to gather greater power for the even more defiant challenges to the Pahlavis which were yet to come.

The Shah's advice that his twin accept Mossadegh's order was, undoubtedly, a most difficult decision for him. But it was completely in keeping with the picture of his character being developed here. In the face of a challenge by a powerful adversary, the Shah's immediate response would be not to back down. That pattern began with his responses to his father. Reza Shah would not tolerate challenges—either from his political allies, his enemies, or his family. (The defiance of his first wife in the face of his decision to take a new, young bride, then, is all the more remarkable.) That the son, Mohammad Reza, would develop a propensity to accommodate, a propensity which became a central part of his character, is no surprise. He could not directly confront his father. Nor could he confront anyone who offered a direct challenge. If Mossadegh were to insist that Princess Ashraf leave the country, thus depriving the monarch of his determined and forceful ally, the Shah would agree.

His willingness to send his sister into exile was also at the heart of another of the Shah's lifelong patterns—one he used in dealing with his political allies, the very individuals to whom he and his dynasty owed the most. He was always willing to sacrifice his allies in the quest for his own political survival. While Ashraf may have been the first example of that pattern, there were many others. The Shah's treatment of Ernest Perron has already been mentioned. The arrest in the fall of 1978 of his long-term prime minister Amir Abbas Hoveyda, who served him from 1965 to 1977, was perhaps the last.

Hoveyda had been the Shah's longest-serving prime minister, assuming that post in January of 1965 after the assassination of Hassan Ali Mansur. Mansur and Hoveyda had been founders of a *dowreh,* or circle, of intellectuals to whom the Shah turned in his quest for a government of "technocrats." Hoveyda had served as minister of finance under Mansur but was elevated to premier when his colleague was assassinated by what we would now call Islamic fundamentalists. Hoveyda served the Shah as prime minister until August 1977 when he was replaced by Jamshid Amouzegar, the secretary general of the Rastakhiz party. Amouzegar's appointment was an effort by the Shah to broaden his liberalization campaign by bringing new and younger officials to the cabinet in the face of widespread discontent then pouring forth from Iran's intelligentsia.

But Hoveyda was hardly disgraced. He was elevated to the post of minister of court, to fill the position vacated by the rapidly weakening Assadollah Alam, who was succumbing to the ravages of leukemia. Yet slightly more then one year later, in the midst of the revolution, the Shah ordered Hoveyda's arrest.[26] But Hoveyda was not alone; the Shah also ordered the arrest of other senior officials. Gen. Nematollah Nassiri was seized. Nassiri was the former chief of SAVAK and the military officer who delivered the imperial rescript dismissing Mossadegh as prime minister in August 1953. Col. Abdul Azim Valian was arrested. He had been the land reform chief and the governor of Mashdad who had found it impossible to obtain instructions on the government's plans for dealing with rioters during the revolution. Former minister of information Darioush Homayoun was also arrested. Homayoun had been instructed by Hoveyda, in early January 1978, to publish a letter impugning Ayatollah Khomeini, resulting in a demonstration by *tullab,* seminary students, in Qum, which was fired upon by the police. The shootings produced the first deaths of the revolution and the initiation of violence which only one year later would force the Shah into exile. In addition, other senior government officials were seized.

The arrests were part of the Shah's attempts to accommodate and appease the wrath of the Iranian people. It was especially necessary for the Shah to accommodate in early November 1978 because the month had begun with a sense of startling revolutionary events. On November 4, students had attempted to topple the statue of the Shah on the campus of Tehran University. Riot police, who had tolerated demonstrations and sit-ins on the campus, moved to break up the demonstrations with gunfire. Some dozen students were killed and more wounded—the first deaths of students on university campuses since the revolution had begun.[27] On

November 5, students spilled out of the campus to riot throughout the city. They were rapidly joined by armed guerrillas and others seeking the opportunity to participate in revolutionary action. Looting became widespread, especially of shops owned by Armenians, Jews, and Baha'is as well as establishments trading in what many Iranians had come to perceive as the hallmarks of Western culture, alcohol and movies. Finally, banks and other financial institutions, the instruments of Pahlavi rule, were attacked. Tehran was left ablaze.

On the next day, November 6, after receiving approval of the U.S. and British ambassadors, the Shah appointed a military government, headed by Gen. Ghulam Reza Azhari. But even in the face of the rabid challenge to his rule, the Shah continued to accommodate and temporize. He did appoint a military government, but he left five of eleven ministries in the hands of civilians. Moreover, in presenting the new order to the Iranian people in a radio address, he was especially self-effacing and apologetic. He referred to himself as *padeshah,* the king, a title he had never before used. Conventionally he was the Shahanshah, the King of Kings. He also assured the Iranian people that their "revolutionary message had been heard." In short, even in the face of his most determined efforts to impose order on the explosive political situation, the Shah provided his people with mixed messages and sought not to suppress but to accommodate.

This pattern, which existed in his relation with his father, was deeply ingrained. It was manifested again and again in his personal and political relations. It contributed to his decision to accede to Mossadegh's order exiling Ashraf. But as with any significant decision, there were other considerations as well. The Shah had his own ambivalence about his twin. She was, certainly, a pillar of political and especially emotional support, an ardent partisan and energetic worker striving to build support for the Shah. But she also built that support in a style both too vigorous and vehement for his liking. And in the process she was constructing networks of supporters throughout the bureaucracies whose primary loyalties, he believed, were to her and not to him. How Ashraf would use those networks was always problematic for the Shah. At the extreme there were those by now constant rumors that, given the Shah's failure to produce a male heir, Ashraf was working to arrange the succession for her own son. More immediately, the Shah appreciated that he was becoming ever more dependent on her for the success of his political plans.

Whatever the Shah's motives, Ashraf's move to Switzerland did not long remove her from a central role in the politics of Iran. She remembers sending clandestine messages to the Shah urging him to be courageous and strong and to resist Mossadegh's acquisition of greater power, for fear of his hostile designs on the monarch.[28]

The British and Americans had different perspectives on the prime minister, perspectives which changed with the changing contexts of the politics of the Middle East and their own domestic politics. The British sought to reclaim "their" oil and feared that a successful challenge to their dominance in Iran would encourage similar challenges throughout the Middle East, resulting in the further erosion of the empire. British diplomats especially feared the demonstration effect on King Farouk of a successful oil nationalization in Iran. British fears were elevated to alarm when Gamal Abdul Nasser came to power as a result of the Free Officers' coup in 1952. Egypt, of course, was not then an oil producer, but England owned and controlled the Suez Canal, a continuous and increasing affront to Egyptian national sensibilities. British diplomats were certain that Colonel Nasser would be emboldened to take action against the canal if Prime Minister Mossadegh succeeded against the Anglo-Iranian Oil Company.

President Truman's concerns were different. He worried over the international oil industry and the stature of U.S. oil firms. But the inauguration of a new Republican administration in 1952—Pres. Dwight Eisenhower and the Dulles brothers, Allan as the director of the CIA and John Foster as secretary of state—changed American concerns. These new leaders feared that Mossadegh was dragging Iran into chaos and the possibility of a Communist takeover. Planning for the coup to oust Mossadegh then began in earnest, and Princess Ashraf was a part of the planning.

She met with the plotters of the coup in Europe. She even few to Iran to enlist her brother's participation in the coup. Princess Ashraf claims that so much publicity greeted her return to Tehran that she was never able to see her brother, passing him a letter instead through Queen Soraya.[29] Kim Roosevelt, the leader of the coup effort, reports that the Shah and his sister were able to meet but, in fear of being overheard, spoke only in platitudes. He concluded that "the attempt to communicate with H.I.M. through his sister had to be written off as a failure."[30] Roosevelt's response to that failure was to take on the responsibility himself. He traveled to Iran and began meeting clandestinely with the Shah.

When Mossadegh was arrested and the Shah returned from Rome to resume his kingly duties, the United States had "recommendations" for him in addition to urging him to oust Perron. They also warned him of the consequences of allowing Princess Ashraf to return to her former prominence as paramount éminence grise in a political system suffused with such figures. But Princess Ashraf was not to be so easily set aside. She returned to Iran and reassembled her networks. Again she installed supporters in key positions throughout the bureaucracies. And again she began to see her brother in frequent meetings.

Ostensibly the meetings were held so that she could report to him on the operations of the organizations she had established. At first she worked to improve the rights of Iran's women, perpetually second-class subjects due to a legal code which gave them few rights. The princess began to establish organizations committed to greater rights for women, drawing the groups together, initially, in the High Council of Women's Organizations, later the Women's Organization of Iran.

The princess was also concerned with the abysmal state of the masses of Iran. She became increasingly involved in individual projects to enhance the health, welfare, and literacy of the millions of Iran's poor. These organizations were joined into the Imperial Organization for Social Services whose very active chair was Princess Ashraf. To raise money for its activities, the government granted the IOSS the exclusive right to conduct a national lottery. Weekly, millions of rials were spent on lottery tickets and many thousands earned their livelihood from selling those tickets. While Ashraf's organization was enriched by the lottery, many in Iran believed that the welfare of the princess was enhanced before that of the poor.

The princess was immersed in the international politics of Iran as well. She made frequent state visits abroad, where she was sent by her brother to conduct delicate negotiations with hostile states. Ashraf, for example, was instrumental in later years in initiating Iran's relations with the People's Republic of China. She also became active in the United Nations and began to serve, as early as the 1950s, as a member of Iran's delegation to the General Assembly. After years of work at the U.N. as Iran's chief delegate to the Commission on Human Rights, she served as director of a number of international conferences on human rights and on women.

About all of these activities she would report regularly to her brother. But she never hesitated in freely offering her advice on domestic politics as well. The Shah, whatever his reservations about her growing power and the ever more widely believed tales of her evil designs and personal corruption which abounded in Tehran's political circles, listened. He resented her, but he listened, knowing that she had the courage and toughness he lacked.

But it became increasingly clear to court regulars that the Shah was becoming irked with his twin. While he would listen to her advice when privately offered, he would tolerate less and less her public performances. At a relatively small dinner party at the beginning of the 1970s, for example, the Shah began to discuss with one of his most senior officials the training he had received as Crown Prince. When he finished, Princess Ashraf, also seated at the table, started to speak. "In my case," she began. But the Shah turned to her and snapped, "Be silent you tiny creature."[31] In later months, the Shah took that official aside and warned him not to listen to the princess, to ignore her interventions, and to prevent her from interfering in the organizations for which he was responsible.[32]

Sometime in the early 1970s there was a showdown between the monarch and Ashraf—a private showdown. He is rumored to have told her he would no longer tolerate her attempts to run a state within the state.[33] It is widely rumored that a good part of the Shah's anger with his twin was stirred by his wife, Empress Farah. She had become increasingly important as a confidant of the Shah and was reported to have resented the princess's ties to him.[34] Court gossips drew parallels with the earlier rivalries between Shams, Ashraf, and Soraya. Wild rumors were circulated about the attempts of Princess Ashraf and the empress to reduce each other's influence. Some suggested, for example, that Princess Ashraf had brought beautiful young women to court dinners in hopes of enticing her brother away from his wife.

Whatever the validity of these rumors, after the early 1970s the princess spent less and less time within the country, devoting herself to her U.N. activities and to her diplomatic missions on behalf of her country. When not at her residence in New York, she would often stay at her estate at Juan-les-Pins in the south of France, one of her "favorite retreats for enjoying the sun and 'getting away from it all.'"[35] It was there, in 1976, that assassins tried to kill her as she was returning from a night of gambling at a casino in nearby Cannes. She was being driven in a Rolls Royce, but had chosen to sit in the front seat. Two friends sat in the rear. As the car approached her house, a black Peugeot sped by them and then blocked the road. Two men leapt from the car and began to spray the Rolls with machine-gun bullets. When the attack was over, Ashraf's female companion—sitting in the rear and apparently mistaken by the gunmen for the princess—had been killed. The princess herself, squeezed down on the front floor of the car, was untouched.

Despite her extended stays abroad and her fall from pride of place with the Shah, the princess remained a major player in Iranian politics. Throughout the 1970s she continued to meet periodically with her brother to report on the organizations within Iran which she still officially directed. She would also report on her U.N. work and her diplomatic missions. But she had clearly lost the rapport and influence with her brother and monarch which she had previously enjoyed.

Instead, she developed other means of access to the levers of influence in Iranian politics. For much of the decade, that lever was to be Prime Minister Amir Abbas Hoveyda. Years before his accession to office, she had befriended him. She had facilitated his rise to power, and once he was in office, she had maintained close ties to him.[36] Through him, she was able to maintain her networks of supporters throughout the bureaucracy, which meant she was usually able to achieve any particular goal she pursued, be it political or economic. Through them and through the prime minister, she continued to influence the course of Iranian politics, at least in those areas of concern to her.

While she was able to retain her extraordinary position in the Iranian system by switching her base of support from the Shah to his prime minister, she was never able to re-create her close ties to her brother. Thus it appears that at his moment of greatest need—during the revolution of 1978—Princess Ashraf played no role whatsoever. When he was most in need of her courage and determination, and especially her ruthlessness, the two had become so estranged that he could not use her strength to bolster his own depleted self.

The princess had been in Iran just before the dramatic events of the revolution began to unfold. She was in Tehran during the famous New Year's visit which Jimmy and Rosalyn Carter paid the Shah at the end of 1977. In her "memoirs from exile," Princess Ashraf includes a photograph from that festive event. Mrs. Carter stands a bit to one side, looking somewhat formally at the photographer. President Carter, looking for all the world like the cat who has just finished off the canary, stands with a champagne glass in one hand and his other arm around a positively glowing Princess Ashraf.

Despite the warmth exuding from that picture, the princess had far more restrained thoughts. She recalled the toast offered by the president to the Shah. Jimmy Carter concluded, "there is no leader with whom I have a deeper sense of personal gratitude and personal friendship."[37] Then the princess mused, "As he spoke, I looked at his pale face. I thought his smile was artificial, his eyes icy—and I hoped I could trust him."[38]

However deep her worries for the future of the dynasty, the princess left Iran shortly after the end of the official visit. She returned to Iran—for the last time, as it turned out—on September 8, 1978. She had been in Alma-Ata in Soviet central Asia for a meeting of the World Health Organization and flew from there to Tehran, to arrive on the very day that martial law was declared. That morning, thousands of demonstrators, unaware of its imposition, gathered in Tehran's Jhaleh Square to protest the rule of the Shah. They refused to disperse and the army fired. What has become known as Black Friday—the massacre—gave the princess an immediate sense of the depths of the revolutionary fervor.

A few days later she was received by her brother, who was, as she tells it, "completely calm on the surface, but . . . extremely anxious."[39] The princess reports the following conversation:

"What will you do?" I asked. "How much longer is there?"

He did not give me a direct answer. Instead he said: "It is not wise for you to be here right now. You know how often you are made the subject of attacks against the regime. I think you had better leave at once."

"I won't leave you alone," I argued. "As long as you're here I'll stay with you."

For the first time in our adult lives, he raised his voice to me: "I am telling you that for my peace of mind, you must go."

So I left Iran and flew to New York, not knowing that it was the last time I would see my country.[40]

At the moment of his greatest need, the Shah's relation with his twin, the person who had been so instrumental in the past in giving him strength and courage and in organizing the political forces of Iran to support both the monarch and the monarchy, had deteriorated to the point where he could no longer derive support from her. This was partly a reflection of the enmity which the princess had earned from him and from so many of Iran's political activists for her decades of meddling in Iranian politics—meddling which was seen as ostensibly for the welfare of the people, but ultimately was understood as corrupt and self-serving. Even more, it was a reflection of the breaking of that special tie between the twins, which had earlier in his life been so crucial a source of psychic support for the Shah.[41]

Assadollah Alam

A third person who had previously been a crucial source of strength for the Shah was also unavailable during the year of his greatest need. Assadollah Alam had died of leukemia in November of 1977, only two months before the first outbreak of revolutionary violence. Alam had been a lifelong associate of the Shah, a man trusted by the Shah as he trusted no other man, a man who was deliberate, but tough and strong, "a constant source of strength" for the ruler.[42]

Alam was born in 1911, the son of Amir Mohammad Ibrahim Khan Alam, Showkat-ul Molk, the owner of hundreds of villages in eastern Iran. A British diplomat posted to that region described the senior Alam as "a genuinely patriotic, public spirited and incorruptible Persian landlord of high degree."[43] The Showkat-ul Molk had, nonetheless, established close ties with the British, who saw the eastern reaches of Iran as the last defense of the British Empire in India from the threat of Russian penetration. The British are reported to have provided him with an annual subsidy to contribute to the maintenance of his private militia.

There were scores of similar militias in Iran before the establishment of the Pahlavi dynasty. Many big landowners armed and trained "their" peasants. Sardar Akram, for example, the owner of hundreds of villages in central Iran, "maintained a fighting force of 800 able to be mobilized in 24 hours. All mounted. And for supplies, an armory of 2000 rifles and 200 French air-cooled machine guns."[44] The major tribes could also field formidable military forces, in some cases consisting of thousands of well-armed mounted troops. But few of these private militias occupied as strategic a location as did the troops of the Showkat-ul Mulk, and few received the support from the British which he was able to claim.

The armed forces under the control of the Qajar shahs were no match for his troops, nor, for that matter, for many of the other private militias. One foreign observer, with some hyperbole, described the Iranian army at the turn of this century.

> The infantry as a fighting force is beneath contempt. At least a dozen different patterns of rifles constitute their armament, consisting of matchlocks, flintlocks, sniders, Martinis, obsolete Russian guns, and a portion of a cargo of nondescript description that was seized some years ago in the Persian Gulf. When it is added that there is not a single round of ammunition to fit any of the above weapons, some idea of the value of their 40,000 man "army" may be formed.[45]

Reza Shah staged his 1921 coup when he was a senior officer in the twenty-five hundred man Cossack Brigade, the most powerful of the Qajar military units. When he seized power, his initial goal was to gain physical control over the entire country. To do so, he followed a dual policy: he built the armed forces of the state while eliminating those forces outside of his control. As his power increased, Reza Shah pursued the goal of eliminating the armed challenges to his rule with heightened vigor. He personally commanded military campaigns against many of the private militias, rebel chiefs, tribal forces, and bandits. Against others he dispatched his generals to assert the command of the central state.

He also forced many of the major landowners out of the security of their fiefdoms into internal exile in Tehran, thus weakening their ties to their peasants and making the mobilization of private armies more difficult. Showkat-ul Mulk was one of those landlords. At Reza Shah's insistence, he spent over six years with his family in internal exile in the capital. It was thus that the Crown Prince, Mohammad Reza, met Assadollah Alam, for many of those landlords were accorded a certain respect by Reza Shah and treated more as conquered rulers than as disgraced captives.

Alam and the future Shah, then, established their friendship in childhood. Alam was to prove that friendship through dedicated public service. After a brief stint in the Ministries of Agriculture and Interior, the Shah appointed him an official of the court in 1945, then governor of Baluchistan—the seat of the Alam properties, Minister of the Interior, Minister of Labor, and, by 1951, guardian of the crown properties. There he was responsible for overseeing the two thousand villages which Reza Shah had amassed during his rule.

Alam, not surprisingly, fell out of favor with Prime Minister Mossadegh in a dispute over the crown properties. The prime minister responded characteristically—he ordered Alam to leave the country. This time the Shah intervened, and Mossadegh relented somewhat. He allowed Alam to retire to his family estate in Khurasan. After the ouster of Mossadegh, the Shah restored Alam to his post as chief of crown properties. But his role was considerably broader than that of a financial manager, and that role was to grow. From then until his death, the boyhood friend of the Shah came to serve as the Shah's principal counselor, someone the Shah could count on—in fact, the only Iranian the Shah could count on to be a loyal adviser and also to execute in a tough and determined fashion the advice Alam himself offered.

The first public demonstration of those qualities was to come in April of 1955. The key figure in Operation Ajax, the U.S.- and U.K.-sponsored coup which ousted Mossadegh from the premiership, had been Gen. Fazlollah Zahedi. Zahedi, a scion of one of the wealthiest landowning families of central Iran, had been one of Reza Shah's most trusted and effective generals. He had been one of the commanders Reza Shah had used to eliminate some of his most powerful and recalcitrant adversaries: Zahedi had been sent to the north to break the military power of the Turkoman tribes. He was sent to the south where he suppressed Sheikh Khaz'al of Mohammorrah (renamed Khorramshahr by the Shah and renamed again by the Khomeini regime as Khuninshahr, "blood city," in memory of the battles fought there with the invading Iraqis in 1980). Sheikh Khaz'al had, under the protection of the British, established a virtually autonomous ministate at the head of the Persian Gulf in Iran's key oil province.[46] Zahedi brought Khaz'al under the control of Reza Shah and, in the process, eliminated a British bastion in the center of the oil industry.

Zahedi was arrested by the British during World War II for his pro-Nazi activities and exiled to Palestine and India. With the allied victory, he returned to Iran to resume his military career. He rapidly won the Shah's support and was appointed chief of the National Police in 1949. Much to the horror of the court, however, Zahedi began to cooperate with Mossadegh and his supporters, facilitating the turmoil they created in pressing for oil nationalization. Mossadegh rewarded the general by appointing him minister of the interior in his first cabinet in 1951.

By 1953, however, Zahedi had become one of the prime minister's chief enemies. A warrant had been issued for his arrest, and Zahedi went into hiding in the mountains above Tehran.[47] The Shah, meanwhile, decided to appoint the tough general who had widespread support in the armed forces as prime minister. The Shah did so as he issued his official rescript dismissing Mossadegh. With the ultimate success of that "countercoup," Zahedi took office.

But it was not long before there was a falling out between the Shah and his independent and strong-willed prime minister. By early 1955, the Shah had decided that General Zahedi was amassing too much power, power which could prove a threat to the Pahlavis. But how to remove the general without provoking him was the challenge. At this delicate moment, the Shah turned to Assadollah Alam. Serving as the Shah's emissary, Alam negotiated the general's retirement. General Zahedi left office and retired to Switzerland, to return only once before his death, in 1957, when his son Ardeshir, of whom more will be heard later, married the daughter of the Shah, Princess Shahnaz.

Alam had proved his importance to the Shah, but his most significant service to the monarchy was yet to come—his role in the June 1963 riots which first made Khomeini a household word in Iran. Before those riots,

Alam had served the Shah as minister of interior and then was appointed secretary general of the Pahlavi Foundation, the organization the Shah had created to administer many of his charitable properties. After Dr. Ali Amini resigned as prime minister in 1962, the Shah decided Alam was ready. He was appointed prime minister. At the time of the 1963 riots, Alam was in a unique position: he occupied the second most powerful formal position in the kingdom while he simultaneously enjoyed the trust of the monarch.

Those facts, along with his decisiveness and toughness, helped him play a crucial role in putting down the riots. When they first broke out in the early hours of June 3, 1963, the prime minister moved into his office, where he was to sleep for the remainder of the crisis. Then he called on a distressed and nervous monarch to report on the spreading violence. Alam later reported to a confidant this conversation between himself and the Shah.

> "What shall we do?" the Shah asked.
> "If you want to get tough," Alam responded, "get tough. But if you take half measures, you will lose everything."
> "Yes, but what shall we do?" the Shah repeated.
> "Don't worry," the Prime Minister answered, "I'll manage it."
> "How?" asked the Shah.
> "I'll weigh the balls of your Majesty," Alam declared, "and see how heavy they are. Then I'll know how to deal with the riots."[48]

With that reply, the Shah understood the determination of his prime minister. He immediately was reassured and regained his royal composure.

The Shah was calmed to the point that Alam received no formal instructions about how to proceed other than to return to his office to monitor the situation. By the time he reached his office, however, major disturbances were occurring in Qum and Tehran and, more menacingly, were spreading to other major cities in Iran. The prime minister realized that unless action was taken and taken quickly, the costs to the regime of restoring order in the more distant future would be far more significant.

The prime minister called the commanders of the armed forces, the police, and the gendarmerie to his office. They lined up, formally, in order of rank before the prime minister. He spoke briefly, but succinctly: "I want the streets cleared."[49] The response from the keepers of the imperial security was dismay. They protested that to clear the streets would require the troops to open fire on the rioters. Blood would be shed. But Alam was firm and insisted that they act immediately to carry out his orders. A very senior military official then challenged the prime minister. The general reminded Alam that he was neither commander in chief of the armed forces—"the responsibility of His Imperial Majesty, the Shahanshah"—nor even in the military chain of command.

The prime minister was furious at the public challenge to his authority, but he also knew the military commander was correct. Alam strode to his special telephone and was quickly connected with the Shah. The prime minister held the phone away from his ear—so the commanders could hear the voice of the Shah—and snapped out the words,

"Your Imperial Majesty, the riots are becoming more severe and beginning to spread to other cities. I have the commanders of the security forces here and believe you should command them to stop the riots by whatever means necessary."

"You mean open fire?"

"That is the only way, Your Imperial Majesty."

There was then silence from the Shah, which lasted a considerable length of time. Finally, he said, "But, Mr. Alam, many might be killed."

"Yes, Your Imperial Majesty, but there is no other way to restore order."

"Mr. Prime Minister, if that is your judgment and you are prepared to take the consequences of your judgment, you may proceed."

The prime minister thanked the Shah, hung up the phone, returned to his place before the commanders, and repeated his order. This time they obeyed. Their troops opened fire with great loss of life. But the streets were cleared.[50]

It was the prime minister who saved the day and, in the process, the throne. It was Alam's strength and courage and the Shah's trust in his commitment to Pahlavi rule which made possible the order to the security forces to end the rioting. It is by no means clear that the Shah himself would have issued the orders for the troops to fire. He needed the strength of Alam to make it possible for him to even countenance such steps from his security forces. Without those orders, the rioters would have won the streets and with them, undoubtedly, the release of Khomeini. The result would have been a far more formidable challenge to the Shah, a challenge which might conceivably have led to an outcome identical to that of the revolution of 1978, but fifteen years in advance.

Assadollah Alam would continue to play that crucial role of encouraging the Shah—giving him the strength to do Shah—for many years. Not long after the riots, Alam was made minister of court, where he had even freer access to the monarch. The two men were to meet nearly every day they were both in Tehran for the next fourteen years. Through all the challenges of the 1970s, Alam was there for the monarch.

Keen observers noted that subtle changes began to occur in the minister of court toward the middle of the decade, however. He grew thinner and began to take large numbers of pills, even in the presence of others.[51] Alam, it was learned, had leukemia. He was dead before the outbreak of the revolution.

These three individuals, over the years, were able to provide the Shah with the strength he did not have. They were the only three individuals whom the Shah trusted personally and whose political judgment he valued. They were, all three, individuals of unusual personal strength, and that personal strength fortified the Shah and helped him function as Shah. By the time of the revolution, however, none of the three was able to perform that vital function. Ernest Perron had died years before in his own country. Princess Ashraf had lost none of her determination, but she and the Shah had had a falling out and he no longer trusted her advice. Assadollah Alam remained by the Shah for the longest period, but he too was gone before the revolution began.

There were, of course, others of great importance to the Shah. His wife, the Empress Farah; Gen. Hossein Fardoust, his boyhood friend and head of his private intelligence bureau; Ardeshir Zahedi, his former son-in-law and ambassador to the United States; and William Sullivan, the U.S. ambassador to Iran—all were available to the monarch, especially during the final months of his rule. The Iranians were all personally close to the Shah, and the American was committed to saving his throne. But the Shah took none of them into his confidences. He did not trust their political judgment even if he was assured of their loyalty to his throne and dynasty. They could not serve as important objects with whom the Shah could psychologically merge, from which he could derive strength from a cohesive and enhanced self.

Empress Farah remained by the Shah to the end of his rule and his life. In the final months of his rule, in fact, she was doing whatever she could to mobilize support for the regime. Only two months before the royal couple left Iran, she told an interviewer that, in fact, Iran had "two monarchs," the Shah and herself, "each acting independently" to control the mounting opposition, to rally the loyalists, and salvage the throne.[52]

The Shah had a complex relation with his queen. They had married on December 21, 1959.[53] Within a year she had given birth to the Shah's first male heir, named Reza, who they both thought would assure the continuity of the dynasty. In 1967 the Shah took a step without precedent in Iranian history. He formally designated his wife the chair of a newly established Regency Council. If the Shah were to die before his heir reached majority, Empress Farah would become, in effect, regent—the first woman so designated in Iranian history. As she was to put it later, by that act the Shah thus gave "very great proof of his trust" in her.[54]

That trust was manifested in Farah's assuming ever wider public responsibilities. In her autobiography, she puts it this way:

I could not write in detail of all the organizations over which I preside and in which I take a very active part, in the realms of education, health, culture, and social matters. It would need a further book. A simple list would perhaps give some idea: the Organization for Family Well-Being—nurseries for the children of working mothers, teaching women and girls to read, professional training, family planning; the Organization for Blood Transfusion; the Organization for the Fight against Cancer; the Organization for Help to the Needy; the Health Organization . . . ; the Children's Centre; the Centre for the Intellectual Development of Children . . . ; the Imperial Institute of Philosophy; the Foundation for Iranian Culture; the Festival of Shiraz; the Tehran Cinema Festival; the Iranian Folk-lore Organization; the Asiatic Institute; the Civilisations Discussion Centre; the Pahlavi University; the Academy of Sciences.[55]

These organizations, moreover, were fully functioning. In many cases they provided extraordinary, valuable services to thousands of recipients. Pahlavi University was one such example, an institution of higher education patterned on American lines and meant to challenge the dominance of the French-oriented University of Tehran. The empress devoted considerable time and resources to it. Another example was the Farah Pahlavi Foundation, again, only one of her many charitable ventures. That foundation took responsibility for providing care to over eight thousand orphans.[56]

Farah was not merely the titular head of these organizations, supplying them legitimacy through her patronage. She was, in fact, deeply involved in their day-to-day activities. The empress was as absorbed in the responsibilities of administration as were all the other officials of the regime. She too was overcommitted. Her days began early, with a meeting to discuss city planning or urban beautification or the unveiling of a new statue, and ended late with a series of meetings to plan a conference on Iran's pre-Islamic culture or to supervise a program to send health care workers to Iran's villages or to translate foreign children's tales into Persian.

Hers was a working life. But as should be clear from her own account, it was work dedicated to the "realms," as she puts it, "of education, health, culture, and social matters." Politics was not one of her concerns. The trust which the monarch developed for her did not extend to the political realm, nor did it extend to her political judgment. He never came to see her judgment in politics as comparably trustworthy to her other instincts. The Shah appears not to have taken his empress into his political confidences. He did not seek her political advice, and she did not offer it.

At the height of the revolution in the fall of 1978, she intervened to stem the collapse of the dynasty without the knowledge and approval of the Shah. Empress Farah did what she could to preserve her husband's throne, but she did so by acting alone. She was not able to provide him with any direct support—any psychological support which would have allowed him to act more effectively as his own esteem and courage ebbed away in the face of his growing sense of rejection by his people and abandonment by the political elite.

To the contrary, there are accounts of those last months which suggest that even she was excluded in the midst of the Shah's deepening self-inflicted isolation and withdrawal. As the urban riots grew and it became clear to him that the military government, which he had installed in November 1978, would not be able to suppress the mounting violence, the Shah began to fear for his life. He did not fear that the mobs would storm his palace and win the revolution by seizing the executing him. He knew that his security forces were still too united and powerful to allow that, and he also knew that his enemies in the streets were aware of that as well. They were far from ready for a direct confrontation in that chilling month of November, even as military rule was unraveling and making palpably manifest to even the most committed observer that the Pahlavi system was incapable of arresting the ever more rapid erosion of its royal authority.

Then it was not the enemies without whom the Shah came to fear, but the allies within. He began to suspect that a member of his entourage, a court insider, would seek to end the entire drama by assassinating the monarch and attempting to seize power for himself. The Shah ordered his personal guards to admit no one to his presence without a thorough body search, to ensure against weapons being brought into the imperial presence. The empress learned of the Shah's new ruling when she called on him in his private quarters. To her horror, his guards insisted on searching her before she was allowed to enter the Shah's rooms.[57]

Thus at his moment of greatest need, the Shah was alone. Even his empress, the mother of his heir, the designated regent of his realm, the most loyal of all his subjects, was not free from his suspicion. In short, however significant a role the empress played, she was not able to serve as a substitute for those—Ernest Perron, Princess Ashraf, and Assadollah Alam—who had done so much in earlier years to strengthen the Shah's will. This was even more true for other significant court figures who had served the Shah for decades before the revolution.

One of the most mysterious of those figures was Gen. Hossein Fardoust. For years he had served as director of the Special Bureau, an intelligence office located within the Ministry of Court and, after 1976, as director of the Imperial Inspection Commission. Fardoust's responsibility, in essence, was to keep the intelligence organizations honest. One way the Shah chose to do that was by maintaining multiple sources of information on both the domestic and political activities of his subjects. SAVAK, of course, had principal responsibility. But the armed forced maintained their own intelligence services and did not restrict their activities to Iran's military security. They too were allowed to gather intelligence on politics.

These intelligence sources fed their reports directly to the Shah during the regularly scheduled weekly audiences which the Shah held with their chiefs. But their more detailed reports and the less essential matters which they uncovered were sent to the Special Bureau. There, General Fardoust would analyze the reports, send instructions for additional intelligence gathering and analysis, and, where he thought appropriate, ask his own staff to gather—outside conventional intelligence channels—information of special importance to the monarch. In short, in the final analysis it was General Fardoust who was "the eyes and ears" of the monarch, as earlier Iranian shahs had referred to their intelligence organizations, and not SAVAK or military intelligence.

Fardoust had come by his position of extraordinary importance by dint of two facts. For one, he had been a personal friend of the Shah longer than anyone in the court. For another, Fardoust was that rare Iranian—self-effacing and intensely personal—who made every effort to remain anonymous even to other court insiders.

He had first befriended the Crown Prince when the future monarch was six, and he was selected by Reza Shah to accompany the Crown Prince to Switzerland. Hossein and Mehrpour Teymourtash were Mohammad Reza's Persian peer group. Later, when Mehrpour's father fell from Reza

Shah's favor with such disastrous consequences and the boy was called back to Tehran, Reza Shah sent his second son, Ali Reza, to join the group. But Hossein was to remain with the Crown Prince for his entire five-year stay at Le Rosey. When they returned from Switzerland, Fardoust maintained and even deepened that friendship, going to Iran's military academy with the Crown Prince, and he began to assume significant responsibilities on behalf of the new monarch.

Years later the Shah told one of his biographers of the effect of his near ouster at the hands of Prime Minister Mossadegh: "There was a sharp break in my life after 1953. I came to realize I could not have the same relations with my friends. Friendship involves the exchange of confidence between two people, but a king can take no one into his confidence. I have even had to put some distance between myself and my old friend, Hossein Fardoust, whom I trust implicitly."[58]

Despite this distance which the Shah imposed, however, he lost none of his trust in Fardoust. To the contrary, he entrusted his old friend with overall responsibility for generating and monitoring the intelligence crucial to maintaining his throne.

All the while, Fardoust went to extraordinary lengths to maintain his anonymity. He demonstrated that passion frequently. An example can be drawn from one of Iran's periodic crises with Iraq. The relations between the two countries had been strained ever since the 1958 Iraqi Revolution, which resulted in the killing of King Faisal and his prime minister, Nuri al-Said. The new Iraqi regime was stridently anti-Western, antimonarchical, and pro–Arab nationalist, all commitments incompatible with the stance of the Shah. Given the number of issues outstanding between the two countries, it was not surprising that the strain turned rapidly to a series of full-scale crises marked by military mobilizations and border conflicts.

The two most sacred shrines of Shi'ite Islam, the cities of Najaf and Kerbala, are located within Iraq. They shelter the tomb of Ali ibn Abi Taleb, the son-in-law of the Prophet—for Shi'ites, the first of the "rightly guided" caliphs—and the tomb of Hussein, the son of Ali and the grand martyr of the Shi'ite faith. Those tombs have become the principal pilgrimage destinations of Shi'ites, competing even with Mecca in sacred importance. Najaf and Kerbala are also the homes of major Shi'ite seminaries where eminent theologians train their successors and write their learned treatises. It was to Najaf that Ayatollah Khomeini had gravitated after his exile from Iran in 1964 and where he lectured until the revolution.

Thus the major Shi'ite holy places were outside the control of the Iranian state, an anomaly given that Iran's constitution formally designated it a Shi'ite state, the only Shi'ite state in the world.

There were other sources of strain as well. Iraq's Kurds, some one-quarter of its total population, felt themselves increasingly disenfranchised by the new regime. They resented, for example, the development of Iraq's oil industry surrounding Kirkuk, Iraq's major Kurdish city, while the oil revenues flowed to Baghdad. Little benefit from that wealth accrued to the Kurds themselves. But an even larger number of Kurds lived across the border in Iran. As the Kurds began their political activities, eventually to bloom into full-scale guerrilla warfare, their Iranian brethren were to provide not only sanctuary, but far more active assistance.[59]

Finally, Iran considered the southern border of the two countries a perpetual offense. The internationally recognized border between the states had been established under pressure by the British. To ensure that their tankers could pass unchallenged from the head of the Persian Gulf to Abadan, then the site of the world's largest oil refinery, the British insisted that the border not be the thalweg, or midpoint, of the Shatt al-Arab River, the confluence of the Tigris and the Euphrates, but rather the low watermark of the river on the Iranian side. Iraq thus had a legal claim to control the entire waterway marking the border between the two countries. Iran considered that inequity an offense to their national sovereignty.[60]

These three issues—Iraqi control over the Shi'ite shrines, the Kurds living on both sides of the border between the states, and the demarcation of the river border in the south—were the most troublesome of a much larger number of controversies. Beginning in the early 1960s, all of these issues became significant for the new rulers of Iraq. The result was a major confrontation, including significant military clashes between the two states. One of those crises occurred in early 1966 when the Shah was on a state visit outside his country. Prime Minister Hoveyda called an emergency cabinet meeting. One of the ministers at that meeting remembers that a stranger entered the room and sat at the table. Although the only person in the room not a member of the cabinet, he was never introduced. Throughout the session, the stranger remained silent. At its conclusion, he rose and silently left the room, not pausing to exchange pleasantries or even to bid farewell to the prime minister—an unusual breach of decorum in Iran, where one's social graces are counted essential to ensuring the structure of personal and social life. The cabinet minister asked the prime minister about the mysterious stranger. "That," said the premier, "was General Fardoust."[61]

Fardoust maintained that mysterious isolation throughout the Shah's rule. One of the United States' ambassadors to the imperial court recalls a party to celebrate the Shah's birthday. The ambassador had come to know all the court regulars and passed comfortably among the small groups of courtiers enjoying the festivities. Then he noticed a complete stranger, dressed unassumingly, and pressed into a corner of the reception room, standing completely alone. He approached the stranger and introduced himself. General Fardoust introduced himself in turn. A short time later the general left the party, as alone and unassuming as he had attended it.[62]

Fardoust, then, served the Shah in the most sensitive of positions in a fashion bound to engender the ruler's trust. The Shah, in turn, trusted Fardoust "implicitly." He depended on him to provide a crucial service for the well-being of the throne, but he never used the general as confidant or adviser. Despite the fact that this boyhood friend remained with the Shah until the end, Hossein Fardoust did not serve the monarch in the way in which the Shah most needed service. Fardoust could never provide any of the direction and psychological strength of which the Shah was so desperately in need as the revolution closed about his throne.

Both the Shah and Princess Ashraf, as well as many others, came to believe that at the end General Fardoust betrayed the monarch. They came to believe that in the last months of tottering Pahlavi rule, Fardoust had gone over to the opposition. "Although my brother is always very reluctant to believe the worst of anyone, especially a man he treated like a brother," wrote Princess Ashraf, "I am convinced that Fardoust must have withheld vital information from the Shah and was, in fact, in active negotiation with Khomeini during the last years of the regime."[63] But the Shah had come to believe the worst. In the Shah's last major formal interviews, those given to David Frost from the Panamanian island of Contadora, the Shah's eyes welled with tears when he was asked about Fardoust.

When the Pahlavi regime fell, senior court officials who had not fled the country were rounded up and imprisoned. Many were subsequently executed. But nothing was heard of Fardoust. Some months later, it was announced that he had been appointed director of SAVAMA, the National Security and Intelligence Service, the new regime's replacement for SAVAK. With the radicalization of Iran's politics which followed the capture and incarceration of the U.S. diplomats, Fardoust dropped from view once again, remaining characteristically silent.

At the end, there was one other in the dramatis personae who, along with the empress, struggled to save the throne and the Pahlavi dynasty. Ardeshir Zahedi, the Iranian ambassador to the United States, served as a key link between the U.S. government, and particularly Zbigniew Brzezinski, the national security adviser of President Carter, and the Shah. As the depths of revolutionary sentiment in Iran became clear, Zahedi left his post in Washington, flew to Tehran, and immersed himself in the unfolding revolution, seeking to bolster both the Shah as well as his flagging supporters.

Ardeshir had impeccable credentials. He was the son of General Zahedi, the first post-Mossadegh prime minister. During the planning for the ultimately successful "countercoup" of 1953, Ardeshir served as the key link among the court, the Americans, and his father. With the Shah restored to unchallenged power on the throne, Ardeshir was rewarded with an appointment as civil adjutant to the Shah. Not long after, the Shah gave permission for the wedding of his only child, Princess Shahnaz, to Zahedi. The Shah then appointed Zahedi to a brief term as Iranian ambassador to Washington and then to an even shorter term as Iranian foreign minister. With the election of Richard Nixon, the Shah once again appointed Zahedi ambassador, despite the fact that by then he had divorced the princess. Zahedi served in Washington for the remainder of President Nixon's tenure as well as through the presidencies of Gerald Ford and Jimmy Carter.

Thus when he returned to Tehran in the fall of 1978, to lend his strength to the faltering monarch, Zahedi had spent the entire decade of the 1970s in Washington. He was far more knowledgeable about the politics of the United States than of his own country. Worse, none of the key actors in Iran trusted him or put much stock in his judgment.

Throughout the fall of 1978, the Shah warned Ambassador Sullivan to ignore Zahedi because he did not understand Iran or the dynamics of the revolution.[64] Later the Shah explained his mistrust of Zahedi on different grounds.

I was ill-served by Ardeshir Zahedi's inaccurate reporting. He had been in Washington too long and was closely identified with the Nixon and Ford Administrations. He pretended to have access to the highest authorities but his reports could never be confirmed. His outgoing temperament was unsuited to the straight-laced

Carter White House and I should have replaced him. In any event, protocol was not observed and I was not told the truth.[65]

The Shah appears to have been wrong about Zahedi in at least one respect. Zehedi did have access in the United States—to Brzezinski, at least. The president's adviser spoke often with the ambassador before his departure from Washington and occasionally by telephone after he had arrived in Tehran. On the basis of these conversations, Zahedi thought he had authorization from the United States to undertake his last-ditch efforts to save the throne.

He may have had that authorization from Brzezinski, but he never succeeded in convincing the Shah. Nor did he convince the U.S. ambassador on the scene.

Zahedi did not strike me as what the French would call a "serious" person. He spoke often in broad philosophical terms, heavily tinged by his open profession of faith in Islam. Whether this covered a razor-sharp mind or whether it was a screen for less than met the eye, I could never really determine. My conclusion ultimately was that Zahedi was shrewd, able to determine where the main interests of his country and his future lay, and masterly at manipulating Americans. However, I do not believe he had a brilliant, analytical mind or that capability to conceptualize much beyond the guidelines that were laid out to him from Tehran.[66]

Lacking the trust or respect of both the Shah and Ambassador Sullivan, Zahedi's efforts "to put some backbone in the Old Man," as he confided to his friends, and to bolster support for the throne failed.[67] Despite his best efforts, Zahedi was no more effective than Empress Farah, the only other person close to the Shah who struggled to serve as a source for the restoration of his collapsing courage and hope.

At the end, the Shah had only one person with whom he could talk—the U.S. ambassador, William H. Sullivan. The ambassador reported on a meeting he had with the Shah at the end of August in 1978.

This rather tense conversation seemed to be cathartic to the shah. Although he appeared somewhat drawn, I felt he was at least more at ease when I rose to take my leave. This meeting established a pattern for frank discussion of political events in Iran that would be followed on a regular basis from that day until the shah eventually left the country. It was clear that he had no one, with the possible exception of the empress, with whom he could talk as he had just talked to me.[68]

The U.S. ambassador then, given the Shah's reservations about the political judgment of his empress, was in those final debilitating months the only person with whom the Shah could talk. Yet the ambassador, striving to remain faithful to his own ambiguous and occasionally contradictory instructions from Washington, was not able to provide the Shah with clear and forceful policy advice. As a result, the Shah's own confusion was exacerbated. Even from exile, the Shah was able to reconstruct his sense of betrayal at the hands of the United States.

The messages I received from the United States while all this was going on continued to be confusing and contradictory. Secretary of State Vance issued a statement endorsing my efforts to restore calm and encouraging the liberalization program. Such Herculean fantasies left me stunned. President Carter's National Security Advisor, Zbigniew Brzezinski, at least had his priorities straight. He called me in early November to urge that I establish law and order first, and only then continue our democratization program.

. . . I thanked Brzezinski for his expression of support. The next day I sought confirmation of the message from Ambassador Sullivan. As usual the American envoy promised to cable Washington, but when I next saw him, he said gravely that he had received no instructions. This rote answer had been given me since early September and I would continue to hear it until I left the country.[69]

Thus, for the last five months of his rule, the Shah's circle of trusted counselors had been narrowed to one—the U.S. ambassador. But the ambassador, remaining faithful to his responsibilities as the representative of his government, would not exceed the limits of his own instructions. He could not be the person the Shah most needed.

How did it come to be that after thirty-seven years on the throne, the Shah ended his rule alone? Poignantly, even tragically, the ruler of the Peacock Throne, who had ascended to kingship in 1941 and ruled longer than any other living monarch, found himself struggling against the mounting revolution without a single trusted counselor. The responsibility for this state of affairs was, of course, entirely his own. For ultimately it was the Shah who could not bring himself to trust any of his countrymen. He could not allow them to serve him as counselors because of his fear, well grounded in his character structure and in his political experience, that they would pursue their own interests as distinct from his. Even more importantly, he had come to believe that any Iranian who had the qualities he might seek as a counselor—personal courage, deep insight into the nature of the Iranian people, a shrewd and analytical capacity to weight the key political forces, and the wisdom to make sensible judgment—would be a threat to his rule. Those counselors were a threat not so much because they might choose to seek his ouster, although during periods of his rule there were such individuals. They were a threat, rather, because those qualities called into question—in his own mind first and foremost—his own qualifications to rule. They were not so much a political threat as a threat to his own psychological well-being.

The Shah, of course, could not acknowledge his inability to tolerate the closeness of the very people he so desperately needed. Instead, he described his policy as a reasoned lesson he had learned from observing his father.

I do not employ advisers in the usual sense of that term. To do so is, I think, dangerous for any head of state. One of the few mistakes my father made was to rely on a narrowing circle of advisers. Fearing Reza Shah, they flattered him rather than telling him the truth, and I am sorry to say they were not always incorruptible. My system is entirely different. In lieu of advisers I obtain information from many quarters and then strike my own balance sincerely and solely in the light of the public interest. Let me add that in no way do I regard myself as the one true repository of knowledge and enlightenment. On the contrary I use my multiple intelligence channels to draw upon the judgment of many wise men. Furthermore, if I see the problem is unusually serious or complex, I instantly start enlarging my network of information channels.[70]

It should now be clear that by and large, the Shah did follow that system. When he was feeling emotionally strong or when he was confronted by few significant crises, the system in place worked quite well. If it did not always produce wise decisions, it did serve to limit challenges to the Shah's capacity for untrammeled rule.

But a considerable number of crucial political events proved to be exceptions to the Shah's conception of his own system, exceptions from which he never drew the appropriate lessons. On many occasions, in addition to those mentioned above, the Shah did rely on specific others. He relied on others not merely for advice, but for leadership as well. In fact, he played a subsidiary role while nonetheless claiming to have been the moving force behind the policies of the day. For example, when British and Soviet troops invaded Iran in August of 1941 and demanded the ouster of Reza Shah, Mohammad Ali Foroughi, a wise and courageous prime minister, served to negotiate the transfer of power from the father to the son. When the Soviets refused to pull their troops out of Iran following World War II but instead backed the establishment of two "independent" republics in their occupation zone, the cunning and tough Prime Minister Ali Ghavam helped convince the Soviets that their future in Iran would be brighter by withdrawing than by occupying. Mohammad Mossadegh led the struggle to nationalize Iran's oil while the United States and United Kingdom arranged the details of his ouster and the Shah's return. During the combined economic and political crises of 1960–61, the Shah was able to call on Dr. Ali Amini, a tough, honest descendant of the Qajars, to restore the authority of the system.

Because the Shah could abide men of powerful character as little as he could abide advisers, however, these men were exceptions. The Shah did nothing to find and cultivate such men. Worse, when a political figure seemed to demonstrate those qualities, his career would soon reach its end. Either he was dismissed from office or, more likely, he was "elevated" to a sinecure—either in an Iranian diplomatic post abroad or in one of the many bureaucracies which the government or the Pahlavis had spawned. Better to have such individuals safely absorbed within the system than sullen outside it.

The consequences for the Shah, however, were devastating. By the time of the revolution, there was no one the Shah could trust. The three individuals whom he had been fortunate to be able to use for psychological merger and those from whom he could derive personal strength as well as political counsel had each passed from the scene. Ernest Perron and Assadollah Alam had died. Princess Ashraf had, effectively, been exiled. The Shah never found substitutes for their strength and wisdom. When they were gone, there was no one else who could fulfill their functions. Empress Farah came close, but the Shah never came to value her political judgment. Ardeshir Zahedi volunteered for the responsibility and, like Empress Farah, even undertook to act as if the Shah had extended it to him. But the Shah had no faith in his former son-in-law.

Two inexorable consequences followed. First, there was no one the Shah trusted from whom he could seek advice on how to deal with the escalating crises threatening his regime. Second, there was no one left whose strength the Shah could draw from to bolster his own dwindling reserves. Earlier in his life and rule, the Shah had confidants from whom he could derive the strength and courage which he needed to rule. He also could count on powerful figures to act decisively during crises. But he lost his throne alone.

Mohamed Heikal reports that in 1951, when the Shah was told of the assassination of Prime Minister Razmara, he was stunned. What he uttered then would have been equally appropriate for the denouement of the revolution: "I can't believe it. I can't believe it. . . . I don't know what to do. . . . I am all alone. Nobody understands my problems. Everybody is in a conspiracy against me; some of them deliberately and some unconsciously. But it is I who have to pay the penalty."[71]

The Shah did pay, of course. He lost everything. In the approximately eighteen months between his last flight from Iran and his death, he lived in exile, with one adviser—Robert Armao, a young American public relations specialist who had been introduced to the Shah during the revolution by his old friend David Rockefeller. After nearly four decades in power, the Shah had no one else, no Iranian, to ease his fate.[72]

6

Cancer: The Failure of Divine Protection

The Shah was the single most important contributor to the collapse of his own rule. In the 1970s the Pahlavi system came to be a reflection of his personal grandiosity. In turn, the majesty of the system reflected back onto the Shah, making him more grandiose. This spiral of mutually reinforcing grandiosity resulted in an impersonal system that became more and more offensive to the Iranian people.

The Shah then contributed to the cracking of his authority by initiating a withdrawal from the system he had created. When the revolution began he found himself increasingly paralyzed as his principal sources of psychic support collapsed. And eventually he lost his belief in another of those sources—his divine protection. But before this belief collapsed, when the Pahlavi system reflected the Shah's grandiosity, he could easily imagine that his good fortune was a reflection of his special relation to the Divine. He had told Oriana Fallaci of it.

A king who does not need to account to anyone for what he says and does is unavoidably doomed to loneliness. However, I am not entirely alone, because a force others can't perceive accompanies me. My mystical force. Moreover, I receive messages. I have lived with God beside me since I was 5 years old. Since, that is, God sent me those visions.[1]

The claim of divine protection was not merely a mode of presentation for foreigners. In a book published in Tehran whose audience was the Iranian people, the Shah declared, "In whatever I have done and whatever I do in the future, I consider myself merely as an agent of the will of God."[2]

Unlike other statements by the Shah which were meant to construe the

Pahlavi dynasty and his rule in their most favorable public light, this was one claim the Shah truly believed. Queen Soraya recounted how the Shah would often talk of his mystical dreams and of his visions of Ali, the son-in-law of the Prophet Muhammad and the central figure in Shi'ism. He told her that in his rule he believed he had merely surrendered to his religious fate.[3] In more recent years, visitors to the court were assured by Empress Farah that not only the Shah, but she too, had come to accept the legitimacy of his visions and belief in divine protection.[4]

The Shah had also come to understand his political victories, his successful responses to the past challenges to his rule, as reflections of such divine power. When musing over the challenge of succeeding to the throne of his formidable father, as a twenty-one year old, the Shah told one of his biographers: "never in my life had I been in a more confused and perplexed state of mind. But, as always, some mysterious force came to my rescue to guide me through this traumatic period. You know, my mystical faith in a divine power."[5] And when Mossadegh defied the Shah's dismissal order and the Shah fled to Rome, only to be restored to the throne by a popular uprising instigated by Kim Roosevelt and the Shah's Iranian supporters, the Shah understood that "once again the mysterious divine power came to my rescue, made my people revolt against Mossadegh and his forces, overthrew him, brought me back to my country and restored to me my crown and kingdom."[6]

Not only did the Shah come to believe that his own personal political longevity was the result of God's will, but he came to believe that he had become God's instrument for the salvation of Iran: "I believe in God and that I have been chosen by God to perform a task. My visions were miracles that saved the country. My reign has saved the country and it has done so because God was on my side."[7]

Many Iranians, even those close to the Shah, believed that these claims were used by the Shah as a political device. They saw them as his means of capturing religious legitimacy while undercutting the appeal of the clerics. But the possession of divine protection is not a conventionally defined manifestation of religiosity in either Islam in general, or Shi'ism in particular, and the Shah's claims were met by virtually universal skepticism. If they were a political device used by the Shah, it was clearly an unsuccessful one.

In fact these claims were not intended to win political support. The Shah actually believed in his divine mission. He repeated it too often to too many diverse audiences—Iranian as well as foreign—for it to be merely a political device. More importantly, he made the claim to those with whom he had the most intimate ties, his spouses among them. The most plausible assumption about the Shah's claim to a mystical, divine force is that he deeply believed it. It was yet another source of the psychic strength which he drew on for "doing" Shah.[8]

In his 1960 autobiography the Shah offered the first public statement of his belief, which emanated from the visions he had had during his near-fatal childhood illnesses.

From the time I was six or seven, I have felt that perhaps there is a supreme being who is guiding me. I don't know. Sometimes the thought disturbs me because then, I ask myself, what is my own personality, and am I possessed of free will? Still, I often reflect, if I am driven—or perhaps I should say supported—by another force, there must be a reason.[9]

In this first public account of his childhood visions and divine protection, the Shah is quite tentative. In comparison with his later assertions, he is initially quite reserved in the strength of his claim. In part this may have been the result of a certain embarrassment in acknowledging what he sensed his Western readers would find farfetched. But it seems more plausible that, as the Shah felt more secure on the throne and his grandiosity mounted, his belief in his divine calling was strengthened. His commitment to that belief was both a product of his growing political strength and a contributor to it, at least indirectly. For the belief served to encourage the Shah in facing both the challenges to his rule and the challenges of his ruling.

Both sets of challenges were to mount in the 1960s and 1970s. In 1960 and 1961 the Shah was forced to cancel the results of two parliamentary elections, following rioting over allegations of widespread election fraud, exacerbated by Iran's faltering economy. In 1963, serious rioting erupted following the arrest of Ayatollah Khomeini. In 1965, Prime Minister Hassan Ali Mansur was assassinated, and shortly thereafter a member of the Imperial Guards sprayed machine gun bullets on the ground floor of the Marble Palace while the Shah worked in his office on the floor above. The guardsman was finally killed as he mounted the stairs to the Shah's private office. Numerous other less dramatic attempts on the life of the Shah occurred as well.

The Shah believed that behind many of these attempts was the hand of Gen. Teymour Bakhtiar, the first chief of SAVAK. Fearing a military coup from Bakhtiar, he exiled the general in 1962. Bakhtiar spent the remainder of the decade traveling the Middle East, attracting supporters, and being arrested on arms trafficking charges in Lebanon.

On August 23, 1970, General Bakhtiar was shot while on a hunting expedition in Iraq. He died a few days later. His companions on that trip were two Iranians who had only shortly before hijacked an Iranian airliner to Baghdad so they could join Bakhtiar in his struggles against the Shah. Two stories of Bakhtiar's death emerged. One had it that the shooting was accidental. That was the official account told by both Iraq and Iran. But the Shah boasted that the killing was a SAVAK operation and that even the hijacking had been staged so its agents could ingratiate themselves with Bakhtiar. "Who assassinated Bakhtiar?" one of his biographers asked. "We did," the Shah replied. "The SAVAK did."[10]

Even with the general's removal, the challenges to the Shah's rule would continue. Matching the style of violence sweeping the rest of the world in the 1970s, the Shah was no longer challenged by assassination attempts but by guerrilla terrorism. In February 1971, the first armed attack against the regime occurred, on a gendarme post at Siakhal near the Caspian Sea. From there the terrorism moved into the cities, where periodic attacks against military officers, police officials, and American civilian and military advisers continued through the decade.

Through all these challenges, the Shah responded with uncharacteristic vigor and determination. He had, he thought, the support of his people. He had the counsel and support of powerful advisers. Iran's oil revenues were mounting to previously unimagined levels. The Shah was backed by the United States and even lauded by President Nixon and Secretary of State Kissinger. And, obvious to him, he still was blessed with the divine protection first revealed to him in his childhood.

As the 1970s unfolded, it appeared that despite the guerrilla attacks, the Shah was becoming more powerful and the Pahlavi system more firmly institutionalized in the political life of the country. Then, in April 1974, the Shah discovered he had cancer.

Until that time, the Shah, as an adult, had suffered from a range of minor medical problems. On his first trip to the United States, in 1949, he had checked into Cornell University's New York Hospital, where he underwent a complete examination. The senior attending physician, Dr. Claude E. Forkner, gave the thirty-year-old monarch a clean bill of health.[11]

In August 1951, not long after he had acceded to overwhelming political pressures and officially designated Dr. Mohammad Mossadegh prime minister, the Shah was struck with appendicitis.[12] A medical team dispatched from Cornell performed a successful appendectomy on the Shah. Queen Soraya, however, fared less well. Just before her scheduled marriage to the Shah, she was struck by typhoid in late 1950. The marriage date was postponed, but by February 1951 she was judged sufficiently well to go ahead with the ceremony. Yet the lingering effects of her own illness, in addition to the burdens of the political tensions surrounding Mossadegh's premiership, left her in a weakened condition. The Shah's operation proved the final straw. The doctors who had treated the Shah expressed alarm over her health, and her own physicians insisted she "go to Switzerland for a rest cure."[13]

Both members of the royal couple regained their health in short order, and the Shah appeared, at least to the casual observer, to be immune from further medical problems. But in fact the burdens of rule took their toll. In later years, the Shah told one of his legion of biographers that he never touched alcohol—only Vichy water—"because of my liver troubles." He added that "I can no longer have the dishes I like, because of the diet I have to observe on medical grounds. No more rich foods, which are not easily digested. I prefer simple fare."[14]

In Iranian culture, "liver troubles" is one of those generic labels used to identify a wide range of "dis-ease" and identified by Western medicine as a variety of particular illnesses. Some time before, the Shah had informed an American adviser that he suffered from dyspepsia.[15] (Thus did the Shah indicate his command over Western culture. Dyspepsia, or indigestion, is the English version of the "liver problems" of Iran, which the French, in turn, label a *crise de foie*, defined by a Frenchman as "the remorse of a guilty stomach.") The Shah later confided to that same American that his indigestion had, in fact, been diagnosed as ulcers. The Shah was to monitor his diet ever after.

But these medical problems were to pale to insignificance with the drama of his cancer. Over the 1974 Iranian New Year's holiday, celebrated on March 21, the spring equinox, the royal family had gone to their home on the Persian Gulf island of Kish. While walking on the beach, the Shah felt a swelling under his rib cage.

A few weeks later, a call went from the imperial court to Prof. Jean Bernard, the "pope of French hematology."[16] He and his colleague, his onetime student Dr. Georges Flandrin, flew to Tehran and in the palace examined the Shah as thoroughly as those surroundings allowed. For fear of stimulating rumors, the Shah categorically refused to visit a Tehran hospital.

Even in the absence of sophisticated clinical equipment, it appeared to the physicians that the Shah had lymphatic leukemia. But the Shah's personal doctor, Gen. Mohammad Ayadi, forbade them to use words such as "cancer" or "leukemia" before the imperial patient. He judged those too harsh for the Shah. Just as the Shah had created a system whereby he was often shielded from the political truth, so it was with his own medical condition. In deference to Ayadi, Bernard and Flandrin informed the Shah that he had Waldenstrom's macroglobulinemia. While a mild cancer of the lymph system, Waldenstrom's does not bear the dreaded name of cancer. More, it was the disease from which Georges Pompidou, the president of France, suffered. All that helped remove the sting. Flandrin and Bernard informed the Shah that his illness was certainly not necessarily fatal and could be controlled with medication. They prescribed daily doses of the drug chlorambucil.

When his French physicians informed the patient of their diagnosis, they were far from confident in their conclusions. They had explained to the Shah that a certain diagnosis of his illness could be made only after exploratory surgery, minimally a biopsy of his spleen. But the Shah refused any surgery, however minor. He informed them that, more than the disease itself, he feared the political consequences of its public exposure. They would have to do the best they could without the surgical procedures they knew to be essential to a conclusive diagnosis and, thus, an optimal treatment.

Years later, in 1979, after he fled his country, the Shah was treated for gallstones at Cornell University's New York Hospital, occupying the same rooms he had stayed in during his 1949 examination. There, a lymph node was removed from his neck and biopsied. The diagnosis was histiocytic lymphosarcoma, a serious cancer. That diagnosis indicated that his French physicians, without the possibility of surgery, had erred in their original diagnosis. The Shah, in fact, had suffered all those years from lymphatic lymphoma, a cancer related to, but more deadly than, Waldenstrom's macroglobulinemia. At the very least, a different treatment regimen was indicated.[17]

Whatever the validity of the original diagnosis, however, it is reasonable to conclude that the Shah was devastated by the news of illness. There is no conclusive evidence that he understood he had cancer, but he took the news of his illness with the utmost seriousness. He informed the physicians that their findings were to be treated as a state secret. They were to inform no one of his condition, not the French security services, not even his wife, Empress Farah. All court insiders knew at the time was that by the mid-1970s he began to take large numbers of pills. During the weekly meetings of the High Economic Council, for example, tea was served promptly at 3:30 in the afternoon. The Shah would then take a number of different-colored pills. He informed his prime minister that they controlled his "stomach gas."[18] None of the other regulars had the courage to ask.[19]

There were other subtle signs that something was amiss. A number of interviewers reported in the mid-1970s that the Shah seemed depressed or discouraged. *Time* magazine, for example, noted in 1974 that "the highly active 54-year-old monarch sighed frequently as he talked, his voice sometimes dropping to a whisper, as though betraying the burden he feels as the absolute ruler of Iran's 34 million people."[20]

That in 1974 the Shah should have felt oppressed by the burden of rule seems unlikely, for that year was the peak of his grandiosity. The Shah had been appointed by Nixon and Kissinger as chief U.S. proxy in the Persian Gulf and been given presidential permission to buy any non-nuclear U.S. weapon system he wished to acquire—an astounding offer. Domestically, Iran's oil-driven economy was booming. At the time of his *Time* interview, Iran's oil revenues had catapulted to nearly $25 billion per year. In short, it is difficult to find reasons of state to account for the Shah's generally depressive tone.

A more plausible reason was the Shah's reaction to the news of his cancer. For the first time in the history of his rule, the Shah began to speak of his own mortality. In the *Time* interview in which the Shah dropped his voice "to a whisper," he said, "I hope that this leadership [his own rule] will continue until everybody is not only literate, but has a good life."[21]

Not until early March 1975, however, did the Shah refer to his own death in a speech before an Iranian audience. He had already startled his listeners in that speech by announcing his intention of introducing a single-party political system into Iran. Not that the idea of a single-party system was itself startling. There were already scores of countries which could boast of such political arrangements. Nor was the surprise occasioned because the idea was necessarily bad for Iran. In fact, the capability which such single-party systems had demonstrated elsewhere for mobilizing the population to support its regime and participate in national development suggested beneficial possibilities for the state. The surprise, instead, came because the Shah had earlier renounced, with great vehemence, the idea of a single party.

After announcing his intention of forming the Rastakhiz party, he startled his audience a second time. That second surprise was less noticed, but was ultimately far more significant. It was a reference to his own death. "No human being is immortal," the Shah noted, "and I am a human being. While I am talking to you now, there is no reason that I will be here with you tomorrow. Nothing can be predicted because man's life is in the hands of God."[22]

Apparently the Shah envisaged the need to institutionalize his own rule through the single party from his awareness of his own mortality.[23] Few were sufficiently sensitive to the nuances of the Shah's speech to have even noted the reference. But the passage of time must have brought the Shah to yet more stark visions of that mortality. With those visions came the willingness to share them with his countrymen, however unwitting such references may have been. The Shah began to refer to the possibility of his own death with increasing frequency. Many of those references, however, appeared in inappropriate contexts—almost slips of the royal tongue. In 1975, for example, the Shah held a news conference to discuss the significant arms buildup which he had launched. The Shah justified the billions Iran was spending on arms and reiterated that he would continue Iran's acquisition of weapons "in accordance with Iran's needs and national interests."[24] To that point the Shah's remarks seemed focused on the criticism of his military buildup and was matter of fact. But in the midst of his discussion of types of aircraft and numbers of tanks, the Shah suddenly began to talk of the dangers of military weakness. He warned that "weakness was tantamount to death" and in a startling non sequitur went on to add, "we have no intention of dying. There is much work to be done to ensure the glorious future which will commit this nation to history."[25]

Months later, in a speech commemorating the fiftieth anniversary of the establishment of the Pahlavi dynasty, the Shah majestically announced, "We have arisen from among the Iranian nation. We have been born in this sacred land, where we will be buried."[26]

In addition to referring to his own death, the Shah even more frequently began to allude to his retirement. In an interview after the formation of Rastakhiz, the Shah discussed, for the first time, some future transition of rule from himself to his son: "Our struggle now lies in the construction of a new Iran . . . in the construction of a better country for my people and for my son who will ascend the throne after me. At his age, I used to dream of Iran's far future and I wish to deliver the dream as a concrete reality into his hands."[27] From that date onward, the Shah spoke of the day when he would step aside in favor of the Crown Prince.

The Shah's withdrawal from the Pahlavi political system appeared, then, to have been driven by his illness. The threat to his life was so great that he began to contemplate, publicly as well as privately, the day he would not be present. Those public messages were to prove serious in suggesting to the people of Iran that the Shah was withdrawing commitment from his own political system. In this he failed to fulfill Iranian cultural definitions of a leader and, in effect, encouraged the Iranian people to withdraw their own support.

The Shah explained his commitments to retirement and the transition to his son as statecraft. It was, undoubtedly, statecraft born of the knowledge of his cancer. For all the clues which he gave, there is no evidence that anyone in Iran, or the foreign capitals so concerned with matters of state in Iran, came to appreciate that the Shah was ill.

The principal indication of how devastating the news of his cancer must have been to the Shah was not so much that he made veiled references to his retirement and death or that he treated the news as a state secret, but that he held the news as a personal secret as well. Empress Farah did not learn of the cancer until 1977—three full years after the Shah himself had learned of his illness, two years after his cancer had worsened and his chemotherapy increased, and only after Assadollah Alam had fallen ill with leukemia.[28] (It is a mark of his estrangement from his twin that even in the summer of 1979, Princess Ashraf had not learned of her brother's cancer.)

By 1977, it appears, the Shah had come to appreciate that he was seriously ill. But he could not himself bear to deliver his horrible news to his wife. Bernard and Flandrin gave the news to the empress. They told her the full story of his illness. They also informed her that by then they had told the Shah "everything" but without ever mentioning the word "cancer."[29] Thus it was that the Shah's physicians came to participate in the delusionary system which enveloped the Shah in so many realms.

It appears that the years of private suffering between his learning of his illness and his courage to inform his wife were necessary for the Shah to integrate his intellectual understanding of his medical condition with his emotionally unshakable belief in his divine protection. The "Waldenstrom's disease" must have been an unmistakable sign that his divine protection had been lost. And that is what the Shah must have found so impossible to accept.

As challenging as the cancer with its daily chemotherapeutic reminder was to the Shah's view of his own divine protection, his condition apparently worsened in early 1978. His French physicians are said to have traveled to Iran and diagnosed the cancer as more serious than before.[30] Reportedly, they altered his treatment and began to administer the drug prednisone, a considerably more powerful drug than chlorambucil. Prednisone can affect the mental processes. It slows reaction time and the ability to think clearly. It induces depression and lessens decision-making ability. Thus his cancer-fighting drugs would have deprived the Shah of what he most needed—the ability to think clearly. Later medical reports deny the Shah took prednisone during the revolution.[31] Whether he did or did not take powerful chemotherapy drugs during the revolution is incidental to the fact that as early as the first months of the disturbances—shortly after the initiation of revolutionary violence in Qum in January 1978—the Shah appeared to courtiers to be not thinking clearly.[32] As the revolution swept up ever larger numbers of the Iranian people, the Shah's cognitive functioning appeared to diminish—when he most needed his mental acuity.

By the spring of 1978, rumors that the Shah was not well began to sweep Tehran. Few of the rumors alluded to cancer, but all suggested that the Shah was withdrawing from rule at precisely the time when the unfolding revolution most demanded his concentrated presence. The imperial court itself was responsible for the beginning of those rumors. In early May 1978, the court announced that the Shah was canceling a long-scheduled trip to Hungary and Bulgaria. It attributed the cancellation to the Shah's "persistent cold."[33]

While the court was informing the public that the Shah had a bad cold, he was telling senior officials that he felt ill because he had bad pains in his legs.[34] In the late spring, U.S. ambassador Sullivan noticed that the Shah was limping. When the Shah became aware of the ambassador's stare, he became flustered and deeply embarrassed. He told the ambassador that he had hurt his leg water skiing at the Caspian Sea.[35]

In a matter of a few weeks, the Shah withdrew physically from the politics of Tehran. He and his family spent virtually the entire summer of 1978 in seclusion at the royal residences on the Caspian. His absence drove the rumor mills to frenzied levels. Some were sure the Shah had been wounded in an assassination attempt and had removed himself to recuperate. Others "knew" the Shah was ill. His cold, some said, had turned into pneumonia. Others hit on the idea that he was dying of cancer. Leukemia and lung cancer were the favorite diagnoses.[36]

The rumors were so widespread that court officials came to believe that something had to be done to convince the public that the Shah was healthy. One day in July, all of Tehran's newspapers published a picture of the Shah and the empress walking on a Caspian beach. But in the unsettled atmosphere sweeping the capital, the picture had the opposite effect. For next to the royal couple were two pairs of beach clogs, and the rumors had it that the court had airbrushed from the picture the two aides who were allegedly walking on either side of the Shah to prop him up. The beach clogs, as most beachgoers would assume, were actually those of the Shah and the empress.[37]

The number of rumors and the certainty with which they were believed were a mark of the extent to which the Shah's authority had been "cracked"—a sign of his rapidly dissipating command over the politics of Iran. The people of Iran had already begun the psychological steps necessary to envisage rule without the Shah.

The government of France apparently learned of the Shah's illness from his physicians, and it is plausible that the United States was not informed. It is less plausible that the British could have learned of his cancer and kept that secret from its principal ally. Nevertheless, there are assertions that Shahpour Reporter, a confidant of the Shah and a British subject, knew of the illness and informed Sir Douglas Home during the mid-1970s.[38] Yet until dangerously late in the revolution, the U.S. government had no knowledge of the Shah's cancer. When it learned that secret is still unclear, but apparently it did not learn conclusively of the illness until the fall of 1978, when the United States was "enlightened by French intelligence."[39]

Pierre Salinger recounts how the French came to learn that truth.

A high ranking official of a major foreign power was at a reception at the residence of the nation's chief executive one day in June of 1978 when he was approached by one of the country's most famous doctors. "I must see you urgently," the doctor said, at which point he pulled the government official into a quiet corner. "You must communicate to the President that the Shah is very, very ill. Not only is he ill, but his illness renders him incapable of making decisions."[40]

It was not literally true that his illness made him "incapable of making decisions." But cancer specialists readily acknowledge that the emotional burden of the illness coupled with the drug prednisone, if that were, in fact, the drug being administered, would combine to produce powerfully debilitating effects.[41]

The claim being made here is that those two factors, the burden of cancer and the drugs used to combat it, produced far more powerful effects in the Shah than would be true for other patients. The crucial additional factor for the imperial patient was his grandiose commitment to his divine protection. The cancer was one of the principal factors which made it difficult to sustain that belief and left him depressed, withdrawn, and vacant. On November 21, 1978, U.S. Treasury Secretary Michael Blumenthal called on the Shah in Tehran; he was one of a number of official American visitors traveling to Tehran to attempt to assess the prospects of the rapidly unfolding revolution and bolster the Shah's confidence through their presence. He reported to President Carter, "This man is a ghost."[42]

This account of the Shah's struggle with cancer is meant to explain his loss of the support of his people, his powerful confidants, and the United States, and his failures to act and act decisively to preserve his throne. But his final and ultimately unsuccessful struggles with the disease can be told in short order. After visiting Egypt and Morocco, on the third stop of his search for a home in exile, in the Bahamas, the Shah developed swollen lymph nodes on the left side of his neck. Dr. Georges Flandrin, his French physician, flew to his side, performed a biopsy, and determined that the Shah had a new and usually fatal form of cancer, Richter's syndrome. Flandrin believed the Shah should enter a hospital for proper diagnosis and treatment, but the Shah still refused to reveal his condition. "He evidently thought that he could still influence the course of events in Iran; he told Flandrin that if those still loyal to him learned he was ill, then morale would suffer. Could he not continue with his secret treatment?"[43] Flandrin acceded to his patient's wishes. The Shah stayed in the Bahamas. Flandrin prescribed MOPP, a powerful combination of anticancer drugs, and the Shah's swollen lymph nodes and spleen began to shrink.[44]

In August 1979, when he had settled in a rented villa in Cuernavaca outside Mexico City, the Shah's skin began to turn yellow. Mexican doctors were called and, in the absence of any information about the Shah's medical problem, diagnosed him as suffering from malaria. The Shah failed to respond to their treatment. Georges Flandrin visited the Shah as well and altered the Shah's chemotherapy dosage. By the end of September, Robert Armao, the Shah's American adviser, concluded that the Shah was seriously ill. Knowing nothing of either his cancer or chemotherapy, Armao concluded that the Shah must have contracted malaria or hepatitis, or both, during his stays in Egypt, the Bahamas, and Mexico. Armao telephoned Joseph V. Reed, later to serve as U.S. ambassador to Morocco but then a senior aide to David Rockefeller, who had originally suggested to the Shah that he name Armao as a public relations specialist and aide.[45] Reed in turn called Dr. Benjamin Kean, who had treated for diarrhea both Armao and Mark Morse, his assistant who had stayed by the Shah in Mexico. Kean was a parasitologist and pathologist who had "a fashionable private practice on Park Avenue and an office and lab at Cornell University Medical College, New York Hospital."[46]

Kean flew to Mexico, examined the Shah, and quickly concluded that the Shah did not have the malaria for which Mexican physicians had been treating him for weeks. But Kean could not make a conclusive determination of the Shah's illness without more testing than was available at the Shah's residence. Amazingly, the Shah did not tell Kean of his cancer and even refused to let him take blood tests. Kean left his patient to return to New York, urging him to seek better, local medical care or to recall his French physicians.

Two weeks later, Armao once again called Dr. Kean in New York and informed him that the Shah's condition had worsened. Moreover, the Shah had admitted, finally, that he had been treated for cancer for years. Kean flew back to Cuernavaca and described what he found.

There was no longer any doubt. The atmosphere had changed completely. The Shah's appearance was stunningly worse. . . . Clearly he had obstructive jaundice. The odds favored gallstones, since his fever, chills, and abdominal distress suggested an infection of the biliary tract. Also he had a history of indigestion.

Besides the probable obstruction—he now had been deeply jaundiced for six to eight weeks—he was emaciated and suffering from hard tumor nodes in the neck and a swollen spleen, signs that his cancer was worsening, and he had severe anemia and very low white blood counts.[47]

It was clear to Kean that the Shah required immediate hospitalization, extensive medical tests, and, perhaps, surgery—surgery which would be extremely complicated given the number of life-threatening illnesses from which the Shah suffered.

On the basis of those considerations, Kean and the Shah decided that the most suitable medical treatment would be available at Cornell's New York Hospital, where Kean was a consulting physician. Kean then set in motion the process which would result in President Carter's personal approval of the Shah's admission to the United States. On October 22, 1979, the Shah entered the country and went directly to the hospital. Within twenty-four hours the Shah was operated on to remove gallstones which were blocking his bile duct and causing obstructive jaundice. A lymph node was removed from his neck and biopsied. But the Shah's swollen spleen was not removed.

On the basis of the biopsy, Dr. Morton Coleman, an oncology expert at Cornell, diagnosed the Shah's cancer as histiocytic lymphoma of an advanced stage, but one in which the potential for cure still existed. What was called for, he determined, was an extensive eighteen-month program of much more aggressive chemotherapy than the Shah had yet experienced.

The Shah's doctors formulated a new medical plan. He would recuperate from the gallbladder operation and then prepare for a second operation, which would remove his cancerous and dangerously swollen spleen. He would recuperate from that operation and begin the new chemotherapy treatments. But two obstacles arose which were to disrupt those plans, and eventually, shatter the United States' relations with revolutionary Iran.

After the Shah's gallbladder operation, x-rays revealed that one gallstone had been left in place and was blocking the Shah's bile duct. The Shah was too weak for another operation, but unless the stone was eliminated, his life would be endangered. It was decided to prepare the Shah for a new procedure which would crush the stone without surgery. Those preparations, however, would take weeks of planning and set back the scheduled removal of his spleen.

Then on November 4, 1979, zealous Iranian students, acting "in the line of the Imam," scaled the walls surrounding the U.S. embassy in Tehran, captured the chancery, and with it the U.S. diplomats, the Marine guard, and the Iranian staff.[48] The United States immediately was elevated to the status of the "Great Satan" of Iranian politics.

Only three days earlier in Algiers, on November 1, Mehdi Bazargan, Iran's prime minister, and his foreign minister, Dr. Ibrahim Yazdi, had met with Zbigniew Brzezinski, President Carter's national security adviser. That meeting in Algiers and the embassy takeover in Tehran proved to be the factors which tipped the political balance and led to the irretrievable radicalizing of Iranian politics. Bazargan and his cabinet were the first victims. He resigned his office and effectively paved the way for direct clerical rule. The United States' relations with the Islamic Republic and the U.S. diplomats who were incarcerated for those excruciating 444 days were also its victims. President Carter was another victim. His immersion in their fate and his inability to free the captives contributed to his 1980 electoral defeat.

But the Shah was to suffer as well. His presence in the United States, even for the treatment of his life-threatening illnesses, was seen by the Carter administration as the major impediment to the release of the American diplomats. Rather than allowing the Shah to remain in the United States to recuperate from his gallstone surgery so that his cancerous spleen could be removed, he was, in effect, expelled from the country. When he had recovered sufficiently, he was moved from New York Hospital to Lackland Air Force Base in Texas. There, Dr. Kean reported, "his cancer was coming back with a vengeance."[49]

Meanwhile, the government of Mexico had decided that his return to Cuernavaca was incompatible with its national interest. Only Gen. Omar Torrijos, the ruler of Panama, was willing to admit the Shah, where he flew after a brief stop in Texas.

But General Torrijos was not willing to allow Kean to treat his patient's worsening cancer as the doctor prescribed. Kean had determined that the Shah could be guaranteed quality medical care only at Gorgas Hospital, a U.S. facility in the Canal Zone. But General Torrijos, apparently with the consent of the United States eager to slake the passions of the Iranians, ordered the Shah to his own hospital, Paitilla Medical Center, in Panama itself. He also insisted that only Panamanian surgeons would be allowed to operate on the Shah's spleen.

Dr. Kean by then understood that he had left the medical realm for the world of international diplomacy. He brought Dr. Michael De Bakey of Houston to Panama, hoping that his international reputation would sway the Panamanian ruler.[50] He intervened with Lloyd Cutler, special counsel to President Carter. He got messages to General Torrijos. But the general refused to bend. The Shah could be operated on in Panama, but only at General Torrijos' own hospital in Panama proper, not at Gorgas in the Canal Zone, and only by Panamanian surgeons, not even by Dr. De Bakey.

Meanwhile, Iran's new government demanded that Panama arrest the Shah and extradite him to Iran. According to the Shah, the Panamanians "hastened to assure us—in secret—that there was no way I could be extradited since such extradition would violate Panamanian law."[51] Nonetheless, it became clear to the Shah that Panamanian officials were in contact with the new regime and were "playing extradition games with Iran."[52]

The combination of health and politics was to prove decisive. Kean was alarmed at the prospect of further delay in removing the Shah's spleen, yet he feared for his patient's safety in what he regarded as an inadequate and poorly staffed hospital. The Shah feared as well, but he also was concerned about the possibility of Panama and the United States cutting a deal which would return him to Iran in exchange for the U.S. diplomats.

On March 23, 1980, the Shah fled Panama. Pres. Anwar Sadat had extended an invitation through his wife, Jihan, to the empress, and with it a promise of protection. The Shah chartered the only jet he could find—a Boeing 707—and flew to Egypt. On March 28, Dr. De Bakey arrived from Houston and removed the Shah's spleen. Dr. Kean recalled the results.

The operation went beautifully. That night, however, was terrible. The medical team—American, Egyptian, French—was in the pathology lab. The focus was the Shah's cancerous spleen, grotesquely swollen to 20 times normal. It was one-foot long, literally the size of a football. But I was drawn to the liver tissues that had also been removed. The liver was speckled with white. Malignancy. The cancer had hit the liver. The Shah would soon die.[53]

He did, on July 27, 1980. "The tragedy," as Dr. Kean concluded, "is that a man who should have had the best and easiest medical care had, in many respects, the worst."[54]

The death of the Shah, like his overthrow, need not have happened at the time and in the way it did. There are no heroes in that death, perhaps with the exception of the medical personnel who struggled to minister to a sick and broken man within the inhospitable context of international politics. But no one else acted with valor and decency. The Shah's illness presented the United States with a dilemma. Its obligations to the man who had served as a faithful ally during the thirty-seven years of his rule were contradictory to the commitments of the new leaders of Islamic Iran. Those in the revolutionary regime who were willing to deal with the United States—the Bazargans, the Yazdis, and their allies—were themselves swept away by radical forces unleashed by Ayatollah Khomeini. In dealing with this dilemma, which it neither fully understood nor satisfactorily resolved, the United States itself lost its pride of place in Iran. The United States acted toward the Shah with considerable dishonor and in the process was devastated by Ayatollah Khomeini.

But as was true as well of his overthrow, the Shah also bore great responsibility for his death. He never allowed his French physicians the kinds of medical procedures they would have needed to establish a conclusive diagnosis after their initial discovery of cancer in 1973. He never shared the knowledge of his illness with his wife or others within Iran who might have been able to help him deal with the emotional burden of the cancer and its symbolic significance. Neither would the Shah allow the news to be passed to his principal foreign ally—the United States.

Later, when his cancer became more severe, he continued to repeat these errors, maintaining secrecy while not seeking and demanding the finest medical attention. For the Shah, the cancer was as a sign that his divine protection had been withdrawn.

7

Xenophobia and Emulation: The Iranian People, The Shah, and the West

Along with the support he derived from the people of Iran, from his identification with powerful others, and from his belief in his divine protection, the Shah maintained his psychological equilibrium from his deeply held belief in the special relationship which existed between him and the United States. As with his other sources of psychological strength, so it was with his relationship to the United States: at the crucial juncture when he most needed to maintain the firm conviction that the United States was his ardent supporter—in fact, that he was "their man" in the Middle East and the Persian Gulf—that conviction became impossible to sustain. So did his capacity to rule. Even before the first shots of the Iranian Revolution had been fired in Qum on that Iranian winter day in 1978, the Shah had already lost much of his capacity to make the difficult decisions which would be so necessary in the coming months.

Henry Kissinger, with his typically shrewd sense of others, knew this about the Shah. He recalled that the Shah

had been restored to the throne in 1953 by American influence when a leftist government had come close to toppling him. He never forgot that; it may have been the root of his extraordinary trust in American purposes and American goodwill, and of his psychological disintegration when he sensed that friendship evaporating. On some levels excessively, even morbidly, suspicious of possible attempts to diminish his authority, he nevertheless retained an almost naive faith in the United States.[1]

The former secretary of state was right on two counts. The Shah lived his life with an "extraordinary trust in American purposes and American goodwill," and he underwent a "psychological disintegration when he

166

sensed that friendship evaporating." The emphasis here is on the psycho-logical. Many observers of Iran noted the deepening tie between Iran and the United States during the thirty-seven year rule of the Shah, but most of them understood that tie in terms of politics and economics. They saw Iran under the Shah sharing the regional perspectives of the United States and understanding the constellation of forces in the Persian Gulf, South Asia, and the Middle East in the same terms as did American policymakers. They saw the Shah's massive buildup of his armed forces as an effort to serve as a surrogate for U.S. power in the region. His efforts to force the international oil companies to pump ever greater quantities of Iranian crude, in order to enhance the revenues of the state, also made it appear that the Shah served Western interests as well. All these steps made it easier to see Pahlavi Iran as politically and economically tied to, if not dependent on, the United States.

That view of the relations between the states misses the subtleties in the ties, especially in the 1970s—a topic taken up in the next chapter. The view also completely misses the point that underlying the political and economic ties was a special psychological relationship which the Shah had developed with the United States and its presidents. They were, fatherlike figures for the Shah, psychic substitutes for his own father, whom the Shah perceived to be so rejecting, so threatening, so ultimately dissatisfied with his own son. The Shah believed he had never won the love and unconditional ap-proval of his father. Failing that, he would win that approval from the United States. In psychoanalytic terms, the United States and its presi-dents were selfobjects with whom the Shah replayed the psychological dramas of his own childhood. He struggled to rework with them his earlier experiences with his father and through their repetition to rectify the in-justices to which he had been subjected by his father. If he could not rectify those injustices, he could hope, in his relations with those legendary, powerful leaders of the most powerful nation in the world, to master the hurts and injuries he had experienced with his father. The Shah would use those U.S. presidents as selfobjects. He could bolster his own psychic equi-librium through a merger with them. He would be strengthened by their mirroring of his own sense of self, by his idealization of their strength and power, and he would flourish by a sense of twinship with the leaders of the world's most powerful nation.

The United States, then, especially as embodied in its national leaders, served the Shah as stand-in for the depreciating and unaccepting father of his childhood. He sought to alter the unalterable past by winning their approval and acceptance. Failing that, he could hope to repeat the rejections again and again until he was able to lessen their sting, to master them. Thus he could demonstrate to himself, in the first instance, that in fact he needed neither the United States nor Reza Shah Kabir, the Great. Mastery would, at the least, be a demonstration that he had achieved true political and economic independence, which in turn was a cover for the deeper and more highly prized psychological independence to which he directed his life.

The Shah never succeeded in that quest. His failure, of course, was to be expected, for the consequences of his relationship with that stern, demanding, and angry father had been sealed in his own youth. The Shah could not undo what had been done in those early and formative years. But, of course, he did not know that. Moreover, the impetus to rectify the failings of his youth was immense. That inner pressure helped sustain the fantasy that he could undo what was undoable. In his relations with the United States, he found the arena for that struggle.

As ruling monarch at the age of twenty-four, the Shah met the first of those eight U.S. presidents. In 1943, Franklin Delano Roosevelt made the long journey from Washington to Tehran to meet Stalin and Churchill and deliberate on the future of the war. As the fifty-six year-old ruling King of Kings, the Shah visited the last of that series of U.S. presidents, Jimmy Carter, in Washington in 1977. Then on New Year's Eve 1978—the last full year in which he would rule—the Shah welcomed Jimmy Carter to Tehran, where he was so fulsomely toasted by the American.

Those U.S. presidents represented both political and psychological support for the Shah. The Shah saw the United States as a powerful protector. In fact, he saw the United States as the most powerful of protectors. In the early days of the revolution, not long after the first serious violence had occurred in Qum, the Shah told an aide, "as long as the Americans support me, we can do and say whatever we want—and I am immovable."[2]

Such faith in the efficacy of the United States and in the steadfastness of its purposes was not surprising, for the United States was more than the most powerful ally of the Shah and of his country. The United States was the power ultimately responsible for the withdrawal of Soviet troops from Azerbaijan and Iranian Kurdistan in 1946. The United States was responsible for the 1953 coup which overthrew Prime Minister Mossadegh and restored the Shah to his throne. The United States proved massive military and economic assistance that allowed the Shah to stay in power after his restoration to the throne. The United States selected Iran to serve as regional superpower as part of President Nixon's reassessment of U.S.

global commitments. The United States was the principal external force which transformed the Shah from the diffident and terror-filled young ruler to the Light of the Aryans.

Not only was that powerful nation the most important political supporter of the Shah, but the United States also served crucial psychic functions. The Shah's own sense of well-being and esteem would rise or fall with its fate and especially with its support for his rule. When those eight presidents held the Shah in high esteem and valued his role as King of Kings and especially his status as the "policeman of the Persian Gulf," the Shah was personally aggrandized. For they permitted and even, unwittingly to be sure, encouraged the Shah's merger with them. In turn, the merger provided the Shah with psychic strength that contributed to his ability to function as the ruling monarch, to do Shah and not merely to be Shah.

As the decades of American support continued and his stature was enhanced through the Nixon-Kissinger designation of the Shah as U.S. proxy, his relation with the United States became an important contributor to his grandiosity. That relationship, the astounding new oil revenues, and the military equipment largely purchased from the United States with which the Shah was able to realize his ambitions for the Imperial Iranian Armed Forces contributed to a massive enhancement of the ruler's self-esteem. By the middle of the 1970s, his grandiosity was at its height—grandiosity which proved so deeply offensive to the Iranian people.

But that grandiosity which so contributed to his projection of power and even ruthlessness was virtually entirely external. It depended for its maintenance on the Shah's ability to sustain his belief in his selfobjects. When, for example, the Shah suspected that the esteem in which he was held by a U.S. president was diminished, so was he diminished. For the consequence of the U.S. president becoming a selfobject for the Shah was that the most significant aspects of the relationship between Iran and the United States occurred within his own mind.

The Shah had experienced damage to his self-esteem from a number of the U.S. presidents. Franklin Roosevelt would not leave his residence to call on the Shah when he visited Tehran for his meetings with Stalin and Churchill. Truman refused the Shah's requests for foreign assistance. Kennedy depreciated the Shah, calling him a despot. But the most damaging loss of esteem the Shah suffered from a U.S. president was from Jimmy Carter. The Shah believed that Carter sought to weaken the special relationship which the Shah had fashioned with so many of Jimmy Carter's predecessors. Whatever President Carter intended, there is no doubt that the Shah understood Carter's program to signal the waning significance of the Iranian-American relationship for the new U.S. president. With this waning significance, the American selfobject no longer served its primary function for the Shah—sustaining his self-esteem.

The decline in the value of the American relationship as a selfobject for the Shah was the fourth and final factor which destroyed his psychic structure. Regrettably for the Shah, for many of the Iranian people, and certainly for the United States, these four pillars of the Shah's psychic structure were all diminished at the very time when the opposition to the Shah in Iran was mounting, and specifically when armed opposition to the Shah was beginning. When the Shah most needed that structure, he could call on the fewest inner resources.

The relations between the U.S. presidents and the Shah were unusual in at least two respects—the number of U.S. presidents whose tenure spanned his rule and the intensity of the relationships between them and the Shah. But as an indicator of the extent of foreign influence in Iranian affairs, their relationships were not in the least unusual. It is impossible to grasp the nature of the tie between the Shah and those U.S. presidents only through psychoanalytic theory. Nor is it possible, in that way, to understand what the Shah's ties to those foreign leaders meant to the Iranian people, for a culture of deep ambivalence toward foreigners and foreign powers had been created in Iran. A contrary mix of deep xenophobia and profound admiration is the product of centuries of Iran's foreign dealings.

Those centuries of history have left the Iranian people with a conviction that foreign states use Iran for their own purposes, that their interference is at the expense of the collective interests of the Iranian people. Yet foreign interference has been perceived as so pervasive and so insidious that individual Iranians could best assure their fortune by linking their fates to foreign powers. As Firuz Kazemzadeh, a scholar of Iranian-British-Russian relations, could justifiably generalize about the nineteenth century, "Internal Persian political forces do not operate until there are assurances that external political forces will support and legitimize them."[3] While the Shah raised the involvement of the United States to a new level, it was a pattern which had long pertained in Iranian history. The Islamic Republic of Ayatollah Rouhollah Khomeini with its attacks on the "Great Satans"—the United States and the USSR—and its governing ideology toward the outside world—"neither East nor West"—sought to break the pattern of Iranian ambivalence to the outside world. That pattern of ambivalence began at least in the sixth century and has been reinforced by Iran's dealings with the outside world to the present.

As early as A.D. 590 or 591, for example, Chosroes II assumed the Sasanian throne of Iran, defeating the usurper Bahram Chubin, with the aid of troops sent by the Byzantine emperor Maurice.[4]

Foreign powers intervened in Iranian affairs with the intention of reaping benefits. They soon began to demand their price. Tahmasp II, for example, sought the assistance of the Russians in restoring his authority after the invasion of Iran and the overthrow of the Safavid dynasty by the Afghans in 1722. "On September 23, 1723, a treaty was signed whereby in return for the expulsions of the Afghans and the restoration of his authority, Tahmasp undertook to cede to Russia the Caspian provinces of Gilan, Mazandaran, and Gurgan and the towns of Baku, Darband, and their dependencies."[5]

The almost constant intervention of foreign powers into the affairs of Persia did not begin, however, until the despatch of a mission to Iran by Napoleon in 1798. From that date on, Iran found itself immersed in Great Power politics, as an arena on which the Europeans and later the Americans played out part of their rivalries and aspirations for domination and control. The French mission succeeded in wooing the Shah with the promise of financial assistance. The Treaty of Finkenstein between Iran and France followed in 1807. Article 8 of the treaty specified: "De son côté, S.M. l'Empereur de Perse, s'engage à interrompre avec l'Angleterre toutes communications politiques et commerciales, à déclarer la guerre immédiatement à cette puissance."[6] Article 12 of the treaty provided for the free passage of French troops through Persia to India.

Despite the explicitness of article 8, little of substance followed from the treaty other than British panic at the French threat to the Indian Empire. The result was immediate British attention to wooing the Shah away from his association with the French. In this task the British succeeded, largely through their willingness to subsidize the Persian throne. Treaties were signed between Iran and Great Britain in 1809 and 1812, with a definitive treaty being signed in 1814. In that treaty, specifically declared to be defensive,

all alliances between Persian and European nations were prevented from entering Persia, if hostile to Great Britain. The Shah was furthermore bound to induce the rulers of Khwarazm, Tataristan, Bokhara, and Samarcand to oppose any army which might attempt to cross in case of aggression, and the limits between Persia and Russia were to be determined by Persia, Russia, and Great Britain.[7]

In return for ceding some of his sovereignty to Great Britain, the Shah was amply rewarded. The British agreed to pay the Persian throne 150,000 pounds annually. The money was to be spent under the "superintendence" of the British minister.[8] Sir Gore Ousely, who negotiated the treaty for Great Britain, commented on its adoption: "It is now my sincere opinion that, having the safety of our Indian territories solely in view, it would be better policy to leave Persia in her present state of weakness and barbarism, than pursue an opposite plan."[9]

Meanwhile, Fath Ali Shah, the Persian ruler, had begun a war with Russia in 1804 in an attempt to recover the province of Georgia. Instead, Iran suffered a disastrous defeat and accepted the disadvantageous Treaty of Gulistan in 1813. Iran renounced all claims to Georgia and other territories by then under Russian control, but Iran also ceded to the Russians Baku and other areas still under Iranian control. Further, Iran agreed to maintain no navy on the Caspian Sea, thereby ceding future dominance to Russia. Russia, for its part, agreed to support Abbas Mirza, the Crown Prince, to secure his succession. "Thus," as Sir Percy Sykes put it, "for his personal advantage, the heir apparent conceded to Russia the whole of the territories in dispute."[10]

The difficulties between Iran and Russia were far from settled with the signing of the Treaty of Gulistan. Russian imperial expansion continually ran up against territories considered by the Shah to be under Iranian suzerainty. After Russia seized one of these territories, war broke out again. Once again Iran was defeated and, on February 22, 1828, accepted the Treaty of Turkmanchai, "the most disastrous treaty ever imposed on Iran."[11]

The treaty imposed such onerous financial obligations on Iran that the country incurred its first foreign debt to make the requisite reparations to Russia. In addition, the treaty gave Russia extraterritoriality—the right to try Russian citizens accused of crimes in Iran in Russian courts, thus effectively removing them from Iranian sovereignty. Once Russia won that prerogative, the other European states were quick to demand, and receive, comparable privileges. Worse, Iranian religious minorities, claiming they could not receive justice in Islamic courts, sought and received protection from the foreign states. Thus did the Treaty of Turkmanchai establish the rationale for the intervention of the great powers in the affairs of Iran. For the remainder of the century, indeed, for the remainder of the rule of the Qajars and the Pahlavis, until the success of the Iranian Revolution in 1979, that foreign intervention occurred with dismal regularity.

Intervention, not surprisingly, was portrayed as advancing the best interests of Iran. Indeed, it often did. But the issue was not, in the first instance, in whose interest the Great Powers were intervening. The question was who would decide—Iranians themselves or foreign diplomats— what the best interests of Iran were and how they could be most effectively advanced. Not long after the signing of the Treaty of Turkmanchai and the establishment of a pattern of British and Russian intervention, a resolution of that question was demonstrated. Fath Ali Shah had died and the succession was in doubt. Abbas Mirza was not to succeed his father, as had been specified in the first Iranian-Russian treaty, for he had already passed away. Instead, a succession struggle erupted between Muhammad, the son of Abbas Mirza, and his uncles, two of Abbas Mirza's brothers, Farman Farma, the governor of Fars Province, and Zill ul-Sultan, the governor of Tehran. Sir Percy Sykes explains what happened.

Fortunately for the rightful heir, the British Envoy, Sir John Campbell, was at Tabriz [the traditional seat of the Persian Crown Prince and the home of Abbas Mirza and his son, Muhammad], and by his assistance, both material and moral, and that of the Russian representative, the new Shah was able to march on Teheran at the head of a considerable force commanded by Sir Henry Lindsay Bethune. The circumstance that he was accompanied by the Ministers of Great Britain and Russia caused the desertion of Zill ul-Sultan's adherents, and the Pretender hastened to submit and was present at the coronation of his nephew. Farman Farma was a more dangerous rival, and the English General was soon marching south to attack him. Isfahan [the capital of Fars Province] was reached by a forced march and shortly after, the rebel army was surprised in a fog near Kumishah. I have visited the site of the battle, which was decided by artillery fire against which the nomad horsemen would not stand. Farman Farma fled, but was captured and died on the way to prison at Ardebil.[12]

With the coming to power of Muhammad Shah in 1834, the British initiated a pattern of intervention in the affairs of Iran, particularly in matters of succession, which gave them unparalleled influence over the domestic politics of the country. As Lord Curzon, the British foreign minister, was to observe in later years,

It may safely be predicted that any extravagant or savage exercise of the royal prerogative such as has been a familiar incident in the Persian history of the past, will rarely occur, if at all, in the future, and that in any case, it will prove an exceptional, instead of a normal feature of government. This remarkable change is to be attributed to the permanent presence of foreign ministers and the electric telegraph.[13]

The British, who controlled the telegraph spanning Iran and linking London with New Delhi, were dominant. The Russians struggled for power but were no match.

The presence of "foreign ministers" in Iran gave rise to another practice which demonstrated the significance of foreign powers for Iranian domestic politics. The Iranians long had the custom of taking *bast*, refuge, at religious shrines. Traditionally such shrines were considered inviolable to the political authorities. But increasingly, in the nineteenth century, the representatives of the crown took it upon themselves to enter the grounds of Iran's most sacred religious sites to capture a suspect. Perhaps the most celebrated case of violating the sanctity of *bast* on the grounds of a religious site occurred in 1891, when Seyyed Jamal ed din al Afghani sought escape from the rage of the Shah by taking refuge on the grounds of the Shah Abdul Azim mosque. Nasr ed din Shah ordered al Afghani arrested, and he was dragged from the mosque.

As the state refused to recognize the sanctity of religious sites for the taking of *bast*, Iranians fled to places under the control of foreigners. Foreign legations and even British telegraph stations became places of inviolable sanctuary for Iranians. They were used for that purpose as early as 1848, when Iranians seeking to escape the wrath of the chief minister fled to the British and Russian legations.[14] But the practice culminated in typical Persian excess during the Iranian Constitutional Revolution of 1905–7. In July 1906, Seyyed Abdullah Behbehani, one of the most outspoken religious leaders demanding a "House of Justice" and a constitution from the Shah, elicited British aid and received permission to use the parklike grounds of the summer British embassy for the taking of *bast*. Some eighteen thousand Iranians camped throughout the embassy grounds, paralyzing the economic life of the capital and enacting a revolution through a foreign protected sit-in. The British chargé d'affaires of necessity became a mediator with the monarch, seeking to protect the grounds of his embassy. Thus it came to be believed, by Iranians and foreigners alike, that the British were responsible for the Shah's granting a constitution to his subjects.[15]

The constitutionalists, or "liberals" as they came to be called, were to be disappointed shortly after the Shah consented to the granting of the first constitution to be prescribed in the Middle East. For those who sought to limit the power of the Shah came to realize that the Great Powers very much had their own agendas. On August 31, 1907, the so-called Anglo-Russian Convention was signed at Saint Petersburg. The convention divided Iran into three zones; the largest zone in the north included the cities of Tabriz, Kermanshah, Isfahan, Mashhad, and the capital, Tehran. It was designated the "Russian sphere of influence." The British sphere was restricted to a relatively small zone in southeastern Iran along the border with Afghanistan and the territory between Iran and the British Empire in India. The rest of the country, including much of the Persian Gulf coast, was designated the "neutral sphere."

In their formal declarations the two states pledged to "respect the integrity and independence of Persia"and to provide "equal advantages for the trade and industry of all other nations."[16] They then proceeded to deny to each other or to "the subjects of third powers" any commercial access to the other's "spheres of influence."[17] Despite the mutually declared intentions of Britain and Russia, the Persians reacted with outrage when news of the convention first appeared in Iran on September 4, 1907. The outrage in Tehran was so great that the British minister, Sir Cecil Spring-Rice, submitted an official document to the government of Iran, explaining and attempting to justify the convention. He assured the Iranian government that

hitherto antagonism has existed between England and Russia, each of whom has endeavored to prevent the continuation of the other in Persia and had this antagonism been prolonged in the present uncertain state in Persia, one or both of these two powers might have been tempted to interfere in the internal affairs of Persia, so as not to allow the other to profit by the existing state of things. . . . This Agreement is injurious neither to the interests of Persia nor to those of any other nation, since it binds only England and Russia not to embark on any course of action in Persia calculated to injure the interests of the other, and so in the future to deliver Persia from those demands which in the past have proved so injurious to the progress of her political aspirations.[18]

Whatever the promises made by the British minister, few in Tehran accepted his assurances. Instead, it was believed that the two states had initiated a process for the ultimate dismantling of Iran and the incorporation of its parts into the encroaching empires of Britain and Russia.

Actually, the dismantling of Iran does not appear to have been the goal of Russia and Great Britain. By then, they understood the value of buffer states between their two empires. Buffers would minimize the possibilities of direct conflict arising between their expanding domains. They maintained the independence and neutrality of Afghanistan for this purpose, even appending territories not previously part of Afghanistan—the Wakhan corridor—so there would be no common border between the two empires. So, apparently, they would keep Iran unified and neutral.[19] But this did not mean that the politics of Tehran would be left to the wishes of the Persians. If Iran was to serve as a buffer between the two states, then the regime in Tehran had to act to maintain its buffer status.

The brilliant Russian minister Count Witte wrote in his memoirs that he always considered the 1907 Convention a testimony to the weakness of Russia following its defeat in the Russo-Japanese War and the turmoil of the 1905 Revolution. Count Witte argued that the Russians conceded two crucial points to the British. First, the northern zone of Iran had traditionally—in his own words, "from time immemorial"—been a Russian sphere of influence. Furthermore, "with the conquest of the Southern parts of the Caucasus, formerly provinces of Persia and Turkey, the Northern part of Persia was naturally destined, so to speak, to become a part of the Russian Empire. To prepare that eventuality, we sacrificed a great deal of our blood and treasure."[20] By signing the convention, Witte argued, Russia gained nothing it did not already have and in fact abandoned the hope of annexing northern Iran to its empire.

But this was not the only flaw in the convention for Witte. In addition, there was an even more serious shortcoming. "As for the Persian central Government," he wrote, "it was to be controlled by Russia and Great Britain acting jointly. Since Teheran, the seat of the central Government, is situated in the North, this meant British influence in the North as well as in the South."[21] Since none of the published articles of the 1907 Convention indicates a decision by the two powers to share responsibility for the management of the Iranian central government, the two powers must have shared unpublished understandings. Thus was realized the deepest foreboding of the Iranians.[22]

Whatever the nature of the understandings reached between Great Britain and Russia, their bitter rivalry for domination in Iran continued. In fact, the convention does not appear to have even moderated their bitter competition for control over Iranian politics. The revelation of the convention's signing served to undermine the status of Britain in Iran, status it had won among the constitutionalists for providing its embassy grounds for *bast* and its minister for negotiations with the Shah. Of Russia, few Persians, except perhaps for the Shah, expected anything different.

In February 1908, a bomb was placed on the roof of the royal automobile believed to contain Muhammad Ali Shah. The Shah was in fact ensconced in a carriage immediately behind his limousine. The bomb exploded, slightly injuring the Shah's French chauffeur while convincing the Shah that the constitutionalists now sought his life and no longer merely his political prerogatives. With the encouragement of the Russians and, eventually, with their insistence and that of Colonel Liakhoff, the Russian commander of the Persian Cossack Brigades, the Shah ordered the elimination of the constitutionalists. The Cossack Brigade bombarded the Majles, destroyed its records, arrested and executed the leading constitutionalists, and looted their homes and property.

But the constitutionalists were far from eliminated. In fact two separate "armies" were raised, one drawn from the Bakhtiari tribe in the south and another from Tabriz in the northwest of Iran. They began simultaneous marches to Tehran, and despite intervention by Russian troops despatched from Baku as well as by the Cossack Brigade, constitutionalist forces entered Tehran in July of 1909 and deposed Muhammad Ali Shah.[23] Accompanied by a combined guard furnished by the British and Russian legations, the constitutionalists installed as Shah the deposed ruler's twelve-year-old son, Ahmad.

The British and Russians entered negotiations with the government of Iran on behalf of Muhammad Ali. Through their intervention, he was awarded an annual stipend and allowed to leave Iran, under the British and Russian flags, for exile in Odessa. The removal of the Shah did not, of course, result in the removal of the influence of the British and the Russians. The latter, in fact, appear to have refused to give up on the possibility of restoring Muhammad Ali Shah to his throne and in 1911 actually facilitated his efforts to return to Iran, from Russia, with a force of armed men. The Persians withstood his efforts, and the former Shah once again retreated north, back to Russia. In contravention to the accord signed at the time of his deposition, the British and Russians insisted that the Iranian government maintain his pension. Thereafter, finally, the former Shah disappeared from the historical record.

Between the defeat of Muhammad Shah's efforts at restoration and the outbreak of the Great War, there were continued efforts by the Russians and the British to maintain a dominant hold over the politics of Iran. Both powers had their allies in the capital. Those allies could be mobilized to ensure continued British-Russian dominance over the politics of Iran. An example of the domination of the Great Powers and the ways in which it was maintained was baldly demonstrated in the case of Morgan Shuster, an American.[24] Shuster was brought to Iran in May 1911 by the "Democrats," who then dominated the Persian government. Shuster was given near-dictatorial powers to rectify the appalling financial situation of the central government and especially to provide it with the revenues it would need to reduce its dependency for regular financing on loans from Britain and Russia. The loans further deepened the control of those states and progressively undermined the independence of Iran. This was especially the case inasmuch as the British and Russians took control of the customs houses of Iran to ensure that their receipts were used directly to pay the interest due foreign loans. But Shuster became an intolerable threat to the interests of the two states when the Majles granted him the authority to establish a Treasury gendarmerie to command the force necessary to collect the taxes due the government of Iran.

When Shuster decided to confiscate the property of the brother of Muhammad Ali, the ex-Shah, on the grounds that he had assisted his brother's efforts to force his return from Russia to seize the throne, the Russians acted. Claiming that the prince owed money to the Russian Bank, the Russian ambassador forbade the confiscation of the royal wealth. Shuster sent his gendarmes against the orders of the Russian diplomats. In short order, the Russians demanded the ouster of Shuster, an ultimatum refused by the Majles. When the Russians despatched their troops to march on the capital, the Iranians succumbed and the treasurer general, after an eight-month effort to wrest control over the financial affairs of Iran, was formally dismissed.

While the British and the Russians clearly dominated Iran, the Russians were in the superior position inasmuch as their troops were stationed in major garrisons throughout their sphere of influence in the northern third of Iran. Their domination was demonstrated in 1912, when the Russians sent troops to the city of Mashhad, site of the shrine of Imam Reza, the tomb of the eighth Shi'ite Imam and the most holy place in Iran. The Russians complained that an Iranian supporter of the former Shah had taken *bast* in the shrine in order to build support for the return of Muhammad Ali Shah. That the former monarch was in exile in Russia and the troublemaker was a Russian agent provocateur did not dissuade the Russians from using the ruse to demonstrate their power. Russian troops bombed the holy shrine, having already spirited their agent out of its precincts, flaunting their military superiority and political dominance.

The British did have strong support from the tribes of the south; their military power had chastened the Cossack Brigade in the showdown over the constitution preceding the deposition of Muhammad Ali. But the power of the tribes was no match for the Russian army stationed in Iran, much less the Russian troops stationed immediately across the border.

The British regularly protested the Russian "occupation" of Iran. And the Russians periodically withdrew troops from northern Iran. Thus in the spring of 1914, Sir Grey reported to Parliament that the Russians had 14,200 troops in Iran, having withdrawn some 3,300 in the course of the past year.[25] But despite the periodic withdrawals, it was increasingly clear that Iran was rapidly losing its independence. The Constantinople Agreement of March 1915 seemed to seal its fate. In the agreement, reached between Russia, Great Britain, and France—dividing the anticipated spoils of the Great War—Russia was given permission to annex Constantinople, European Turkey, and the straits between the Black Sea and the Mediterranean. Moreover, it was recognized that Russia "should gain full freedom of action in her own zone of influence."[26] "Full freedom of action" had that ominous ring of annexation, an entirely plausible goal given Russia's past behavior in the Caucasus and central Asia, as well as in Iran and Turkey. In return, Russia agreed to allow the inclusion of the neutral zone of Iran in the British sphere.

A German adventurer was dispatched to Iran to raise the tribes against the British and Russians while harassing their troops and destroying their bases. He sought to do for the Germans in Iran what T. E. Lawrence was doing for the British in Arabia.[27] The Russians bore the burden of the fighting against the Ottomans in the west and north of Persia. The British did not become a factor until 1916, when they managed to despatch troops from India into their sphere of influence in southeastern Iran. Acting under the provisions of the Constantinople Agreement, the British launched operations throughout the neutral zone as well.

What saved Iran, at least in the short run, was the Bolshevik Revolution and the decision of the revolutionary regime to withdraw from the war. The Treaty of Brest-Litovsk, signed on March 3, 1918, specified among its other provisions that both Ottoman and Russian troops should withdraw immediately from Iran. This the Russians proceeded to do, more through the disintegration of their armed forces than the orderly march of a disciplined force. The Ottomans continued their military action in the Russian territories east of the Caspian Sea and the British invested the rest of Iran, even sending a force under the command of Maj. Gen. L. C. Dunsterville to Baku to prevent an Ottoman (or Bolshevik) capture of that Russian city on the Caspian.

Dunsterville was unable to defend Baku from the Ottomans but managed an orderly withdrawal by sea to the Persian port of Enzeli. From there he stretched his forces across northern Iran, to prevent incursions by either the Ottomans or the Bolsheviks. The British then organized a fleet of warships on the Caspian Sea, in 1918, which it used to capture the dockyards of Baku. When the Ottomans withdrew from the city, the British captured it, in the process aiding the anti-Bolshevik Central-Caspian Dictatorship which had succeeded in ousting the Bolsheviks from the surrounding territory. The British navy on the Caspian then attacked all Bolshevik vessels on the Caspian, and "every Soviet vessel that dared to show its nose outside of the Port of Astrakhan was either sent to the bottom, or driven back to their refuge, from whence they did not attempt to venture again."[28]

Within Iran, British troops attacked and ultimately destroyed the military force of Kuchik Khan, called the *jangalis,* the jungle dwellers, after their refuge in the tropical rain forests along the Caspian coast of Iran. Kuchik Khan was committed to expelling all foreign powers from Iran and restoring the independence of the state. To achieve that end, he was not averse to accepting aid from the Germans, the Ottomans, or the Russians. But there is little doubt that he was an instrument of none of those powers. When he attacked the British forces in northern Iran in 1917, his troops were devastated by British guns. His defeat marked the end of his threat to both the British and the government of Iran.

In the midst of all the fighting by foreign forces across the countryside, it was remarkable that there remained any Iranian government whatsoever. In affect, it was a government in name alone. Its power was limited by the absence of a bureaucracy through which it could extend its writ, especially an armed force, and, most decisively, by the control of the Great Powers and, after the withdrawal of the Russians, by the British alone. As the British minister wrote to London in early 1917,

possibly no country on earth suffers so much from the Legation Government as does Persia. It is doubtful if a single Prime Minister has been appointed in Persia during my stay at this post except at the request and earnest demand of some Legation. Even Governors of Provinces are almost universally appointed through Legations. Of course, such activity is usually confined to the British and Russian Legations.[29]

Shortly after the British minister had made his observations, "Legation Government" was to be left exclusively to the British. In a stirring decree issued over the signatures of Lenin and Stalin, the Soviet Council of People's Commissars proclaimed:

Mohammadans of the East! Persians, Turks, Arabs, and Indians . . . ! We declare that the secret treaties of the deposed Tsar are now null and void. The Russian Republic and its Government . . . are opposed to the annexation of foreign lands. Constantinople must remain in the hands of the Mohammedans.

We declare that the treaty for the division of Persia is null and void. Immediately after the cessation of military activities . . . the Persians will be guaranteed the right of free self-determination.[30]

By the end of the First World War, then, British power and prestige in Iran were at a peak never before attained, nor ever to be attained again. The Russians had withdrawn and the Bolsheviks were still an unknown quantity. The Germans and Ottomans were defeated. The French and Americans exerted a diplomatic presence, but an inconsequential one. Finally, the British had infested Iran with troops. The South Persia Rifles, the Baghdad Command, the East Persian Cordon Field Force, and General Malleson's Mission effectively controlled the Iranian countryside. General Norris and his flotilla had made the Caspian Sea a British lake.

All that was left for the British was to control the politics of the center. This they attempted to do through formulating a treaty which would make Iran a virtual satrapy of Great Britain. Lord Curzon had concluded that a treaty with Iran would guarantee British control of India indefinitely and provide Britain with a security zone stretching across the underside of Soviet Russia. To fashion the treaty with Iran, he sent Sir Percy Cox, an official of the government of India. Cox began his work by ensuring the friendship of the government with which he would have to negotiate the proposed treaty.

In May of 1918, the British began paying a monthly subsidy of fifteen thousand toumans to the Shah as long as he retained Vossugh ud-Dowleh as prime minister.[31] Vossugh, it is not difficult to imagine, was known as the most pro-British politician in Iran. There was no better negotiating partner for the British. After nine months of discussions, the "Agreement between the Government of Great Britain and Persia" was signed on August 9, 1919. Lord Curzon informed his cabinet colleagues of the purpose of the agreement:

To come to some arrangement with the Persian Government by which British interests in that part of the world should be safeguarded in future from a recurrence of the recent shocks, and by which Persia, incurably feeble and unable to stand by herself, should be given support that would enable her to maintain her position among the independent nations of the world.[32]

After the mandatory pledge on the part of the government of Great Britain to respect the independence and integrity of Persia, the agreement went on to specify that after consultation, the government of Great Britain would provide advisers for whatever part of the Persian government might require assistance. Britain would also supply officers and munitions for the formation of a centralized military institution, would help Iran revise its tariffs, construct roads and railways, and would also loan two million pounds sterling to the government of Persia which could be used to pay the British for the advisers and material they were supplying until such time as the revenue sources of the government of Iran could be sufficiently ordered so that they would be able to pay these costs directly.

It was clear that this agreement was an extraordinary piece of work. In return for an insignificant loan, the government of Persia agreed to cede dominance over its internal affairs to another government. As an astute observer of Iran noted, the agreement could easily have been the vehicle for "converging Persia into a semi-autonomous part of the British Empire."[33] The Shah used his subsidies from the British to finance his royal pleasure through foreign travel. When Sir Percy Cox in Tehran received confirmation that the September installment of the subsidy had been paid to the Shah's British bank account, the Shah left for an extended tour of Europe. He spent the entire fall in Great Britain and the winter in the south of France before returning to Tehran in the spring, through Baghdad, where he received full British honors.[34]

In addition to the beneficence of the Shah, guaranteed through his retainer, the British cause was most facilitated by the participation of the three senior Iranian politicians known as the most Anglophile of the Persian elites. Vossugh ud-Dowleh, the president of the Council and the prime minister; Prince Firuz Mirza, the foreign minister; and Prince Akbar Mirza, a grandson of Nasr ed din Shah, were the triumverate who negotiated and signed the treaty on behalf of Iran. As Sir Clarmont Skrine commented, "they were known to have the ear of the British Minister and profited personally from that knowledge; like Chinese warlords they had funds salted away in foreign territory; and it is a fact that . . . they were promised asylum within the 'British Empire' should the necessity arise."[35]

While it appeared to all that the 1919 Agreement was a "done deal," the two governments made what later proved a fatal mistake. They failed to submit the treaty for the approval of the Majles, approval required by the constitution of Iran. The Persian triumverate were not eager to convene the Parliament which had not met since 1915 because to do so would necessitate submitting their resignations. And even in Persian politics, their resignation might be followed by a refusal of the Majles, always the first (and last) line in the defense of Persian nationalism, to reappoint them, especially after their signing of what was increasingly coming to be seen as a scandalous betrayal of Persian sovereignty.

The United States did not help the British cause. The U. S. minister in Tehran issued a statement which was to embolden the domestic opposition to the agreement. He declared that "the American Government is surprised to learn of the recent Anglo-Persian Treaty which would seem to indicate that Persia does not wish America's aid or support."[36]

But the decisive foreign blow to the treaty was administered by the British themselves. They proceeded to implement the provisions of the treaty without its having been approved by the Majles. British personnel and money began to arrive in Iran. The Soviet government confirmed its renunciation of all the inequitable treaties which had previously been forced on Iran by the Czar. It reiterated its intention to abolish the hated practice of capitulations, or extraterritoriality. In that system, foreign nationals and Persians who were able to acquire the protection of foreign embassies were tried in foreign courts for offenses committed in Iran. The Soviet Union announced its intention of signing a new treaty with Iran which would codify these understandings between two equal partners.

Then quite inexplicably to the principal actors in Iran, the British determined to trim their commitments and announced their intention to begin pulling their armed forces out of Iran. Whereas the British had been able to boast a line of troops from Baghdad through India, the Persian link was largely removed. Only General Dunsterville was left to hold Azerbaijan, bordering the USSR, with a force of five hundred men, renamed Norperforce. Winston Churchill saw the danger in such a policy and complained bitterly to Lord Curzon in a letter dated May 20, 1920.

There is something to be said for making peace with the Bolsheviks. There is also something to be said for making war upon them. There is nothing to be said for a policy of doing all we can to help strengthen them, to add to their influence and prestige, to weaken those who are fighting against them, and at the same time leaving weak British forces tethered in dangerous places where they can easily and suddenly be overwhelmed. I do not see how anything we can do within the present limits of our policy can possible avert the complete loss of British influence throughout the Caucasus, Transcapia, and Persia. . . . I should have been only too ready to have helped you with a different policy which, properly supported, would now have ended this criminal regime in Russia. But in view of the decisions which were taken . . . and in view of the uninstructed state of public opinion, I think that is impossible. . . . I must absolutely decline to continue to share responsibility for a policy of mere bluff.[37]

In this, as in so many matters, Churchill's prescience was soon to be demonstrated. In the spring of 1920, the Soviets landed a large force at the Persian port of Enzeli. In the process they destroyed the remnants of the former British fleet on the Caspian which had since been turned over to the White Russian leader, General Denikin. Norperforce, confronted by an enemy of overwhelming superiority, withdrew, leaving the Soviet force to occupy the Caspian region.

Meanwhile, a religious leader, Sheikh Muhammad Khiaban, who had lived in the Caucasus during one of its more revolutionary periods, proclaimed an independent state in the Persian province of Azerbaijan, named Azadistan, the Land of the Free. The principal plank in Khiaban's platform was the elimination of British influence from Tehran.[38] To the British, these events had implications which went far beyond the relatively insignificant territories in northern Iran. The advancing Soviet troops, by British calculations, "will, no doubt, make every effort to establish close relations with the Republic of Azerbaijan and the Turks with the object of securing the Baku oil fields . . . and to form a coalition of Mohammedan states for the overthrow of British rule in India, Mesopotamia, and Egypt. . . . This is their last and chief aim."[39]

The combination of the Russian advance, the demands of the separatists, and the unpopularity of the 1919 Agreement resulted in the collapse of the pro-British triumverate and the installation of Moshir ud-Dowleh as the new prime minister. This put the British in a dilemma. The British had paid a subsidy to the Shah for retaining the Anglophile politicians. Moshir was no Anglophile. The British ambassador proposed maintaining the subsidy. The Shah, he cabled London, "is now thoroughly well disposed towards us and determined to work with us in his rather odd way. Best method of keeping him in this frame of mind is to give him or obtain for him as much money as we can for that is what he loves most in the world."[40]

The Shah may have been favorably disposed, but as one of his first governing acts the new prime minister announced his refusal to submit the 1919 Agreement to the Majles for ratification, thus decisively ending Great Britain's hopes of controlling the internal affairs of Persia and establishing a cordon of dominated states across the southern reaches of the new Soviet Union. Moshir then despatched a mission to Moscow which negotiated a treaty originally proposed by the Soviet government. The 1921 Agreement, which established formal diplomatic relations between the states, assured the Soviets that the government of Iran would not allow Persian territory to be used by any forces hostile to the USSR. In the event such forces occupied Iran, the agreement gave the Soviets the authority to send their troops into Iran to eliminate the enemy forces.

The stature of the British had taken the most remarkable turn. From a position of apparently unassailable dominance the British had fallen, in the course of slightly more than one year, to losing any standing in Iran whatsoever. Lord Curzon quickly grasped the implications of these new developments.

Three conclusions seem now forced upon us: (1) that the Anglo-Persian Agreement will never be genuinely accepted as it stands; (2) that Persia will not be able, in our lifetime, to raise an army fit to oppose an external enemy; and (3) that any policy involving direct financial or military assistance on our part, must inevitably prevent growth of that nationalist spirit which is, in the long run, our real defense against the incursion of Bolshevism. . . .

As regards external enemies, as soon as Persia realizes that she must look after her external defence herself, she will make shift with her own Oriental methods of diplomacy. Our own disappearance into the background will rob Bolshevism of her one valid excuse. . . .

In short, we should leave Persia to work out her own salvation.[41]

The British announcement came shortly thereafter. Beginning April 1, 1921, all British troops would be removed from Iran. Widespread insecurity and fear swept the country with the realization that no military force would exist to impede the southward sweep of Bolshevik forces, perhaps aligned with Sheikh Khiaban. The British considered a variety of measures to prevent the advance of the Bolshevik forces once their own military was removed. They discussed the possibility of establishing a new dynasty in the hands of the Bakhtiari tribe in southern Iran but rejected the idea on the grounds that the Bakhtiari leaders were hated for their rapacious and oppressive rule.[42] The British also contemplated the establishment of a republic, a possibility they rejected on the grounds that any republic in Iran would shortly assume the form of a Soviet republic.[43] What they were certain of, however, was that the "GREAT DIFFICULTY is that all measures to be taken must be devised and carried out in agreement with a Government and Medjliss who know that any sign of Anglo-Persian cooperation may furnish Bolsheviks a pre-text for aggression, which for several months, at least, after withdrawal of British troops there will be no means of resisting."[44]

Actually, the British had long ago concluded what means were necessary for the salvation of Iran. Shortly after the turmoil of the constitutional revolution and the signing of the 1907 Anglo-Russian accord on Persia, at least one British observer of the Iranian scene had concluded that "Persia is not yet, and will not for a couple of generations to come, be fit for representative institutions. Persia stands in need of a strong man to prevent her falling to pieces from her own inherent weaknesses; but, so far, no such man has been found."[45]

It appears that by early 1921, such a man had been found. Forbes-Leith, a British subject living in Iran at the time, noted that "the British cooperated with Reza Khan and Zia ed Din, rendering every assistance to the former and enabling him to collect some sort of an army from the rag tag and bobtail forces in Kasvin. Everything that they lacked in the way of arms and ammunition was found for them by the British."[46] It is impossible, of course, to establish conclusively that this interpretation of the events of the February 21, 1921, coup is valid. On that day, Reza Khan, a senior officer in the Cossack Brigade, and Seyyed Zia ed Din Tabataba'i, a prominent, pro-British journalist, marched from Qazvin to Tehran, overthrew the existing government, and forced Ahmad Shah to install them as minister of war and prime minister, respectively. But it strains credulity to believe that they were able to marshal their forces or stage their coup without the consent if not the participation of the British. For one thing, British troops were garrisoned in Qazvin and the coup plotters would never even have been able to begin their march on the capital without consent from the British. Little in the way of direct evidence from either governments validates this view of the coup, but there is a great deal of indirect evidence. For example, the British emissary in Tehran reported a series of conversations which he had with Seyyed Zia after the coup. The new prime minister stressed that in order to avoid the enmity of the Soviets, "the pro-British character of the new administration should for the present as far as possible be disguised."[47]

No one, of course, was more concerned with rumors of the English authorship of the coup than Reza Khan. On its first anniversary he issued a proclamation "intended to put a final end to all speculation about the event."[48] Reza stated:

Since, unfortunately, meaningless words have taken the place of facts, and personal spite has been working to hinder progress, some of the newspapers have now, after a full year, begun discussing the question of the coup d'etat of February 21, 1921, and its author. . . . Is it not ridiculous to search for the author of the coup in my presence? . . . I advise these journalists to take thought and not to pretend to believe that anyone could make a coup d'etat. Only men could take such a step who had realized the extent of foreign oppression and the incapacity of our statesmen; men who had spent their lives in the army; men who had perceived the evil designs of foreign advisers aimed at the destruction of the country; men who had risked their lives in deserts and mountains in the service of their country; men who deplored the fact that mean and incompetent politicians were managing to use all these sacrifices for their personal gain.

. . . This idea could never have been initiated on promenades, in parks, in gardens, or in heated rooms. A man was needed who had experienced the poverty, misfortunes, and sufferings of the military as opposed to the luxury and irresponsibility of the ruling class in Tehran. Do not make a mistake. Do not blindly fumble in search of the author of the coup d'etat. I consider it an honor to declare myself to be the real author of the coup d'etat. It was I who took this path and it is I who has no regrets about it. . . .

This idea had not entered my mind only last year on the 21st of February. The idea was never put into my mind. It was very long ago that I became aware of the appalling misery of my compatriots. . . . I could not stand for the sale of my unhappy countrymen to foreigners. . . . I could not be a mere spectator of the tragic conditions of Gilan . . . ruined by the brutality of a group of bandits [Sheikh Khiaban]. . . . It was beyond my power to be content with seeing the destitute widows of Kerman and Baluchistan paying 5 million tomans every year for the army while there were robbers at Qom, Kashan, and even at the gates of Tehran, plundering the people and purchasing immunity from government officials in the capital.

Nobody with the least sense considered it fair that the army, from private to officers, should be mowed down by regiments in fighting foreigners and others while the government devoured their salaries and sold military ranks to the highest bidders. The nation and the government disgraced themselves in the eyes of foreigners and the blood of the self-sacrificing troops froze with shame.[49]

Reza Shah clearly did not succeed in countering the charge that the coup was a foreign product. What he did manage to do through his words, but much more effectively through his actions, was to disabuse the people of Iran that the coup was the creation of other Iranians, in particular Seyyed Zia, whom he quickly ousted from power in the postcoup government.

It was considered, ever after, a serious offense to suggest the existence of any connection between the British and the coup d'etat. Thus the trial of Dr. Mohammad Mossadegh, following his overthrow in August 1953, was interrupted by the presiding judge when the former prime minister explained why he had refused to remount the statues of Reza Shah after they had been pulled down by angry demonstrators. "If we were once again to place the statues upon their pedestals then it would have hurt the prestige of the Iranian nation, because the late Shah was directly supported by the British."[50]

What is important about the testimony of the former prime minister is that he articulated a widespread belief in Iran that not only was Reza Shah somehow an agent of the British but that the coup was, in fact, engineered by the British. There is, of course, a great deal of difference between the coup being engineered by the British or merely being supported by it.[51] But that distinction was lost on many Iranians for whom the legitimacy of the Pahlavi dynasty, from its inception, was suspect because it was seen as the product of another foreign stratagem to control the destiny of Iran.

Of profound significance for any understanding of Iran is an appreciation of what issue lay beneath the suspicions of British complicity in the 1921 coup—a profound ambivalence about the role of foreigners in Iranian affairs. While it was assumed that all Iranian events of significance could be linked to foreign powers, there was also a thirst for freedom. As a British observer of Reza Shah's coup put it, "Persia is now sick of foreign interference."[52] But however much Iranians may have been "sick" of foreign interference, very few believed Iran could ever hope to escape it.

The ouster of Reza Shah, similar to the inception of his rule, strengthened the Iranian dual view of the role of foreigners. During his reign as Reza Shah Pahlavi, following his 1925 ouster of the Qajar dynasty and his crowning himself monarch, Reza Shah largely isolated himself from the intervention of foreign states. He could not free himself completely from dealing with the British because his principal source of revenue remained the Anglo-Iranian Oil Company which held the lease on Iran's producing oil fields. But Reza Shah strove to free Iran of foreign influences and translate the growing economic and military strength of the central government into a guarantor of Iranian independence. That attempt was shattered by the August 1941 invasion of Iran from the north by the Soviet Union and from the south by Great Britain.

By that date, the Nazis had swept to the outskirts of Moscow and Leningrad and German U-boats were decimating Allied relief shipments to the Soviet Union. In June of that year a coup demonstrating pro-Axis sympathies had taken place in Iraq. Reza Shah, meanwhile, had established close trade and political relations with Germany. The Allies wished to ensure that Iran did not fall to the Germans. One of the many scenarios which plagued the Allies was the possibility of a Nazi turn to the south within the USSR, a dash for the Soviet oil fields and Baku, and a continued march through Iran to the Persian Gulf, capturing the Iranian fields as well and, in the process, depriving the British of Iranian oil.

To prevent a German takeover of Iran and to turn Reza Shah's greatest physical feat—the construction of the trans-Iranian railroad—into an Allied asset for shipment of war materials to the USSR, the British and Soviets determined on a preemptive takeover of the country. No efforts were made to negotiate with Reza Shah, in advance of the invasion, to ascertain his willingness to cooperate with the Allies against a German threat. Instead, British forces from Iraq and by sea from the Gulf moved through southwestern Iran as the Soviets moved in from the northwest. After three days of desultory fighting, the Iranian armed forces collapsed. Reza Shah's twenty-year dream of building an army which could guarantee the independence of Iran was shattered. With it was also shattered his rule. The victors demanded his abdication. He gathered his family, with the exception of the Crown Prince and his twin, the Princess Ashraf, and left for the Persian Gulf and exile in South Africa.

On September 16, 1941, the Crown Prince appeared before the Majles to swear his loyalty to the Constitution of 1905 and to announce his investiture as Mohammad Reza Shah Pahlavi, the reigning monarch. Thus, in the eyes of many Iranians, Reza Shah left power as he had entered it—a pawn of the Great Powers. His son suffered the same fate. He was placed on the throne by the British and the Russians, who saw his kingship as a useful device for their control of Iran. He would be the king, while the two occupying powers would retain the power to make the crucial decisions affecting their welfare in Iran. The Shah and his government could be entrusted with only the insignificant matters of governance. The Shah began his rule under the same cloud of suspicion as had his father—as a tool of foreign powers who had determined that his kingship suited their interests. The British, the Soviets, and the ruling dynasty were involved, in the eyes of many Iranians, in a *folie à trois,* each needing the other, each suspect. The Shah was the most berated of all, for he was seen as serving the interests of his foreign masters at the expense of the Iranian people. His authority derived from them, and to them, many Iranians argued, would go his principal fealty and service. It was not an auspicious beginning.

The pattern of involvement between the United States and Iran, at least initially, was totally different than that between Great Britain and the Soviet Union. The United States and Iran had signed a Treaty of Friendship and Commerce on December 13, 1856. The treaty pledged "sincere and constant good understanding" between the governments and peoples of the two states, provided for the establishment of diplomatic relations and consulates in both countries, and accorded most-favored-nation trading status to the goods of each country.[53] Despite the treaty and subsequent agreements, the United Sates was basically not involved in the politics of Iran until the Second World War.

Until then, the U.S. reputation in Iran was built not by any official diplomatic presence. Rather a small number of individual Americans had come to be widely known in Iran and highly esteemed for the selfless service they were perceived to have performed for the people of Iran. Perhaps the first American to have established a reputation for sacrifice in the cause of justice for Iran was Howard C. Baskerville. He was a teacher in the Tabriz Boy's School run by the American Presbyterian Mission. During the struggle between the constitutionalists and Mohammad Ali Shah, the ruler who had ordered the bombardment of the Majles and then disavowed the constitution, the nationalists had seized Tabriz, the second largest city in Iran and the seat of the Crown Prince. The Shah ordered loyal forces to lay siege to the city and starve the nationalists from their refuge. In an attempt to break through the siege and open a road through which food could be brought into the starving city, Baskerville was killed by the cossacks.

W. Morgan Shuster was another American who came to be seen as sacrificing his well-being in the disinterested service of the Iranian people. He accepted the post of treasurer general and reached Iran in 1911. His brief if ardent efforts and his failure to rationalize the finances of Iran have been noted above. His dismissal was due to British and Russian pressures on the Shah and the Majles. He clearly impinged on what they considered their rightful prerogatives. Again, the Iranians saw an American who had sacrificed for their well-being.

Yet another American was brought to Iran to reorganize its finances. Dr. Arthur C. Millspaugh arrived in Tehran on November 18, 1922, with full powers over Iranian government receipts and expenditures. Millspaugh served with distinction, ending his mission only when Reza Khan became prime minister and refused to tolerate Millspaugh's control over the finances of the government.

Elgin Groseclose was another American whose services to Iran are still remembered. He was a relief worker in Iran and the Caucusus after World War I. During World War II he returned as treasurer general of Iran to devise means of controlling the crippling inflation caused by Iran's foreign military occupation. He succeeded in bringing the inflation under control and helped revive Iran's shattered economy.

Perhaps the most revered American to serve Iran was Dr. Samuel Martin Jordan. Dr. Jordan devoted his life to the cause of education in Iran. In 1899 he became principal of Alborz College, Iran's only secondary school offering a "modern," that is, Western, curriculum. He served in that position until 1940 when Reza Shah insisted on the "Iranization" of all educational institutions. Many prominent Iranian officials and men of letters graduated from Alborz and remember, with reverence, the contributions Jordan made to Iran.

It was through the example of these Americans that the United States acquired a reputation in Iran as a disinterested party seeking no particular collective advantage, but rather the well-being of the people of Iran and their independence from the Great Powers, which sought only to establish their own dominion over the country. With the onset of the World War, however, the United States government became an active participant in the affairs of Iran, and from then onward, the U.S. reputation was altered. Inevitably, the United States came to be seen as another foreign player in the game of Iranian politics. And foreign players were not playing in the politics of Iran for the benefit of the people of Iran. The British and Russian invasion had been a starkly bold demonstration of the willingness of powerful states to alter Iranian political realities to suit their purposes. On January 29, 1942, the British and Russians, this time with Iran as a signatory as well, concluded the Tripartite Treaty of Alliance. Article 1 dutifully stated that the United Kingdom and the USSR "jointly and severally undertake to respect the territorial integrity, the sovereignty, and the political independence of Iran."[54] Despite these assurances, the treaty appears to have struck Iran much as did the news of the 1907 Agreement between the two powers, which had resulted in the parceling of Iran into spheres of influence. The first American troops arrived in Tehran by December of 1942. Known as the Persian Gulf Command, some thirty thousand Americans were stationed in Iran, moving goods from the Persian Gulf to the Soviet Union. The Americans maintained a truck convoy system from the Gulf directly to the Soviet Union and also operated the trans-Iranian railroad. By the end of the war, the trucks had carried over four hundred thousand tons of war material, and the railroad over four million tons of supplies to the USSR.[55]

Shortly after the arrival of American troops in Iran, the United States became a formal signatory to the Tripartite Treaty. A memorandum from the Division of Near Eastern Affairs of the Department of State set out a new vision for U.S. policy toward Iran.

The United States, alone, is in a position to build up Iran to the point at which it will stand in need of neither British nor Russian assistance to maintain order in its own house. If we go at this task whole-heartedly, we can hope to remove any excuse for a post-war occupation, partition, or tutelage of Iran. We can work to make Iran self-reliant and prosperous, open to the trade of all nations and a threat to none. In the meanwhile, we can so firmly establish disinterested American advisers in Iran that no peace conference could even consider a proposal to institute a Russian or British protectorate or to "recognize the predominance" of Russian or British interests. If Iran needs special assistance of a material character, we can provide it and so remove any cause for claims for compensation by other powers. We can forestall loans carrying with them control of the customs or other servitudes upon the Iranian Government. If railroads, ports, highways, public utilities, industries are to be built, we can build them and turn them over to the Iranian people free of any strings.[56]

What was never stated in the memorandum which laid the ground work for the next thirty-five years of U.S. policy toward Iran was the possibility that absent an Iran fully capable of standing on its own, the United States would replace Britain and the Soviet Union as the principal foreign protector of the integrity of Iran. While the proposed policy was premised on the idealism which drove U.S. policy, its full consequences went unexamined. U.S. policy was launched on a course from which it would veer only slightly during the rule of Mohammad Reza Shah. The United States largely succeeded in freeing Iran from the domination of Great Britain and Russia. It pursued a policy which also went a long way to freeing Iran from the domination of the United States. But, finally, the United States replaced those two Great Powers as the principal foreign power in Iran. It did not control the Shah as those states had the Qajar monarchs, but the relationship which was established between Mohammad Reza Shah and the United States was so intense that American influence was paramount, if not always explicitly exercised or consciously followed.

The arrival of President Roosevelt for the Tehran Conference in November 1943, along with Churchill and Stalin, was another stage in the movement of the United States toward dominant influence in Iran. The Allies issued a declaration pledging the evacuation of Iranian territory after the conclusions of the hostilities and pledged to aid Iran in the reconstruction of its economy following the trials of the war years.

In addition, President Roosevelt invited the Shah to meet with him at the British embassy, where Roosevelt stayed in the interests of security. (Not only would the president not have to move through the streets of Tehran for the meetings with his counterparts, but the grounds of the Soviet embassy abutted those of the British embassy; thus leaders would not need to leave the security of the diplomatic compounds.) In his meeting with the Shah, President Roosevelt, in effect, announced the newly formulated U.S. policy toward Iran.

The first significant manifestation of that policy was to come in the Azerbaijan crisis of 1946. The Allies had agreed to remove their troops from Iran within six months after the conclusion of the hostilities of war. But before that deadline, the Democratic party of Azerbaijan announced the establishment of an autonomous state in the northwestern province of Iran. Soviet troops in the province prevented Iranian government forces from entering the territory of the new republic while Iranian military garrisons were attacked and overwhelmed. The Iranian government took its case to the Security Council of the United Nations, the first case to be heard by the new international body. The conventional account of what happened next is that Pres. Harry Truman, already alarmed by reports that the Red Army was pouring fresh tanks and men across the border into Azerbaijan, was jarred into action. He sent what he later called "a blunt message" to Stalin: Get your troops out of Iran in six weeks or the United States Navy will sail into the Persian Gulf and land American forces. A few days later, Andrei Gromyko, the Soviet delegate to the Security Council, rose to announce that the Russian troops would be out of Iran in five weeks—and so they were.[57]

In fact, no record of that "blunt message" has ever been found. The direct role of the president is unclear, but the United States was, nonetheless, exerting its power at the United Nations to pressure the Soviets into withdrawing from Iran. The Iranians were also busy applying all their negotiating skills to induce a Soviet withdrawal. In February of 1946, Prime Minister Ahmad Qavam fashioned an agreement with the Soviets whereby they would withdraw their troops within six weeks and Qavam would submit a proposal to the Majles for the formation of a joint Iranian-Soviet venture to explore the oil resources of northern Iran.

Iranian diplomatic and political finesse was a major factor in the decision of the Soviets to withdraw, a factor frequently ignored by both Americans and Iranians. In fact, over the years of intense U.S. involvement with Iran, the myth grew that everything of significance in Iran was determined by the United States. More then a decade after the Iranian Revolution, many Iranians continue to believe that the success of the revolution was the result of a U.S. decision to depose the Shah in favor of the more stridently anti-Soviet Ayatollah Khomeini. But whatever the precise role of the United States in the Soviet troop withdrawal of 1946 and the subsequent collapse of the "independent" republic of Azerbaijan, the United States earned much credit in Iran, and especially with the Shah, for preserving the territorial integrity and independence of the Iranian state.

The Shah was not to make his first trip to the United States until November 1949.[58] The official visit was a grand tour, with the Shah visiting many parts of the country, being feted at numerous formal dinners and honored at the armed services academies, checking into a hospital for a complete round of medical examinations, and undergoing the rigors of a full-blown Washington diplomatic welcome. Still, from the Shah's perspective, the visit was not successful. He was unable to convince the United States to provide significant financial assistance for the first five-year plan drawn up by the Iranian Plan Organization. Looking back at the visit some two decades later, Dean Acheson, secretary of state during the Shah's visit, remembered it as a "disappointment" and recalled that "twenty years ago the Shah was not as experienced or wise as he is today. . . . The plans, military and economic, were too ambitious for the means available."[59]

The Shah was dismayed by his failure. During his visit, he cabled Minister of Court Hussein Ala in Tehran: "If America does not provide military aid, I will have no further responsibility for keeping Iran independent."[60]

The Shah's failure to lure the United States into deeper involvement was not to be a permanent condition. Four years later it was the United States and Great Britain which took the initiative to remove Mossadegh from the prime ministership and, with him, the principal threat to the rule of the Shah. President Eisenhower and the Dulles brothers had come to fear a Communist takeover of Iran. The rationale for the coup was spelled out, at least indirectly, by the president.

According to the Shah, by the summer of 1953, Mossadegh had become "absolutely mad and insanely jealous like a tiger who springs upon any living thing that it sees moving about him." Mossadegh, the Shah thought, believed that he could form an alliance with the Tudeh party and then outwit it, but in doing so, the Shah recognized, Dr. Mossadegh would become to Iran what the ill-fated Dr. Benes had been in Czechoslovakia—a leader whom the Communists, having gained power, would eventually destroy.[61]

The overthrow of Mossadegh would, in fact, fulfill two U.S. foreign policy goals. It would eliminate what was perceived as an immediate Communist threat and would secure a stake in Iranian oil for U.S. companies.[62] Having achieved those goals, the United States set out to secure the throne for the Shah and eliminate, in the process, the long-term Communist threat as well. The new prime minister and leader of the coup, Gen.

Fazlollah Zahedi, made the case directly to President Eisenhower only days after the restoration of the Shah: "The assistance which the United States is already rendering Iran, helpful as it, is unfortunately not sufficient in amount and character to tide Iran over the financial and economic crisis. . . . The Treasury is empty; foreign resources are exhausted; the national economy is deteriorated. Iran needs immediate financial aid to enable it to emerge from the state of economic and financial chaos."[63]

The United States responded with a program of emergency economic and military assistance for Iran. From 1953 to 1957, President Eisenhower channeled $500 million to Iran. In all prior history, the United States had extended only $59 million.[64]

The abundance of U.S. assistance was a mark of the close ties which the restoration of the Shah had fostered between Iran and the United States. The burgeoning bureaucracies which the United States established in Iran to administer the vast aid programs were a tangible demonstration of American influence. But finally, of course, that influence was exercised directly through the Shah. When John F. Kennedy was inaugurated as the new activist U.S. president committed to the internationalization of liberal reform, the Shah was one of the first to sense the new winds blowing from Washington. The Shah panicked. He tried confrontation. He sent his prime minister to Moscow in an attempt to play off the two superpowers for his benefit. He also gave extraordinarily tough interviews to American publications in which he stressed the significance of a friendly Iran for U.S. foreign policy.[65]

But the new president was not to be intimidated. When Kennedy turned his attention to Iran, he became deeply concerned that the Shah's throne rested fundamentally on Iran's security forces—the army and SAVAK. The Iranian economy appeared to the Americans to be on the verge of collapse, despite the high levels of U.S. aid and the oil revenues, and the crowds were in the streets, demanding reform.

On May 7, 1961, the Shah abandoned confrontation with the United States and appointed Dr. Ali Amini prime minister. Amini had served as minister of finance in the last cabinet of Mossadegh and still had credentials with the Shah's opposition. He had remained on as finance minister after the ouster of Mossadegh and negotiated Iran's new agreement with the oil consortium. As a reward, he was appointed ambassador of Iran to the United States, where he came to be held in high esteem. But he was no longer so esteemed by the Shah. In 1957 the Shah dismissed Amini as ambassador; there were widespread rumors linking Amini with an unsuccessful coup against the Shah spearheaded by General Qarani.[66]

Other rumors enveloped Amini. Given the Shah's mistrust of the man, it was alleged that he had been appointed prime minister on orders from Washington. Amini, it was suggested, was an agent of the CIA. In one of the earliest exposés of the Central Intelligence Agency, the author claimed that a few days after Amini was appointed prime minister, a newspaperman asked a CIA agent at a bar in Istanbul about the new Iranian prime minister. "Oh, he's all right," replied the CIA man. "He is fine. He's one of our boys."[67] What is clear is that the Shah appointed Amini knowing he was the choice of the United States.[68] The Shah later told the Egyptian journalist Mohamed Heikal that he regarded pressure from Kennedy as "more or less an American coup directed against him."[69] There is little doubt that the Shah received many direct and not so direct messages about his standing with President Kennedy. For example, Edward R. Murrow had accepted JFK's offer to become director of the United States Information Agency. Upon learning that the Shah had ordered a USIA film about Iran to be shown throughout Iran, Murrow had the film canceled. Murrow explained that "anything that pleases them so much as that can't be completely accurate reporting."[70]

In a state visit to Iran, Vice President Lyndon Johnson communicated the precise U.S. position to the Shah and to the Iranian people. At departure ceremonies at Tehran's Mehrabad Airport in April of 1962, the vice president asserted: "we are sure that the leaders of this valiant nation can have no doubt of the fidelity of the devotion of the United States to Iran's cause."[71] The Shah must have wondered just who were the leaders of Iran other than himself. The vice president then made clear that the United States intended to press the Shah for additional reforms. "We shall walk beside you toward the new horizons of human dignity," he informed the Shah and all Iranians. "Let me assure you that as long as you walk this road, you will never walk alone."[72]

The Shah later complained that the United States had attempted to "impose your type of regime on other people. You started almost on the same path of old Queen Victoria's British policy. Your worst period was in 1961 and 1962. But even before that, there were your great American liberals wanting to impose their way of democracy on others, thinking their way is wonderful."[73]

However personally bitter and intimidated the Shah was over U.S. pressures and signs of disdain, when Amini took office he immediately instituted far-reaching changes, the most ambitious of which was a program of land reform spearheaded by his minister of agriculture, Hassan Arsan-jani. In addition, Amini struggled to deal with the socioeconomic crisis he had inherited. Nonetheless, when Amini became embroiled with opposi-tion to his reforms, opposition to which the Shah himself contributed, and when Amini made the mistake of blaming Washington for the financial dif-ficulties with which his government was struggling, the Shah seized the opportunity. He dismissed Amini and appointed his longtime friend As-sadollah Alam.

By this time the United States had managed to work itself into the worst of all positions. Most observers of Iran had come to believe that the Shah was the creation or tool of the United States, yet the Shah took any U.S. instructions as "intolerable interference."[74] An unusually wise re-port, written in early 1961 by Kenneth Bowling, a State Department official, assessed the domestic political situation of the Shah and alter-native U.S. foreign policies. After reviewing a variety of options, from sponsoring a military coup to overthrow the Shah to working with the Shah's "Mossadeghist" opposition, the report concluded:

It would appear preferable that the United States would be best advised to con-tinue its present policy of reassurance to the Shah of United States sympathy and support, along with persistent but delicate inferences by our Ambassador to the ef-fect that the Shah should devote his attention to his internal political problems rather than to foreign and military affairs. . . . We should, of course, continue to be on the alert for the rise of competent and creative alternate leadership in or out of the military, which might allow a reconsideration of our alternatives.[75]

In short, in the 1960s the United States had responsibility for the state of Iranian affairs without the power to exercise that responsibility. Yet the Shah feared American interference in internal Iranian politics. The United States could always choose to undermine his rule by making common cause with those who had supported Prime Minister Mossadegh or by identifying a military officer with whom to sponsor a military takeover. The Shah's response was to lavish praise on the United States—in public, at least—and to declare his commitment to American goals. In April 1962, for example, in an address to a joint session of Congress, shortly after the ouster of Amini and in the midst of continuing tension with President Ken-nedy, the Shah declared:

Our experience over Azerbaijan proved to us that in the present state of the world, no country, still less a country in our geographical position, can afford to remain neutral. We, therefore, decided to throw in our lot with the countries whose system of government, whose civilization and culture, whose way of life and manner of thinking resembles our own and to associate ourselves with them whether it be for good or ill.[76]

The members of Congress and the American people, of course, were deeply gratified by the faithful commitment of the Shah. And he was strengthened by their appreciation. The Shah was psychologically enhanced by the mirroring, idealizing, and twinship relations he fostered with the United States. In turn, the increasing strength which he experienced through his selfobject relations with the United States facilitiated his ability to press two policies on the West—higher oil production to generate more government revenues and increased levels of U.S. assistance, particularly for his armed forces. In 1962 the Shah urged David Lilienthal, whose company was involved in a massive development project in Iran's province of Khuzestan, to help Iran win more U.S. aid. "I hope your Government will make up its mind about Iran," the Shah urged. "Iran could be the showcase for the whole of Asia. America can spread its assistance into every country. . . . But here is the place with the best prospects of a great transformation.[77]

With President Kennedy's assassination, the Shah was relieved of a leader he perceived as both a rival and a threat. The Shah was displeased at the palpable popularity JFK enjoyed among Iranians.[78] The Shah also "strongly resented the fact that Kennedy, who was two and a half years younger than he, would attempt to advise him on how to run his kingdom."[79] Despite the hostility he felt toward Kennedy, the Shah used the assassination to elaborate further his psychological attachment to the United States. The Shah transformed his public evaluation of the U.S. president. In 1967 he was asked by an Italian journalist of his most painful memory. Without hesitation, the Shah responded, "The assassination of President Kennedy, not only because he was the President of the United States and, therefore, the most powerful man in the world, but also because he was young and a father. He died during the best days of his life. Like myself, he was the father of young children."[80]

With the assassination of JFK, the Shah would not receive another substantial scare from a U.S. president until the 1976 election of Jimmy Carter. In a 1964 state visit to Washington, however, the Shah came close. President Johnson told the Shah in private meetings in the White House that he would not authorize higher levels of military assistance because the United States questioned Iran's ability to integrate the sophisticated weapons into the Iranian armed forces. Within a week, however, LBJ made an unscheduled trip to the United Nations for a special meeting with the Shah. There he told the monarch that he had changed his mind about the weapons. The Department of Defense had urged him to supply the weapons the Shah wanted because the United States needed the Shah.

Iran's relations with Washington continued to change in the direction sought by the Shah. As the United States became ever more entangled in Vietnam, the Shah remained a steadfast ally. Then, in 1968, two events propelled the Shah to the forefront of American strategic thinking in the Persian Gulf. The Tet offensive signaled that the Vietnam War had become a hopeless morass, and the British announced their intention to abandon their military commitments east of Suez by 1971. The looming presence of Iran became ever more significant in U.S. strategic calculations.

Riding the wave of America's new appreciation for Iran's strategic value and, in turn, experiencing that appreciation on a psychological level, the Shah pushed to advance Iran's interests. Along with an unlikely bedfellow, Colonel Qaddhafi, the Shah perpetrated the 1970s "leapfrogging" of oil prices. Shortly after the September 1969 coup by which he achieved power, Colonel Qaddhafi had won price increases from the international oil companies. He had urged that Libyan crude oil supplies were much closer to European markets, making them more reliable and far less expensive than Persian Gulf oil. After the colonel won new revenues, the Shah responded with his own arguments. As the bastion of support for the West in the Persian Gulf, he was owed no less than revolutionary Libya. That argument succeeded as well. But when the Shah received new revenues, the colonel would restate his original argument. Another round of the leapfrogging would begin.

Then in 1971, at the Tehran OPEC conference, the Shah proposed a significant increase in the price of petroleum, a price increase adopted by all the producers. The increase was at least partially accepted by consumers because Iran under the rule of the Shah had become still more significant to the United States. The extent to which that was true was demonstrated in May of 1972 when President Nixon and his secretary of state Henry Kissinger paid their now notorious if brief visit to the seat of the Peacock Throne. It was on that trip that the U.S. president authorized the Shah to buy any non-nuclear U.S. weapons system he fancied.

Former Secretary of State Kissinger has denied this blanket authorization. In his memoirs he wrote, "Nixon ordered that decision on these aircraft purchases [the F14 which was to be ready in 1973 and the F15 which would be delivered in 1976 or 1977] and their timing should be left to the Government of Iran. In the context, that is the meaning of the oft-quoted directive, which ended with a general obiter dictum that the Pentagon not try to second-guess Iranian decisions on what equipment to select."[81]

Kissinger often returned to the subject. "Later, when our interests were beyond salvage," he recognizes, "it grew fashionable in America to exorcise guilt feelings by blaming Iran's fate on Nixon's decision in 1972 to sell advanced weapons to our ally."[82] Or again, "In the perspective of a decade, the Shah's overthrow had little to do with his purchases of military equipment. Indeed, had America played its hand differently when that upheaval started, Iran's military establishment might have provided a political counterweight to radicalism during the period of the monarchy's disintegration."[83]

While, as discussed in the final chapter, Henry Kissinger is correct that the possibility for a different outcome of the Iranian Revolution was contingent on a different U.S. foreign policy in 1977, his assessment of the 1972 decision is overly simplistic. A U.S. Senate investigation took a harsher view of the 1972 decision which had been transmitted in writing to the U.S. foreign policy bureaucracies. "The decision not only opened the door to large increases in military sales to Iran." the Senate report concluded, "but also effectively exempted sales to Iran from the normal arms sales decision making processes in the State and Defense Departments. In so far as is known, the May 1972 decision [was] never formally reconsidered, even though the large oil price increases in 1973 enabled Iran to order much more than anyone anticipated in 1972."[84] But the most significant dimension of that decision was not the skewing of Iran's budgets to strengthen the military at the expense of other sectors nor the siphoning of technical personnel from civilian sectors of the economy to the vastly enhanced military. Of far greater significance to subsequent events in Iran is what the decision told the world, and more importantly the Shah, about where he stood in the eyes of the United States.

The Nixon and Kissinger "announcement" of the Shah as U.S. proxy in the Persian Gulf was both a product of and contributor to a fundamental and decisive alteration of the traditional pattern of Iranian foreign policy. Since 1798, Iranian foreign policy had been to play one foreign power off against the other in order to maximize its freedom of maneuver and maintain its independence. Throughout the nineteenth century, the Qajar shahs set Great Britain against Russia to preserve Iran from entrapment within either empire. However great the influence those states were able to exercise in Iran's internal affairs, Iran, unlike so many other states in Asia and Africa, preserved its independence.

Reza Shah modified the pattern following his seizure of power. Thereafter the role of both foreign powers was diminished, but certainly not eliminated. Reza Shah pitted the Soviet Union, France, and later Germany against the pressures of Great Britain. The British and Soviet invasion and occupation during World War II were a repetition of an earlier era, even though the United States joined the occupying powers.

But under the Shah, the United States and, to a far lesser extent, the United Kingdom came to monopolize influence over the Shah. While there were occasional efforts by the Shah to resurrect the old pattern—he began buying weapons from the Soviet Union in the 1960s, for example— the 1972 decision confirmed what many had expected. The Shah had fully attached his country to the United States and would preserve its integrity and his role by exploiting the interests of the United States. The Shah was able to exercise "reverse leverage" with Washington and use it to enhance dramatically his role not merely in the Persian Gulf, but throughout much of the Middle East, Africa, and Asia.[85] The United States global role had been so weakened by the tragic debacle of Vietnam that it not only supported the Shah's global ambitions but contributed to their realization. Kissinger detailed the reasoning.

There was no possibility of assigning any American military forces to the Indian Ocean in the midst of the Vietnam War and its attendant trauma. Congress would have tolerated no such commitment; the public would not have supported it. Fortunately, Iran was willing to play this role. The vacuum left by British withdrawal, now menaced by Soviet intrusion and radical momentum, would be filled by a local power friendly to us. Iraq would be discouraged from adventures against the Emirates in the lower Gulf, and against Jordan and Saudi Arabia. A strong Iran could help damp India's temptations to conclude its conquest of Pakistan. And all of this was achievable without any American resources, since the Shah was willing to pay for the equipment out of his oil revenues. To have failed to match the influx of Soviet arms into neighboring countries would have accelerated the demoralization of the area, including Iran's. I daresay that it might have prevented or made far more difficult Sadat's later turn towards the West.[86]

There is ample testimony to the Shah's new stature as head of a regional superpower dependent on the United States, but his new psychic strength allowed him to conduct policies opposed to American interests. He was the first head of state, in 1973, to advocate a sharp rise in the price of oil. After Arab producers embargoed oil shipments to punish the West for aiding Israel, the Shah urged unlimited sales but at dramatically higher prices. On December 22 and 23, OPEC's Persian Gulf members met in Tehran. King Fahd had instructed his representative, Sheikh Ahmad Zaki Yamani, to accede to an end of the embargo but only on the condition that OPEC's new price not exceed $7 per barrel. The Shah pushed for far higher levels. He carried the day and the new price was set at $11.65—a nearly fivefold increase over the pre–Yom Kippur/Ramadan War price.

What the Shah had succeeded in achieving for himself was a degree of freedom from the dictates of Washington. He had managed to establish considerable leeway to fashion a foreign policy for Iran. But by and large, after his 1972 appointment as American surrogate in the Persian Gulf, the Shah appears to have acted with concern for the best interests of the United States, given the political strength of the larger forces impinging on his freedom of action. And given the psychological significance of the United States for the Shah, this is no surprise. Thus the Shah could have taken a line against any substantial price hike for OPEC oil, but he would not have served well the financial interests of his own country, nor would he have been able to withstand the voices of those states demanding more extreme measures. But ending the oil embargo while achieving higher revenues for Iran without at the same time succumbing to the voices of extremism within OPEC left him in an admirable position. He was able to do well for Iran while doing good for the United States.

In short, within the context of the political realities he confronted, the Shah acted as a loyal and faithful ally of the United States. He carried this role to such extremes, however, that he earned the reputation, first and foremost among his own people, as an agent of the United States. This reputation for serving U.S. interests at the expense of Iran appeared long before his 1972 meeting with President Nixon and Secretary of State Kissinger. In 1963 the National Security Council reported that "it must not be forgotten that the Shah's greatest single liability may well be his vulnerability to charges . . . that he is a foreign puppet."[87] By the 1970s, the Shah came to be defined, by virtually the entire politically aware sector of Iranian society, as a tool of American global interests.

The Iranian people had emerged from their nearly two-centuries-long involvement with the states of Europe and the United States with a profound ambivalence toward the outside world. On the one hand, Iranians manifested a startlingly intense admiration for the outside world. They demonstrated a longing for foreign ways, a determination to master and adopt the ways of the outsider. That was the pole of the duality most visible to the foreigner in Pahlavi Iran. The pursuit of Western fashions, the passion to travel to Europe and the United States, the eagerness for foreign study, and the adoption of Western culture made the thirst for the outside readily apparent.

Less obvious was the other pole of the duality—the profound xenophobia which was simultaneously present even in many of the people most ready to seize on foreign customs. That xenophobia fed the cataclysm of hatred articulated so eloquently and convincingly by Ayatollah Khomeini. Iran then identified virtually the entire world as its enemy. The "Arch Satan," the United States; the "Great Satan," the USSR; and all the "lesser Satans," especially Iraq, Israel, Egypt, Saudi Arabia, and Kuwait; and the Zionists, Baha'is, and Christians—all are enemies of Iran. The vigor with which the Khomeini regime pressed its apoplectic xenophobia was a recognition of its appeal in Iran, but also of the intensity with which xenophobia had to be pressed in order to overcome that contrary impulse. During much of the reign of the Shah, only the intense admiration of the West was obvious. Americans on visits to Iran would be struck by Iran's pursuit of the West. The "golden era" of the United States in Iran was as one-sided as is the current hatred. Neither period gave full vent to the rage or ambivalence with which an Iranian confronts the foreign.

In the narrowest sense, the struggle many Iranians have with the foreign is only an extension of the Iranian struggle which begins outside the immediate boundaries of the self. For as difficult and complicated as are relationships with foreigners, the relationships of Iranians with each other are comparably complex. Relations with the immediate family, the extended family, the representatives of the governing powers, and the Shah are all instances of the "outside world." The foreign powers who came to woo and manipulate, to recruit and control the Shah, were, initially at least, hardly more outside than those other institutions. The ambivalence Iranians felt toward those foreign forces was paralleled by their responses to the entirely domestic forces that, being outside their own selves, impinged on their ability to lead their lives as they chose.

The ambivalence toward power outside the self—the rejection of externally imposed restrictions and limits while yet admiring and yearning for authority firmly exercised—is the hallmark of Iranian character. Fereidoun Esfandiary, an Iranian writer living in the United States, captured the ambivalence brilliantly in his novel *Day of Sacrifice*.[88] The book recounts the struggles of a young man attempting to break the control over his life exercised by his father, while at the same time struggling to free Iran from what he and his political companions perceive to be the oppression of the Shah. Because of the hero's ambivalence to that control and oppression, however, he fails to act decisively at the moment when decisive action is essential. As a result, he fails his comrades, his father, and himself.

The entire Iranian people are passing through a comparable struggle under their new regime. The power of that struggle is accounted for by the fact that the impetus for rage against control is a combination of cultural and characterological factors. The authority structure of the Iranian family is a powerful and rigidly hierarchical one. There is no democracy in that institution.[89] In some sense, all Iranians are struggling with the power of their fathers, not just the hero of the *Day of Sacrifice*. In this sense the story of the Shah's efforts to free himself from the powerful emotional domination of Reza Shah is archetypal. Much of the emotional power with which Iranians reject their leaders and struggle against political control can be understood as deriving at least some of its force from the struggle to break the bonds of the domination of the father. There is, of course, a good deal of ambivalence about the struggle as well. Just as the failed political activist of *Day of Sacrifice* could not bear, finally, to break with his father, so many in Iran cannot carry through the ultimate rejection of authority figures.

It is striking the extent to which Iranian youth have been captivated by elderly political leaders. Both Prime Minister Mossadegh and Ayatollah Khomeini won widespread support among the young. Clearly, neither age nor political control per se are necessary sources for hatred by the young in Iran. To the contrary, great political leaders in Iran understand—in whatever way great leaders are able to empathize with their followers—the ambivalence of their followers to political power. They succeed at relating to their followers in a way that makes their leadership acceptable.

In addition to the characterological bases of ambivalence to others in Iran, there is as well a deep-seated culturological ambivalence to authority. To no small degree, that cultural ambivalence stems from Iran's experience with attempts by foreign powers to control its politics. The personal, psychological response by Iranians to those attempts at control become irretrievably mixed with their characterological responses to ambivalence over their authoritarian family structures. The transferences and displacements—from family to political leaders to foreigners—become tangled.

In the 1960s and 1970s in Iran, three voices articulated the most consistently xenophobic positions—Jalal Al-e Ahmad, Ali Shari'ati, and Ayatollah Khomeini. Jalal Al-e Ahmad was a former schoolteacher and principal who became the most famous Iranian man of letters of his day. His essay *Gharbzadegi,* awkwardly but accurately translated as "Weststrucked-ness," is a stinging attack on those Iranians who "severed [their] ties with the essence of society, culture, and custom" and "follow the directives of the oil companies and the western countries."[90]

Ali Shari'ati was a French-trained sociologist who made, perhaps, the decisive contribution to the intellectual roots of the Iranian Revolution. In his speeches and writings from 1967 to 1972 at the Husseinieh-i Ershad, a religious assembly hall in Tehran, Shari'ati argued that

all Shi'is, irrespective of time and place, had the duty to oppose, resist, and even rebel against overwhelming odds in order to eradicate their contemporary ills . . . world imperialism, international Zionism, colonialism, exploitation, oppression, class inequality, cartels, multinational corporations, racism, cultural imperialism, and *gharbzadegi.*[91]

For Decades Khomeini railed against the evils of foreign domination of Iran. Perhaps the single most important theme in his writings is the destructiveness of foreign influences on Iran. According to Khomeini, those foreign influences destroyed not only religion, but the very brains of Iranians as well. The Iranian people, as a result of foreign oppression, had become mimics of the West. His solution was to turn to Shi'ism, which promised liberation from oppression and foreign domination.

Reza Baraheni, a professor of comparative literature at Iranian universities, a visiting professor at American universities, a prisoner of the Shah and, after the revolution, of Khomeini, captured the Iranian ambivalence to the West, with emphasis on the hatred.

First we are alienated from the West because the Colonial calamities bred by the Western world have been thrust upon us without we ourselves being or having become Westerners; second, the West plunders and destroys all our languages, literature, folklore, the identity of all our positive visions, poetic, and artistic rhythms without replacing them with something that can originally be called Eastern.[92]

The consequence of the Iranian embrace of xenophobia was disastrous for the Shah and proved disastrous, in quite different ways, for Khomeini, and Iran as well. Despite the fact that the Shah vigorously articulated an Iranian nationalism which called for Iranian economic and military development and that he was the principal OPEC spokesman for higher revenues for the oil producers, the Shah's regime was understood by Iranians to be totally invested—most in Iran by 1978 came to think of it as infested—in the West and, in particular, the United States. But no one anticipated the intensity of the storm of xenophobia which would break over the Shah, his regime, and Iran. Neither Iranian nor American observers appreciated the xenophobic rage which would erupt throughout Iran in the mid-1970s. For example, John Stempel, a U.S. foreign service officer in Tehran who spoke Persian and possessed a keen sophistication about Iran, missed the power of the building rage. In a cable to Washington, Stempel discussed the ways in which the Shah and his ministers would cope with the mounting difficulties of the Iranian economy. He astutely anticipated that

the GOI [Government of Iran] is likely to blame foreigners for their failure to correctly impart Western techniques and methods. This is already taking place—there are charges of communist intrigue with domestic opponents of the regime; assertions that foreigners are polluting Iran's culture; and increasing expressions of belief that Western technology is ineffective and not worth the social price being paid for its presence. . . . The inevitable criticism of foreigners means that the reorientation of Persian values that must take place if Iran is to operate its modern industrial structure will have at least a modest anti-foreign animus.[93]

But what Stempel missed—as did virtually all other observers of Iran—was the depth of the "anti-foreign animus" and the rapidity with which it was manifest. The Shah, despite his attacks on the West and his efforts and those of his officials to foist the failings of their rule onto foreigners, never managed to convince the Iranian people that they were not part of some foreign conspiracy to crush Iranian culture. The opposition to the Shah managed to capture the enraged xenophobia as its issue. With the deaths of Al-e Ahmad and Shari'ati, Ayatollah Khomeini remained to propound the most ardent xenophobic message of the opposition. Moreover, he succeeded in linking the message of liberation from foreign oppression to the message of liberation from all oppression. He thus tapped into the central theme of Iranian political culture. When he monopolized that issue, the Shah was doomed.

Empress Farah Diba Pahlavi and her new husband at their wedding celebration. December 21, 1959. AP/Wide World Photos.

The people of Tehran celebrate the birth of the Shah's first son and heir, on October 31, 1960, surrounding a newspaper which, undoubtedly, none of them can read. Magnum Photos.

The Shah in a horse-drawn carriage shortly after the ceremony in which he was formally crowned. October 28, 1967. AP/Wide World Photos.

With the royal family after the coronation ceremony. The Shah (on a riser) stands with Empress Farah and his officially designated heir, Crown Prince Reza II and their daughter Princess Faranaz. To his right is his daughter Princess Shahnaz and his twin sister Princess Ashraf. To the Empress's left is Princess Shams. October 28, 1967. AP/Wide World Photos.

By the beginning of the decade, the Shah had assumed the trappings of the imperial monarchy. July, 1971. AP/Wide World Photos.

An official photograph issued by the Ministry of Court portrays the Shah in his grandiosity. July, 1971. AP/Wide World Photos.

The Shah, with tears in his eyes, prepares to board his plane for a flight to Egypt and exile in the face of the popular revolution which demanded his ouster and his death. January 16, 1979. AP/Wide World Photos.

President Anwar Sadat and the Shah performing prayers in Egypt. The Shah already looks wan and ill. January 19, 1979. Bettmann Archives.

Fearful of being turned over to the Ayatollah, and unable to get the medical care he desper-
ately needed, the Shah fled Panama for Cairo where he underwent surgery and died on
July 27, 1980. This is one of the last known photographs of the Shah. July 16, 1980.
AP/Wide World Photos.

8

Dependence on the United States

Shortly after he arrived in Tehran in June 1977 to assume his position as U.S. ambassador, William H. Sullivan turned his attention to what for him had been the single most troublesome issue concerning Iran since his first briefings on that country. He was convinced that the Shah's industrialization program was overambitious—exceeding the economic, technological, and manpower capacities of the country. The result of the Shah's efforts to propel Iran into the forefront of the world's industrialized nations, in the ambassador's mind, was certain to be economic disaster and social chaos.

The ambassador commissioned studies and "tasked" U.S. agencies to investigate Iran's industrialization drive. But all his instructions resulted in few studies and no conclusions germane to his concerns. The ambassador decided then to proceed on his own, on the basis of the intuition he had developed during his years of diplomatic service in the Far East. While his instincts about the flaws in Iran's development drive were sound, his sense of what to do with those concerns was, perhaps, better suited to the Far East. It certainly was not in keeping with SAVAK-permeated Iran.

He proceeded to call Iran's principal economic policy-makers to a private dinner at his residence, where he laid out his concerns and asked for their views. The ambassador's remarks were greeted with stunned silence, followed by a speech from the senior economic figure present who launched into a spirited defense of the Shah's plans for Iran. With unanimous agreement, the rest of the Iranians present concluded the dinner by celebrating the economic triumph of Iran and the wisdom of the Shah in determining Iran's economic course.

Ambassador Sullivan was by then aware that his approach had failed and little would be gained from its pursuit. "Consequently," he later wrote, "I broke up the working aspect of the dinner, retired to the library with my guests, passed around brandy and cigars, and finished off the evening with small talk."[1] But much to his amazement, as the ambassador ushered his guests to the door, each took him aside to support his concerns. Each guest apologized for his inability to criticize the Shah or his plans, and each guest urged Ambassador Sullivan to take his concerns directly to the Shah himself.

Emboldened by the recommendations of Iran's leading economic figures, the ambassador raised the subject at his very next audience with the Shah. The Shah's response was predictable; he became alternately defensive and angry.

He listened very intently and then responded rather querulously. He did not raise his voice, but he asked a number of somewhat petulant questions. He slumped lower in his chair and seemed to react peevishly. He permitted himself a little rancor by pointing to the economic difficulties that were currently besetting the United States and the industrialized world, but in general he tried to brush off my questioning of his industrialization program as irrelevant.[2]

After this audience, the Shah broke his normal routine of calling the ambassador to appear for an audience approximately every ten days. The ambassador came to believe that he must have hurt the Shah and been banished from the imperial presence. Yet the ambassador reports, after a long period with no word from the Shah at all, he began to hear that the Shah had, in fact, taken action.

It seems that the Shah had called his economic ministers for a complete review of the industrialization program and other aspects of economic policy. This review went on in a series of meetings with the economic cabinet over a period of three or four weeks. At the end of that time, the Shah let it be known that some changes were in order. Shortly thereafter the cabinet resigned, and the prime minister [Amir Abbas Hoveyda] was made minister of court. Jamshid Amouzegar, the former head of the single [Rastakhiz] political party, was brought in to be prime minister and to introduce a program of austerity that cut back sharply on the industrialization investment and that also limited significantly the generous credit rules that had buoyed the economy into high inflation. Such measures as crackdowns on corruption and bribery were also announced.[3]

The ambassador, in reviewing this sequence of events, never reached a conclusion on the connection, if any, between his dinner soiree, his conversation with the Shah, and the Shah's subsequent volte-face on his industrialization program. In fact, Ambassador Sullivan made it clear that "I frankly preferred not to find out, because of the implications of it troubled me. It suggested that the Shah had no really well articulated economic program and that a brief word of concern from a friendly outsider could alter significantly the course of his nation's economic future."[4]

It may not be too dramatic to suggest that the ambassador's flight from the truth of the Shah and the nature of his leadership was the single most significant event in that sequence of significant events which led to the downfall of the Shah. For had the ambassador pursued his insight, he would have learned not that any "friendly outsider" who uttered "a brief word of concern" could have fundamentally changed the Shah's plans for Iran. Only one "friendly outsider" could have done that—the official representative of the government of the United States of America. For the Shah had come over his years of rule to depend on the United States for general guidance and orientation, for specific advice and even instructions, and to a significant extent, it is argued here, for a source of his psychological well-being.

The Shah's relationship to the United States was, of course, more complicated than slavish admiration. It was a mixture of the xenophobia and admiration of foreign powers and foreign cultures which had come to characterize Iran by the time he assumed the throne. Richard Cottam, an astute observer of Iran, put this ambivalence somewhat differently.

Until Mossadeq's time . . . Iranians simultaneously believed that (a) all of Iran's ills could be ascribed to foreign interference and hence foreign interference per se was evil, and that (b) foreign interference was inevitable and Iran needed a disinterested foreign power which would support Iranian independence against the avarice of the British and the Russians.[5]

The Shah understood these lessons from Iranian history at least as well as any other Iranian. He must have come to suspect the British contributed to the success of his father's coup. He likely did not learn of this from his father, but there was no way the Shah could have escaped the speculations about their part in the coup. Nor, obviously, could the Shah have not been keenly sensitive to the fact that what the British did in 1921, they undid twenty years later. The joint invasion which brought about the exile of his father and his own assumption of kingly authority was the product of foreigners whom the Iranians could not possibly bend to their will. The near loss of Azerbaijan to Soviet-backed separatists and the defeat of those separatists were believed by Iranians, ultimately, to have been due to the firm stand taken by President Truman. Without his anti-Soviet toughness, all the cleverness of Prime Minister Qavam and the good intentions of the Shah would have been inadequate to have overcome the determination of the Soviets to maintain the regime of their puppets. Other events as well, the overthrow of Mossadegh foremost among them, led the Shah to believe in the efficacy of foreigners and, particularly, the United States.

But when President Nixon and Secretary of State Kissinger designated the Shah as the principal representative of the Nixon Doctrine for the Persian Gulf, the Shah came to believe that he was indispensable to the United States.[6] With that indispensability, it has been argued above, also came the sense of his own grandiosity, a reflection of the fact that he had been selected by the revered United States to be "its" man in the Persian Gulf, the energy heart of the world. With that selection and grandiosity came a further sense of infallibility. The Shah believed that he could not make an unwise decision in the areas of oil, defense, and foreign policy. He totally stopped listening to the counsel of others.[7]

By the early 1970s, in short, the Shah had thrown his psychic lot in with the United States; with that psychological commitment went, as well, his commitment of the Iranian state to American foreign policy goals. He derived immense psychological benefits from his relationship with the United States as Iran derived immense material benefits. In terms of the psychoanalytic system created by Heinz Kohut, the Shah established three transferencelike selfobject relationships with the United States—transferencelike relationships which were embodied by the Shah's personal ties with those eight U.S. presidents and their many ambassadors. He fashioned mirroring, idealization, and twinship relations with those leaders. From those transference relations between his self and selfobjects, he derived immensely enhanced self-esteem and, thus, enhanced psychic strength.

The Shah had managed to establish mirroring relationships with the United States. Its representatives and leaders told him in words, as well as in financial and military assistance, as well as in diplomatic and political support, that he was a central figure to the security and well-being of the United States.

Through the decades of his rule, the Shah clearly idealized the United States and its presidents. That was, moreover, an idealization which the United States did nothing to discourage. To the contrary, the Shah's idealization was encouraged as an indication of the close connection between the two states and as a way of cementing U.S. influence over the fate of Iran. That idealizing relationship to the United States allowed the Shah to merge or identify with the United States and, from that, to gain strength by sharing in its strength.

The third self-selfobject relation the Shah was to fashion with the

United States was the twinship relationship. His formation of twinship transferences with others has already been described in detail above. But in addition to the twinship ties he formed with other Iranians, there was a twinship quality in his relationship to the United States. In the initial stages of his rule, of course, a partnership, let alone a twinship, was inconceivable to either the Shah or the United States. Iran was simply too poor, too unstable, and the Shah too weak to allow for even the contemplation of such a relationship. Yet as the Shah became more established in his kingship and enhanced his control over domestic Iranian politics—especially after the overthrow of Mossadegh and the establishment of SAVAK—as the economy of Iran began to grow, first in the 1960s with new industrialization and than in the 1970s with massive infrastructure projects, and as the Shah was able to build a powerful armed force in the 1970s, the contemplation of a more significant role for the Shah and Iran seemed less absurd.

Indeed, when Nixon and Kissinger designated Iran as the defender of U.S. interests—defined, of course, in terms of issues such as "the free world" and democracy—it was possible for the Shah to imagine Iran in a twinship-like relationship with the United States. That is not to imply that either of the parties to this relationship imagined that the United States and Iran were equal partners. But nothing in the twinship relationship necessitates equality—the metaphor of fraternal rather than identical twins would capture the connection of the Shah to the United States.

Whatever the appropriate metaphor, throughout his relationship with the United States in the 1970s the Shah came to believe that he shared certain qualities with those U.S. presidents and that under his rule Iran had come to share certain qualities with the United States. From that similarity grew a twinship relationship which provided the Shah with another psychological pillar from which he derived the psychological strength necessary to rule. These selfobject, transference-like relationships of the Shah's were crucial components of his psychological well-being. It has been argued that as long as those relations functioned to produce and sustain useful selfobjects, the Shah functioned as ruler. But as the Shah regressed from the threats of his illness, the pressures of the unfolding political opposition in 1977, and the blossoming of violence in 1978, his need for psychological strength increased. Since he derived that strength from his selfobjects, the Shah found it necessary to sustain and even strengthen his ties with his selfobjects during the periods of his regression. It was precisely at a period of great regression, when the Shah was most in need of his relationship with the United States for the mirroring, idealization, and twinship so central to his mental equilibrium, that he sensed the ebbing of that relationship.

The Shah's troubles were exacerbated because the Iranian people understood that he was becoming more desperate in his pursuit of his selfobjects. As the Shah struggled for the reinforcement of those selfobjects, the Iranian people came to sense the extent to which the Shah was a psychological captive, particularly of the United States. The people of Iran were themselves deeply ambivalent to the United States and the West. They admired the wealth and prosperity and the power. Many admired its vitality and believed jeans, Italian and French fashions, and rock and roll to be sure signs of Western cultural superiority. But for most Iranians, there was simultaneously another dimension. The sexuality and violence of the West were stimulating but also indicators of a certain moral bankruptcy. More menacing were the "invasion" of some fifty thousand Americans and the Shah's continued commitment to the United States, both of which threatened to undermine the culture of Iran with those same admired yet disdained practices of the West.

Many in Iran understood that the "reverse leverage" the Shah was able to exercise politically over Washington had nothing to do with the psychological dependency the Shah continued to feel so deeply. They appreciated that the economic boom of Iran did not serve to change his underlying psychological reality.

They came to detest the Shah for not having the strength to break the chains of dependency which they themselves felt so strongly. For many Iranians, the Shah failed because he was not able, after all, to translate the economic, political, and military strength of the Iran he had done so much to construct into a psychological independence from the West in general and the United States in particular. Reza Shah had understood that. "The Persian character," he declared, "has got to be hardened. For too long my countrymen have relied on others. I want to teach them their own value, so that they may be independent in mind and action."[8] That was also what Ayatollah Khomeini promised to do for the Iranian people. To a significant extent, he succeeded. In psychological terms, it can be argued that he substituted Islam and God for the United States as the principal, institutionalized selfobjects of the Iranian regime.

The differences between the Shah and the Ayatollah in terms of their relation with the West were substantial. Both the Shah and the cleric accepted the fundamental dualism or dichotomy which existed between Iran and the West. The Shah saw the dichotomy in the superiority of the West and the need for Iran as a state and for Iranians as individuals to adopt Western characteristics to minimize the dichotomy.[9] In the 1970s the Shah adopted a new tone, berating the West on the grounds that it had gone soft. But few in either Iran or the West understood the Shah to have changed his basic position.

The Ayatollah dealt with the dichotomy in a different way and in the process provided the Iranian people with a more satisfying way of dealing with their ambivalence. He too accepted the West as superior to Iran in terms of science, technology, and economic well-being. But he argued that those criteria were inadequate and morally bankrupt. Under the banner of Islam, Iran and the entire Third World could be superior to the West. The "oppressed," as he referred to those to whom he directed his message— thus appealing as well to their deeply felt ambivalence about authority— must develop an Islamic morality. Islam would then lead to the formation of a community of the faithful which would provide a life superior to anything available in the West. There were many in Iran who embraced the Ayatollah's formula for breaking their ambivalence and venting their hatred of foreigners. The Shah was never able to provide as satisfying a formula because he depended on the psychological rewards derived from maintaining selfobject relationships with the United States.

This argument attempts to turn on its head the explanation Henry Kissinger has advanced to explain the intensity of the relationship between the United States and the Shah.

There have been many falsehoods about America's relationship with the Shah. The impression has been created that personal friendships or a predilection for authoritarian rulers shaped American support for the Iranian leader. Reality was far more complex; a relationship that thrived under eight American Presidents of both political parties must have resulted from deeper causes than personal idiosyncracy.[10]

It is telling that he felt the need to deny the significance of the "personal idiosyncrasies" of the Shah (or the U.S. presidents) as the basis for the close ties between the two countries. It is true that other factors are crucial components of that relationship. But without the personal input of the Shah, the relationship would never have taken the form and assumed the intensity it did.

To a large extent, the self-selfobject ties the Shah forged with the United States emerged from the meetings he had with the eight U.S. presidents. Five of them made state visits to Iran, beginning with Franklin

Delano Roosevelt's trip to the Tehran Conference in 1943. President Eisenhower arrived in Tehran on December 14, 1959. As President Kennedy's vice president, Lyndon Johnson visited the Shah in August of 1962. President Nixon and his secretary of state arrived on May 30, 1972. President Carter and his wife spent New Year's Eve of 1978 enjoying the hospitality of the Shah.[11]

The Shah, however, made far more trips to the United States. He visited the United States on thirteen occasions, beginning with his first trip on November 17, 1949, and concluding with his last trip on November 16, 1977. On each occasion he conferred with the president.[12] He never made a secret of the importance to him of their respect and admiration. In fact, after his overthrow, when the Shah felt it necessary to justify his rule and account for his failure to hold his throne, it is telling that his writings were published only in French and English.[13] It was to the West and particularly to his American transference figures that he owed an accounting. Nothing was to be published in Persian. The hurt of the rejection by his own people was undoubtedly too great for him to make an accounting to them.

The Shah's father, Reza Shah, never felt the need to make an accounting of his rule to foreigners, and he certainly never attempted to celebrate the support he received from foreign powers. In fact, despite the origins of his rule, one of his main aims as monarch was to free Iran from its dependence on Great Britain and the Soviet Union.[14] Reza Shah was explicit in his desire to end Iran's dependency on foreigners. He frequently lectured the Iranian people against the evils of foreign interference in the internal affairs of Iran and, worse, the predilection of Iranians to welcome and even invite that interference. In one speech, Reza Shah said,

I consider myself duty bound to warn the public of the incalculable harm of such dependence and to demand its immediate cessation. No civilized person anywhere in the world should take upon himself the shame of appealing to foreigners in order to attain his aims. It is incumbent upon every Iranian to maintain the glory of Iranian history by learning to rely upon himself and upon the powerful force of the nation. The Iranian should be of an independent mind, and should live with an independent will. Compatriots! It is a thousand times better to starve in poverty and destitution rather than prostrate yourselves in humiliation before foreigners. Everybody knows that in an independent country there is nothing more despicable than becoming the instrument of foreigners, or allowing foreign interference in the country's political affairs.[15]

Reza Shah then was sensitive to the dangers that could befall Iran from the interference of the Great Powers and devoted much of the resources of his rule to protecting himself from those eventualities. That he was to fail utterly in achieving that goal—that his son was to achieve the throne by his father's failure to guarantee the independence of Iran—undoubtedly was another set of factors in leading to the Shah's attraction to foreign powers and particularly the United States.

In his memoirs from exile, the Shah struggled to justify his own rule. Had the dead Shah been able to read his son's text, he would have been unsettled. For the Shah attempted to legitimize his own rule and his pursuit of foreign legitimation in a variety of ways—even by remembering the foreign support his father had received. He recalled the recognition granted by his father by Ataturk in Turkey, the only foreign trip Reza Shah made: "Just how . . . much admiration his efforts garnered from the man he had sought to emulate, Ataturk, came some years after his coronation when he went on a state visit to Turkey and the honor guard's standard bearer knelt before him."[16]

But mostly the Shah recounted the esteem in which he had been held by the U.S. presidents. "President Eisenhower," the Shah recalled, "sent me a letter expressing his personal appreciation for my efforts in resolving the oil problems caused by Mossadegh's government."[17] President Eisenhower also praised the Shah, as the Shah remembered, "in an address to the American people." The president recalled the threat of a communist take-over in Iran during the Mossadegh period. "Under the courageous leadership of the Shah," Eisenhower declared, "the people of Iran met that danger. In their efforts to restore economic stability, they received indispensable help from us. . . . Iran remains free. And its freedom continues to prove of vital importance to our freedom."[18] President Kennedy was also remembered for acknowledging the significance of the Shah to the United States. "On a visit to the U.S. in April 1962, Kennedy stated that he considered me to be . . . a vital force in maintaining the independence of [my] country. . . . So when we welcome the Shah here we welcome a friend and a very valiant fighter."[19] Kennedy's successor is quoted as well. "Upon my visit to the United States, in August 1967, President Johnson also declared: 'The changes in Iran represent very genuine progress. Through your "White Revolution,"' Johnson continued, 'Iran has risen to the challenge of new times and new generations . . . without violence and without any bloodshed.'"[20] The point here is not the sincerity or astuteness of the evaluations of the Shah by the presidents. It is that even after being exiled by his own people—after having lost his throne in one of the great revolutions in world history—the Shah could take comfort in the praise which had been lavished on him by American leaders.

The attachment of the Shah to the United States began early and strengthened over the tenure of his rule. Many factors sustained that attachment and the formation of selfobject relationships with both the United States and its chief executives. The U.S. ambassador in Tehran, for example, reported the Shah's gratitude for American assistance in the 1946 liberation of Azerbaijan Province from occupying Soviet troops. The ambassador cabled the secretary of state that the "principal reason for sudden collapse of Azerbaijan movement in Shah's opinion, was (1) surprising weakness of Tabriz military organization, (2) high morale and determination of Tehran forces, and (3) most important, conviction by all concerned (Soviets, Iranians, and Azerbaijanis) that the United States was solidly supporting Iranian sovereignty."[21]

But the consolidation of American influence over the Shah and the Shah's utter dependency on the United States did not occur in earnest until the overthrow of Prime Minister Mossadegh. President Eisenhower recalled the effect his restoration had on the Shah. "The Shah is a new man," he wrote. "For the first time, he believes in himself because he feels that he is the King of his people's choice and not by arbitrary decision of a foreign power."[22] At that point, the United States was still maintaining the position that there had been no outside, and certainly no American, involvement in the August 1953 demonstrations which led to the ouster and arrest of Mossadegh. The coup was still portrayed as a popular referendum against the prime minister and in favor of the Shah.

There was, of course, outside involvement and specifically American involvement in the coup. With the success of that operation, the future of the Shah's regime was cast.

This initial dependence implied a narrowing of the regime's policy options to a pro-Western, mainly pro-American, stance in both its domestic and foreign policy behavior. The regime committed itself to a formal alliance with the West, and tied not only Iran's foreign policy but also the country's socio-economic development to the interests of the capitalist world. These constituted the basis for the development of Iran's "dependence relationship" with the United States.[23]

The coup established the initial dependence. For the rest of the 1950s, Iran under the Shah entered into a series of agreements with the United States which consolidated that dependence.

There were programs of massive economic and military assistance entailing the dispatch of American technical experts to Iran to ensure the proper use of American aid. Cooperation was especially close in the security field. American military personnel set about the reconstruction of the Iranian military through the professionalization of its standards and the modernization of its standards and the modernization of its equipment and training.[24] Iran responded appropriately. On October 11, 1955, the Shah formally joined the Baghdad Pact, the anticommunist alliance between Britain, Iraq, Turkey, and Pakistan. When a revolution swept Baghdad in 1958 and ousted the pro-Western monarchy, the revolutionary regime withdrew from the pact, causing profound embarrassment for the West. Nonetheless the pact was reformed, with the United States taking an active rather than passive role, and renamed CENTO, the Central Treaty Organization. Iran promptly transferred its membership.

The dependence was fostered as well by the oil consortium agreement of November 1954. The government of Iran continued to own Iran's oil. It delegated the responsibility for exploiting that resource to a government agency, the National Iranian Oil Company. NIOC, in turn, on the basis of a system of fixed percentages established by the 1954 consortium agreement, let contracts to the international oil companies for the lifting of Iranian crude. Thus, Western oil companies were effectively restored to their controlling place in Iran's oil industry. American oil companies managed to win a 40 percent stake in Iranian oil from which they had previously been completely excluded on account of the British monopoly. The British, who had controlled 100 percent of Iranian oil through the Anglo-Iranian Oil Company, saw their share reduced to 40 percent, with the remainder divided between the French and Dutch. The myth of Iran's nationalization of its oil industry was maintained, but for all practical purposes the contracts with the foreign oil companies constituted Iran's implicit surrender of its sovereignty over oil.

"This extensive American involvement in Iran," according to Amin Saikal, "brought with it a great increase in Western social and cultural influence. . . . This influence consolidated the overall structure of Iran's dependence on and vulnerability to the United States."[25] By the end of the decade, then, the United States had consolidated its influence over Iran, and the Shah had not merely acceded to that influence as being in the best interests of his country but had welcomed it as being in the best interests of his regime and himself as well. But with that influence went obligations. The Shah was quite aware of the lengths to which he would have to go to please his foreign patrons.

Toward the end of the decade, the Shah formed two political parties, to be headed by courtiers. Assadollah Alam formed the Mardom party while Manouchehr Eqbal was instructed to form the Melliyun party; both men were closely attached to the court and the Shah through their personal loyalty and years of service. Nonetheless, they contested the parliamentary elections of 1959 with great vigor, even if the range of their debate was highly constricted. When asked by a confidant why he had gone to the trouble of establishing this charade of democracy, the Shah was quite forthright. "They were started in 1959, helped by a kind of sentimental desire on the part of the Americans and the British to have a Westminster type of democracy here."[26]

What had become clear to thoughtful observers was that the influence of the United States in Iran had not, in fact, been consolidated as the Shah suggested in his cynical explanation of the formation of his tweedle-dum and tweedle-dee political parties. It was not simply the intrusiveness of the United States and Great Britain, forcing themselves on Iran. American influence was consolidated because the Shah sought that influence. As Henry Kissinger had put it, the Shah "was for us the rarest of leaders, an unconditional ally."[27] An American analyst assessed the Shah at the beginning of the 1960s, the decade in which American influence over the Shah had been consolidated. "The Shah, although highly intelligent," he concluded, "is emotionally insecure and shares with other Iranians a deep suspicion that the West may abandon him in the course of detente with the U.S.S.R. or by supporting his internal opposition."[28]

The Shah feared the loss of the support of the United States because of his realpolitik appreciation of the significance of foreign actors in Iranian politics and because of a psychological attachment steeped in transference. The Shah particularly agonized over the possibility of abandonment by the United States under the vigorous new U.S. president John F. Kennedy. The U.S. ambassador to Iran, Julius Holmes, explained to a visitor why the Shah had become so bothered: "What really upset the Shah was what Kennedy had said in his speeches. . . . The U.S. was for 'revolution'—that was the word. . . . The Shah interpreted these words to mean just one thing: we were going to support a revolution in Iran."[29]

When it became clear to the Shah that Kennedy did not intend his overthrow, when Vice President Johnson was despatched to Tehran to assure the Shah of U.S. intentions, when the Shah was able to dismiss Ali Amini—the American choice as reformist prime minister—and install instead his longtime friend and confidant Assadollah Alam, he felt less threatened. Feeling more secure in the support of the United States and increasingly confident in his ability to master the storms of internal Iranian politics, the Shah instituted his White Revolution. As with all his reforms from the throne, the White Revolution was meant to forestall demands emanating from the society itself, demands which might prove less manageable than those resulting from the reforms from above.

The decade of the sixties, then, was totally different for the Shah than the preceding ten years. The decade was marked by no challenge comparable to that posed by Mossadegh. The Shah did have to deal with bloody demonstrations that spread to major cities following his order to arrest the troublesome Ayatollah Khomeini in June of 1963. But while many were killed, those protests never developed into a systemwide threat. Furthermore, when Khomeini was exiled to Turkey, the problem seemed resolved. Certainly little which appeared to be politically significant was heard from the Ayatollah or his supporters for the remainder of the decade. Meanwhile, the Iranian armed forces were being effectively modernized with the assistance of U.S. advisers and U.S. equipment. SAVAK appeared to operate effectively in rooting out domestic opposition. The economy was growing steadily, at times explosively, as oil revenues increased and as the Iranian bourgeoisie invested more and more of their funds in Iran rather than expatriating them to Europe and the United States.

By the end of the 1960s, in short, it appeared to all observers of Iran that the Shah was firmly in control of his country and its people and that his throne was secure from internal as well as external challenges. On political grounds, the Shah appeared to have consolidated the independence of Iran from all foreign powers as well as his own ability to remain immune from foreign pressures. Yet a diplomatic cable sent from the United States embassy in Tehran to Washington in 1971 suggested that little about the Shah himself had changed.

Lately he has shown signs of trying to take a few pages out of General de Gaulle's book, searching for a way to assert his "independent nationalism" in foreign affairs. (He told a recent visitor that he had developed a real personal friendship and serious basis of cooperation with de Gaulle.) This recent disposition has not, however, as yet taken on any important substance. He continues to consult closely in the first instance with the U.S. . . . in all important matters of global policy.[30]

In fact, even after the boom in oil prices and the flow of billions of dollars of oil revenues to Iran, the basic dimensions of the Shah's dependency on the United States did not change. Of course, there was an ostensible change. The Shah manifested a grandiosity and arrogance toward the West—as he did toward his own people. He was fond of lecturing the West on its decadence and its failure to keep its own house in order, in comparison with his own country whose future was assured. But, in fact, the

Shah's basic dependency on the United States did not, in the first instance, stem from political or economic or security or strategic considerations but from psychological transferences. Therefore, alterations in the balance of power between Iran and other states, or indeed, the entire world, could not substantially affect the Shah's psychological dependency, at least for a substantial period of time.

For the remainder of his rule, the Shah—in public, at least—talked very tough. When Jimmy Carter was U.S. president, the Shah was asked what he thought an American president committed to extending human rights around the world and curbing American arms sales abroad would mean for Iran. The Shah minced no words.

> Relations between Iran and the United States are good and I do not think they could be otherwise. . . .
>
> Whenever a new administration takes over, there are those who imagine that everything will be changed. But it is only individuals who change; the long term interests of a nation cannot change. What is important is that everyone should know that if anyone wants a third or fourth rate Iran, we shall not tolerate that. We shall not accept anything less than a first class position for Iran.
>
> If they accept this, then they should meet our demands. If they do not accept that . . . then I will sit down and make up my own mind about the best means of safeguarding my country's interests, always remembering that Iran must have a first class status.[31]

The talk was tough. But in private the Shah had changed little from the diffident and dependent monarch about whom so many diplomats had cabled Washington for so many years. Even at the height of his grandiosity and arrogance, at the height of his bitter attacks on the West and especially the United States, U.S. diplomats reported the Shah was still in constant need of "hand holding."[32]

For ultimately, beneath the tough talk and the veiled and occasionally not so veiled threats to the United States, the Shah, like so many of his countrymen, was ashamed of Iran and its backwardness and personally humiliated by what he perceived to be the disdain in which Iran was held by the West. These complex feelings about the West—a mixture of admiration and resentment, a longing for acceptance and a fear of rejection, coupled with an almost preemptive rejection of the West—lay at the heart of Iranian xenophobia.

Farhad Kazemi, in his study of poverty in prerevolutionary Iran, presents a typical example of the way that complex of feelings toward foreigners worked among the lower classes of Tehran society. He describes the life of Hamid, a Tehran slum dweller who began selling fruit from the top of a box set up in front of his squatter settlement.

In a few days, the local police officer asked Hamid for regular extortion payments. Since Hamid could not pay the fee, he was taken to the police station and charged with obstructing traffic. Hamid protested at the station that selling fruit was not illegal and that others in the same location made a similar living. The police captain retorted that "the filth and irregular" life of Hamid and others like him in the settlement and other parts of the city has [*sic*] caused the foreigners to think that Iran was a backward country. Hamid responded: "Then, your highness, why doesn't the government build houses and find work for us so that foreigners would not have such thoughts about us?"[33]

The issue here is not the depredations of the local police or the role of the government in the social and economic life of Iran. Rather it is that a felt embarrassment over the opinions of foreigners was a constant feature of everyday life in Pahlavi Iran. This was, of course, not exclusive to Iran under the rule of Shah Mohammad Reza Pahlavi. Reza Shah, for example, after his return to Tehran from his state visit to Turkey, met Great Britain's ambassador to Iran, to whom he asserted that he would never visit Europe. According to the ambassador, Reza Shah "dreaded" seeing the contrast between the developed West and his own country.[34] In this case it was Reza Shah himself who dreaded the consequences of his personal evaluation of the West. Psychologically, the pain from a self-evaluated derogatory contrast with the West could be as painful as a derogatory evaluation made by a foreigner. Iranians, from the Shah on down, were subjected to both kinds of derogation—inflicted by themselves and by foreigners as well.

The empress of Iran, Farah Pahlavi, for example, recalled with bitterness her days as a student in Europe and, in particular, France. She remembered being asked in the 1950s, where she was from: "When I told them Iran, . . . the Europeans would recoil as if Iranians were barbarians and loathsome. But after Iran became wealthy under the Shah in the 1970s, Iranians were courted everywhere. Yes, your Majesty. Of course, your Majesty. If you please, your Majesty. Fawning all over us. Greedy sycophants. Then they loved the Iranians."[35]

The Shah echoed these sentiments. He told a royal courtier, "Now we are the masters and our former masters are our slaves. Every day they beat a track to our door begging for favors. How can they be of assistance? Do we want arms? Do we want nuclear power stations? We have only to ask, and they will fulfill our wishes."[36]

The Shah and his empress clearly relished their newfound national— and personal—power vis-à-vis the West. That new national power brought with it the possibilities for the expression of both dimensions of the ambivalence which Iranians had so long felt toward the West. On the one hand, there was the rage at the West for the control which had been exer-

cised and for the denigration which Iranians had for so long experienced in
contact with the West. But the converse of the disdain was the profound
admiration and awe for the achievements of the West, the achievements
which served as the basis for the power which the West had been able to
exercise over Iran for so many centuries. No one better expressed the ambivalence than the Shah. In an interview with *Der Spiegel* in early 1974, at
the height of his grandeur, the Shah declared, "I would like you to know
that in our case, our actions are not just to take vengeance on the West. As I
said, we are going to be a member of your club."[37]

This ambivalence—I want to beat you and be you, simultaneously—has
been a deep-seated feature of Iranian culture, and of long duration. Certainly the wealth of Iran, the policies of the Shah, and the speed of jet travel
contributed to making the ambivalence of Iranians toward the outside
world far more acute. For these three factors brought a huge increase in the
number of interactions between Iranians and foreigners—both foreigners
in Iran as well as Iranians traveling and living abroad. Even in the early
1960s, intense interaction with foreigners, at least among the upper classes, had been occurring for decades. In an earlier study of Iran by this
author, it was found that almost half of the most politically powerful members of Iran society had spent a minimum of ten years outside of Iran, while
fully one-third of the political elite had spent more than fifteen years outside their country.[38] But the interaction of Iran and the West increased
with a vengeance in the 1970s. As Iran's wealth blossomed, the Shah's
cherished infrastructure and developmental projects brought tens of thousands of foreigners to live in Iran. Iranian students went abroad in equal
numbers, and for the first time, tens of thousands of Iranians could afford
foreign travel. Contact with the West became an everyday feature of Iranian
life, a feature no longer restricted to the upper classes.

International tourists visiting Iran were one immediate source of foreign culture. In 1962, fewer than 75,000 foreign tourists traveled to Iran.[39]
By 1975 the number had increased to 600,000. More American tourists
arrived in 1975 than had tourists from all countries only a dozen years previously.[40] In the first six months of 1976, 40 percent more tourists arrived
than in the comparable 1975 period. As foreigners came to Iran in ever-
increasing numbers, the flow was matched in the opposite direction. Iranians toured Europe and the United States. Some 350,000 Iranians went
abroad in 1975. In 1976, 40 percent more Iranians traveled abroad.

The interactions were facilitated not only by foreign travel. The mass
media played their part. American television programs were constant fea-

tures of Iranian life. Iranians could learn the latest in American folkways and mores whether via "Dallas" or "Wheel of Fortune," or slightly more dated sources of American ways, courtesy of say, "Jeannie." Then there were the Americans themselves. While no precise survey was taken, approximately 50,000 Americans were living in Iran at the outbreak of the revolution.

Of course the exposure of Iranians to these bearers of foreign culture differed, primarily on the basis of their social class. Iranians with relatively poor education, living in relatively remote areas of the country, would see fewer Americans. But by the mid-1970s, virtually all the wealthiest Iranians seemed to crave travel abroad.[41] And irrespective of social class, more and more found the means to do it. Those who could not afford more, boarded air conditioned buses in Tehran and made the long overland journey through Turkey to Istanbul and then on to Munich and even Paris and London. But many found the funds to fly directly to Europe and the United States. Finally, there were those Iranians studying abroad. America was the favorite place, and by the time of the revolution, more students from Iran than from any other country were studying in the United States.

Yet another indication of the extraordinary growth in ties between Iran and the West, especially between Iran and the United States, was the rise in telephone communications between the two countries. James Bill gathered astounding data from AT&T on telephone calls from the United States to Iran.

In 1973, a total of 53,597 telephone calls were completed from the United States to Iran. This number increased to 122,477 in 1975, but by 1977 the number of calls had exploded to an astonishing 854,382. In these five years, the number of calls completed from the United States to Iran had increased by over 1,600 percent. In 1973 the 50,000 calls totaled almost 9,000 hours of conversation; four years later the annual hours of conversation had risen to over 134,000. In response to an unprecedented demand, the telephone company had increased the number of U.S.-Iran circuits from six in January 1973 to ninety in December 1977. By 1978 Iran had become the fourth largest revenue producer in the World for AT&T.[42]

The 1970s were years of increasingly intense interaction between Iranians and the outside world, primarily the West. As Iran's interactions with Europe and the United States became more intense and more salient, the meaning of those interactions became more problematic for the Iranian people as well as for the Shah. The Shah clearly felt the ambivalence to the West as deeply as did any Iranian. And insofar as the West and the United States were transferencelike relations for the Shah—objects onto which he displaced feelings more appropriately directed at significant figures in his own life—then the power of his "foreign" relations would be all the greater. It is clear that the Shah could point to a series of hurts which he had experienced or, more importantly, believed he had experienced in his dealings with the West.

A primary hurt and probably the initial significant experience with the denigrating control of the West must have been the invasion of Iran by the British and the Russians in August 1941. His feelings about the invasion, it is reasonable to suppose, although there is no direct evidence, must have been deeply ambivalent. He must have decried the violation of the territorial integrity of Iran as well as its political sovereignty. It must have been a blow to witness the armed forces, which his father had so laboriously and expensively constructed and from whose officers' school he had been graduated, collapse before the joint onslaught of the two great powers. But the Shah, however unconsciously, might well have taken some pleasure in seeing his powerful and punishing father finally receive what must have appeared to the Crown Prince as his long overdue comeuppance. In the process, of course, his father was deposed and Mohammad Reza offered the throne. The Great Powers were aptly named, for they had the power to make and unmake kings.

The Shah experienced other slights at the hands of the West, slights which accumulated over the years into a compendium of hurts. A major slight to the Shah occurred when the three Allied leaders appeared in Tehran in November 1943 for their wartime conference. Remarkably, no Iranian, including the Shah, had known they were to meet in Tehran until after they had arrived.[43] President Roosevelt, moreover, as recounted above, declined to call on the Shah, but agreed to receive him for a private meeting at the British legation, as if the young ruler were not the sovereign of the host country. Months later, President Roosevelt sent the Shah a letter about his impressions of Iran, impressions which were extremely distant from the concerns troubling the Shah.[44]

The White House

My Dear Shah Mohammad Reza: Sept. 2, 1944

Of course, I do not pretend to know Iran well on account of the shortness of my visit, but may I write you about one of the impressions which I received on my air trip to Teheran?

It relates to the lack of trees on the mountain slopes and the general aridity of the country which lies above the plains.

All my life I have been very much interested in reforestation and the increase of the water supply which goes with it.

May I express a hope that your Government will set aside a small amount for a few years to test out the possibility of growing trees or even shrubs on a few selected areas [and] to test out the possibility of trees which would hold the soil with their roots and, at the same time, hold back floods? We are doing something along this line in our western dry areas and, though it is an experiment, it seems to be going well.

It is my thought that if your Government would try similar small experiments along this line it would be worthwhile for the future of Iran.

I do not need to tell you how much I am interested in that future, and the future of the people of Iran.

With my warm regards,

Cordially yours,

The Shah's relationship with the United States did not improve appreciably under the presidency of Harry S. Truman. While the Shah believed Truman's firm stand to have been responsible for the Soviets' decision to pull their troops from Azerbaijan, the United States refused to come to the financial assistance of Iran. The Shah's principal purpose in making his first trip to the United States in 1949 was to acquire that longed-for U.S. financial and military aid. He returned from the United States "completely empty handed," and even after he made more vigorous reform efforts, the United States still refused substantial aid.[45]

The Shah assessed the consequences: "Such a serious setback to our hopes convinced many of my people that the United States had deserted them, and anti-American sentiment developed, with a corresponding strengthening of the National Front Party."[46] In short, the Shah was arguing that the American failure to offer him assistance was responsible for the rise of Mossadegh and the nationalization of the oil industry. The implications the Shah was trying to spell out at the time were clear—American money will keep Iranian internal politics on a course compatible with American interests. (Of course it is also not unreasonable to imagine that when the Shah spoke of the sense among his people of having been deserted and the concomitant growth of anti-American sentiment, the Shah was referring to not only his people but himself as well. He also had these responses to the U.S. decision not to provide Iran with assistance.)

With the overthrow of Mossadegh, the Shah was in a far stronger position to receive substantial aid. By eliminating his chief opponent and placing the Shah firmly on the throne, the United States was obligated to strengthen his hold so that he could remain there. The Shah finally had the initial reverse leverage which he would later develop so successfully. President Eisenhower, in a period when the United States was still denying its involvement in the coup, explained its effects on Iranian-American relations.

> The Shah is not bitter, but does feel that both Britain and America—but especially Britain—have made mistakes and have interfered unwisely in Iran in the past. He also feels that promises have been made to him by the United States which were not honored. He recognizes now his debt to us and hopes, as he puts it, that we have a realistic understanding of the importance of Iran to us.
>
> Like General Zahedi, he stressed the urgent need for prompt and substantial economic aid. He also spoke to me of military aid, a subject on which he has become more realistic in recent years. He no longer talks of jet planes and hundreds of tanks, but does talk of the assistance and training needed to produce crack mountain troops. He is fully aware of the importance of the army to the security of his country.[47]

By then the Shah owed to foreign powers both his initial accession to the throne as well as his retention of that throne in the face of the greatest threat to his kingship. With the ouster of Mossadegh, the Shah had his throne, but there were no oil revenues to finance it or the government. The British had succeeded in preventing the Iranians from enjoying the benefits of the oil nationalization for which Mossadegh had been responsible in 1951. Iranian oil revenues had been reduced to a trickle for more than two years. The Shah was forced to seek funds from the United States and to accept an agreement with the international oil companies which gave them control over both the level of Iranian production as well as the price they would pay for Iranian oil. After the restoration, the Shah had little influence over the fate of his regime or its financial well-being or security. To the contrary, the foreigners, in particular, the United States, called the shots.

All of those issues of crucial dependency were embedded in the Shah's memory. He found them compatible with his fundamental character structure. But they also grated. It was, he well understood, unseemly for the Shahanshah of Iran to be in the psychological need of the praise and sanction of the United States. Yet he understood that he was. It made for an extraordinarily delicate, yet complicated relationship between the United States and the Shah. The Soviet ambassador to Iran claimed that "in his heart, the Shah thought the Americans despised him and that he tried to pick quarrels with them on minor issues as a way of releasing his frustrations and complexes."[48]

In the mid-1960s, the United States and Iran were engaged in difficult negotiations over the sale of U.S. weapons to Iran. These negotiations were always troublesome because, despite the Shah's early interests in "crack mountain troops," thereafter he consistently pushed the United States for the most advanced weapons in American inventories. The Pentagon believed that Iran had little use for such sophisticated weapons and no technological capability to deploy them effectively. And no U.S. president had authorized the Shah to buy the weapons system of his choice, as would President Nixon in 1972. In 1966 the negotiations were intense because the Shah insisted on purchasing the advanced F-C fighter plane. In the face of U.S. reluctance to sell the Shah that aircraft, Assadollah Alam, then minister of court, complained to the U.S. ambassador that the Shah felt he was being treated by the United States as its "lackey."[49]

That feeling would never leave the Shah. He felt diminished—even humiliated—by his association with the United States.[50] Undoubtedly, he was. If this assessment of the psychological relationship between the Shah and the United States is accurate, then for him any association with the United States, even if the result was enhanced self-esteem for the Shah, would be diminishing in the sense that it was a regressive experience for the Shah insofar as the relationship entailed transference issues from his relationship with his father. Furthermore, no matter how the Shah's self-esteem was enhanced by the United States, it was always insufficient. His demand for psychological enhancement and well-being was so profound that it was unlikely he could have ever received satisfaction commensurate with his needs.

As a result, he felt demeaned, like a lackey. So on those rare occasions when the tables were turned, when the Shah had the opportunity to diminish the United States, he found it difficult to resist the opportunity. Oil prices were the realm in which that opportunity was most frequently presented. Oil prices were the most significant issue to the United States over which the Shah had some control. Simultaneously, of course, oil prices were the most crucial issue for Iran. Over the years, the Shah's demands for higher oil revenues for Iran had been frequently rebuffed by the oil companies. They always gave the Shah the same two answers. They declined to offer him a higher price for each barrel of Iranian oil pumped on the grounds that what they offered Iran would have to be offered to all oil producers—an arrangement which would be impossible given international economic realities. Failing a higher price, the Shah urged that oil companies lift a larger volume of Iranian oil, at the same price. This they frequently refused as well, on the grounds that additional Iranian oil could be sold only at the expense of other producers, most notably Saudi Arabia and Kuwait. The oil companies argued that they could not deprive those states of revenues in order to enhance the revenues of Iran.

By the early 1970s, however, the world had developed a ravenous appetite for oil, especially for the oil of the OPEC producers. When Arab oil producers enacted an embargo on oil shipments to states which supported Israel, during the Yom Kippur/Ramadan War, the Shah refused to join their ranks. In fact, he offered the oil companies as much oil for the West as they could lift from Iran, while leading the demand for higher prices. As a former U.S. diplomat with access to the Shah put it, "The Shah remembered with the greatest clarity every single time he had asked the oil companies for an extra one-fourth of a cent per barrel and they turned him down. Then, when he could move on prices he didn't give a shit what anyone else said. The Shah was really tough on this one."[51] The Shah was "tough on this one" because oil prices were the weapon with which he could flay the West, and especially the United States, for the hurts he believed had been inflicted on him.[52]

The final indignity was yet to come, however. In his memoirs, the Shah makes it clear that he considers the loss of his throne was not his responsibility. Rather, the Shah has argued at considerable length that the Pahlavi dynasty fell because of the failures of the United States. As one of the most astute U.S. diplomats who was witness to the Iranian Revolution put it, "Perhaps this ungracious attempt to gloss over his own flaws by criticizing his friends is the final legacy of America's intimate relationship with Iran during the reign of Mohammad Reza Pahlavi."[53]

What is being argued here is a bit more complex, however. Responsibility for the failures of the Shah rests ultimately with the Shah himself, but the United States is not without its own responsibilities. The United States failed to appreciate its significance for the Shah. Had it done so with appropriate sensitivity, it could have dealt with the Shah differently than it did and, in the process, contributed to the psychological strength of the Shah and thus to the longevity of his regime. An examination of this suggestion requires a more careful reading of the record of the Carter administration in its dealings with the Shah.

Paradoxically, as it may seem, when the brilliance of the Pahlavi dynasty appeared the most vivid, when the Shah's power appeared to be at its height, when he was less willing than ever to listen to the advice of others, the psychological need of the Shah for the United States was more acute than ever. What appeared paradoxical, as is usually the case with the paradoxes of politics, was not especially paradoxical after all. For, simply put, the Shah had lost his other sources of psychological strength and needed more desperately to rely on the United States.

Not surprisingly, he was not aware of this reality. Indeed, if it had been brought to his attention, he would have bridled at the thought that he "needed" the United States in any way other than as a source of the weapons he believed would allow him to transform his country, through the use of petro-dollars, into a first-rate military power. But irrespective of his insightfulness, it was precisely at the time when he appeared the most invulnerable that his relationship with the United States was the most crucial for him.

By the 1976 U.S. presidential election campaign, the Shah had, as one of his confidantes said, "put all his eggs in the American basket."[54] However unable or unwilling to articulate this idea they might have been, all those responsible for administering the Shah's regime knew that as well. For example, one of the Shah's most senior officials proposed a new policy that dealt entirely with matters internal to Iran. The Shah's only response was to ask, "but do you think the Americans will accept this."[55] When Richard Helms was ambassador to Iran, the Shah decided to shut down the radio and television stations which he had earlier authorized the U.S. armed forces to establish in Iran. When the U.S. ambassador protested, the Shah responded, "We have to take them over, but we will guarantee you the same hours of American programming as before."[56]

Countless similar examples demonstrating the significance of the United States for the Shah could be offered. But as the Shah's psychological dependence on the United States crystallized, two events occurred. On the one hand, as the Shah had done years before, the United States stopped "minding the store." On the other, the 1976 election campaign and the election of Jimmy Carter exacerbated the Shah's worst fears.

Former CIA director, Richard Helms, was appointed ambassador to Iran after Watergate. By the time he reached his post, the Watergate hearings had begun. From early 1973 to the end of 1976, the ambassador returned to the United States on thirteen occasions to testify at the investigations of the scandal.[57] Those years bracketed what is described above as the high water mark of the Shah's grandiosity. With the Shah ostensibly unassailable, close scrutiny of Iranian politics seemed relatively unimportant. The U.S. ambassador was in Washington, there were few Persian-speaking foreign service officers in Tehran, and the United States relied on SAVAK for its intelligence on internal Iranian affairs. The United States lost touch with Iranian political realities.

Precisely at this time—at the moment the Shah was most desperately in need of American support—Jimmy Carter became the Democratic presidential candidate. It is not the intention of this book to detail the political relationship between the Shah of Iran and the United States during the presidency of Jimmy Carter. Nor is it the aim of this book to offer a detailed account of the Iranian Revolution. Both those stories have been told at great length by former officials of the Carter administration, including the president of the United States,[58] by former officials of the Shah's regime, including the Shah himself,[59] by officials of foreign governments,[60] as well as by scholars, journalists, and others.[61] Consequently, only certain aspects of the history of 1977, the crucial year preceding the revolution, and of 1978, the year of the revolution itself, will be recounted here. Those aspects are the few details drawn from the swirl of events and actions, conversations and intentions, which serve to illuminate the psychological state of the Shah.

As the 1976 U.S. presidential campaign unfolded, the Shah would become increasingly disquieted. For Carter struck the Shah as the embodiment of that piety which could prove damaging to the Iran-U.S. bond the Shah had so assiduously cultivated for thirty-five years. Carter, after all, stood for a foreign policy with two pillars. He sought the internationalization of the American concern with human rights, and he sought severe limitations on the international arms race, especially the sale of weapons to the third world.

Both of those policies chilled the Shah because they seemed aimed at his rule. No country in the world was the subject of more attention for its alleged or actual violations of human rights than Iran. And no third world country was buying more weapons or developing its armed forces at a faster pace than Iran. When Jimmy Carter talked of human rights and arms sales, the world, but especially the Shah, thought he was talking about Iran.

The actual extent of human rights violations in Iran during the 1970s will never be known. The victors of the revolution have proved unreliable witnesses to Pahlavi history. The fate of SAVAK records is uncertain, and although officials of the Khomeini regime reported their intention to publish the complete files of both SAVAK and the Foreign Ministry, reports issued by the revolutionary regime would be suspect. The accounts of former Pahlavi officials are equally suspect. But as in so many other phenomena, what is germane here is not some quantitative measure of the status of human rights in Iran under the Shah, but the common perceptions of that status. About that there is no doubt.

With the vigorous championing of human rights organizations, as well as committed Americans and Iranians, the Shah was portrayed in the 1970s as the world's most vicious ruler. Martin Ennals, the secretary general of Amnesty International, announced that "no country in the world has a worse record in human rights than Iran."[62] Finally, in the 1970s, it was Iran—not Haiti or China or the USSR or Vietnam or Paraguay or any other state whose viciousness toward dissent was well known—which became the focus of worldwide concern for its violation of human rights.[63]

Similarly, there was no doubt in the minds of thoughtful persons that when Jimmy Carter deplored American arms sales abroad, he was referring, in some principal way, to Iran. For example, the first sentence of the 1976 report *U.S. Military Sales to Iran*, prepared by a subcommittee of the Committee on Foreign Relations of the United States Senate, made it clear that "Iran is the largest single purchaser of U.S. military equipment."[64] In this realm as well, then, there was little doubt that Jimmy Carter was referring to Iran.

The result was that the Shah as well as his opposition—in fact, all thoughtful Iranians—saw the campaign of Jimmy Carter as a significant threat to the Pahlavi system and to the close relationship the Shah had managed to establish with the United States. The Shah did not keep his concerns to himself. In an interview with Mike Wallace before the 1976 elections, the Shah expressed his doubts about Jimmy Carter, who "fails to fully comprehend Iran's role in the defense of American interests."[65] Nonetheless, with the announcement of the election results, the Shah sent a cable of congratulations to the president-elect. The text of the cable was released to the Iranian press, which dutifully published the congratulations of the Shah. But there was no text of any cable in reply. The weeks passed and still Jimmy Carter failed to respond to the Shah's message. Both the Shah and the politically aware in Iran were struck by the absence of any message of thanks from President-elect Carter. By the end of 1976, the perceived snub of the Shah was the talk of Tehran. No message, in fact, was ever received.

The British ambassador to Iran could not help but observe the growing strain in the relationship between the Shah and the United States. "The Shah," observed Sir Anthony, "made no secret of his apprehension at the victory of President Carter."[66] Perhaps in response to that apprehension and the snub he perceived from his failure to receive any correspondence thanking him for his good wishes, the Shah took steps to demonstrate that he had no intention of being pushed around by the new U.S. president. In a repeat of his response to the election of that other Democratic president in 1960, the Shah sent his vice minister of war, Gen. Hassan Toufanian, to Moscow in December 1976. General Toufanian was in charge of arms purchases for the Iranian armed forces. While he rarely made decisions about precisely what to buy, he executed the decisions made by the Shah. By sending Toufanian to Moscow, the Shah was signaling that there were sources of weapons available to Iran other than the United States.

Again, after Carter's election, but before the inauguration of the president, the Shah communicated another important message to the United States. On December 15, 1976, the oil ministers of OPEC had their regularly scheduled meeting. The Shah made it clear that Iran would take, by far, the most radical stance in the defense of producer interests. At the meeting, the Shah had Iran's delegate argue for an immediate 15 percent increase in oil prices. Saudi Arabia had asked for a 5 percent increase. Jimmy Carter had been asked his opinion and had warned that a 15 percent increase would be a serious blow to the industrialized world. By the end of the meeting, the Shah had backed off from his original demands, and Iran settled for a 10 percent increase, reserving the right to ask for an additional 5 percent on July 1, 1977. Saudi Arabia refused to accept the higher level of increase and raised its own prices only by 5 percent.[67] But once again the Shah indicated he did not intend to be intimidated by the United States. It was, of course, not easy to appreciate his psychological dependency in the face of what appeared to be a brusquely anti-American stance, especially the elaborate minuet he was dancing with the U.S. president-elect.

As the inauguration of President Carter approached, the anxiety level among Tehran's ruling circles was high and the sense of expectation among all Iranians was acute. The U.S. ambassador was later to characterize that anxiety. "When the Carter administration took office," he cabled Washington, "the Shah and Government of Iran were uncertain about its interests in this part of the world, its commitments to previous agreements, and its attitude towards the Shah as ruler."[68] In his inaugural address, President Carter did nothing to alleviate the Shah's mounting anxiety. Rather, he returned again to the principal themes of his campaign. He warned against the dangers of indiscriminate arms sales and of the importance to his new administration of protecting human rights everywhere in the world.

Iranians listened intently to that message and believed their judgment was confirmed. Jimmy Carter would be a president like JFK. He would pressure the Shah for reforms and liberalization. And the Shah, irrespective of his new petro-power, would have to respond positively. As the British ambassador saw it,

the reaction of the Shah's opponents, particularly the large and vociferous student community in the United States and the *ci-devant* political leaders in Tehran (whose fortunes had briefly prospered in President Kennedy's day), was precisely the reverse. They took comfort and courage from what they rightly detected as a potential weakening of the absolute support which their enemy had received from Washington for so many years.[69]

Sometime after his inauguration, Jimmy Carter held a reception for the foreign diplomatic corps. As he moved down a line of foreign ambassadors, receiving the congratulations and best wishes of their governments, he stopped opposite Ambassador Ardeshir Zahedi and asked him to thank the Shah for his best wishes. Tehran's newspapers headlined Carter's thanks to the Shah. That those thanks were—at least by the dictates of Iranian protocol—inexcusably late and inexcusably rude for not having been tendered directly to the Shah, was not mentioned. But the headlines indicated the significance the regime attached to the idea that the Shah was important to, if not blessed by, the U.S. president. That relationship was precisely what was important to the Shah.

The ambiguity in the evaluation of the Shah communicated by the new U.S. president had two important negative consequences. For one, it powerfully affected the Shah. Jimmy Carter undoubtedly was deeply concerned about reports of human rights violations in Iran and about the consequences for both regional conflict and internal political turmoil from the vast arms purchases of the Shah. But ambiguity in the American stance was, it is suggested here, precisely the wrong way to communicate that concern. The ambiguity weakened the Shah's faith in the commitment of the United States. With a weakening of his faith in that commitment, there was a weakening of his self-esteem.[70] For the Shah would have believed that the selfobject from which he derived such an important contribution to his psychological well-being was no longer functioning according to the patterns by which he had come to form that selfobject. In effect, the United States—as embodied in President Carter—was rejecting the idealization and mirroring which he directed toward the United States. With that rejection came a diminution in the usefulness of the selfobject as an instrument of esteem. With that diminution came a further erosion in the Shah's esteem and his capability to rule.

The perceived weakening of the American commitment to the Shah had yet another major consequence in Iran: that perception served to embolden the opponents of the Shah. As suggested above, the Iranian people resembled the Shah at least insofar as they held ambivalent feelings toward the United States. One of the components of that ambivalence was to believe in the power of the United States to determine Iranian politics. What the United States wished, they had come to believe, would happen.

One of the principal goals of Ayatollah Khomeini was to break that culturally cherished belief. He struggled to give Iranians the sense that they are the masters of their fate. Thus, during all those months when the revolutionary regime held fifty-two U.S. citizens captive, the favorite slogan of Ayatollah Khomeini and his followers became, "The U.S. can't do anything." It was repeated so often and so ritualistically that it came to seem a magical incantation. But its use by the Ayatollah was in the service of breaking a pattern of Iranian culture and Iranian character. If the Iranians repeated it often enough, it would come to be believed and, perhaps, the United States would not somehow be able to destroy the revolutionary regime. At the very least, the Iranian people would take courage from the courage of the Ayatollah and be able to maintain their anti-American resolve (and hatred) in the face of their fear of U.S. retaliation.

What Jimmy Carter managed to do, in short, was to weaken the resolve of the Shah by fostering doubt in the commitment of the United States to his rule, while simultaneously encouraging the opposition to the Shah to believe that the United States would support their efforts to alter the balance of power in domestic Iranian politics. As one of President Carter's new National Security Council staff members for the Middle East put it in a characteristically understated fashion, "It was quite apparent in Washington that the Shah was apprehensive about the new Carter administration."[71] Despite that appreciation, the steps which the new president took only served to exacerbate the apprehension. For months after his inauguration, no announcement was made of the president's choice of a replacement for Ambassador Richard Helms who had left Tehran. Then in April 1977, President Carter announced his choice of Ambassador William H. Sullivan to be sent to Tehran. But with the delays in the ambassador's leaving his Manila post and the Washington confirmation and briefing processes, he did not arrive in Tehran until June.

Besides his delay in naming of a new ambassador, the president took other steps which appear to have troubled the Shah. An entry in the diary of the Shah's ambassador to London gives the flavor of one such occurrence:

Sunday, May 22, 1977: President Carter makes a speech at Notre Dame University and says America must abandon its inordinate fear of Communism and its attempts to contain it world-wide. That policy, he says, led America to embrace any dictator who opposed Communism. Vietnam is cited as an example. Bloody hell! What does HIM [His Imperial Majesty] think of these remarks, I wonder?[72]

In a subsequent entry, Ambassador Radji answered that question. In his notes for July 6, 1977, Radji recounts that in a meeting between Secretary of State Vance and the Shah in Tehran, the secretary of state had fed back to the Shah criticisms of the Shah's record on human rights which had originally been formulated by a leading Iranian civil rights spokesman, Haj Seyyed Javadi. The Shah was taken aback, and as a result, "the Shah is more insecure in his relations with the Americans than ever."[73]

On the very next day, July 7, 1977, the president of the United States notified Congress of his intention to sell seven AWACS reconnaissance aircraft to the Shah for more than $1.2 billion. Despite the support shown by President Carter, the Shah could take but slight comfort from the announcement. Controversy arose almost immediately. Opposition on diverse grounds came from different sources. Some objected to the further militarization of the Persian Gulf. Others complained about the amount of money Iran was spending on weapons instead of the development of the country. Still others feared the possibility of loosing to the Soviets the sophisticated American technology included with the airplanes. But perhaps most damaging to the Shah were the widespread complaints in the United States that the Shah's regime was unstable and more American weapons would both contribute to that instability as well as be lost in the event of a change in the regime. The House Foreign Affairs Committee voted against the sale, and President Carter, anticipating defeat by the full Congress, inflicted another blow to the Shah by withdrawing, on July 28, 1977, his proposal to sell the AWACS to Iran.

Ambassador Sullivan explained the failure of President Carter to convince Congress of the merits of the proposed AWACS sale on two factors—successful lobbying of Congress by human rights activists as well as congressional pique at White House ineptitude in its insistence on determining the congressional calendar against the wishes of the congressional leadership.[74]

It was Ambassador Sullivan's duty to inform the Shah of this new turn of events. The ambassador recalls what happened: "When I told him why I had come, he began a long, pained monologue about the fatuity of the

United States Congress, the treachery of the American Press, and the ordeal that seemed to result from being friendly to our country. I let him get it all out of his system and waited until he seemed ready to discuss airplanes and radars."[75]

What followed were two months of intensive negotiations between the White House and congressional leaders over the conditions the sale would have to meet before it could be approved and equally arduous negotiations with the Shah to receive the security guarantees the leaders of Congress had demanded. The president resubmitted the proposal which, ultimately, was approved in October of 1977. From a political point of view, it was a pyrrhic victory. The congressional debate had stirred the deepest American concerns about the Pahlavi regime. In turn those concerns had fed back into the congressional deliberations and then been broadcast on American television and published in American newspapers. They were then disseminated throughout the world.

The effects on the Shah and on the Iranian opposition were electrifying. The Shah understood the message from the United States as saying he needed to transform his regime. The president of the United States, the Shah had concluded, was demanding that he liberalize. Indeed, U.S. diplomats in Tehran were counseling Washington to pressure the Shah to make greater progress toward liberalizing his regime. In a cable to the State Department, they concluded:

Urge continuing US concern for human rights in Iran both in terms of Iran's image as a de facto ally of the US and for Iran's own future stability in which the US is interested. Avoid ex cathedra denunciations, or excessive USG [Government] support for critics of Iran's human rights situation, but work consistently with Iranian policy makers and the bureaucracy to identify areas in which liberalization of Iranian law or practice will not hurt internal Iranian security but indeed help it in the long run.[76]

Not surprisingly, liberalization was precisely what the Shah turned his attention to doing. The year 1977 was characterized by a reciprocal process of demands and concessions largely between the intelligentsia and the Shah. Whereas in the past the demands they made would have been met with repression, in 1977 the demands were either granted or, with certain glaring exceptions, allowed free expression.[77]

By the middle of the year, it was clear the Shah was on the defensive.[78] Liberalization appeared less and less a coherent policy for opening the system to assure its political base than a means to placate the new U.S. president and appease the opposition. But the scent of appeasement only served to stimulate the passion of the opposition. In early August, the Shah used the periodic electrical outages then sweeping Tehran to justify replacing Prime Minister Hoveyda, after more than twelve years of service, with the secretary general of the Rastakhiz party, Jamshid Amouzegar, who, despite his party credentials, was widely known as a nonpolitical technocrat committed to better management of Iran's economy. The promotion of the chief party official suggested to many that its role in Iran's political life was being enhanced. Amouzegar's appointment seemed to signal an institutionalization of liberalization. Shortly after his appointment, the *Kayhan* newspaper seemed to confirm that sense. It launched a lengthy front-page series entitled "What is Wrong." The series was initiated with a warning that people expected the government "to act decisively to eliminate evils like water and power shortages, traffic congestion, telephone failures, inefficiencies in agriculture, low productivity, shortages of skilled labor, lack of modern public transport facilities, corruption, bribery, red tape, addiction, educational problems, profiteering, and so on."[79] The press had served faithfully, since the overthrow of Mossadegh, as an instrument of the regime. Now it appeared to be continuing in that role, but in a different capacity—as a transmitter of the flaws of the system rather than its strengths. The paper was inundated by letters criticizing aspects of Pahlavi Iran and urging changes.

The liberalization continued despite the outpouring of resentment against the Shah and despite the arrest of Ayatollah Teleghani and the killings at a Tehran squatter settlement. To strengthen the Shah's resolve and to lay to rest some of the rampant speculation about the Shah's standing with the United States, the ruler was invited to Washington for a state visit in November 1977. The positive results which the United States so eagerly sought from the visit were not to be realized, in public at least. For weeks before the visit, Iranian and non-Iranian groups opposed to the Shah targeted the state visit as the perfect occasion to express their disdain for the Shah and their resentment at American support for him. The word went out among student groups and opposition activists that the anti-Shah action would occur outside the White House on November 15, the day of the formal White House ceremonies welcoming the Shah and the empress.

Supporters of the monarch had learned of these plans weeks in advance and were determined to organize pro-Shah demonstrations. They rallied their followers to demonstrate before the White House. None of this was unknown to security officials of the United States government, who reacted with increasing alarm over the possibility of violent confrontations between supporters and opponents of the Shah. Security officials were certain they could protect the president and his foreign guests, but they were less certain of their ability to protect the demonstrators from each other. Their concerns were well founded. While President Carter was welcoming the Shah and the Emperess, the demonstrators broke through the police lines separating them from each other and a wild melee broke out opposite the White House. The police responded by firing tear gas into the midst of the clashing demonstrators.

As Ambassador Sullivan, who had returned to Washington for the occasion, put it:

The world was treated to the spectacle of the President of the United States and the Shah of Iran dabbing at their eyes with their handkerchiefs, tears streaming down their cheeks as they made their formal presentations of respect. Under the circumstances, both chiefs of state retained their composure well and completed their statements as scheduled. The rest of us did our best to contain our tears and coughs as the ceremony moved to its completion.[80]

The official initiation of the state visit, in short, was a public relations disaster. But President Carter apparently did much to rectify the dismay the Shah must have felt on the lawn of the White House. The National Security Council staff man for Iran, Gary Sick, reports that at the state dinner, President Carter toasted the Shah with "a brief but heartfelt statement about the importance of Iran to the United States and the need to preserve the relationship," after which "the Shah had tears in his eyes."[81] When the Shah returned to Tehran, Secretary of State Vance remembers receiving from the embassy in Tehran "glowing reports of his new mood of confidence and satisfaction."[82]

That new confidence may have been demonstrated in the regime's response to the major test of its liberalization policy. Shortly after the Shah returned from Washington, courage bolstered, SAVAK destroyed the hopes of many for peaceful change when club-wielding thugs put an end to a meeting, outside Tehran, called to form a united political opposition. The Shah had, apparently, returned from Washington strengthened to show a different face to the opposition. But his liberalization policy was dealt a fatal blow. It was by then startlingly clear that liberalization was to be restricted to approved regime channels of communication and was to be limited to expressions of dismay. Meaningful political activity against the government seemed no more possible at the end of 1977 than it had at any time since the 1963 crackdown.

The final day of the year gave proof to this new reality. President Carter had decided to press the momentum engendered by the visit of the Shah to the United States. He proposed a New Year's Eve stopover in Tehran between state visits to Warsaw and New Delhi. Ambassador Sullivan reports, "The Shah was thrilled at the prospect. It would not only demonstrate internationally that the close relations between the two countries continued; it would also show his critics in both the United States and Iran that the great American champion of human rights considered his regime worthy of personal endorsement."[83]

It was during that fateful visit that Jimmy Carter made the first toast of the 1978 New Year to the Shah.

I think it is a good harbinger of things to come that we could close out this year and begin a new year with those in whom we have such great confidence and with whom we share such great responsibilities for the present and for the future.

Iran, because of the great leadership of the Shah, is an island of stability in one of the most troubled areas of the world.

This is a great tribute to you, Your Majesty, and to your leadership and to the respect and admiration and love which your people give to you.

We have no other nation on earth . . . closer to us in planning our mutual military security. We have no other nation with whom we have closer consultation on regional problems that concern us both. And there is no leader with whom I have a deeper sense of personal gratitude and personal friendship.[84]

Nine days later Iranian police fired on a crowd of religious demonstrators in Qom, killing between six and a hundred people, depending on whose count is believed.[85] The "island of stability" rapidly disintegrated into revolution.

9

Revolution and Collapse

Two of the Shah's pillars of support failed him before the revolution. His divine protection and his psychic twins were gone. The revolution was a brutal demonstration that he had lost the support of the people of Iran. What was left to him was his relationship with the United States. There were two American perspectives on the Shah. Some in the United States continued to see him as he had been seen in the past—as the monarch who needed constant "hand holding" by Washington in order to bolster his resolve. But the predominant view of the Shah had been transformed; the "reverse leverage" argument had taken hold in Washington.

It is obvious how the United States could have concluded that the Shah had become a "forceful personality," a powerful monarch who had shaken off his ambivalence, weakness, vacillation, and general paralysis of will.[1] As long as the Shah's sources of psychic strength functioned—as they did so effectively in the 1970s—the Shah cut a formidable figure. He projected a sense of personal power and forcefulness whether in private audiences with U.S. officials or in public ceremonial functions. All throughout the 1970s, he appeared to act with decisiveness and vigor. He seized the opportunity presented to him by President Nixon and Secretary of State Kissinger to expand Iran's power by placing massive orders for military hardware from the United States. With seeming ruthless determination, he cracked down on urban "guerrillas" who had conducted terrorist operations in cities throughout Iran. His secret police launched a vigorous campaign to eliminate the domestic opposition which had turned to violence, and they unleashed a wave of torture against their prisoners.

The reporting from the U.S. embassy in Tehran in the 1970s repeatedly amplified these themes and helped foster the impression in Washington that the Shah was, finally, his own man.[2] In addition, the activities of Iranian exile groups in the United States and Europe contributed to the image of the Shah as a ruthless and determined tyrant. One such group, for example, published posters which contained three photographs: One showed a row of stakes to which blindfolded men were roped, waiting for the volley of bullets which would bring death. A second picture showed a firing squad executing other blindfolded prisoners. And in a third photographs, almost looking on and seeming to relish these spectacles, was a smiling Shah in his most ostentatious ceremonial regalia. Bedecked with medals, sashes, hanging pendants, a jeweled belt and covered by a golden embroidered cape, wearing a spectacular jeweled crown, and carrying a gold and jewel encrusted staff, the Shah strode before a phalanx of Iranian military officers bearing drawn swords and resplendent in ceremonial uniforms. The poster, published by an organization called the Committee for Artistic and Intellectual Freedom in Iran, which boasted prominent American intellectuals on its board, was devastatingly effective.

The Shah's presentation of self, the reporting from Americans "in the field," and the activities of opposition groups in Europe and the United States all contributed to the belief that the Shah was a decisive leader. To many who sympathized with the challenges he confronted and the solutions he had adopted, he had become a tough and decisive leader. To his opponents, he had become a tyrant. In both cases, his supporters and detractors agreed that in the 1970s, he had become, in effect, a new man.

That view of the Shah led to four beliefs in the minds of American policymakers. These beliefs, in turn, were to have crucial consequences for U.S. policy during the Carter administration. First, the Shah's demonstration of an apparent new sense of personal power and determination led to the belief that the United States was no longer responsible for the fate of the Pahlavi dynasty. Second, this view of the Shah led American officials to believe that their active involvement in preserving the Pahlavi throne was less necessary than in the past, given the Shah's own capabilities. Third, certain Carter administration officials were led to believe that given the Shah's personal power, substantial pressure could be brought against him in order to ameliorate Iran's political problems. Finally, these three views contributed to the belief that it would be desirable for the United States to distance itself from the regime of the Shah.

The internal opposition to the Shah had yet a different view of Iranian political realities. Its members had a highly elaborated understanding of the role of the United States in Iran. They had never accepted the notion of "reverse leverage" nor believed that the lines of significant influence ran from Tehran to Washington. The Shah, in their view, was still the creation of the United States. The meaning of dependency to the opposition was obvious—the Shah was the puppet whose strings were pulled by the Americans. Orders, in short, came from the U.S. ambassador. The Shah was merely the executor of the will of the United States. For those political activists, the source of political change in Iran was Washington, and the way to bring about political change in Iran was to influence Washington's perceptions of Iranian realities.

The first year of the Carter presidency had been a mixed year for Iran and for the Shah. Each of the principal actors seemed to have confirmed their understandings about the ways in which Iranian politics worked.

The Shah must have felt very much as he had in the first year of the Kennedy administration. Then the new Democratic president had singled out Iran for special attention and insisted on reforms which would broaden the base of the Shah's rule and bring genuine popular acclaim to the monarchy. The Shah, deeply anxious, nonetheless embarked on a series of reforms. He survived those reforms, and most importantly, in the process of instituting them, he managed to escape further pressure from Kennedy. In 1977 the Shah did something of a repeat of 1961: he instituted a series of reforms and eased censorship; he appointed reform-minded personnel and shunted some of the old elite to the sidelines. For these changes, he apparently managed to win the support of President Carter and to reestablish the bonds between Iran and its chief patron.

The United States pressed him to change policies, to ease repression and allow political forces freer expression, to broaden the base of meaningful political activity. When it felt the Shah was weakening or that the opposition sensed the United States to be abandoning the Shah, the Shah was invited to Washington for a state visit. When it was clear that the visit had done much to sustain the Shah, yet another official visit was arranged for the leaders of the two countries. Jimmy Carter's visit further sustained the Shah. The U.S. ambassador was able to report that as a result of the New Year's visit, the ruler's "uncertainties have been totally dissipated. In the aura of this situation, I feel I have been able to develop a relationship of trust and confidence with the Shah. I regularly have long talks with him on a whole range of subjects and these discussions are marked by candor on both sides."[3]

Only the opposition felt betrayed. Where they had anticipated a year of fundamental changes in the distribution of power in Iran, they saw the changes of 1977 as entirely the gift of the Shah, made under the duress of American pressure. With the exuberant toast of the U.S. president, they imagined that it would be back to business as usual—that the "gifts" extended by the Shah would be withdrawn by the Shah.

The end of 1977 appeared, on the surface at least, to be marked by far less fervor than its inception. Tehran was largely calm. The visit of the president had done much to allay the anxieties of the Shah and to quiet as well as disappoint the heightened expectations of the opposition for further change.

The decisive year of the revolution began with the ruler reassured of American intentions but nonetheless wary of the moralistic U.S. president. His wariness was made the more acute because he had already lost three of the pillars of his psychological well-being. The opposition was wary because they perceived the United States to be repeating the pattern it had followed so consistently in the past. After a period of pressuring the Shah to liberalize and enact popular reforms, the United States would retreat in the face of the Shah's determination to hold unfettered power. Finally, the United States was wary as well. The United States had not begun to worry over the Shah's physical health because it was unaware that the Shah had cancer. Nor did it worry about the erosion of the Shah's psychological strength because no one thought about the Shah along those lines. But it was clear that 1977 had been marked by unprecedented political turmoil. The economy was overheated, with inflationary pressures, massive bottlenecks, and supply disruptions. Yet oil revenues were plummeting, and the government had resorted to international borrowing to meet its deficits. Finally, the Shah's old nemesis, Ayatollah Khomeini, was back in the news. In the fall, students at the secular universities had called for his return from Paris. Then in November his eldest son, Mostapha, had died in Iran. Allegations of SAVAK responsibility for his death, allegations which had also widely circulated at the times of the deaths of Jalal Al-e Ahmad and Ali Shari'ati, swept the country. It was clear that the Shah's liberalization had not exorcised the passion of the political opposition. Instead, the genie was out of the bottle.

The first deaths of the revolution occurred in 1978 on that January day in Qom when students and clerics protested the publication, on January 7, 1978, in the newspaper *Ettela'at*, of an article entitled "Iran and Red and Black Colonialism." The piece was a scurrilous defamation of Ayatollah Khomeini. By then, the four principles guiding U.S. policy toward Iran appear to have been firmly in place. As a result, it followed that the United States no longer had to assume operational responsibility for the perpetuation of the Pahlavi throne. When junctures in the revolution crucial to the fate of the regime were reached, the U.S. ambassador, backed by the Department of State and others in Washington, concluded that the Shah himself was the person most capable of dealing with the challenges and, more importantly, most capable of deciding which challenges to meet and how to meet them. John Stempel, a State Department officer in Tehran during the revolution, put it most directly: "Reduced to its essentials, President Carter decided to leave the crisis to the Shah to handle. . . . Having decided that 'the Shah knows best,' the administration drifted into a 'minimalist' strategy of as little direct involvement as possible."[4]

This tendency was exacerbated by a growing split within the Carter administration about how to deal with the revolution. The State Department and the National Security Council differed markedly in their understanding of the nature of the revolution and their solutions for its resolution. More accurately, Secretary of State Vance and National Security Adviser Brzezinski differed bitterly about how to deal with the revolution. There were, of course, lower-level functionaries in both institutions who shared a common view of the nature of the revolution and the nature of the policies which should be followed by the United States. But it was not often that those common views were matched by agreement at the top.

Simply, the president's National Security Adviser developed a "Saudi-centric" policy toward the Iranian Revolution. The basic premise of his strategy was that the United States had to support the Shah of Iran to the end, no matter how bitter that end turned out to be for either the Shah or the United States. Any abandonment of the Shah would communicate a powerful message to all U.S. allies and all other states which looked to the United States for support. That message would portray the United States as a fickle ally, unreliable in times of crisis, willing to abandon those who had been committed to the principles of American foreign policy. The result, according to Brzezinski, would be an erosion of support for the United States all over the world and particularly in Saudi Arabia. The turmoil in Iran made Saudi Arabia even more significant to the realization of U.S. interests in the world, and a withering of Saudi confidence in the United States would lead to its accommodating the enemies of the United States. For Brzezinski the course was clear: the United States had to stick with the Shah to the end.[5]

In the State Department, there was much more hope for an accommodation with the demands of the Shah's political opposition. Initially that opposition was seen principally in the remnants of Dr. Mossadegh's National Front. It was believed that those aging proponents of constitutionalism could be brought into the Pahlavi system if it were genuinely opened and the powers of the Shah curtailed in conformity with the 1905 Constitution. The inclination of the Department of State, in short, was to advocate human rights and the further liberalization of the Pahlavi system.

The differences between State and NSC in terms of the most appropriate U.S. responses to the revolution and the perceptions of what was at stake in Iran mask two important issues. First, the position of National Security Adviser Brzezinski was devoid of policy substance. To stay with the Shah to the end was not a substantive action policy. It was a policy devoid of content, of action for preserving the Shah's position in the face of the escalating demands of the growing opposition. It was a policy which gave support to the charges of the Shah that Ambassador Sullivan was able to offer him nothing but vague assurances of U.S. support with no specific advice for action.

The policy of the Department of State was in its own way equally devoid of content, for liberalizing a political system without institutional mechanisms for processing and absorbing those demands would result, inevitably, in challenges to the entire system. Moreover, liberalizing in the face of escalating opposition demands served not to co-opt and temper those demands but only to stimulate them. The Iranian opposition perceived the Shah's liberalization as an indication of his weakness. They were emboldened to up the ante every time there was an indication that they might achieve their previously stated goals.

Yet another aspect of the U.S. problem in dealing with the Shah and the revolution was that Ambassador Sullivan came to be distrusted by the National Security Council and the White House because he was perceived, and correctly, to be "Vance's man" in Tehran. In the chain of command, Sullivan's superior was the secretary of state, and it was to the secretary that Sullivan reported. But the accusation that he was "Vance's man" meant more—it meant he had bought into the accommodationist vision of the Department of State. Therefore, those in the U.S. government who believed it was possible and appropriate for the Shah to crush his opposition were reluctant to work through the ambassador. The result was that the ambassador always believed there were backdoor channels from Washington to Tehran which did not include him.

In the final months of the revolution, at least one of those backdoor channels was Ardeshir Zahedi, the long-serving Iranian ambassador to the United States. Zahedi determined perilously late in the revolution that the Shah was drifting aimlessly. He believed that more than anything else the Shah needed a firm hand in Tehran, so Zahedi resolved to return to Tehran and "put some backbone in the Old Man," as he confided to his friends.[6] Once in Tehran, he initiated a vigorous campaign to preserve the throne of his sovereign and former father-in-law. He met with supporters and enemies alike. He met with the Shah and his family. He maintained direct communications with NSC chief Brzezinski, bypassing the ambassador and the U.S. State Department. But he was unable either to rally members of the opposition to the side of the Shah or to convince military officers to prepare for a military solution to the revolution. Despite Zahedi's best efforts, Ambassador Sullivan reported that

the Shah would regularly speak to me about Zahedi's activities and tell me that he did not approve of them. He would say that we should not be deceived into thinking that Zahedi's course of action was a fruitful one. He asked me to inform Washington that Zahedi did not understand the domestic situation in Iran and that, although his heart was in the right place, he was out of touch with reality.[7]

Other channels bypassed the ambassador as well. Late in 1978, Gen. Robert "Dutch" Huyser, deputy commander (to Gen. Alexander Haig) of U.S. forces serving in Europe, received a telephone call from the office of the chairman of the Joint Chiefs of Staff asking his opinion of sending a U.S. military man to Iran. Huyser had spent considerable time in Iran and knew the Shah personally, having gone to Iran in April 1978 at the Shah's request. Huyser had been back to Iran in August of 1978 to report to the Shah on the "mission" he had been asked by the Shah to perform.[8] In early January 1979 he was again ordered to Iran, over strenuous opposition by General Haig, in order to maintain the unity of Iran's senior officer corps behind the rule of the Shah, to prevent any unauthorized use of the military against the opposition, and to prepare for the possibility of a coup on behalf of the Shah. General Huyser reports that when he checked in with Ambassador Sullivan,

he almost immediately handed me a wire he had received from Secretary Vance. The message directed that I ignore all previous instructions. It seemed I was not to make contact with the Iranian military leaders as originally instructed. I was to do nothing until I received further word from Washington. This was not a good omen. It made me realize there was not unity of effort in Washington. It was obvious the State Department had one view of the situation and the Department of Defense and Executive Branch another.[9]

Eventually, Huyser received authorization to proceed. He was to spend nearly four weeks traveling through Tehran wearing a bulletproof vest, and meeting with senior military officers to mobilize their resources and commitment to the rule of the Shah. At the end of each day, the general would return to the embassy where he stayed with the ambassador. After a discussion during which they relayed their daily activities and impressions, each would retreat to a secure telephone. The general would report to Secretary of Defense Harold Brown, who would report to National Security Adviser Brzezinski. The ambassador, meanwhile, would do the same with Secretary of State Vance.

Besides being mistrusted by segments of the U.S. national security bureaucracies and having to cope with the existence of multiple channels of communication between Washington and Tehran, the ambassador operated under other handicaps. Ledeen and Lewis note that Sullivan's

political independence had earned him the suspicion of successive American administrations. Nixon thought that he was a "Johnson man"; the Carter people considered him a "Kissingerian." Thus Sullivan was forced to be purer than Caesar's proverbial wife, meticulously following instructions, attempting to change the views of those with whom he disagreed by subtle methods rather than by direct challenge, and generally maintaining a low profile.[10]

Stempel agrees with the consequences of their assessment. He does not explain why "Sullivan himself realized the Carter administration was uncertain about him," but he makes it clear that the result was that the ambassador toed the administration line, which, of course, was the line of his boss, the secretary of state.[11]

As a result of these factors, the ambassador was never certain that the policies he was receiving from the Department of State were, in fact, the policies of the president. He knew that the secretary of state and the national security adviser shared no common view of the Iranian problem and that the president seemed to be giving contradictory signals about his wishes. Sullivan also knew that he did not have the personal authority to make his own policy. As the Shah himself put it,

For the balance of the year I received numerous messages from various people in and out of the Carter administration pledging U.S. support. Whenever I met Sullivan and asked him to confirm these official statements, he promised he would. But a day or two later he would return, gravely shake his head and say that he had received "no instructions" and therefore could not comment. Sullivan appeared to me always polite, always grave, always concerned. He came to see me several times a week. He seemed to take seriously everything I said to him. But his answer was always the same: I have received no instructions.[12]

The effect of these differences of perception within the U.S. government and the relationships between the ambassador and Washington were of extraordinary significance for the Shah. Together they produced a relationship with the Shah totally different from those which had existed with previous U.S. ambassadors. In 1978, Ambassador Sullivan laid out the options for the Shah "many, many times."[13] But the ambassador never explicitly told the Shah what the United States believed he should do and what in its judgment was the most effective means to preserve his throne.

Most significantly, the United States could never bring itself to the point of suggesting that the Shah use force to preserve his throne. Despite the fact that there were frequent encounters between the armed forces and protesters, relatively few casualties occurred during the revolution. The revolutionary regime would boast of the 60,000 to 100,000 martyrs whose deaths contributed to the overthrow of Pahlavi tyranny. Eqbal Ahmad, an observer sympathetic to the revolution, put the number of deaths at 70,000.[14] James A. Bill, citing studies by Ahmad Farokhpay, calculates that 10,000 to 12,000 persons were killed during the revolution.[15] Said Arjomand estimates "about three thousands killed in the whole of Iran," from Black Friday in September 1978 to the collapse of the Imperial Guards, and with them, the Pahlavi System, in February of 1979.[16] Ervand Abrahamian, who throughout the revolution closely studied the newspapers from all cities of Iran as well as the publications of the opposition, counted all the reports of casualties from throughout the country. The casualty toll by midsummer had resulted in less than 1,000 dead.[17] It is difficult to suppose that more than 5,000 died in the entire struggle to overthrow the monarchy. In fact, as with the atrocities of SAVAK, the number of casualties during the revolution will never be known with assurance. But what appears remarkable are the relatively small number of deaths which occurred during the fourteen months of violence preceding the return to Iran of Ayatollah Khomeini.

There were some notable days in which many were killed. Black Friday, as it has come to be known, was a day of death during which military units opened fire on some 20,000 demonstrators who had gathered in Jhaleh Square for speeches by religious leaders. Unbeknown to many of the demonstrators, the previous evening the government had imposed martial law to begin early on the morning of the 8th. That decision had been made in response to the unprecedented demonstrations of September 7, the end of the Islamic celebration of Ramadan. On that day, processions superbly organized by religious leaders and containing vast numbers of marchers—

well over 100,000—had intimidated the authorities into imposing martial law.

That decision was communicated to opposition leaders. The secular leaders sought to avoid confrontation with the armed forces, but the religious leaders, including the current president, Hashemi-Rafsanjani, pressed for a showdown. The religious leaders carried the day. On September 8, there was an early morning debate in Jhaleh Square between military officers and opposition leaders, during which the officers urged the leaders to disperse their followers. Meeting with a complete refusal, the officers issued a formal order to obey the martial law and disperse. Still the crowd refused the budge. The order was then given to fire, and the armed forces shot into the crowd. For the rest of the day the shooting continued, as the military sought to oust all the demonstrators who had infested the neighborhood around Jhaleh. When the day ended, the military had succeeded, but only at high cost. While the count of the government differs markedly from that of the opposition, it appears that some few hundred demonstrators were killed and 3,000 to 4,000 were treated for injuries.[18] The shootings electrified the country. More Iranians were driven into the ranks of the opposition, and those already there began to escalate their demands. For the first time, moderate secular opposition leaders began suggesting that the Jhaleh massacre meant that reform of the Pahlavi system was impossible. The Shah would have to go.

The high number of dead and wounded at Jhaleh was an exception, however. There were, of course, other days in which many were killed. There were far more days in which some were killed. But over the course of the revolution, the regime acted with surprising restraint. It clearly had a decisive monopoly of armed might, yet it did not use that asset effectively to preserve itself. Basically, after Jhaleh, the Shah refused to allow the use of deadly force against the Iranian people.[19] Thereafter he consistently warned against the use of force, even to save the Pahlavi dynasty.

The role of the United States in contributing to the Shah's resolve to avoid the use of force is difficult to establish with certainty. Gary Sick, the NSC staff member with responsibility for Iran, has recounted the telephone call President Carter made to the Shah shortly after the Jhaleh massacre: "Carter told the Shah that he was calling to express his friendship and his concern about events. He wished the Shah the best in resolving these problems and in his efforts to introduce reform."[20] Other commentators have suggested that the call conveyed its message far more strongly. Ledeen and Lewis, for example, claim that "Carter told the

Shah . . . that he hoped there would be no further lives lost in the streets of Tehran and that the regime would be increasingly liberal in its treatment of its opponents."[21] It is not difficult to imagine that the Shah heard the telephone call as supporting his own sense of the need to avoid further loss of life.

Not long after the Jhaleh massacre, Ambassador Sullivan reports that he and the U.K. ambassador Sir Anthony Parsons began seeing the Shah on a regular basis. The Shah told them that he had

considered the use of the military option and rejected it. He felt he could suppress political dissidence by military force and keep it suppressed so long as he was personally on the throne. But then, in the first allusion to his ill health, he said he would probably be turning over authority to his son, the crown prince, in the course of the next few years, and after his departure from the scene the young man would not be able to continue to rule by military force. He felt, therefore, that it was essential for him to move rapidly to establish a democratic political system that would sustain the dynasty after his own departure.[22]

The Shah retained this policy against using deadly force for the remainder of the revolution, even after he ordered the installation of a military government in early November. Some weeks after its formation, on December 21, Gen. Gholem Reza Azhari, the prime minister, requested a visit from the U.S. ambassador. Ambassador Sullivan arrived and was shocked to find the prime minister bedridden, having recently suffered a heart attack. The general warned that while his condition was not serious, that of the regime was: "the troops had now been in the streets for four months and . . . were becoming badly demoralized. The effect of their orders, which permitted them to fire only in the air, no matter how badly they were abused or how heavily they were pressed, left them in a state of shock."[23]

The Shah's refusal to order the use of deadly force continued even after he received a message from National Security Adviser Brzezinski urging that the Shah do what was necessary to defend his regime. The message was delivered to the Shah by the majority leader of the Senate, Robert C. Byrd of West Virginia, whose son-in-law was Iranian. Prior to his audience with the Shah, the senator met with Ambassador Sullivan. When informed of the president's message, the ambassador said, "The Shah is going to ask you, 'Does this mean you're for shooting people?'" The ambassador knew the Shah. That was the question he asked the senator. The Shah never changed his policy.[24]

The refusal of the Shah to order his troops to action was a decisive factor in his defeat. The Shah knew his people as well as anyone knew them. He understood that his refusal to order deadly force would become known to the opposition. They would be emboldened by the knowledge, not constrained by it. In effect, the absence of the threat of government force was to contribute to the frenzy which swept the country in the late fall of 1978. Only after he had lost his throne did the Shah make it clear that he understood this consequence. After reiterating his decision not to "spill blood," the Shah was asked if he thought that policy had been a mistake.

That should have been any government's attitude—to establish law and order. The mistake was not to establish law and order. It's not a question of spilling blood or not. Either you have law that any government must enforce or you don't. In our case, it was becoming a lawless country. Now many people say that if my government had enforced law and order there would have been a hundred times less casualties than there have been in the past 15 months.

I think the one mistake was to adopt this policy [of not spilling blood] . . . because then the opposition saw that now we were surrendering under duress and pressure and they decided they could go all the way.[25]

In the face of the Shah's reticence to order that the military actually use weapons to preserve his throne, the Carter administration could not bring itself to counsel the Shah to do so.[26] The closest the United States came to advocating that policy occurred in a by-now notorious telephone call from Zbigniew Brzezinski to the Shah. On November 2, 1978, Tehran had been rocked by its single worst day of destruction. Crowds had roamed the city, setting fire to symbols of "Western decadence and corruption," including liquor shops, banks, government offices, and a wing of the British embassy. They met no resistance from the Iranian armed forces, who had been ordered not to intervene by the commander of the army and Tehran martial law administrator Gen. Gholam Ali Oveisi. The general had apparently sought to force the Shah's hand and thus bring about a military government with himself as its chief. Instead the Shah "did the worst thing possible. He brought in a military government, but one that was military in name only. The Shah bypassed the hard-line Oveisi and instead appointed an ineffectual parlor general, Azhari, who soon earned himself the rhyming sobriquet, 'eshali,' diarrhea-ridden."[27]

The next day, the president's national security adviser telephoned the Shah and recalls what he told the ruler:

"The U.S. supports you without any reservation whatsoever, completely and fully in the present crisis. You have our complete support. . . . Secondly, we will support whatever decisions you take regarding either the form or the composition of the government that you decide upon. And, thirdly, we are not and I repeat, not encouraging any particular solution." . . . The Shah responded to the effect that he was very appreciative of the message "but it is a very peculiar situation," and went on to suggest that he had been made to feel that "extreme measures, if at all possible, should be avoided."

I then responded by saying, "well, you in effect, it seems to me have a problem of combining some gestures which would be appealing in a general sense with a need for some specific actions which would demonstrate effective authority." The Shah simply said "yes." I went on to add, "It is a critical situation, in a sense, and concessions alone are likely to produce a more explosive situation."[28]

Apparently, the Shah hung up from this conversation with the national security adviser understanding that he had been urged to restore order first and to liberalize later. The Shah telephoned Ambassador Sullivan for clarification. "As usual," the Shah later described it, "the American envoy promised to cable Washington, but when I next saw him, he said gravely that he had received no instruction."[29] In his memoirs the Shah provides a torturous (and tortured) explanation of why he did not pick up the telephone directly and call President Carter for "clarification." He did not do so, the reader is assured, because the Shah always scrupulously followed "the protocol of international diplomacy."[30]

The Shah did, however, reach one firm conclusion from the lack of specific instructions from Washington. "The fact that no one contacted me during the crisis in an official way explains everything about the American attitude . . . the Americans wanted me out."[31]

The fact is that the Shah was contacted on numerous occasions "in an official way." The U.S. ambassador, by the Shah's own account, called on him several times a week. In addition, National Security Adviser Brzezinski telephoned the Shah the day after the worst crisis of the revolution to pledge American support for a get-tough policy, support which the Shah claims he understood. In addition, the Shah received a telephone call directly from the president of the United States.

This last telephone call is, perhaps, the most interesting of all the official communiqués between the ruler and the United States because the Shah had absolutely no memory of that conversation. In his book written in exile, the Shah remembered the telephone call he received from President Carter at Lackland Air Force Base in Texas, where he had flown to regain strength following his cancer treatments in New York and there reached an agreement with the White House on his eventual departure from the United States. On December 13, 1979, President Carter telephoned. "He warmly wished me good luck," the Shah recalled, "and reiterated the assurances of his aides. It was the first and only time I had spoken with the President since wishing him farewell on New Years Day 1978 when he visited Tehran."[32]

In fact, that was not the first time the two leaders had spoken since the president's departure from Tehran. President Carter had called the Shah to offer his support on September 10, 1978, after the Jhaleh massacre. Carter had interrupted his meetings at Camp David with President Sadat and Prime Minister Begin to speak with the Shah.[33] Ambassador Sullivan reported from Tehran that the telephone call had delayed the Shah from attending an audience with a group of American businessmen. When they saw the ambassador later in the day, they reported that the call from the president had left the Shah "considerably buoyed."[34]

The Shah may have been buoyed at the time, but in the unwelcome leisure of his exile, he could not recall the conversation with President Carter. At that point the Shah was seeking to avoid responsibility for the fall of his dynasty by shifting that responsibility to the Americans, who, in his mind, had abandoned him in his months of need.

What is essential here, however, is not to assign blame but to analyze complex historical processes. In this analysis, the Shah's failure to remember his conversation with the president, his inability to understand appropriately the telephone conversation with the national security adviser, his refusal to call the president or any other U.S. official for explicit clarification, and his refusal to use the U.S. ambassador in Tehran to help fashion policies toward the unfolding revolution are all indications of how hopelessly befuddled the Shah had become. In the waning months of the revolution, the Shah had experienced a massive psychic regression which brought with it a psychological paralysis entailing memory losses and an inability to act.

There were occasional indications of the Shah's failing capacities throughout 1978. In March, on the occasion of the Iranian New Year celebrations, the senior Israeli diplomat in Iran was invited to visit the Shah at his Persian Gulf retreat on Kish Island. The diplomat was shocked by the Shah's depression and indecision. He concluded that the Shah was lost because he was incapable of running the country.[35]

When Ambassador Sullivan returned to Tehran from his summer vacation, he immediately requested an audience with the Shah. He reported that the Shah appeared "tanned, healthy, and relaxed" after spending the summer at the Caspian Sea.[36] Yet despite the appearance of health, the Shah talked in a very different way. He told the ambassador that he had

figured out how the demonstrations, strikes, and protests which had swept
Iran for the preceding months had occurred. The Shah had

concluded that the actions that he had just outlined represented the work of foreign
intrigue. What bothered him, he said, was that this intrigue went beyond the capabilities of the Soviet KGB and must therefore also involve the British and the
American CIA. He said that he could understand the British intrigue to some extent, because there were those in the United Kingdom who had never forgiven him
for nationalizing the oil industry. . . . What bothered him the most, he continued,
was the role of the CIA. Why was the CIA suddenly turning against him? What had
he done to deserve this sort of action from the United States?[37]

The Shah's resort to extraordinarily fanciful conspiracies to explain the
outbreak of popular resentment which had characterized 1978 was an
important indicator of the plummeting state of his mental capacities.[38]

White House personnel who heard the telephone call between President
Carter and the Shah after the Jhaleh massacre were aware of the Shah's
failing capacities. "Most of the call," Gary Sick later reported, "was a virtual monologue by the Shah. [He was] speaking in a flat, almost
mechanical voice."[39] Sick also reported that during that call the Shah
sounded "stunned and spoke almost by rote."[40]

The British ambassador, Sir Anthony Parsons, had his own acute observations of the Shah. Sir Anthony returned from his summer leave after the
Jhaleh riots and did not call on the Shah until September 16. The ambassador was "horrified by the change in his appearance and manner. He
looked shrunken: his face was yellow and he moved slowly. He seemed exhausted and drained of spirit."[41]

Sir Anthony also received a briefing on the Iran situation from former Prime
Minister Hoveyda, who had recently been dismissed as minister of court.
Hoveyda thought "the main problem . . . was the Shah's inability to make up
his mind and to show the people that he was directing a clear policy."[42] Sir
Anthony came to understand firsthand what that acute observation meant, for
shortly thereafter he joined the U.S. ambassador for meetings almost every
other day with the Shah. In those meetings the Shah would engage in long
discourses on the various courses of action open to him. While he was clearly
inclined to press his liberalization program and save his throne through further
democratization, he never had a program for democratization which would
mobilize the people to his side. Rather ironically, the liberalization gave the
opposition the opportunity to strike at his regime. In the meanwhile, he never
removed the martial law he had imposed after the Ramadan procession. The
messages were both mixed and confused.

The Jhaleh massacre appears to have consolidated and sealed the Shah's psychological regression. In their first meeting after Black Friday, Sir Anthony Parsons reported that the "Shah then asked plaintively why it was that the masses had turned against him after all that he had done for them."[43] A few days later, the Shah, again receiving Sir Anthony in a private audience, informed him that "he was worried that the Americans might be plotting with his opposition" and that "he was no longer sure that his regime would survive."[44] The Shah's remarks immediately after Jhaleh suggest that the final two pillars of his psychological well-being had been decisively damaged. The Iranian people whose admiration he had held as a matter of faith had, he appropriately realized, turned against him. Finally, he had come to believe that the Carter administration sought his ouster as well. When the final props of his capacity to function were destroyed, as he believed they had been by the Jhaleh massacre, he was no longer able to do Shah. As Said Arjomand notes, "There can now be no doubt that the collapse of the man preceded the collapse of . . . the monarchical regime."[45]

There are many indications of the Shah's paralysis. Perhaps the most telling is his inability to order his armed forces to shoot to preserve his throne. On one notable previous occasion, in June 1963, the Shah had been willing to "spill blood" to save his throne: he had sanctioned Alam's orders to the army to clear the streets of demonstrators protesting the arrest of Ayatollah Khomeini. The troops opened fire and in three days, after considerable loss of life, they broke the resistance. Those orders, however, as recounted above, were originally conceived by Prime Minister Alam. The Shah consented to them, but only because it was Alam who had formulated them and given them to the military commanders for execution. During the Iranian Revolution, there was no Assadollah Alam to issue such orders. The Shah could not do so alone. But not only did he fail to give orders to use deadly force to quell the revolution, he consistently gave orders not to use force. When he decided to institute martial law in early September, he telephoned General Oveisi who was to be martial-law commander. "Begin applying the martial law tomorrow," he told the general, "but I do not want anybody's nose to bleed."[46]

The Shah was to urge restraint for the remainder of his rule. Arjomand notes that, "the Shah frequently scolded Oveisi for fatal shootings, and commanders in Qazvin, Mashhad, Tabriz, and elsewhere who disobeyed Tehran and ordered their men to shoot to kill in self-defense in October were reprimanded."[47] In exile, however, the Shah tried to make a virtue out of his inability to save his throne through force. When he was asked why he chose to leave the country for exile, he replied, "To avoid bloodshed. That is the difference between a king and a dictator."[48]

In addition to his inability to use force, the reports of virtually everyone, Iranian and foreigner, who had the opportunity to meet with the Shah after Jhaleh came away stunned or at least distressed, depending on the extent of their premeeting briefings. The Shah was described as depressed, indecisive, vacant, and listless. In November 1978, court insiders assured me that the Shah was "no longer functioning" and that virtually all his kingly duties had been assumed by his wife, Empress Farah, "the one with the guts," as Hoveyda described her.[49] In December 1978, General Azhari concluded his meeting with Ambassador Sullivan with the words, "You must know this and you must tell it to your government. The country is lost because the king cannot make up his mind."[50]

The United States, however, continued to deal with the Shah after Jhaleh as if he were still a functioning political leader. Thus National Security Adviser Brzezinski believed that a telephone call of considerable ambiguity would be sufficient to embolden the Shah to take the forthright action many believed would still be sufficiently timely to save the Pahlavi dynasty. But the Shah could no longer hear messages of that sort from the United States, and he had already ruled out the use of force against the mounting revolution. What was needed, instead, was far more direct intervention by the United States in the affairs of Iran.

That position was reached too late in the revolution. On January 4, 1979, the notorious "Huyser mission" was launched.[51] Considerable ambiguity clouds the Huyser mission to this day, but by the time General Huyser arrived in Tehran, the Shah had long since ceased to function as ruling monarch. In response, General Huyser worked with senior military officers separately from and even without the knowledge of the Shah. But their unity and their commitment to the Pahlavi dynasty were rapidly unraveling and virtually disappeared when the Shah flew from Iran on January 16, 1979. He had asked the senior generals not to come to Tehran's Mehrabad Airport to witness his departure and had refused to leave instructions for the chief of staff to communicate with him in exile.[52]

Finally, it was the United States which failed the Shah. Not so much by the conflicting messages which reached the Shah from Washington. Not by the inability of the U.S. ambassador to supply the Shah with the kinds of answers he sought. Not by General Huyser working without the Shah's knowledge with his own armed forces. And certainly not because the United States ever worked with his opposition, despite the Shah's belief in the treachery of the Carter administration—a belief that had been established in the early days of the 1976 presidential campaign and nurtured during the Carter administration, especially by the pressures the Shah felt to liberalize his regime. Ultimately it was the behavior of the United States during the revolution of 1978 which confirmed the Shah's belief that he had been abandoned by his most significant ally. During the revolution, Ambassador Sullivan refused to give the Shah specific advice on how to deal with the burgeoning unrest and violence against his regime. "You're the Shah," the ambassador was telling the ruler. As Ambassador Sullivan was to recall some years later, "The Shah had obviously been used to getting advice from the United States on internal politics and, therefore, he may have been justified in believing that he was being given the brush off."[53]

But the Shah's certainty that his fate was sealed came directly from President Carter. On December 7, 1978, the president was asked at a news conference in Washington if he expected the Shah to survive the revolution. The President's reply was

I don't know, I hope so. This is something in the hands of the people of Iran. . . . We have never had any intention of trying to intercede in the internal political affairs of Iran. We primarily want an absence of violence and bloodshed, and stability. We personally prefer the Shah maintain a major role in the government, but that is a decision for the Iranian people to make."[54]

By equivocating in its support for the Shah, both privately and in public, the United States effectively, if unwittingly, destroyed the psychological capacity of the Shah to act. The Shah later mused about this equivocation in a pathetic fashion: "Is it any wonder that I felt increasingly isolated and cut off from my Western friends? What were they really thinking, and what did they want—for Iran and of me? I was never told. I never knew."[55]

In the midst of the stress induced by the threat to his rule posed by the revolution, the Shah had been particularly dependent on U.S. support because his three other bases of psychic strength had been eliminated. Not only were they gone, but the stress of the revolution had induced a regression in the Shah whereby he became all the more needy of American support. But it was precisely at that time that the United States chose to ignore its historic commitments and, effectively, to abandon the Shah. Having been abandoned by the United States, the Shah collapsed. With his collapse came the entire edifice which had been so laboriously built by father and son and by those eight U.S. presidents whose photographs, taken with the Shah on official state visits, continued to adorn the U.S. embassy until November 4, 1979, when the "students in the line of the Imam" leapt the walls and crashed the doors to capture the embassy and its diplomats in a way that would forever change world history.

10

Lessons for U.S. Foreign Policy

Had the United States conducted its foreign policy in Iran in a different fashion, the regime of the Shah might have been saved. There are many who would question the desirability of that outcome. Although they are hard to find in the United States, there were many admirers of Ayatollah Khomeini who remained dedicated to his leadership to his death. There are others who believe that the Khomeini regime was a necessary stage through which Iran had to pass if it is to complete its progress from oppression to democracy. While the Khomeini regime may have been worse than that of the Shah, these people argue, the revolution was positive because it broke the Pahlavi regime. The rule of the clerics will prove to have been an interregnum.

This work takes a different point of view. It is difficult to know whether the rule of the clerics will be an interregnum in the near term. In some sense, of course, every regime is. But the Pahlavi dynasty lasted fifty-four years, from 1925 to 1979. Interregnums, particularly in Iran where every important political process appears to occur with all the deliberateness of a highly refined and delicate ritual performance, can last for a very long time.

Such regimes can also do a very great deal of damage. Iran has suffered incalculable harm under the reign of the clerics. Millions of Iranians fled the turmoil of the revolution and settled in Europe and the United States. Those Iranians appear to have been the most highly educated and technically skilled. They also included a large number of the entrepreneurs who had driven so much of Iran's economic development. The clerics also imposed a reign of terror on Iran which resulted in far more deaths and far more imprisonments and vicious tortures than were imaginable under the Shah. The clerics have also done staggering harm to the education system,

258

including the comprehensive system of higher education which, in the last years of the Pahlavis, had just begun to produce a cadre of trained and technically competent men and women to lead the development of the Iranian economy. The clerics, through their imposition of Ayatollah Khomeini's vision of an Islamic society, have reversed the considerable social progress which had been made under the Shah. Perhaps the most serious loss to Iranian society has been the full participation of its women. While women remained in the labor force because of the manpower shortage brought about by the lengthy war with Iraq, Ayatollah Khomeini frequently articulated the role he considered proper for them—homebound wives and mothers. The result has already been a loss of the productive energies of a major proportion of the population, as women have moved away from many of the professions which they had begun under the Shah.

Perhaps the most devastating human cost of the clerical regime was its refusal to settle the war with Iraq, save on terms imposed by Ayatollah Khomeini. Within a few weeks of its would-be "blitzkrieg" invasion of Iran in September 1980, the Iraqi onslaught had become mired in the wastes of Iran. By June of 1982, the Iranians had succeeded in expelling the last Iraqi troops from all but the disputed border areas. Iran then faced a monumental choice. It could seek to bring the war to an honorable close, having repulsed the invasion and liberated its territory. Or it could move the war into Iraq to punish the aggressors. With Khomeini at the helm, there was little surprise that Iran chose the latter course.

For the next six years, Iran incurred hundreds of thousands of dead and wounded. Through frontal assaults against the Iraqi defenses before Basra, the "war of the tankers," and the devastating "war of the cities," the Ayatollah sought vengeance. Only when Iran had suffered a series of startling battlefield reverses in the spring of 1988—fleeing the Fao Peninsula and the Majnoon Islands, and fearing full-scale American involvement on behalf of Iraq—did Iran accept a cease fire.

In addition to the stunning loss of life, there were massive nonhuman costs as well. Because of the continuation of the war, all available economic resources were devoted to its pursuit. The economy suffered dramatically. Iran reverted to the status of a middling third world power. The economic progress which Iran had experienced under the Shah was arrested. The entire infrastructure of the Iranian economy—roads, communications, plant, and equipment—suffered as investment capital was diverted away from postponable expenditures to the more immediately pressing needs of the war. As a result, there are vast, financial requirements confronting the country which will impede its future development as well as divert its manpower.

In short, it is hard to argue that the ouster of the Shah was a progressive act, given what followed. But not every outcome of the revolution was negative. Perhaps the most important positive outcome was the psychological well-being the Iranian people derived from reasserting control over their own destinies. The sense that the Shah had sold his fate, and with his fate, that of his people, to the Americans had become nearly universal in Iran. The revolutionary process, including the capture and incarceration of American diplomats, was an important catharsis for the Iranian people. Just how short-lived it was, however, can be seen from the Iranian view of the Iran-Iraq War. It is referred to in Iran as the "imposed war." The Iranian people are taught to believe that it is a war which the "arch-satan," that is, the United States, zionism, and imperialism, have forced on Iran through their principal agent, the Iraqis. In short, the rest of the world is somehow so taken with Iran's significance that it cannot let go. Iran is too much a treasure and a prize to the rest of the world to leave it to its own devices. The grandiosity of the Shah, in short, is repeated again and again by the Iranian people. It is, after all, their grandiosity which justifies the idea of an "imposed war," thus placing blame for the perpetuation of the war elsewhere while absolving themselves of all responsibility.

Given the many negative and few positive lasting achievements of the revolution, it is possible to argue that Iran would have benefited from a perpetuation of the regime of the Shah. Had his regime been preserved, especially with its gradual liberalization to foster more widespread participation and true democratic features, the Iranian people would have been better off. Certainly the United States would have been.

It is a central thesis of this work that the United States was deeply implicated in virtually every phase of the rule of the Shah and of the revolution of the Iranian people which so decisively rejected that rule. The United States bears responsibility for what happened in Iran because it was so deeply enmeshed in the Pahlavi dynasty. It is a further thesis of this work that had the United States acted differently at different stages during the rule of the Shah, the outcome of that rule would have been different. The United States contributed, perhaps in decisive ways, to make the Shah into the tyrant he became. It fostered his grandiosity by building his rule economically and militarily. It did the same psychologically by allowing the Shah to use it and its presidents as selfobjects. They even encouraged the

Shah to use them and their country for the mirroring, idealization, and merger functions he needed so desperately to operate as Shah.

Having contributed so much to the construction of His Imperial Majesty Mohammad Reza Pahlavi Shahanshah, Aryamehr, "Light of the Aryans," the United States also benefited greatly from his rule. As Henry Kissinger has pointed out again and again, the Shah was the rarest of allies, a personal as well as a political friend. The United States enjoyed the rewards of that friendship—whether in the form of guaranteed petroleum supplies or the stability of the Persian Gulf, which his foreign policy and Iranian naval might did so much to ensure, or the pursuit of parallel policies toward the Arab states and the USSR, which in the latter case led the Shah to grant the United States listening posts along the Soviet border. Actually, the benefits the United States gained from its association with the Shah could be extended at far greater length. Suffice it to say that it was deeply implicated in his regime, both through its participation in imposing and sustaining the rule of the Shah as well as through the immense benefits it derived from that imposition.

Given the inescapable depths of U.S. responsibility for his regime, it was necessary for the United States to be aware of the complex dimensions of that responsibility and to act toward the Shah from an appreciation of that responsibility. This analysis has suggested that the United States did neither. The United States contributed to the burgeoning grandiosity of the Shah, but it did nothing to protest or modify the policies pursued by the Shah—policies which flowed from his own grandiosity and which proved so deeply offensive to the Iranian people. When they began to articulate their dissatisfaction with his rule, the United States not only added its voice to their complaints but failed to provide the Shah with the counsel expected of a steadfast friend. It pressured him, but without specific guidance as to how he might most effectively quiet the outrage of his people. Instead, his policies unleashed even greater rage. When that rage became violent, the United States failed to appreciate its seriousness and failed to suggest ways by which the Shah could control it. Again, the Shah's efforts to subdue the violence of his people exacerbated their rage. In short, the United States will forever bear significant responsibility for his fall.

This conclusion is predicated on the belief that a different U.S. policy could have made a difference to the outcome of the revolution. There are two broad dimensions in which this was the case. Preceding the revolution, the United States might have intervened with the Shah to mitigate his grandiose policies which so deeply enraged his people. The Shah was obviously not a person comfortable with any interferences with his intentions. But he also demonstrated, time and time again, a willingness to listen to others, especially to the ambassadors of the United States and Great Britain, if they understood how to phrase their concerns appropriately. The United States certainly could have modified the Shah's policies which contributed so significantly to the rage of the Iranian people.

Furthermore, the United States could have intervened far more effectively during the months of the revolution. Had it understood that the bases from which he derived his strength had one by one deserted him, it might have had a better sense for how crucial his ties to the United States had become. It might also have understood how tenuous was his psychological capacity to function as Shah.

The United States, by continuing to serve as a selfobject for the Shah, could have strengthened that hold rather than undermine it. Politically, Jimmy Carter could have articulated a message of continued appreciation of the crucial significance of the Shah as a political and personal ally of the United States, all the while seeking to encourage the Shah's further emulation of Western human rights practices.

During what was virtually a year-long demand of the Iranian people for greater civil liberties, the United States could have provided the Shah with the guidance he needed to be responsive to those demands, without, in the process, stimulating more demands. During the subsequent year-long revolution, the United States could have strengthened the Shah and suggested ways for him to deal with the violence increasingly meant to destroy his throne. Even after the Shah's collapse following the Jhaleh massacre, the fate of the revolution was not yet decided. Firm rule from the center may have preserved the rule of the Shah, although certainly not restoring royal authority as it had been at the zenith of its imperial splendor. But by maintaining the Pahlavi dynasty, the seizure of power by Khomeini would have been prevented.

Had the United States chosen to intervene more forcefully after Jhaleh, it would have had to assume responsibility for making the hard decisions which the Shah could no longer make for himself. Zbigniew Brzezinski appears to have misunderstood this early in the fall of 1978, but came to a keener appreciation of the dilemmas not much later. He writes that "the Shah wanted the United States to take responsibility for the painful decisions needed to keep Iran intact, and particularly for the decision to use Iranian military force against the opposition."[1] The point the national security adviser misses here is that the Shah could not make the decisions himself. It was not that he sought to evade the responsibility for making the difficult decisions. He was psychologically incapable of making them. Brzezinski came to recognize that reality by mid-December: "it was becoming increasingly doubtful that the Shah could act on his own."[2] As it was, the empress assumed ever more of the day-to-day responsibilities of the monarchy. Toward the end, with the Huyser mission, the United States did so as well. But what had been needed was U.S. willingness to assume responsibility for making the hard decisions, far earlier in the revolution. Had the United States been prepared to do so, even after Jhaleh, the Shah might have pulled through. Even after the psychological regression and collapse which Jhaleh fostered—its destruction in turn having destroyed any vestiges of the Shah's belief in the love of his people—the United States may have been able to strengthen the Shah's resolve sufficiently to pull him through the task of reasserting kingly authority while assembling a coalition of opposition figures willing to work within the strictures of a vastly altered Pahlavi system.

That would not have been easy. The opposition had minimal faith in the Shah. They remembered all too well what had happened to Prime Minister Mossadegh, whose memory most of the secular opposition revered. They recalled, as well, how the Shah, no longer having to appease the United States, dumped Ali Amini. There were profound and widespread doubts that the Shah's commitments would be more reliable in 1978 than in the past. Had the United States been deeply implicated in the negotiations for a redefinition of the distribution of power, the opposition might not have been any more willing to trust the Shah. But a U.S. guarantee of a newly brokered arrangement for power sharing may have been sufficiently appealing to break the inexorably growing unity of the opposition.

Just when the Shah's situation became hopeless is difficult to assess. It is fascinating to recall a story told by Mohamed Heikal. When he visited the Ayatollah, newly arrived from Iraq to the suburbs of Paris in October 1978, the Ayatollah's aides asked for his help. They wanted Heikal to find a country which would receive the Ayatollah after the expiration of his six-month French residency visa. They needed a home for the Ayatollah in April 1979. Even they could not imagine that the Ayatollah would return to Iran in triumph in February.

Certainly by the time of the imposition of the military government in early November, the situation of the Shah had become desperate. But in the two months between the first week of September and the first week of

November, there was still opportunity to reassert the Shah's control over the fate of his nation. It was in that period that the United States had one last opportunity to restore the Shah to a level of functioning which would have allowed him, in concert with Iranian and American advisers, to make the decisions necessary to have retained his throne. The possibility of that policy succeeding after the institution of a military government in early November, however, was exceedingly slim. It might have been possible for the United States to have provided the Shah with so much psychological and moral support that he would have been strengthened. But a U.S. failure at that late stage of the revolution would have brought no more hostile revolutionary forces to the fore after its success. More to the point, a more effective U.S. foreign policy would have prevented the fate of the Shah and, with him, that of the United States from having come down to that final phase of the revolution.

A vast number of factors impeded the fashioning of an effective U.S. foreign policy toward Iran in the final years of the Iranian Revolution. One was the absence of coordination among foreign service bureaucracies. The National Security Council is meant to serve the president by fulfilling that function. But instead, as has happened again and again since its establishment, the NSC became an independent actor. In the case of the Carter administration, the structural rivalries between the foreign policy bureaucracies were exacerbated by personal conflicts. The two foreign policy principals, Vance and Brzezinski, were especially likely to compete because they represented conflicting approaches to international relations. In that conflict, they embodied Jimmy Carter's two orientations to the world— Christianity, human rights, and international order versus power and naval, nuclear engineering. Vance and Brzezinski, in some important way, represented an externalization of President Carter's internal conflicts over the nature of international relations. That externalized tension was not to end until April 1980, when Vance resigned to protest the hostage rescue mission.

The consequence of the Vance-Brzezinski conflict was to heighten the structural conflicts in the foreign policy bureaucracies. The result was that the two bureaucracies and their chiefs came to see the Iranian situation in different ways, came to compete for control of Iran policy, and occasionally even subverted each other's efforts to effect solutions to the turmoil. The National Security Council staff was no coordinating body but a full-fledged player.

U.S. foreign policy also suffered from insufficient communication between senior policy officials and the staffs of the foreign policy bureaucracies. These officials acted as if there were not vast U.S. government foreign policy bureaucracies and as if there were no accumulated wisdom about Iran in those bureaucracies. Thus Brzezinski depended on Ardeshir Zahedi as a major source of information about Iran. He also recounts how he had periodic meetings in Washington with "various Iranians."[3] He despatched to Tehran a U.S. businessman who had once been CIA station chief in Iran.[4] Brzezinski turned to former Undersecretary of State George Ball for a reassessment of the Iran situation.[5] Brzezinski also depended on his own evaluations of the Shah, based on their two meetings during the state visits in Washington in November 1977 and Tehran in December 1977.[6] The search by the NSC for independent information was partially a reflection of their unwillingness to trust the Department of State (or the CIA, whose intelligence NSC found virtually useless). But it was as if everything about Iran had to be learned for the first time.

The fact is that there was precious little useful information about Iran in the files of the U.S. government. Despite the dominant position which the United States had occupied in Iran since the 1953 coup, or perhaps because of it, there were no data about Iran which proved useful to policymakers during the revolution. Or in the words of a U.S. House of Representatives study on intelligence performance in Iran:

From an analyst's perspective, "until recently you couldn't give away intelligence on Iran." . . . CIA intelligence reporting on the Iranian internal situation was minimal before late 1977. No reports based on contacts with the religious opposition had appeared during the previous two years, and there was absolutely no reporting on the internal situation based on sources within the opposition during the first quarter of 1978.[7]

Partly this is attributable to the fact that there are only three parts of the vast federal foreign policy bureaucracies which actually do research on strategic, political matters: the Bureau of Intelligence and Research of the Department of State (INR), the analytic sections of the Central Intelligence Agency, and the Defense Intelligence Agency. Virtually all other foreign policy bureaucracies are concerned with the management of the day-to-day international relations of the United States. There is no place in the government other than INR, CIA, and DIA where thoughtful research analyses, free of the constraints of day-to-day policy, can be done.[8]

Another reason U.S. foreign policy bureaucracies could offer National Security Adviser Brzezinski and Secretary of State Vance little useful information on Iran stemmed not from structural factors of the organization of the foreign policy bureaucracies, but rather from decisions which had been made years before. Simply, the United States, in order not to offend the Shah, had chosen to circumscribe, within narrow limits, the freedom of action of its personnel. A conscious decision had been made not to collect data on Iran, data which would subsequently prove to be of crucial significance for policy-making.

This decision was embodied in the sorry story of William G. Miller, a brilliant foreign service officer whose first post was Iran. When Miller finished his initial assignment at the U.S. consulate in Isfahan, he was sent to Tehran as a political officer. There, in the early 1960s, he befriended a number of younger Iranians who were members of the National Front, the residue of the coalition which had formed around Prime Minister Mossadegh and which the Shah considered to be his most threatening enemies. It was easy to befriend members of the National Front; virtually all the younger members of that opposition group were essentially the same kinds of people as the Americans attracted to the U.S. foreign service. The members of the National Front were middle class, well educated, sophisticated, avowedly secular, politically and culturally au courant, and pro-Western, although not without their profound criticisms of the role of the United States in Iran. But Bill Miller ran afoul of the Pahlavi system, and of the Shah himself, when SAVAK reported that he had "been meeting" with the Shah's opposition.[9] The Shah informed the U.S. ambassador, who chastised Miller. Eventually, Miller became so unpopular with the Iranian authorities that he was informed by the ambassador and by senior officials of the U.S. State Department that his career at State was essentially over—that he would never receive a meaningful assignment or promotion again. Miller, who had done nothing more than establish personal friendships with members of one of the groups about which the United States most needed to know, resigned.

Shortly thereafter, he accepted a senior position in the Peace Corps. In the course of his new responsibilities, he traveled to Iran to survey the operation of the Peace Corps there. His old friends from the National Front invited him to dinner, a purely social occasion. However social it might have been, it infuriated the Shah, who learned of it shortly thereafter; thus did SAVAK establish a reputation for omniscience and omnipotence which later would lead the Iranian people to outrage against its ultimate chief, the Shah. The Shah called the ambassador and suggested that if the Peace Corps became an instrument for U.S. officials to encourage his most hated opposition, the American Peace Corps would no longer be welcome in Iran. The result, of course, was the firing of Miller.[10]

From that time on, the word went out to U.S. personnel that CIA and State were no longer to cover the internal Iranian political scene. The United States would depend for its information on SAVAK. The CIA itself would concentrate its resources on five areas: the Iranian armed forces, Iranian oil, the Soviets and Iran, the Iranian Communist party, and Iranian foreign policy.[11] But no CIA attention would be paid to the Shah, the operation of the Pahlavi system, the opposition to the Shah, save the Communist opposition, or the Islamic clergy.

The Shah appeared to be firmly in power in Iran. He was willing to share with the U.S. ambassador and the CIA station chief whatever he knew about internal politics. Furthermore, SAVAK appeared to be both effective and efficient in penetrating the Shah's domestic opposition. Focusing the efforts of the CIA appeared a cost-effective way to cover a wide range of subjects of undoubted significance to the United States. In the process, however, the United States put itself at the mercy of SAVAK.

The congressmen investigating the U.S. intelligence failure put it somewhat differently.

The cultural weakness in intelligence collection on Iran has been the lack of widespread contact with Iranians of various persuasions, leaders and followers alike. . . . U.S. close identification with the Shah limited the opportunities for U.S. officials to hear from Iranians who opposed him, thereby causing Iran to resemble a closed society from the U.S. perspective, with even clandestine collection on Iranian politics discouraged.[12]

When the opposition to the Shah mounted during the 1970s, and the SAVAK generals were busy "doing real estate," the United States had barely a clue as to the identity of the opposition and what they wanted. John Stempel, then serving as a foreign service officer in Tehran, reports that until March 1978, "there were no direct encounters between embassy officers and religious leaders" and that it was not until January 1979 that "the first face-to-face discussion with influential Khomeini proteges" occurred.[13] Stempel also claims that it was not until September 1978—after Jhaleh and after the collapse of the Shah—that "the embassy diversified its sources and . . . Farsi-speaking officers knew personally at least one leader of all the dissident groups except the communists behind the Tudeh Party and the most radical Fedayeen faction."[14] The Shah, Stempel hastens to assure us, "understood the merit of this policy."[15]

In short, senior foreign policy personnel had to rely on an assortment of "old hands" or emissaries hastily despatched to Iran. The United States, after restoring the Shah to his throne in 1953 and having pride of place for the next twenty-five years, did not have the information or the analytic capacity to supply policymakers with useful information.

Not surprisingly, given the failures to collect adequate data and the capabilities to appraise accurately those which were available, U.S. intelligence assessments during the revolution were wrong.

Five Intelligence Appraisals were produced on Iran by DIA in the first nine months of 1978. . . . They concluded as recently as the September 28 "prognosis" that the Shah "is expected to remain actively in power over the next ten years." . . . State Department's Bureau of Intelligence and Research . . . produced no Intelligence Reports on Iran in 1978. . . . Two major long-term analyses by CIA provided valuable insights into many of the trends, forces and relationships that underlay current events in Iran, but they failed entirely to prepare consumers for the gravity of recent popular disturbances. . . . *Iran After the Shah* . . . published in August 1978 . . . proved to be highly misleading with its preface, which asserted, "Iran is not in a revolutionary or even a 'prerevolutionary' situation."[16]

The crucial U.S. failing in Iran was its "Shah-centric" policy. It allowed the Shah structure a relationship in which, effectively, all contacts with Iranian society had to pass through his person or the institutions which were part of his system. The assumption grew, as the Shah appeared to grow in stature and power, that as long as the United States was right with the Shah, its position would be assured since the Shah was right with Iran.

There were five bases to the Shah-centric policy of the United States. First, in the minds of virtually all U.S. officials, the Shah had been Shah forever. He had come to power in Iran in the distant past, increasingly even before the younger U.S. officials had been born. More to the point, he was the Shah before they had begun their Iran tours, and he remained Shah after they had completed those tours. The Shah had become, in the minds of most Americans, conceptually coincident with Iran itself. The House Intelligence Subcommittee on Evaluation referred to "the implicit priorities of policy makers who for years increasingly premised U.S. policy in the Persian Gulf on a judgment of the Shah's permanence, while showing little interest in questioning his performance."[17]

Second, the Shah personally controlled U.S. access to valuable assets. For example, the United States had established sophisticated electronic monitoring stations in Iran which collected data on Soviet missile launchings. The Shah had to be pleased for fear he might "deny U.S. access to its technical collection sites or restrict other forms of technical cooperation."[18]

Third, U.S. policy was Shah-centric because over the years he had been such a faithful ally. He consistently followed policies consonant with American interests. He remained staunchly anti-Soviet. His diplomatic agreements and weapons deals with the USSR never threatened U.S. policymakers. In addition, the Shah was especially strident in his opposition to pro-Soviet or Marxist "liberation" movements. The Shah sent Iranian troops to Oman to aid the sultan in quelling the Dhofar rebellion supported by the Soviets and aided by the Marxist-dominated People's Democratic Republic of Yemen. No nonaligned movements decrying "imperialism" or "colonialism" for the Shah. In short, the Shah willingly served as a regional superpower, and under the Nixon doctrine, striving to ensure regional stability and the perpetuation of pro-Western regimes.

Fourth, the Shah made significant contributions to the U.S. economy. While he was a "price hawk," always striving for higher oil revenues, he never restricted Iranian oil output. He used his staggering oil income in the 1970s to buy billions of dollars of American goods—civilian as well as military—and he paid his bills.

Finally, the Shah had spent the better part of two decades cultivating American opinion leaders. He and the empress in Tehran received and entertained countless Americans—senior political figures, captains of industry, media stars, and intellectual luminaries. His "point man" in Washington, Ambassador Ardeshir Zahedi, pursued American opinion leaders even more assiduously.[19] As a result of their cultivation, the many contributions the Shah made to advance U.S. foreign policy, the palpable economic development which Iran experienced under the Shah, and the economic ties between the two countries, a powerful ideology had been fostered. That ideology conceived of the Shah and Iran as virtually identical.

Two fatal errors were ensconced in that way of doing business. When the Shah ceased to function effectively, as he lost the four pillars of his psychological strength, and when the Shah enraged the Iranian people, as he did increasingly during the 1970s, the United States had no independent access to Iran whatsoever. While Iran was by no means the only country in the world in which the ruler had (tacitly or explicitly) put constraints on the operations of American foreign policy bureaucracies, neither was it the only country in the world in which the United States (tacitly or explicitly) accepted such constraints.

But one of the implications of Iran for the United States is that mechanisms independent of every host state must be established for the collection of data on indigenous political forces. The United States must find ways to avoid the wrath of rulers who believe that any American contacts with those forces constitutes at least a tacit endorsement. The United States must also establish an analytic foreign policy capability which can monitor the long-term pulse of any political system. Such capacity should be "out of the loop" of immediate policy analysis and formulation and be relatively isolated from the day-to-day needs of the foreign policy bureaucracies. Instead, such a unit should be charged with establishing theoretical frameworks for the assessment of political stability and change. It would be responsible for providing early warning of political instability and with having models of any given political system which provides an empirically as well as theoretically grounded understanding of the sources and nature of the political opposition.

In this era of U.S. budget deficits and a cost-cutting Congress intent on slashing State Department funding, it appears utopian to seek greater foreign policy analytic capacity. But if the United States is to continue to maintain its global commitments, especially in an era of financial stringency, it must demonstrate a far more sophisticated and efficient capacity to understand political forces.

In addition to creating the capacity for performing different analytic policy functions, the foreign policy bureaucracies must do more effective analyses. Psychoanalysis, a mode of analysis barely present in U.S. foreign policy bureaucracies, served as the basis of this work. Psychoanalytic thinking can usefully serve as one of the theoretical frameworks within which foreign policy analysis is conducted. It can also usefully serve as part of the process of monitoring the "pulse" of a political system. This work has used psychoanalytic thinking in its most common and easily applicable form—the investigation of the individual leader. In those political systems where there is a dominant figure, modes of psychoanalytic thinking can be productively used for political analysis. Psychoanalytic modes of thinking can also be used to investigate group phenomena. The relations of leaders to followers, group psychological processes, and the psychological bases of historical and social changes have been studied through psychoanalytic theories.[20]

But psychoanalytic modes of analysis are not part of the foreign policy analytic capacity of the United States. There are psychiatrists and perhaps even psychoanalysts in the service of the foreign policy bureaucracies. And they are occasionally charged with responsibility for evaluation of intelligence. For example, when the intelligence community had reason to believe that Colonel Qaddhafi had made death threats against the president of the United States, a psychiatric assessment of Qaddhafi was requested.

The psychiatrists were asked whether the colonel was psychologically capable of ordering the assassination of the president of the United States.

Only rarely, however, are government psychiatric personnel asked to participate in the more broad-ranging investigation of a political system as done here. There are no ongoing psychologically based assessments of political systems. There are, moreover, virtually no U.S. government foreign policy analysts with psychoanalytic training. But if this work has demonstrated the utility of such an analysis for understanding both how the Shah came to offend the Iranian people and how he was unable to respond appropriately to their complaints, it has also demonstrated that there is a place for psychoanalytic investigation in the ongoing work of the U.S. foreign policy bureaucracies.

A final lesson of the Iran debacle for the United States is the need for timely focusing of the attention of senior policymakers on pressing foreign policy problems. In the Iran of the 1970s and during the revolution itself, inadequate attention by the wrong personnel was paid at the wrong time. Partly this can be explained by the extraordinary rapidity with which the Iranian Revolution unfolded. But it can also be explained by the demands made on the senior members of the U.S. foreign policy bureaucracies. The capacity of the system to process crises is limited by the extraordinary demands made on policymakers as a result of the global commitments of the United States and of the structure of the foreign policy bureaucracies. Just as the Defense Department has attempted to broaden the capability of the U.S. military to conduct simultaneously more than a single military operation, so must the foreign policy bureaucracies develop the capacity to facilitate the system's simultaneous response to more than one foreign policy crisis. Mechanisms need be created whereby the attention of the very senior political and bureaucratic figures responsible for foreign policy formulation can be focused on more than a particular problem at a particular time.

These failures of the U.S. bureaucratic system contributed to the fall of the Shah. We cannot know if the Shah could have been saved had the United States operated differently. But the purpose of any analysis, after all, is not to change the past, but to learn from it.

Notes

Introduction

1. *New York Times,* April 20, 1979, p. 12.

2. Sigmund Freud, *Leonardo da Vinci: A Study in Psychosexuality* (New York: Random House, 1947); idem, *Moses and Monotheism* (New York: Alfred A. Knopf, 1939); William Runyan, *Life Histories and Psychobiography: Explorations in Theory and Method* (New York: Oxford University Press, 1902).

3. For psychological studies of great leaders, see the following: Sigmund Freud and William C. Bullitt, *Thomas Woodrow Wilson: A Psychological Study* (Boston: Houghton Mifflin, 1967); Vamık D. Volkan and Norman Itzkowitz, *The Immortal Ataturk: A Psychobiography* (Chicago: University of Chicago Press, 1984); Alexander L. George and Juliette L. George, *Woodrow Wilson and Colonel House: A Personality Study* (New York: Dover, 1956); Bruce Mazlish, *In Search of Nixon: A Psychohistorical Inquiry* (Baltimore: Penguin Books, 1973).

4. Fred Weinstein and Gerald M. Platt, *The Wish to Be Free: Society, Psyche, and Value Change* (Berkeley: University of California Press, 1969). Also see Committee on International Relations, *Self-Involvement in the Middle East Conflict* (New York: Group for the Advancement of Psychiatry, 1978).

5. Sudhir Kakar, *The Inner World: A Psycho-analytical Study of Childhood and Society in India* (Dehli: Oxford University Press, 1981).

6. See Bruce Mazlish, ed., *Psychoanalysis and History* (Englewood Cliffs, N.J.: Prentice Hall, 1963).

7. The impressive work by James A. Bill, *The Eagle and the Lion: The Tragedy of American-Iranian Relations* (New Haven: Yale University Press, 1988), is a careful examination of consistent U.S. foreign policy errors in dealing with Iran.

Chapter 1. Flying Fantasies

1. U.S. Congress, Senate, Committee on Foreign Relations, *U.S. Military Sales to Iran,* 94th Cong., 2d sess., July 1976, p. 25.

2. Ibid., p. 28.

3. Ibid., p. 7.

4. The Shah never made a secret of his reason for the air force. In 1975 he told Egyptian journalist Mohamed Heikal:

Presently we primarily emphasize the development of our own power. We want to turn the Imperial Air Force into an invincible power against all threats and acts of aggression. We must develop the air combat capability to destroy any enemy aircraft at a distance of two to three hundred kilometers from our border. In a nutshell, we intend to be a power to be reckoned with in the region.

Interview originally in *An Nahar*, Beirut; as reprinted in *Khayan International*, September 16, 1975.

5. William Green and John Fricker, *The Air Forces of the World: Their History, Development and Present Strength* (London: Macdonald, 1958), p. 164.

6. Ibid., p. 7.

7. For references to the Azerbaijan crisis, see George Lenczowski, *Russia and the West in Iran, 1918–1947: A Study in Big Power Rivalry* (Ithaca, N.Y.: Cornell University Press, 1949); Gen. Hassan Arfa, *Under Five Shahs* (New York: William Morrow, 1965); Sir Clarmont Skrine, *World War in Iran* (London: Constable, 1962).

8. For a thoughtful analysis of the U.S. role in the Azerbaijan crisis, see Ruhollah K. Ramazani, *Iran's Foreign Policy, 1941–1973: A Study of Foreign Policy in Modernizing Nations* (Charlottesville: University Press of Virginia, 1975), pp. 109–53, esp. pp. 138–39.

9. Mohammad Reza Shah Pahlavi, *Mission for My Country* (New York: McGraw-Hill, 1961), p. 56.

10. For one who believes that the order of the telling is a clue to the significance of the told, it is worth noting that the Shah titles chapter 3 of his autobiography "My Unconventional Childhood." In that chapter he recounts four events of his adulthood which confirmed his childhood faith in God as his protector. The first incident to which he refers is the plane crash described here. The others are the Azerbaijan crisis of 1945–56, his survival of an assassination attempt in 1949, and "the miracle . . . of how we in Persia recovered from Mossadegh" (ibid., p. 47), which miracle presumably includes how he recovered his throne in 1953. Not only does he break the chronological order of these events by putting the 1948 plane crash first, but he even confuses the chronological order by referring to the plane crash as the "first" event of adulthood to confirm his childhood faith, even though he then moves on to discuss the second event—the recovery of Azerbaijan—which occurred two years previous to the plane crash.

11. Ibid., p. 56.

12. Gerard de Villiers, *The Imperial Shah: An Informal Biography*, trans. June P. Wilson and Walter B. Michaels (Boston: Little, Brown, 1976), pp. 133–34.

13. In his autobiography, the Shah notes that "Reza Shah decided to provide for me a suitable bride" (p. 218). Most often the Shah refers to his father simply as "my father." I assume that the distancing mechanism of referring to him formally as "Reza Shah" in this very personal instance is an expression of the Shah's persistent unhappiness with his first and forced marriage.

14. Personal interview, March 29, 1983. Because Iran remains politically

unsettled, I have chosen to protect the confidentiality of the many Iranians and others who supplied their insights on the Shah. Their names are not revealed.

15. Pahlavi, *Mission for My Country,* p. 219.

16. *Times of London,* July 21, 1948, p. 1.

17. Personal interview, June 4, 1983.

18. Queen Soraya Pahlavi, *Khaterat-e Soraya* (Remembrances of Soraya), trans. from the German by Musa Majidi (Tehran: Saadat Printing House, n.d.), p. 46.

19. Ibid., p. 63.

20. William H. Forbis, *The Fall of the Peacock Throne: The Story of Iran* (New York: McGraw-Hill, 1981), p. 59.

21. See interview with Reza Pahlavi II, in *Dossier,* vol. 14, no. 3 (March 1988): 43.

22. Forbis, *Fall of the Peacock Throne,* p. 66. The Shah's thoughts about Pan Am are reminiscent of Franz Kafka's *Metamorphosis.* Heinz Kohut has noted, "Some of the most painful feelings to which man can be exposed . . . and observable during the analyses of many people with severe narcissistic personality disorders, relate to the sense of not being human . . . [which] stems, I believe, from the absence of human humans in the environment of the small child." Heinz Kohut, *How Does Analysis Cure?* ed. Arnold Goldberg (Chicago: University of Chicago Press, 1984), p. 200.

23. Mohammad Reza Shah Pahlavi, *Answer to History* (New York: Stein and Day, 1980), pp. 74 and 145–46.

24. Personal interview, January 6, 1981.

25. Pahlavi, *Mission for My Country,* pp. 51–52. It is characteristic of the Shah that he compares Iran, in this case its mountains, to Western countries.

26. Ibid., p. 52.

27. Sigmund Freud, *The Interpretation of Dreams,* trans. and ed. James Strachey, in *The Standard Edition of the Complete Psychological Works of Sigmund Freud* (London: Hogarth Press, 1953; originally published in 1900), vols. 4 and 5. For a similar view, see P. Federn, "On Dreams of Flying," in R. Fliess, ed., *The Psychoanalytic Reader* (London: Hogarth Press, 1950).

28. Jerome Kavka, "The Analysis of Phallic Narcissism," *International Review of Psycho-Analysis,* no. 3 (1976): 277–82.

29. Henry Murray, "American Icarus," chap. 28 in Arthur Burton and Robert E. Harris, eds., *Clinical Studies of Personality,* vol. 2 of *Case Histories in Clinical and Abnormal Psychology* (New York: Harper Brothers, 1955).

30. Jerome L. Weinberger and James Muller, "The American Icarus Revisited: Phallic Narcissism and Boredom," *International Journal of Psycho-Analysis* 55 (1975): 581.

31. Murray, "American Icarus," pp. 632–33.

32. Ibid., p. 631.

33. Ibid., p. 640.

34. Ibid., p. 640.

35. Ibid., p. 639.

36. The difficulty of establishing criteria for determining theoretical signifi-

cance is one of the most consequential issues in the social sciences. Ultimately, the theoretical system one adopts supplies the criteria for determining what is and is not significant. Those who do not accept that set of theories as germane or powerful will in all likelihood not be able to accept the data as useful. But many social science disputes are over the utility of particular data, with too little appreciation of the theories that specify those data as useful. To convince another of the utility of data without first agreeing on a commonly accepted theoretical system is a hopeless task. This does not seem to limit, regrettably, the number of social science discussions which attempt that.

37. Heinz Kohut, "Forms and Transformations of Narcissism," *Journal of the American Psychoanalytic Association* 14: 243–72.

38. Heinz Kohut, *The Analysis of the Self: A Systematic Approach to the Psychoanalytic Treatment of Narcissistic Personality Disorders* (New York: International Universities Press, 1971), p. 144.

39. It needs to be reiterated that to make this claim is not also to claim that Iran's development was only a tangible "realization" of its ruler's fantasies. It can be useful, depending on the context, to think of Iran's development in a variety of conceptual frameworks—economic, political, social, etc. The issue, in other words, is to enhance an understanding of what happened to Iran and to the Shah over the years. And the claim is that the mode of thinking employed here does that in a useful fashion not achieved through other modes of analysis. This latter point is, of course, contestable. It is likely that most readers not convinced of the power of the arguments will do precisely that.

40. "Shah of Iran Addresses the National Press Club," *New York Times,* April 14, 1962, p. 1.

41. While many of the characteristics associated with the narcissistic personality were spelled out by Reich in 1933, it was not until after more recent work on narcissism that a comprehensive understanding of the structure and dynamics of phallic narcissism could be generated. See W. Reich, *Character-Analysis* (New York: Noonday Press, 1933).

42. The description and much of the subsequent discussion of phallic narcissism are drawn from the following sources: Ben Bursten, "Some Narcissistic Personality Types," *International Journal of Psychoanalysis* 54 (1973): 287–300; Weinberger and Muller, "American Icarus Revisited"; Rose Edgcumbe and Marion Burgner, "The Phallic Narcissistic Phase: A Differentiation between Preoedipal and Oedipal Aspects of Phallic Development," in *The Psychoanalytic Study of the Child* (New Haven: Yale University Press, 1975), 30: 161–80; Kavka, "Analysis of Phallic Narcissism"; W. W. Meissner, "Narcissistic Personalities and Borderline Conditions: A Differential Diagnosis," in Chicago Institute for Psychoanalysis, *Annual of Psychoanalysis* (New York: International Universities Press, 1979), 7: 171–201; Max Forman, "The Narcissistic Personality Disorder as a Regression to a Pre-Oedipal Phase of Phallic Narcissism," paper presented to the Chicago Psychoanalytic Society, June 23, 1981.

43. Bursten, "Narcissistic Personality Types," p. 291.

44. Meissner, "Narcissistic Personalities," p. 175.

45. Weinberger and Muller, "American Icarus Revisited," p. 584.

46. For a contribution to the theory of psychic twinship, see Kohut, *Does Analysis Cure?*

47. Benjamin Weiser, "Behind Israel-Iran Sales, 'Amber' Light from U.S.," *Washington Post,* August 16, 1987, pp. 1, A26–A28.

Chapter 2. Childhood and Youth

1. Mohammad Reza Shah Pahlavi, *Mission for My Country* (New York: McGraw-Hill, 1961); Rustom Khurshedji Karanjia, *The Mind of a Monarch* (London: Allen and Unwin, 1977).

2. Margaret Laing, *The Shah* (London: Sidgwick and Jackson, 1977); Freidoune Sahebjam, *Mohamad Reza Pahlavi, Shah d'Iran: Sa vie trente ans de règne (1941–1971)* (Paris: Editions Berger-Levrault, 1971); Ramesh Sanghvi, *Aryamehr, the Shah of Iran* (London: Transorient Press, 1968); Gerard de Villiers, *The Imperial Shah: An Informal Biography,* trans. June P. Wilson and Walter B. Michaels (Boston: Little, Brown, 1976).

3. On the anniversary of the Shah's birth, the Ministry of Court would release accounts of the Shah's life.

4. See Firuz Kazemzadeh, "The Origin and Early Development of the Persian Cossack Brigade," *American Slavic and East European Review* 15 (1956): 351–63.

5. For a discussion of Reza Shah's rise to power, see L. P. Elwell-Sutton, "Reza Shah the Great: Founder of the Pahlavi Dynasty," in George Lenczowski, ed., *Iran under the Pahlavis* (Stanford: Hoover Institution Press, 1978), pp. 1–50.

6. Lord Curzon, then British foreign secretary, wrote his cabinet colleagues to explain the treaty that had just been negotiated:

We come to some arrangement with the Persian Government by which British interests in that part of the world should be safeguarded in the future from a recurrence of the recent shocks, and by which Persia, incurably feeble and unable to stand by herself, should be given support that would enable her to maintain her position among the independent nations of the world.

Documents on British Foreign Policy, 1919–1939, 1st ser., 4: 1120, as quoted in Sir Clarmont Skrine, *World War in Iran* (London: Constable, 1962), p. 59. The British traditionally referred to Iran as Persia.

7. Ibid., p. 64.

8. There are two versions to the still generally accepted account of British complicity in Reza Khan's coup, one less charitable to him than the other. Both versions suggest that the British, realizing they would be unable to control Iran, given the failure of the Majles to ratify the 1919 treaty, and fearful of Soviet encroachments, had concluded that only a strong central government in Iran could maintain Iran's independence. The less charitable version has it that the British had selected Reza Khan for the job because they knew he would achieve that goal, while he and his editor-colleague, Seyyed Zia ed Din Tabataba'i, would nonetheless acquiesce to, or even facilitate, Britain's larger regional goals. This version intimates that Reza Khan and Seyyed Zia were British agents. The more charitable version has the British conceding to the de-

sirability of a Reza Khan–Seyyed Zia coup as the most palatable of all the unpleasant alternatives.

9. Karanjia, *Mind of a Monarch*, p. 231.

10. The book was apparently actually written in the mid-1950s by a visiting American professor of political science, Donald Wilhelm. Wilhelm spent many hours talking with the Shah and prepared drafts which the Shah reworked. Despite Wilhelm's literal "writing," however, the book strongly reflects the Shah's tone and style and should be read as an authentic statement of the Shah's voice.

11. This total is derived from adding all the mentions in *Mission for My Country* to "Reza Khan," "Reza Shah," "my father," as well as "him" or "his" when they unambiguously refer to Reza Shah.

12. In the entire work there are only two references to Reza Shah which can be understood as criticism. On one occasion (p. 44) the Shah refers to his father as "fallible," a quality which seems unimaginable in the midst of the plethora of otherwise overweening praise. Later in the book the Shah refers, only once, to his father's "dictatorship" (p. 76). Significantly, the Shah does not refer to his father's rule as a "dictatorship" until after the Shah tells the story of Iran's invasion by the United Kingdom and the USSR and their forcing Reza Shah to abdicate. It is as if the Shah cannot bring himself to criticize Reza Shah as long as his father is the ruling monarch. Only after his father was humbled by the Great Powers can the "lesser power," his son, allow himself a negative word—literally a single word—about his father.

13. Pahlavi, *Mission for My Country*, p. 10. Fascinating if minor points about the writings of the Shah are the thematic repetitiveness and frequent similarity of wording which characterize the books he authored. For example, the quote in the text was taken from a book written by the Shah in 1958. In a book published in 1977, the Shah is quoted as saying:

Father . . . possessed a most amazing personality. Strong men were afraid even just to look at him. His uncanny gift of instantly sizing a man up made one believe that he had an invisible electronic ray in his eye which could delve deep into a man's mind and heart, spot his strong and weak points, gauge his sincerity or discover his guile and, in a moment, thanks to his marvelous sense of timing, decide what action he should take. (Karanjia, *Mind of a Monarch*, p. 31)

This repetitiveness at least raises the possibility that such recent books were a reworking of earlier material. Another possibility is that this repetition of themes indicates how significant such issues were for the Shah throughout his life.

14. Pahlavi, *Mission for My Country*, p. 36.

15. Ibid., p. 45.

16. Karanjia, *Mind of a Monarch*, p. 31.

17. Mohammad Reza Shah Pahlavi, *Answer to History* (New York: Stein and Day, 1980), pp. 53–54.

18. Pahlavi, *Mission for My Country*, p. 45. Later in the same book, the Shah added: "except with me, I don't think he ever indulged in any informal easygoing humor. Those who came in contact with him either were trembling

before him or looked up to him. . . . Except with me, his mental dominance and force of personality made lighthearted humor impossible" (p. 50).

19. Princess Ashraf Pahlavi, *Faces in a Mirror: Memoirs from Exile* (Englewood Cliffs, N.J.: Prentice-Hall, 1980), p. 9.

20. Queen Soraya Pahlavi, *Khaterat-e Soraya,* trans. Musa Mahjidi (Tehran: Saadat Printing house, n.d.), p. 18.

21. An interesting indicator of the transformation of the Pahlavi system is the title used to designate the Shah's wives. In Persian, both Soraya and Farah were addressed by the same formal title, Awliya Hazrat, which is not translatable. In English Soraya was referred to as empress. That inflation in majesty was but another sign of the grandiosity which increasingly characterized the Pahlavi regime in the 1960s and 1970s.

22. Farah Shahbanou Pahlavi, *My Thousand and One Days: An Autobiography,* trans. Felice Harcourt (London: W. H. Allen, 1978), p. 92.

23. Pahlavi, *Mission for My Country,* p. 228.

24. Ashraf Pahlavi, *Faces in a Mirror,* p. 9.

25. Ibid., p. 10.

26. Karanjia, *Mind of a Monarch,* p. 39. Equally characteristically, the Shah suggested a positive outcome for him personally from the domestic stalemate: "the impression was obviously created in my mind that a woman can also be a human being with an identity of her own, apart from that of a wife" (ibid.).

27. Pahlavi, *Mission for My Country,* p. 228. It is, of course, tempting to muse on the ambiguities in the Shah's form of expression. An "incalculable debt" can be read to imply that the debt is so small as to be beneath calculation.

28. E. A. Bayne, *Persian Kingship in Transition: Conversations with a Monarch Whose Office Is Traditional and Whose Goal Is Modernization* (New York: American Universities Field Staff, 1968), p. 73.

29. Karanjia, *Mind of a Monarch,* p. 174.

30. Ibid., p. 175.

31. Oriana Fallaci, "The Mystically Divine Shah of Iran" (interview), *Chicago Tribune,* December 30, 1973, sec. 2, p. 1. A number of noteworthy points are revealed by the Shah in this section of the interview, besides his bristling disdain for women. In the midst of the interview, after discussing what he has done for women in Iran, the Shah suddenly interjected the memory of his father. He frequently referred to his father in what appeared to be non sequiturs. Two processes seem to be at work. It was as if boasting about himself and elevating his own stature, he became worried over the consequences of all that self-aggrandizement. As a way of reassuring and protecting himself from the internalized, psychic representation of his stern and punishing father, he frequently hastened to assure his listeners—and himself and his own memory—that Reza Shah was, indeed, Reza Shah Kabir, "the Great," and the son was not challenging the father for that honor.

Another characteristic of the Shah revealed in this section of the interview is that when seeking examples to illustrate a point, he would choose non-Iranian, Western examples. To be sure, this interview was to be read by a Western audience and he would communicate with that audience more effectively by selecting illustrations which were meaningful to it. But the Shah fell into the pattern of using

Western examples even in completely domestic speeches and interviews. To his subjects he began to appear more deeply imbedded in and committed to Western history and culture than to Iranian. This was but another way in which they experienced him as increasingly removed and distant.

32. Personal interview, November 29, 1978.

33. The Queen Mother died of heart failure in Acapulco, Mexico, on March 10, 1982.

34. It is important to disabuse the reader of the associations generally made with the word *palace*. To say that the Crown Prince was subsequently raised in a palace is not meant to convey any idea of opulence or grandeur. While Reza Shah himself did live in ever larger residences, his tastes remained spartan and he cared little for luxury or splendor, at least domestically. Clothing, furnishings, decoration, all remained simple throughout his life. In fact, when Soraya became the Shah's bride in 1951, she relates how tasteless and shabby were the furnishings in the "palace" which was to become her home. That home was palatial in size, but in few other senses. Soraya Pahlavi, *Khaterat-e Soraya*, p. 15.

35. This was not the Mme Arfa married to Gen. Hassan Arfa. Cf. Gen. Hassan Arfa, *Under Five Shahs* (New York: William Morrow, 1965).

36. Karanjia, *Mind of a Monarch*, p. 173.

37. Pahlavi, *Mission for My Country*, p. 52.

38. Ibid.

39. Ashraf Pahlavi, *Faces in a Mirror*, p. 15.

40. Pahlavi, *Mission for My Country*, p. 54.

41. In recounting the story to an English-speaking audience—*Mission for My Country* was written and published in English—the Shah related his dream of Ali in a fashion typical of the entire work. He identified Ali as "the chief lieutenant of Mohammed (much as, according to Christian doctrine, St. Paul was a leading disciple of Jesus Christ). Ali was the husband of Mohammed's daughter and one of his bravest followers" (p. 54). Two aspects of this story were typical. The Shah used a parallel to Christianity—in fact, a grossly inadequate parallel—to communicate to his Western audience. Whatever his motives, his refuge in Western metaphors often proved to his Iranian subjects that those realities were more meaningful to the Shah than were the details and realities of the history of his own culture. A second typical aspect of the Shah's writings and speeches was his predilection for denigrating Islam, and Shi'ism in particular. Equating Ali and Saint Paul would produce that sense in any Shi'ite reader, especially because the Shah never mentions Ali as the leader or foremost figure in Shi'ism. The Shah seemed almost incapable of failing to commit such gratuitous insults.

42. Ibid., p. 54.

43. Ibid. Here again the Shah manages to offend orthodox Shi'ite sensibilities while enlightening Western readers. In the Shi'ism of Iran there are no "saints," however revered Abbas and other key Shi'ite figures might be.

44. Ibid.

45. Ibid., p. 55.

46. Shah of Iran, interviewed by Mike Wallace, *60 Minutes*, March 24, 1975.

47. Pahlavi, *Mission for My Country*, p. 222. Some might argue that the Shah

had the facts correct, only the object wrong. After the CIA participation in the Mossadegh coup, the Shah came under the protection of the United States. Of that there is abundant empirical evidence discussed below.

48. Mohammad Reza Shah Pahlavi, *The While Revolution* (Tehran: Ministry of the Imperial Court, 1966), p. 16.

49. Fallaci, "Mystically Divine Shah," p. 1. The Shah may have had the visions correct but his memory was off on his age. He was actually six when first struck by the illnesses and the visions. When the Shah noted that Fallaci appeared puzzled at his claim, he commented, "Oh, I fear you don't understand me." She responded that, indeed, she did not. The Shah then added, "That's because you're not a believer. You don't believe in God and you don't believe in me. Lots of people don't. Even my father didn't believe me. He never did and laughed about it." While the Shah may not remember his age correctly, the memory of his father's refusal to take the young boy seriously is still fresh.

50. Karanjia, *Mind of a Monarch*, p. 89.

51. Soraya Pahlavi, *Khaterat-e Soraya*, p. 66.

52. William H. Sullivan, *Mission to Iran* (New York: W. W. Norton, 1981), pp. 12–13.

53. Ibid., p. 16.

54. Ambassador Sullivan added, "This strip was later to achieve worldwide renown as the place where the American rescue mission seeking to extract the hostages came to an ignominious end in 1980." Ibid., p. 83.

55. Ibid., p. 84.

56. Pahlavi, *Mission for My Country*, pp. 51–52.

57. Sahebjam, *Mohamad Reza Pahlavi*, p. 31.

58. Fallaci, "Mystically Divine Shah," p. 1.

59. Pahlavi, *Mission for My Country*, p. 44.

60. The sophisticated elaboration of language for use as a political device is developed in Iranian culture to the point where it must be considered an art form. For detailed examination of linguistic mechanisms for establishing and maintaining status and power hierarchies, see William O. Beeman, *Language, Status, and Power in Iran* (Bloomington: Indiana University Press, 1986).

61. Personal interview, December 29, 1981. The content and tone of this conversation are extremely rare. The interviewee, for many years, was one of the few Iranians who had access to the Shah and who would presume to speak as bluntly as he did here. This very bluntness was eventually to cost him both his official position and his access to the Shah.

62. Ashraf Pahlavi, *Faces in a Mirror*, p. 61, refers to her father in this way.

63. Foreign Broadcast Information Service, Middle East and Africa, no. 163, August 18, 1978.

64. Pahlavi, *Mission for My Country*, p. 99.

65. The Shah mentions that "I was awarded my diploma" in the spring of 1936. Ibid., p. 63.

66. Ibid., p. 60.

67. Ibid., p. 62.

68. Ibid.

69. Karanjia, *Mind of a Monarch,* p. 173.

70. This particular remembrance had political overtones at the time of its recollection. Many Iranians claimed that the Shah was more comfortable in French than Persian, citing his upbringing from the age of six by a French governess as well as his years of schooling in Switzerland. They used that claim to depreciate the Shah's "Iranianness" and to explain his predilection for closer ties to foreign powers, especially the United States. The Shah's mention of his Persian tutor, then, is a refutation of such claims.

71. Two important points are suggested by this memory. Previously the Shah had implied that the restrictions on his freedom were an unwarranted excess on the part of his guardian. Here he makes it clear that such concern was the tutor's reasonable response to Reza Shah's penetrating scrutiny, exercised even over the great distances from Tehran. Thus Reza Shah proves to be the guilty party. The Crown Prince's stay in Switzerland was a desperately unhappy period because of the control exercised by his father.

A second important, but indirect, point is made by this anecdote. It is a commentary on the relatively primitive state of Iran at the time. Even in the 1930s there was no telephone service linking Iran with Europe, only a telegraph cable originally built across Iran to India in the nineteenth century so that the British might more effectively control that jewel of their colonial empire. But Iran's isolation was marked not only by the absence of telephonic communication. Travel outside its borders was still a relatively rare event. Even Reza Shah made only one trip out of Iran during his entire rule. And that was a state visit to Ataturk in Turkey while his son was studying in Switzerland. One of the things Reza Shah did in Turkey was to take advantage of that country's more highly developed infrastructure: he placed a telephone call to his son at Le Rosey. See Ashraf Pahlavi, *Faces in a Mirror,* p. 23.

72. Queen Soraya recalls that she had learned that Reza Shah, in the interests of making a man of his son, gave instructions that he be treated with more severity than other students at Le Rosey. She also notes that Reza Shah gave the same instructions when the Crown Prince attended the Iranian officers academy after his return from Switzerland. Soraya Pahlavi, *Khaterat-e Soraya,* p. 64.

73. Arfa, *Under Five Shahs,* p. 226.

74. As reproduced in *Kayhan International,* April 27, 1976, p. 4. The letter had been made public in early 1976, having only shortly before been discovered in the court archives.

It was, perhaps, noted by his lonely son at Le Rosey that Reza Shah found it so "difficult" to express "the depth of his suffering" that he never actually did so. It is reasonable to suppose that the boy could have imagined his father's failure to visit as having produced not suffering but indifference.

75. Reza Shah did, however, travel to the Caspian Sea to welcome his son back to Iran. Donald Wilber has described the trip in a fashion which captures the mettle of Reza Shah.

At Chalus he descended from his car into the midst of a group of gardeners who were frantically rushing about in last minute effort to have all in order. He was not pleased with what he saw, struck one of them and had two trees uprooted that had not been planted according to his liking. He was on hand when the ship carrying his son arrived on May 7 [1936] and drew him into a close embrace. Tears of happiness came to his eyes.

Donald N. Wilber, *Riza Shah Pahlavi: The Resurrection and Reconstruction of Iran, 1878–1944* (Hicksville, N.Y.: Exposition Press, 1975), p. 176.

76. Ashraf Pahlavi, *Faces in a Mirror,* p. 22. She also remembers how her brother would talk of what he had learned at Le Rosey other than his academic lessons:

My brother told me how impressed he had been by the democratic attitudes he had seen at school, by the fact that all the boys, whether they were the sons of businessmen or noblemen or kings, were equals within the school community. He talked about how he had come to realize, for the first time, how much economic and social disparity there were among the people of Iran. (P. 22)

77. Personal interview, December 29, 1981. One of the inexplicable aspects of this story is the failure of Reza Shah to expel Perron from Iran. How he was convinced to allow a foreigner, the son of a gardener, and a male ten years older than his son to remain in Tehran as his son's closest friend has been lost to history. Only one inadequate explanation was offered by the many informants interviewed for this book. This account has it that Reza Shah was told that Perron was his son's physical education instructor. And Reza Shah, from his desire to see his still delicate son's physical condition improved, allowed Perron to remain (personal interview, March 23, 1983). But given Reza Shah's shrewdness, it seems unlikely he would have been convinced by that flimsy story.

78. Soraya Pahlavi, *Khaterat-e Soraya,* p. 64.

79. Karanjia, *Mind of a Monarch,* p. 44. The Shah related the nature of those meetings:

During our lunch period, he would acquaint me with various activities of the State in such a simple way as enabled my young mind to absorb what he said without much effort. Of course, he would not discuss politics with me, but he would talk to me about general aspects of life, the paramount need for hard work, the virtue of sobriety, the vices of lavishness and luxury, the necessity of plain living and high thinking, of unremitting industry and dogged perseverance. (P. 44)

80. Pahlavi, *Mission for My Country,* p. 64. The Shah adds a few paragraphs later: "Nevertheless, I, a young man of only some nineteen years of age, frequently spoke my mind to the Shah and the amazing thing was how willing he was to listen to me and how seldom he rejected my proposals" (p. 65). In fact, in the context of the Shah's fear of his father and his other memories of how formidable a figure his father was (and how reticent he himself was as a youth), it seems highly unlikely that he "spoke his mind" to Reza Shah, unless his mind contained basically unadorned praise for and agreement with what Reza Shah was up to.

81. Ibid., p. 219.

82. Ashraf Pahlavi, *Faces in a Mirror,* p. 29.

83. Ibid.

84. Soraya Pahlavi, *Khaterat-e Soraya,* p. 64.

85. In fact, even in Iran where fathers are conventionally more distant and more powerful than their Western counterparts, the relation between Reza Shah and his son Mohammad Reza appears to have been atypical. Little scholarly work has been done on Iranian family structures, but a variety of evidence supports the notion that Iranian fathers are, and particularly in previous generations were, distant, powerful

authority figures. Iranian novels are especially adept at capturing the flavor of these relationships. See, for example, Jalal Al-e Ahmad, *The School Principal*, trans. John K. Newton (Minneapolis: Bibliotheca Islamica, 1974), and Fereidoun Esfandiary, *The Day of Sacrifice* (London: Heinemann, 1960). Reza Shah was a far more awesome father than is or was common, even in Iran. His powerful and tough character coupled with his formal status as the King of Kings intersected to make his role as father all the more awesome.

Rooted in universal, culture-free psychoanalytic theory is the claim that irrespective of the cultural normativity of fathers like Reza Shah, they are likely to produce common effects in their sons, effects which were produced in young Mohammad Reza. That a particular family constellation varies in incidence on a cross-cultural basis, or for that matter, on a cross-class basis within a particular culture, does not mean the psychoanalytic consequences of that given family constellation would differ on the basis of its frequency of incidence. What it suggests is that the incidence of the resultant psychological configurations would vary by the frequency of the family constellations within any given group. Unfortunately, there are still no hard data on the distribution of such configurations across meaningful groups. For a discussion of this issue, see Robert A. LeVine, *Culture, Behavior, and Personality* (Chicago: Aldine Press, 1973), pp. 15–39.

86. Pahlavi, *Mission for My Country*, p. 65. It is interesting to speculate about the Shah's mention of his father's abdication immediately after his own sense of injury. It would be logical—according to the canons of logic pertaining in psychoanalytic theory—to assume that the Crown Prince's injury was followed by rage and a wish for his father's destruction, a wish brought about by Soviet and British action through their 1941 invasion. One result is that psychologically the Crown Prince may have felt some complicity in his father's overthrow.

87. Bayne, *Persian Kingship in Transition*, p. 58.

88. Pahlavi, *White Revolution*, p. 75.

89. Karanjia, *Mind of a Monarch*, p. 51.

90. Personal interview, December 28, 1981.

91. Ashraf Pahlavi, *Faces in a Mirror*, p. 63. It is reasonable to understand the memoirs of Princess Ashraf in the proper context. By recollections such as these, the princess legitimated a central place for herself in Pahlavi rule. However, it is also the case that her memories of Reza Shah's parting words appear accurate given the final words of advice he offered his son.

92. Karanjia, *Mind of a Monarch*, p. 59.

93. Pahlavi, *Answer to History*, p. 69.

94. Pahlavi, *Mission for My Country*, p. 45.

95. Ibid., facing p. 48. Almost as if the obvious and special bond between the father and son was too powerful to acknowledge, the picture is mistakenly labeled. The caption identifies the solitary, lonely figure as Mohammad Reza rather than Ashraf.

96. This argument about the Shah is parallel to an argument about Arab men made in a fascinating and daring analysis by a Tunisian sociologist. See Abdullah Bouhdiba, "The Child and the Mother in Arab-Muslim Society," in L. Carl Brown and Norman Itzkowitz, eds., *Psychological Dimensions of Near Eastern Studies* (Princeton: Darwin Press, 1977).

97. Pahlavi, *Mission for My Country,* p. 248.

98. Soraya Pahlavi, *Khaterat-e Soraya,* p. 76.

99. *U.S. News and World Report,* June 26, 1978, p. 38. In fact, the Crown Prince did depart Iran for pilot training in the United States, but he never again returned to Iran, his father having fled the country while he was still undergoing his training.

100. *Chicago Tribune,* September 13, 1987, sec. 5, pp. 1, 6.

101. Pahlavi, *Mission for My Country,* p. 126.

102. Mohammad Reza Shah Pahlavi, *The Shah's Story,* trans. from the French by Teresa Waugh (London: Michael Joseph, Ltd., 1980), p. 126.

103. Personal interview, December 29, 1981.

104. Personal interview, April 5, 1982.

105. Ashraf Pahlavi, *Faces in a Mirror,* p. 155. The princess goes on to describe some of the details of the law:

It recognized a wife as an equal partner in marriage. . . . It limited a man to one wife . . . by laying down strict conditions which virtually made it impossible for him to marry a second time. . . . The act provided that a woman could seek a divorce on the same grounds open to a man . . . and it created a machinery whereby she could seek, and collect, alimony and child support. In the event of her husband's death, the guardianship of the children would automatically be awarded to the wife; previously, all her male in-laws would have been given preference. (Pp. 115, 156)

106. Personal interview, March 25, 1982.

107. Personal interview, November 11, 1981.

108. Putative descriptions of these adventures are legion among Iranians, as they were during the reign of the Shah himself. Just as the Shah had fixed weekly audiences with his senior officials, so he was alleged to have set aside fixed hours for his amorous liaisons. Those liaisons can themselves be understood as an indication of the Shah's disdain for women—his use of so many of them exclusively as sexual objects.

Chapter 3. Imperial Grandeur

1. Alan Williams, *A Bullet for the Shah* (New York: Popular Library, 1976).

2. Paul Erdman, "The Oil War of 1976," *New York,* December 2, 1974, pp. 39–51.

3. Borozou Faramarzi, *Towards the Great Civilization* (Tehran: Ministry of Information, 1974), p. 1. The author attempts to define the great civilization. First he suggests that to understand it, Iranians need only "consult their heart and their most intimate aspirations, since Shahanshah Aryamehr [the King of Kings, Light of the Ayrans, as the Shah in his grandiosity came to be referred], in letting them have a glimpse of it . . . is only answering their wishes" (p. 21). But Faramarzi cannot resist and goes on to describe the Iran of the future. In addition to all the usual descriptions of material abundance, Faramazi adds such wonders as "international prestige," "knowledge of the biology of love . . . of psychology and metapsychology." He states that "in about twenty years time . . . diseases will have completely disappeared and men and

women will live more than one hundred years" (p. 29). This is typical of the messages from the imperial propaganda machine to which the people of Iran were subject in the 1970s.

4. *New York Times,* March 31, 1974, p. 3.

5. Newspaper headlines raise a particularly important question for students of Iran and other societies. Can newspaper headlines or any comparable phenomena which are not directly produced by the Shah be used as indicators of his grandiosity? Are they not, instead, better indicators of the lengths to which Iranian newspaper editors, for example, would go to curry favor with the Shah? Clearly, headlines were meant to do that. But newspaper headlines also reflect the inclinations of the Shah. Both he or the empress were quite capable of altering them whenever they wished.

There was, in fact, a period during which Farah complained publicly of the accolades being heaped on her and her spouse. She pleaded that schools, hospitals, streets, and squares stop being named after members of the royal family. Yet the practice continued unabated because her wishes never went beyond verbal remonstrances.

Newspaper headlines—again merely one example of many genres of panegyric—reflect the imperial inclination because SAVAK spent so much effort managing, in a most heavy-handed manner, the public image of the Shah within Iran. While the extent of the Shah's micromanagement of SAVAK was exaggerated, he was certainly capable of reducing the panegyrics on which they were so insistent, had he desired.

6. All of the headlines quoted are the lead headlines for the dates listed and taken from *Kayhan International,* a Tehran English-language daily newspaper. The significance of that particular paper is problematic. As a foreign-language paper, it clearly was oriented, in the first instance, to foreigners. As such it was widely believed to be relatively more free of regime controls than dailies aimed at an Iranian audience. A comparison of *Kayhan International* with *Ettela'at,* the principal Persian-language daily, reveals few differences in the headlines for the dates given.

7. A large number of Empress Farah's advisers and an increasing number of influential "technocrats" were Melli University faculty members. The prominence accorded Farah's visit to the campus was not lost on those officials who understood such happenings as important signs indicating the direction of the political winds.

8. Oriana Fallaci, "The Shah of Iran" (interview), *New Republic,* vol. 169, no. 22, December 1, 1974, pp. 16–21.

9. *Kayhan International,* January 2, 1975, pp. 1, 3.

10. From an interview with *Der Spiegel,* reprinted in the *Washington Post,* February 3, 1974, p. c5.

11. Mohamed Heikal, *Return of the Ayatollah: The Iranian Revolution from Mossadeq to Khomeini* (London: André Deutsch, 1981).

12. E. A. Bayne, *Persian Kingship in Transition: Conversations with a Monarch Whose Office Is Traditional and Whose Goal Is Modernization* (New York: American Universities Field Staff, 1968), p. 48.

13. Mansour Farhang, "Resisting the Pharaohs: Ali Shariati on Oppression," *Race and Class* 21 (Summer 1979): 32.

14. *Kayhan International,* January 2, 1975, pp. 1, 3.

15. The one billion dollars he leant France became a major issue of contention between France and Iran in the 1980s. The French government made installment payments on that loan in 1986 and 1988 to win the release of French citizens kidnapped and held captive by Iranian-dominated militias in Lebanon.

16. Interview, *Le Monde,* carried in *Guardian/Le Monde,* English ed., October 16, 1971.

17. Cynthia Helms, *An Ambassador's Wife in Iran* (New York: Dodd, Mead, 1981), p. 69.

18. Farah Shahbanou Pahlavi, *My Thousand and One Days: An Autobiography,* trans. Felice Harcourt (London: W. H. Allen, 1978), p. 95. The sensitivity of the royal family, and of the empress in particular, is demonstrated by her lengthy treatment of the celebrations in her autobiography. Out of a 146-page book, 11 pages describe the festivities. The empress "had been asked to preside over the organization of these celebrations and it had meant considerable work," so it is no wonder she spent so long both describing and defending. She defends the celebrations against all the criticisms with the thought that "the arrival of all these notables, visitors proved to the people of Iran the respect felt by the world for their history, their civilization, and for the present position of Iran in the community of nations" (p. 90).

19. Henry Kissinger, *White House Years* (Boston: Little, Brown, 1979), p. 1264.

20. Central Bank of Iran, *Bulletin* 5, no. 30 (March–April 1967): 1088–89.

21. For a detailed account of how the Shah successfully pressured the oil companies to lift ever-increasing volumes of Iranian oil exports, see Robert B. Stobaugh, "The Evolution of Iranian Oil Policy, 1925–1975," in George Lenczowski, ed., *Iran under the Pahlavis* (Stanford: Hoover Institution Press, 1978), pp. 201–52.

22. The 1973 OPEC meeting led to a major confrontation between Iran and Saudi Arabia and established a pattern of confrontation between the two states which has continued to the present. King Faisal had instructed Yamani to accept a new OPEC posted price of no more than $7 per barrel. The Shah pushed for a $14 price, eventually compromising at $11.65. See Stobaugh, "Evolution of Iranian Oil Policy," pp. 245–46. Saudi Arabia has conventionally sought more moderate prices for OPEC oil, a pattern which has remained long after the ouster of the Shah.

23. Personal interview, March 11, 1986.

24. It needs to be reiterated that this analysis should be understood as distinct from criticism. The issue is not merely that it is all too easy to second-guess others, especially from the comfortable position of hindsight. Even more to the point are the common, all-too-human processes at work. The question, for example, is not why the empress began to mirror the grandiosity of the

Shah—although that issue certainly could be understood in the context of the psychodynamics of her character structure. A more relevant question is who could have withstood the blandishments? From the Shah's perspective, from the empress's perspective, from the perspective of "their" officials, Iran was on a joy ride which promised decades of wealth and power. Very few could have resisted. Many—but certainly not all who did resist—were in fact unable to get in on the division of the spoils. This also applies to many of the religious leaders who, it appears, were the beneficiaries of the millions of dollars Prime Minister Hoveyda distributed to them for many years.

25. Ashraf Pahlavi, *Faces in a Mirror: Memoirs from Exile* (Englewood Cliffs, N.J.: Prentice-Hall, 1980), p. 155. The princess's language is characteristic not only of the defensive style found in the writings of the Pahlavis during the 1970s, but provides a clue to the Pahlavi system and its relation to the Iranian people. That which constituted "progress" was defined by the regime and "given" to the people. The system was thus both paternal and patronizing and increasingly recognized as such by the people.

26. Ibid.

27. Interest rates in the bazaar fell five percentage points, from 21 percent to 16 percent per annum, the day after the land bill was submitted; *Kayhan International*, January 7, 1975, p. 2.

28. Tehran's speculators quickly found alternative opportunities for risk taking. The still-fledgling Tehran stock market reported the value of its transactions in January of 1975 at a level four times greater than the previous high. Much of the increase was attributable to a single large move by the Central Bank of Iran, but even so, a huge record was set. See *Kayhan International*, February 4, 1975, p. 4.

29. Mohammad Reza Shah Pahlavi, *Mission for My Country* (New York: McGraw-Hill, 1961), p. 173.

30. *Kayhan International*, March 3, 1975, p. 2.

31. William H. Forbis, *The Fall of the Peacock Throne: The Story of Iran* (New York: McGraw-Hill, 1981), p. 247.

32. Helms, *Ambassador's Wife in Tehran*, p. 177.

33. Personal interview, March 14, 1986.

34. Forbis, *Fall of the Peacock Throne*, p. 238.

35. *Kayhan International*, September 7, 1975, p. 3.

36. *Kayhan International*, September 11, 1975, p. 3.

37. Mohammad Reza Shah Pahlavi, *Answer to History* (New York: Stein and Day, 1980), p. 126. Interestingly, the Shah gives the date for these tribunals as August and September 1977, rather than 1975 when they actually occurred. No antiprofiteering campaigns were conducted in 1977, with those two months in particular witnessing a remarkable growth in opposition activities among all segments of the opposition. See, for example, Ervand Abrahamian, *Iran between Two Revolutions* (Princeton: Princeton University Press, 1982), esp. pp. 502–4. Why the Shah should have confused the dates of the student antiprofiteering brigades is unclear. But by placing them in the fall

of 1977, he makes the campaign into a two-year-long effort, thus implying both greater continuity of policy than was the case and greater vigor in enforcement of that policy.

38. See Bank Markazi Iran, *Bulletin*, vol. 14, no. 77 (October–December 1975): pp. 264–65.

39. Pahlavi, *Answer to History*, p. 126.

40. James A. Bill, *The Eagle and the Lion: The Tragedy of American-Iranian Relations* (New Haven: Yale University Press, 1988), p. 204.

41. For an elaborate and highly convincing analysis of Iran's nuclear energy program which demonstrated its economic and financial folly, see Zalmay Khalilzad, "The Political, Economic, and Military Implications of Nuclear Electricity: The Case of the Northern Tier," Ph.D. dissertation, Department of Political Science, University of Chicago, 1978.

42. Iran Ministry of Power, *A Survey of Nuclear Power Stations in Iran* (Tehran, 1969).

43. U.S. Congress, House of Representatives, Committee on Foreign Affairs, Subcommittees on International Organizations and Movements and on the Near East and South Asia, *U.S. Foreign Policy and the Export of Nuclear Technology to the Middle East*, 93d Cong., 2d sess., p. 30.

44. *Kayhan International*, February 28, 1974, p. 1.

45. *Kayhan International*, June 2, 1976, p. 3, announced the signing of a contract with Framatome of France for the construction of two 900 MWe reactors. Construction costs were listed at $2.8 billion, with an additional $1.2 billion earmarked for enriched uranium. The two reactors were not only of medium size, rather than the 1,200 MWe which the Shah intended to build eventually, but they were to be located in what were judged to be the optimal locations, thus minimizing additional infrastructure costs.

46. *Kayhan International*, September 4, 1975.

47. *Kayhan International*, September 1, 1975, p. 1.

48. This was not the first time one of the Pahlavis had changed the Iranian calender. In 1925, Reza Shah replaced the Arabic lunar calender with the Iranian solar calender. That, however, was in the service of Iranian nationalism and not imperial grandiosity. See Said Amir Arjomand, *The Turban for the Crown: The Islamic Revolution in Iran* (New York: Oxford University Press, 1988), p. 68.

49. Those who appreciated the readiness of the Shah to pursue Western ways expected he would attempt to join the West by adopting its calendar, a move made decades earlier by Ataturk as one means of propelling Turkey into Westernization. But others, who appreciated the Shah's keen sense of Iranian nationalism combined with his more recent grandiose depreciation of the West, could more readily understand his selection of an entirely new, solely Iranian calendar. Just as no one could crown either Reza Shah or Mohammad Reza Shah except those rulers themselves, so no calendar was fit for Iran except its own.

50. *Kayhan International*, March 15, 1975, p. 1.

51. *Kayhan International,* March 23, 1976, p. 4.

52. In an effort to placate an aroused population whose revolutionary fervor was mounting, the regime restored Iran's old calendar on August 27, 1978.

53. *Kayhan International,* March 23, 1976, p. 4. The notion of a commandership is not as outrageous in the Iranian language as it appears in English. Previous dynasties had issued "commands" or *firmans* or *farmans.* But the term had long since fallen out of use, at least partly because it was out of keeping with both the spirit of the twentieth century and the provisions of the Iranian Constitution, which precluded the Shah's being a command giver.

54. The Shah's creation of a new concept of rulership is similar to an innovation of Ayatollah Khomeini. The cleric created the concept of *velayat-e faqih* or "rule of the jurist," and he occupied the position of ruling jurist from the time of the founding of the Islamic Republic in Iran in 1979. Both the concepts, *farmandehi* and *velayat-e faqih,* were innovations within the existing ideologies of which they were a part. They both also had the effect of giving the ruler extraordinary power. With the new interpretations of the relationship between Islam and the state which Khomeini propounded in early 1979, the *faqih* would seem to have unlimited power. Khomeini declared that the interests of the state took precedence over all other considerations, even of Islam.

Chapter 4. Cracking the Shah's Authority

1. Other students of Iran have recognized this to be true. John Stempel, the U.S. State Department official who spent years in Iran and is the author of an excellent survey of the Iranian revolution, has written:

> Ambivalent feelings of obedience and hostility toward authority are carried over into the political sphere. To understand the concept of being controlled by an all-powerful leader is to understand how Iranians view their government. The Shah's basic approach to ruling—positioning himself as the "father" supervising his "children"—appealed to deep-rooted instincts in the Iranian psychic make-up. Ayatollah Ruhollah Khomeini, far from being the antithesis of the Shah, is merely his mirror image in clerical dress. The Ayatollah succeeded where the Shah failed because he more consistently and successfully played the role of a strong, authoritarian figure who would not compromise.

John Stempel, *Inside the Iranian Revolution* (Bloomington: Indiana University Press, 1981), p. 15.

2. Farid ud-din Attar, *The Conference of the Birds* (*Mantiq ut-tair*), trans. Garcin de Tassy and C. S. Nott (London: Routledge and Kegan Paul, 1954).

3. Myths, of course, are a central component of the cultural heritage of any people. With many—but by no means all—of those scholars loosely referred to as students of "culture and personality," I would argue that myths also reveal important dimensions of the character structure of those for whom the myths are myths and also play significant psychological functions for them as well. To make this claim, it is not necessary to argue that myths are nothing but the projections or externalizations of the psyches of the culture's members. Nor is it necessary (or possible) to specify a single mythic function, e.g., "Myths are

designed to be remembered and repeated in order that the sharing of unconscious fantasies may confirm and consolidate the central identification of members of the society to whom the myths appeal." Sudhir Kakar, *The Inner World: A Psychoanalytic Study of Childhood and Society in India* (Dehli: Oxford University Press, 1981), p. 145.

4. Sadeq Chubak, "The Baboon Whose Buffoon Was Dead," trans. Peter Avery, in *New World Writing* (New York: Mentor Books, 1957), 11: 14–24.

5. Ibid., p. 17.

6. Ibid.

7. This is not the place to document the diverse interpretations of Shi'ism or the ways in which the ruling authorities in Iran under Khomeini's concept of *velayat-e faqih* (rule of the jurist) have succeeded in enshrining one of these sets of interpretations—Ayatollah Khomeini's, of course—as the paradigmatic interpretation. For an explication of these diverse interpretations, see Marvin Zonis and Daniel Brumberg, *Khomeini, the Islamic Republic of Iran, and the Arab World* (Cambridge: Harvard University Middle East Papers, 1987); and idem, "Shi'ism as Interpreted by Khomeini: An Ideology of Revolutionary Violence," in Martin Kramer, ed., *Shi'ism, Resistance, and Revolution* (Boulder, Colo.: Westview Press, 1987).

8. See Marvin Zonis and Daniel Brumberg, "Interpreting Islam: Human Rights in the Islamic Republic of Iran," in *Proceedings of the Symposium on the Relationship of the Baha'i Faith and Islam,* forthcoming.

9. The source for Principle 5 of the Constitution of the Islamic Republic of Iran is *Middle East Journal* 34(2): 181–204.

In early January 1989 the Ayatollah reasserted his absolute power over the affairs of Iran through an extraordinary exchange of documents which began with a request from the president, Ali Khamene'i, to the faqih, Khomeini, to clarify the status of certain legislation. The Majles had passed laws on foreign trade and land reform which the Council of Guardians had consistently found incompatible with Islam, and thus null and void. Khomeini responded to the president with a stinging rebuke which constituted a reformulation of the powers of the faqih. Khomeini's basic position was that the interests of the Islamic Republic of Iran were so pressing that the means for their realization could not be limited. The interests of the state, in short, transcended even the dictates of Islam.

10. Nothing here is meant to suggest that there are not other visions within the complexity of Iranian culture which can be construed as democratic and egalitarian, nor that there are vast numbers of Iranians who subscribe to those alternative visions. The National Front which coalesced around Prime Minister Mossadegh from 1951 to 1953, to survive incarcerations through the Revolution of 1978, and a number of other groups, including those inspired by Dr. Ali Shari'ati in the late 1960s and 1970s, all sought a secular, democratic republic. To be sure those groups agreed on few of the specifics of what would constitute "democratic" government, but the point is that they were committed to the realization in political form of a different cultural vision than the dominant theme explicated here.

11. Mohammad Reza Shah Pahlavi, *Answer to History* (New York: Stein and Day, 1980), pp. 53–54.

12. Certainly innumerable foreign observers have noted the significance for Iranians of such a leader. Writing at the beginning of this century, for example, Donald Stuart had this to say of Nasr ed din Shah, who ruled from 1848 to 1896:

Nasr ed din Shah Qajar was a despot in the truest meaning of the term; if he wanted money he took it from his subjects and if they resented the honourable distinction, he took their lives—and yet his memory is held in reverence by every Persian, for he ruled his country with a rod of iron, and the universal verdict is "mash'allah, he was a man."

Donald Stuart, *The Struggle for Persia* (London: Methuen, 1902), p. 130.

13. Princess Ashraf Pahlavi, *Faces in the Mirror: Memoirs from Exile* (Englewood Cliffs, N.J.: Prentice-Hall, 1980), p. 201. Princess Ashraf continues, "The Carter Administration's insistence on America's vision of 'human rights' had the opposite effect of what was intended: it signalled to the Shah's opponents that the United States had, in effect, made up its mind to abandon him. To give concessions in this atmosphere signalled a weakness born of desperation, rather than a genuine attempt to conciliate and heal." The extent to which the "concessions" offered by the Shah fed rather than extinguished the revolutionary fires and the role of the United States in pushing him toward those concessions is discussed below.

14. Ibid., p. 188.

15. Gerard de Villiers, *The Imperial Shah: An Informal Biography,* trans. June P. Wilson and Walter B. Michaels (Boston: Little, Brown, 1976), p. 284. The Shah's one-time minister of court and earlier prime minister, the most trusted of his officials, Assadollah Alam, had once declared, "In this country, with its 2,500 year history of monarchy, the Shah is the father, everything referred to him, and he has got to be aware of the problem." William H. Forbis, Fall of the Peacock Throne: The Story of Iran (New York: McGraw-Hill, 1981), p. 69. Clearly some claims of this nature must be understood as rationalizations of the distribution of power in Iran and defenses of the Shah's authoritarian or dictatorial rule. But irrespective of the purposes for which the metaphor of "father" was used to characterize that rule, it is striking how often it was used and how those who used it understood that it would make sense to the Iranian people. They understood this nature of power in the Iranian family and were prepared to accept that structure as a paradigm for the national power structure.

16. *Kayhan International,* September 18, 1975, p. 4.

17. *Kayhan International,* March 23, 1976, p. 4.

18. Said Arjomand makes the point that "the decisive person to withdraw his commitment to the preservation of the state was no other than the Shah himself." Said Amir Arjomand, *The Turban for the Crown: The Islamic Revolution in Iran* (New York: Oxford University Press, 1988), p. 114.

19. Personal interview, March 23, 1982. The only group administrative meeting in which the Shah regularly participated after early 1976 was, apparently, the High Economic Council. It met every Monday morning, with senior economic officials reviewing their programs and presenting proposals for the Shah's approval. The members of the council would spend the preceding Sunday afternoon working

out their disagreements so that, next morning, the Shah would be presented with the group consensus. The chances for his having any significant input were, consequently, reduced, and the meetings were, like so much else in Iranian life by the last years of the Pahlavis, largely ceremonial. Part of the reason for the ceremonial nature of these meetings was the Shah's lack of interest in domestic economic matters. In the economic realm, he cared deeply about oil production, on account of the revenues accruing to Iran, as well as about Iran's growing nuclear energy capability. But neither of these issues were the responsibility of the High Economic Council. He never particularly involved himself with what otherwise were their responsibilities.

20. Personal interview, March 23, 1982.

21. Personal interview, March 23, 1982.

22. While it has proven virtually impossible to evaluate objectively SAVAK's ruthlessness, my sense is that its reputation (like many other reputations in Iran) for ruthlessness was grander than its performance. This is not to deny that it used torture to interrogate and intimidate suspects. Nor is it to deny that its members sought to instill terror in the Iranian people by acts of savagery, including beating perceived opponents of the regime and physically breaking up gatherings considered unsympathetic to the ruling order. But it seems to be true that SAVAK did create an aura of terror which came to supersede the reality. The efforts of certain opponents of the regime contributed to this process. They made SAVAK symbolic of the entire Pahlavi system and then portrayed it as an inhuman organization. This practice apparently extended to the point that certain notorious individuals claimed to have been brutally tortured by SAVAK when the actuality is that they were never mistreated.

23. Personal interview, April 11, 1982.

24. Personal interview, February 16, 1982.

25. Personal interview, March 23, 1982. It was not only the Iranian prime minister who failed to be included. James Bill reports that

when President Roosevelt and his entourage traveled to Iran in November–December 1943, the American minister, Louis Dreyfus, was cut out of the deliberations. At an important state dinner given by the British legation on November 30, 1943, Dreyfus was conspicuously absent. Instead, influential confidants such as Harry Hopkins, W. Averell Harriman, and Colonel Elliot Roosevelt were in attendance.

James A. Bill, *The Eagle and the Lion: The Tragedy of American-Iranian Relations* (New Haven: Yale University Press, 1988), p. 45. Bill mentions this bit of arcania in the course of making the point that the U.S.-Iranian relationship was dominated, on the American side, not by official diplomatic representatives but by informal high-level insiders whose Iranian connections were largely limited to the Shah and his senior elite and who had no special knowledge of Iran.

Many accounts of the Shah's conduct of Iran's business tend to confirm the exclusion of the prime minister. For example, Cynthia Helms, wife of the U.S. ambassador to Iran, described the Shah's 1975 state visit to the United States: "The Shah met with the President alone. Although he had a large official group with him, including his Foreign Minister, he preferred to conduct official business himself, and when he went to his meeting in Congress, only Dick [Helms] and Ardeshir Zahedi, the Iranian ambassador to the United States, accompanied him." Cynthia Helms, *An Ambassador's Wife in Iran* (New York: Dodd, Mead, 1981), p. 181.

26. This evolution of the Shah's interests and attention was striking given the Shah's previous comments. He had earlier claimed to be interested in very different areas of government in Iran:

if you want to know me, you must know my convictions as a man and head of state in this seething part of the world. And the plain truth is that I derive my chief satisfactions from grappling with complex economic and other problems. Myself as Shah cannot be separated from myself as a man fervently interested in economic development, agricultural reform, and educational advance.

Mohammad Reza Shah Pahlavi, *Mission for My Country* (New York: McGraw-Hill, 1961), p. 140.

These, of course, were the very areas about which, by the 1970s, the Shah cared little and which he was willing to turn over to the prime minister. In effect, the Shah had abandoned the internal affairs of Iran while he focused on its external relations.

The empress, H.I.M. Farah Pahlavi, has also alluded to the Shah's withdrawal from certain domestic affairs:

my wifely duty is to create about him as pleasant an atmosphere as possible, to be careful to avoid family cares being added to those of the State, to help him find relaxation and repose. I also help him in certain fields with which he has not the time to concern himself personally: education, health, culture, social matters."

Farah Shahbanou Pahlavi, *My Thousand and One Days: An Autobiography,* trans. Felice Harcourt (London: W. H. Allen, 1978), p. 129.

27. Colonel Valian was universally despised in Mashhad. He was widely believed to have been a SAVAK official. With his appointment as governor of Khorasan Province, he was also designated the guardian of the Imam Reza shrine in Mashhad, the burial place of the eighth Imam and the most holy religious site in Iran. That deeply offended the entire religious community. But when the colonel instituted an urban renewal program to create "green spaces" surrounding the shrine, he sealed his fate. In the process, seminaries and scores of traditional buildings were destroyed.

28. Personal interview, January 5, 1982.

29. Farah Pahlavi, *My Thousand and One Days,* p. 51.

30. Ibid., p. 52. The queen would deliver three additional children to the Shah, a girl, Farahnaz (March 12, 1963); a second boy, Ali (April 28, 1966); and another girl, Leila (March 27, 1970).

31. Jonathan Braun, writing in *Parade Magazine* ("An Interview with Empress Farah of Iran," January 12, 1975, n.p.), recognized that significance, although exaggerated it as well:

When Farah gave her husband an heir on October 31, 1960, she also gave him a new emotional security say veteran court watchers. With the future of the dynasty secure in his mind, the Shah began to move in bold, innovative ways. In 1963, he initiated a broad social welfare program—called the White—or bloodless—Revolution.

The link here between social reform and the birth of his son is too direct and simple. Nonetheless, there was some connection.

32. The move to institutionalize the Pahlavi system presented the Shah with a dilemma which was to trouble him for the rest of his rule. Insofar as he retained direct control over the day-to-day details of governing, he was not institutionalizing the system. But insofar as he vested authority in the bureaucracies, he was curtailing his own power. The Shah responded characteristically. He would take one approach, and then, after some time, he would pursue the other approach, thus introducing great confusion into the system.

33. For the economic crisis of 1960–63 and its relation to the revolution of 1978, see Jahangir Amuzegar, *Technical Assistance in Theory and Practice: The Case of Iran* (New York: Praeger, 1966); Robert Graham, *Iran: The Illusion of Power* (New York: St. Martin's Press, 1978); Fred Halliday, *Iran: Dictatorship and Development* (New York: Penguin Books, 1979); and Homa Katouzian, *The Political Economy of Modern Iran: Despotism and Pseudo-Modernism, 1926–1979* (New York: New York University Press, 1981).

34. The Shah always claimed that the United States had forced Amini on him. Amini had served as Iranian ambassador to the United States, where he allegedly cemented his ties to U.S. authorities. When political turmoil and economic decline hit Iran in 1960, the strong-willed Amini was the "logical," "American" choice. See the Shah's interview with *U.S. News and World Report,* January 27, 1969.

35. Amini actually fell from royal favor in 1958. In that year Gen. Bahrullah Qarani, chief of military intelligence, had been arrested on charges of plotting a coup. Amini was alleged to have been aware of the general's plans but had failed to inform the Shah. It appears that what Qarani had actually done was to have drawn up a lengthy report charging senior security officials, including SAVAK chief General Bakhtiar. See Bill, *Eagle and the Lion*, p. 127. What has never been satisfactorily explained, however, is the role of the United States in Amini's fall. Ervand Abrahamian suggests that the United States sided with the Shah against Amini when the prime minister sought to cut the defense budget. See Abrahamian, *Iran between Two Revolutions* (Princeton: Princeton University Press, 1982), pp. 423–24. Other authors have offered other explanations, the most widespread being Amini's inability to raise sufficient foreign aid from the United States. But if he were America's preferred prime minister, it is unclear why the United States would undercut him.

36. Another boyhood friend of the Shah, Gen. Hossein Fardoust, also played a key role in the life of the Shah. Fardoust was one of the young men sent by Reza Shah to serve as companions for the Crown Prince during his years of study in Switzerland. Fardoust was to play other key roles for the Shah, the most important of which was chief of the Special Bureau—a post within the Ministry of Court which served as a crucial link between the ruler and the intelligence services. Fardoust's decision to remain in Iran for some five years after the success of the revolution led many, including the Shah, to believe that Fardoust actually sided with the revolution while he served the Shah.

37. Farah Pahlavi, *My Thousand and One Days,* p. 62.

38. Certain events in the life of Mohammad Reza Shah were so significant to him that he raised his own son with certain parallels. The coronation provides one such example. The significance of his formal designation as Crown Prince in April of

1926 upon the coronation of his father has been mentioned above. Mohammad Reza was then some six months short of his seventh birthday. During his own coronation, he formally designated his son as Crown Prince. His son was a few days younger than seven years of age.

39. *Time,* April 1, 1974, p. 41. The Shah's comparison of himself (favorably) to De Gaulle is fascinating. He had done so on numerous occasions. In his memoirs the Shah mentioned that "it was as a very young sovereign that I first met General Charles de Gaulle. I was immediately captivated by his extraordinary personality. . . . This ardent patriot was a guide for me as a sovereign" (Pahlavi, *Answer to History,* pp. 137–38). Perhaps most telling in the comparison is the differential in their heights. As mentioned above, stature was of great significance for the Shah. And De Gaulle had it. But the Shah, at least in this reference, managed to find a way to make himself superior to the general.

40. *Time,* November 4, 1974, p. 34.

41. For example, in an interview with Mohamed Heikal in 1975, the Shah said:

Our struggle now lies in the construction of the new Iran, in the construction of a better country for my people and for my son who will ascend the throne after me. At his age, I used to dream of Iran's far future and I wish to deliver this dream as a concrete reality into his hands, to place the future in his safe-keeping as a tangible reality which eyes can see and hands can touch.

Interview originally in *Al-Nahar,* Beirut, reproduced in *Kayhan International,* September 16, 1975.

42. The poster which became so omnipresent in Iran in the 1970s—discussed above—where the Shah was portrayed waving to his people against a background of clouds and not obviously standing on anything takes on new meaning in light of his foreboding of his death. On the relatively more manifest level, the Shah is associated with the heavens and, blasphemous as it might be, with God. On a more obscure level, the poster put the Shah in the heavens, which is what was very much on his mind throughout this period.

43. Personal interview with the government official who made this report to the Shah, March 15, 1982. It is worth noting the ambiguity of the communication which the Shah received. Iranian culture is virtually predicated on ambiguity in its verbal communications. See, for example, M. C. Bateson, J. W. Clinton, J. B. M. Kassarjian, H. Safavi, and M. Soraya, "Safa-yi Batin: A Study of the Interrelations of a Set of Iranian Ideal Character Types," in L. Carl Brown and Norman Itzkowitz, eds., *Psychological Dimensions of Near Eastern Studies* (Princeton: Darwin Press, 1977). And as the imperial court functioned as a distillation of Iranian culture, its communication tended to be the most ambiguous of all. What is astounding is not that the system collapsed, but that it functioned as well as it did for as long as it did.

44. Personal interview, March 15, 1982.

45. Pahlavi, *Mission for My Country,* p. 57.

46. Filmed interview with David Frost, "Crossroads of Civilization: An Inquiry into History," 1979. The interview was done, of course, after the Shah had learned of his cancer. His mention of fifteen years is puzzling, since there were as-

sassination attempts in 1949 and 1965, and his cancer was discovered in 1974. Fifteen years previous to the interview, 1963, was the year in which the Ayatollah Ruhollah Khomeini, was arrested for making a bitterly anti-Shah speech. His arrest was followed by three days of rioting in Iranian cities and hundreds of deaths. It was the first major confrontation between the Shah and the Ayatollah. The Shah, perhaps with some foreboding of the immediate future, harkened back to 1963 as the year when death became meaningless to him, when, perhaps, he had seen death right in front of his eyes.

47. Ashraf Pahlavi, *Faces in the Mirror,* p. 40. The princess informs us that she promised to do as her brother suggested. But there was no armed assault by the British or Russian troops on the palace and no suicide attempt. It is striking that the young man's suicide was to be activated by his capture, not by the fall of his country to the foreigners or by the capture of his father the Shah, not even, apparently, by the likely collapse of the Pahlavi dynasty.

48. There are precedents in Iranian history for the flight of a monarch to Europe in the face of uncontrollable domestic political events. For example, Ahmad Shah, the last ruler of the Qajar dynasty which was supplanted by Reza Shah's establishment of the Pahlavi dynasty in 1925, took that course. Reza Shah, then known as Reza Khan, and an Iranian journalist, Seyyed Zia ed Din Tabataba'i, had staged a coup in 1921. Reza Khan initially took the post of defense minister, leaving the prime ministership for Seyyed Zia. But Reza was clearly the most significant power in the postcoup government and was challenging Ahmad Shah. The king chose to leave for Europe, thinking a temporary absence would give the people time to put Reza Khan aside. Thus there are historical, that is, cultural, antecedents to the Shah's flight to Europe, in addition to the psychological forces being articulated here.

49. Pahlavi, *Mission for My Country,* p. 106.

50. The quote is taken from a press conference given by the Shah on the anniversary of the overthrow of Mossadegh, August 18, 1978—in the midst of the revolution which would ultimately succeed in overthrowing him (Foreign Broadcast Information Service, MEA-78-163, August 18, 1978). For the Shah, the obvious and painful parallels between 1953 and 1978 become clear here. And the issue of his failure to act vigorously and assertively also became clear. On some level, he understood his dilemma about activity and passivity. On occasion, and this was one, he indicated that understanding, for he continued his remarks about Mossadegh: "There was no other remedy but that [leaving the country to "crystallize" public opinion]. Some people used to say: 'Why have you been so patient? Why have you not acted before?' But perhaps the course of events in those days did not allow more than that. The Iranian people made their choice." It is undoubtedly true that the Shah must have hoped that another flight from Iran—in the midst of the revolution—would lead the Iranian people to make another choice in his favor.

51. For the story of the coup as recounted by its principal author, see Kermit Roosevelt, *Countercoup: The Struggle for the Control of Iran* (New York: McGraw-Hill, 1979). The countercoup of the title refers to the idea that the Shah was, in

fact, staging a countercoup against the unconstitutional power grab, or coup, first propagated by Mossadegh. Also see Mark Gasiorowski, "The 1953 Coup d'Etat in Iran," *International Journal of Middle East Studies* 19 (August 1987): 261–86.

Another minor actor in the drama was Gen. H. Norman Schwarzkopf, commander of the New Jersey state police at the time of the Lindbergh kidnapping and, in 1942–48, the chief adviser to the Iranian gendarmerie. The general was flown into Tehran on August 1, 1953, to bolster the "flagging self-confidence" of the Shah. Bill, *Eagle and the Lion,* p. 90.

For more information on the Mossadegh era, see James A. Bill and William Roger Louis, eds., *Musaddiq, Iranian Nationalism, and Oil* (Austin: University of Texas Press, 1988).

52. Abrahamian, *Iran between Two Revolutions,* p. 271.

53. Ibid., p. 274.

54. Loy Henderson quoted in Stephen E. Ambrose, *Ike's Spies: Eisenhower and the Espionage Establishment* (Garden City, N.Y.: Doubleday, 1981), p. 203.

55. Roosevelt, *Countercoup,* p. 161. The Shah's recollection of this plan, as revealed by his 1978 press conference (see n. 50 above), differs in at least one respect from Roosevelt's account. The Shah mentions "a great deal of thought," while Roosevelt suggests that the idea for a fallback plan was a virtual afterthought and that the idea of a flight to Baghdad was impromptu. Any political leader wishes to portray his actions as the result of seasoned deliberation. The Shah was no exception. What is striking, however, is the extent to which many of his decisions seem to have been made without substantial forethought.

56. Personal communication, Prof. Fazlur Rahman, April 2, 1982.

57. Pahlavi, *Mission for My Country,* p. 65.

58. At his trial, Mossadegh gave this account:

At 1 A.M., August 16, 1953, I received the Royal Order and I gave a receipt for it. After I examined the Royal Order, I found that there was something wrong in the Shah's handwriting and there were signs of a possible forgery. I found that the text of the Royal Order had been written after His Majesty had signed it. Unfortunately, this Order was stolen the day my house was plundered.

Iran, *Proceedings of the Mossadegh-Riahi Trial* (Tehran: Echo of Iran Publications), November 23, 1963, p. 3. Mossadegh may have been right, at least in regard to the rescript having been stolen. Kermit Roosevelt reproduces the original royal decree appointing Zahedi prime minister (p. 3 of the photographs following p. 124 of the text of *Countercoup*), but does not reproduce the one dismissing Mossadegh.

59. Queen Soraya Pahlavi, *Khaterat-e Soraya,* trans. Musa Mijidi (Tehran: Saadat Printing House, n.d.), p. 92. It needs to be acknowledged that accounts by ex-spouses are not always the most reliable guides to history. Nevertheless, where it is possible to check her version against those presented by other authors, there appears to be no particular violation of the facts.

60. Ibid., p. 95. One sidelight of the Shah's flight to Rome should be spelled out. The planning for the Shah's flight to Baghdad—and subsequent flight to Rome, further from, not closer to the political action in Iran—did not extend to finances. The Shah arrived in Rome with no funds. Moreover, he had no foreign bank accounts from which to draw funds (personal interview, June 16, 1981). His

stay in Rome was apparently paid for by an Iranian businessman who happened to be in that city and gave the Shah money. It is said that he was handsomely rewarded in later years by receiving the exclusive right to certain imports to Iran as well as a monopoly to provide certain services within the country.

Soraya's account bears out reports of the Shah's difficult financial position. She reports that in Rome she asked the Shah if they could live abroad on their income: "He picked up a pencil, and, after making various calculations said, 'If it were just you and I, perhaps. But my family consists of more than 20 persons. That is why I should like to buy a farm. All my brothers could live there and at least they could be fairly sure that their children would be fed'" (Soraya Pahlavi, *Khaterat-e Soraya*, p. 97).

One of the consequences of the Shah's realization in Rome of his financial vulnerability was a lifelong commitment to assuring the financial security of himself and his family, inside as well as outside Iran.

61. Personal interviews, June 16, 1981, and October 15, 1981.

62. Soraya Pahlavi, *Khaterat-e Soraya*, p. 97.

63. Personal interview, March 8, 1981.

64. For his account of those days, see Roosevelt, *Countercoup*, pp. 175–97. Roosevelt's published version omits any mention of his violation of orders but presents both coup efforts as aspects of a single whole. For another eyewitness account of the days surrounding the countercoup, see Jonathan Kwitny, *Endless Enemies: The Making of an Unfriendly World* (New York: Congden and Weed, 1984), esp. pp. 161–77. Kwitny reproduces long excerpts from a firsthand account of the coup by Kennett Love, a *New York Times* reporter who happened to be in Tehran at the time.

65. Peter Avery notes, "The Shah, it seems, was caught off-balance by the sudden conjunction of forces in Mussadeq's favor—his command of xenophobia excited by the oil dispute and his ability to profit alike from the support of the conservative elite, from religious extremists, and from left-wing agitators." The Shah was, of course, caught "off balance" by the confluence of not too dissimilar forces in 1978. Peter Avery, *Modern Iran* (London: Ernest Benn, Ltd., 1965), p. 420.

66. Soraya Pahlavi, *Khaterat-e Soraya*, p. 82. Soraya adds:

After official receptions the Shah frequently asked me questions such as:
"How deeply did X bow to you?"
"Did Y kiss your hand?"
"Did Mrs. Z's curtsey seem to you spontaneous or deliberate?"
I myself attached no significance to such superficial matters, but Mohammad Reza believed at that time that from such symptoms he could diagnose the degree of loyalty of his entourage and could judge whether it was increasing or decreasing.

It was from such small symbolic gestures and actions that much in Iranian politics was understood. The Shah, his political elite, and even the middle and lower classes were adept interpreters of the most minute and, to Westerners, seemingly innocuous, signs. This was a form of Iranian discourse which pervaded Iranian culture. It was pervasive in two senses. First, all forms of communication—speech and other behaviors—had as one component of their transmission of meaning that conveyed by nuance, that delicate variation in the execution of behaviors or articulation of speech at which Iranians are such masters. Second, virtually all Iranians participated in this form of discourse. The result was an extraordinarily complex communication field in which foreigners were grossly inept. For an analysis of some of these nuances in verbal communication, see William O. Beeman, *Language, Status, and Power in Iran* (Bloomington: Indiana University Press, 1986).

67. Pahlavi, *Mission for My Country*, p. 97.

68. Soraya's version is as follows:

In February 1953 he therefore decided to go abroad for an indefinite period. Mossadegh agreed at once, and placed foreign exchange to the value of $11,000 at our disposal to cover our travel expenses. In order not to attract attention we were to leave by land, travelling first to Beirut. We sent our trunks ahead in a palace car, and led the servants to believe that we were simply going skiing. (Soraya Pahlavi, *Khaterat-e Soraya*, p. 85)

Whatever the validity of her claim that the Shah had initiated the notion of his leaving the country, the quote is fascinating for the additional insight it gives on the Shah's financial status. In order to incur a large expense, that is, $11,000, the Shah apparently had to receive foreign exchange from the government. The Shah's failure to do so in August 1953 was responsible for his financial difficulties in Rome. Both examples contribute to the interpretation that whatever assets the Shah and his father before him had accumulated in the name of the Pahlavis, they were neither particularly liquid nor located outside Iran.

Another version of the Shah's proposed February–March 1953 trip can be found in Avery, *Modern Iran*, pp. 430ff.

69. At about this time, Mahmoud Jam wrote a letter to Dr. Qassem Ghani in which he despaired for Iran because the Shah did not think for himself but instead listened to others and then reacted impulsively to events. Jam also lamented that the Shah lacked the courage to implement his own vision for the country. See Qassem Ghani, *Az yaddoshthaye Qassem-e Ghani*, Vol. 9 (London: Routledge and Kegan Paul, 1982), January 28, 1952. I appreciate Cyrus Amir Mokri's familiarizing me with this material.

70. Soraya Pahlavi, *Khaterat-e Soraya*, p. 86. Soraya's description rings true because there have been a number of descriptions of the Shah's crying. For example, one biographer of the Shah was told by the Empress Farah that the "Shah would cry over films about animals or friendship" because he had a "tender heart." Margaret Laing, "Interview," *The Guardian*, February 24, 1977, p. 9. Not surprisingly, the Shah notes this quality in others. For example, he belittles Mossadegh for crying "like a woman." Pahlavi, *Mission for My Country*, p. 126. The softness revealed by the Shah's propensity for tears is consistent with and supportive of the interpretations of the Shah in this work.

71. Personal interview, December 29, 1981. The informant added that Reza Shah would invariably conclude his assessment of his son by adding that in the royal family there was only one man—Ashraf, the Shah's twin sister.

72. The issue of responsibility in a political system is a key issue in its operation. For my views on Iran under the Shah, see Marvin Zonis, "He Took All of the Credit; Now He Gets All the Blame," *New York Times*, January 14, 1979. The issue is sufficiently significant to be the subject of numerous jokes. Richard Nixon, at the height of Watergate, for example, is alleged to have told anyone who would listen, "I accept full responsibility but none of the blame."

Less humorously but no less serious, the Middle East is an especially fitting area in which to analyze this phenomenon. Each of the actors in the Arab-Israeli conflict attributes all of the responsibility for the perpetuation of the conflict to its adversaries. Ayatollah Khomeini was a model for evading responsibility. The problems of the Islamic Republic are attributed to "the Great Satan" (the United States), "the Lesser Satan" (Israel or the USSR, depending on the context), the Zionists, the imperialists, the monarchists, the terrorists, the "hypocrites" (from the Iranian *monafeqin* which the Ayatollah used to refer to the Mujaheddin, a principal opposition group whose name he refused to utter), and on and on. This refusal to accept political responsibility is so widespread in the Middle East and matched by a similar failure in personal life that its roots must be sought in psychocultural, rather than political, factors.

73. Grace Goodell has described how the villagers in a development town in Khuzestan "sought relief from their hunger during the country's 1974 wheat crisis" by requesting a larger wheat allocation from the government, the only source of additional foodstuffs.

To my surprise, they did not take their case to the provincial Ministry of Labor or Health or Rural Welfare or even Water and Power but rather, straight to the regional headquarters of the secret police. They were right. The dreaded SAVAK, housed in an inconspicuous private home on a side street, determined the price, allotment, and distribution of wheat even for our remote *shahrak* (development town).

Grace E. Goodell, "How the Shah De-Stabilized Himself," *Policy Review* 16 (Spring 1981): 67.

74. The referendum—shades of Prime Minister Mossadegh—was virtually as one-sided as that which he perpetrated in 1953. The Shah asked the Iranian people to vote approval or disapproval for his reform package: 5,589,710 voted in favor; 4,115 voted against; none abstained! *Ettela'at* (Tehran), January 31, 1963, p. 1.

75. In his first book, the Shah had observed, "To combat Communist subversion or any other evil, a government must enjoy the backing of the majority of the people, and in the long run, it will only have this if it provides adequate social justice in the broadest sense" (Pahlavi, *Mission for My Country*, p. 129). It is, of course, virtually impossible to separate the political motives of the Shah from his personal motives, when assessing the significance of such a statement. But on the basis of both the personal and political assessments of the man made in this work, it would be reasonable to conclude that the Shah, however cynical, was also genuine about social justice, at least in his definition of the term.

76. Mohammed Reza Shah Pahlavi, interview, *Time*, September 18, 1978, p. 17.

77. "More than two years ago," he said, "I decided that changing conditions in Iran required a program of liberalization. This increase in the freedom of my political opponents has enabled them to be active against me, and because of the liberalization, I have not been exercising my strength." *U.S. News and World Report*, June 26, 1978, p. 37. In this same interview, the Shah was asked, "Will you reinstate tight controls if political demonstrations get worse?" The Shah's answer: "The liberalization will continue and I view law and order as a separate issue." The response was typical of the Shah's utterances and behaviors throughout the revolu-

tion. The message contained no warning or threat against demonstrations, and the meaning of the answer was, at best, cryptic. It was, in short, an example of the "mixed messages" which did so much to crack the Shah's authority.

78. Personal interview, January 5, 1982.

79. Helms, *Ambassador's Wife in Iran,* pp. 204–5.

80. U.S. Congress, House of Representatives, Committee on International Relations, *Reports on Human Rights and U.S. Policy: Argentina, Haiti, Indonesia, Iran, Peru, and the Philippines,* 94th Cong., 2d sess., submitted by the Department of State, December 31, 1976.

81. See Marvin Zonis, "Human Rights and American Foreign Policy: The Case of Iran," in Tom J. Farer, ed., *Toward a Humanitarian Diplomacy: A Primer for Policy* (New York: New York University Press, 1980), pp. 131–76.

82. John D. Stempel, *Inside the Iranian Revolution* (Bloomington: Indiana University Press, 1981), p. 82.

83. Parviz Radji, *In the Service of the Peacock Throne: The Diaries of the Shah's Last Ambassador to London* (London: Hamish Hamilton, 1983), p. 91. Radji, who took the text from an article by Robert Graham in the London *Financial Times,* adds, "No such letter could have been written says Graham, if it were not for the protective umbrella of President Carter's stand over human rights."

84. *Kayhan International,* July 26, 1977, p. 1.

85. *Kayhan Weekly International Edition,* vol. 10, no. 483, August 13, 1977, p. 2.

86. *Kayhan International,* June 15, 1977, p. 1.

87. Anthony Parsons, *The Pride and the Fall: Iran, 1974–1979* (London: Jonathan Cape, 1984), p. 77.

Chapter 5. The Strength of Others

1. Heinz Kohut, *How Does Analysis Cure?* ed. Arnold Goldberg with the collaboration of Paul Stepansky (Chicago: University of Chicago Press, 1984), p. 49.

2. These alter ego or twinship self-selfobject relationships are found frequently in creative persons. The nature of Freud's relationship with Fleiss is one possible example of this kind of relationship. Mary Gedo argues that Picasso helped sustain his creativity through a twinship with Georges Braque. See Mary Gedo, *Picasso: Art as Autobiography* (Chicago: University of Chicago Press, 1980).

3. Gerard de Villiers, *The Imperial Shah: An Informal Biography,* trans. June P. Wilson and Walter B. Michaels (Boston: Little, Brown, 1976), p. 55. Princess Ashraf recalls that on her trip to Le Rosey, when she was sent by her father to visit her brother, he

told me about two new friends he had made. One of these was Richard Helms, who later became director of the Central Intelligence Agency and America's Ambassador to Iran. Another was Ernest Perron, the son of the school handyman, a young man who came to live in Iran and remained my brother's close friend until the day he died in 1961.

Ashraf Pahlavi, *Faces in a Mirror: Memoirs from Exile* (Englewood Cliffs, N.J.: Prentice-Hall, 1980), pp. 22–23. Actually, Princess Ashraf's memory here was faulty. Richard Helms was a student at Le Rosey, but not until several years after the Crown Prince had left the school. The Shah did, however, meet Helms's older brother, whose term at the school overlapped that of the Crown Prince. Personal interview, December 27, 1981.

4. Queen Soraya Pahlavi, *Khaterat-e Soraya,* trans. Musa Majidi (Tehran: Saadat Printing House, n.d.), p. 77.

5. Mohammad Pourkian, *Ernest Perron, Showhar-e Shahanshah-e Iran* (Berlin: Druck und Werbung Ghamgosar, 1979).

6. Personal interview, December 29, 1981.

7. Personal interview, September 15, 1982.

8. Ashraf Pahlavi, *Faces in a Mirror,* p. 53.

9. Ibid., p. 55.

10. Personal interview, December 29, 1981.

11. Sepehr Zabih, *The Mossadegh Era: Roots of the Iranian Revolution* (Chicago: Lake View Press, 1982), p. 41.

12. Personal interview, September 26, 1985.

13. Ashraf Pahlavi, *Faces in a Mirror,* p. 2. One can, of course, read this account of Ashraf's tie to her brother cynically and suggest that she is not so much mourning the tragedy which has befallen her brother and her country since his overthrow as much as the evaporation of her own status as twin sister to the world's most powerful ruling monarch. While it is undoubtedly true that the loss of that status has been a bitter one for her, there is no doubt in my mind, after personal interviews with her, that the quotation here is accurate— that there was a great degree of enmeshment in their lives, not only in many practical ways, but, most importantly, in a psychological way.

14. In these volumes there is virtually no mention of his half brothers and sisters. His own mother and Reza Shah produced four children—the Shah, his twin Ashraf, his older sister Shams, and his younger brother, Ali Reza. With his three other wives, however, Reza Shah produced ten other issue. Only two of them, Gholam Reza, born in 1923 and the son of Reza Shah's third wife, and Abdol Reza, born in 1924 of Reza Shah's fourth wife, were active in official, public roles. The others were increasingly shut out of court life by the Shah.

15. Ashraf Pahlavi, *Faces in a Mirror,* p. 55.

16. Ibid., p. 43. Princess Ashraf remembered that Reza Shah added, "I wish you had been a boy, so that you could be a brother to him now."

17. Ibid., p. 75.

18. Ibid., p. 76.

19. Mohamed Heikal, *The Return of the Ayatollah: The Iranian Revolution from Mossadeq to Khomeini* (London: André Deutsch, 1981), p. 57. While the number of skins seems inordinate, the princess had, only a few years before, traveled overland in Africa where she was, undoubtedly, able to buy large numbers of pelts. That the "Black Panther" collected tiger skins can perhaps be understood as symbolic of her hunting prowess or even more abstractly as a mark of her identification with the jungle cats which made her nickname so appropriate. As for her "passion" for Napoleon, Princess Ashraf admits, instead, to a "passion" for De Gaulle: "Of all the Western leaders I have met, I think

the one I most admired, ever since the days of the French resistance, was Charles de Gaulle, a military leader who was almost fanatic in his patriotism. Whatever France is today I think it owes to De Gaulle" (Ashraf Pahlavi, *Faces in a Mirror*, p. 171).

20. Soraya Pahlavi, *Khaterat-e Soraya*, p. 41.

21. Heikal, *Return of the Ayatollah*, p. 58.

22. Ashraf Pahlavi, *Faces in a Mirror*, p. 110.

23. Personal interview, March 15, 1982.

24. Mohammad Reza Shah Pahlavi, *Answer to History* (New York: Stein and Day, 1980), p. 84.

25. Ashraf Pahlavi, *Faces in a Mirror*, p. 118.

26. The arrest of Hoveyda led to a contretemps between the Shah and another of his close allies, Finance Minister Hushang Ansary, who had been the principal competitor of Amouzegar for the premiership. Ansary was traveling on official business in Europe at the time of Hoveyda's arrest. He reached the Shah by telephone and asked the ruler why, having promised Ansary and even Hoveyda himself that he was safe, the king had then ordered his arrest. Receiving no answer which he found satisfactory, Ansary was never again to return to Iran. Personal interview, December 27, 1981.

27. The first anniversary of the killings on the campus of Tehran University, November 4, 1979, was commemorated by Tehran students through the seizure of the United States embassy and its American occupants. The so-called hostage crisis was launched.

28. Personal interview, December 10, 1981.

29. Ashraf Pahlavi, *Faces in a Mirror*, p. 140.

30. Kermit Roosevelt, *Countercoup: The Struggle for the Control of Iran* (New York: McGraw-Hill, 1979), p. 146.

31. Personal interview, June 6, 1983. Given what has been suggested above about the Shah's own limited stature and his lifelong concern for height, personal and otherwise, it seems clear that a reference to his twin as a "tiny creature" was meant as a serious insult.

32. Ibid.

33. This showdown was reported by a number of Iranian officials and is mentioned in John D. Stempel, *Inside the Iranian Revolution* (Bloomington: Indiana University Press, 1981), pp. 21–22.

34. Personal interview, July 15, 1982.

35. Ashraf Pahlavi, *Faces in a Mirror*, p. 165. She reports that it was at Juan-les-Pins that she first met and entertained Jacqueline and John Kennedy before he became president.

36. Personal interview, July 15, 1982.

37. Ashraf Pahlavi, *Faces in a Mirror*, p. 198.

38. Ibid.

39. Ibid., p. 205.

40. Ibid., pp. 205–6.

41. This conclusion differs from that of other students of the revolution. Michael Ledeen and William Lewis, *Debacle: American Failure in Iran* (New York:

Alfred A. Knopf, 1981), for example, claim that "in the end, the Shah's greatest support came from his wife Farah Diba, his sister, and his ambassador to Washington, Ardeshir Zahedi" (p. 24). I claim here that "in the end" he derived no support whatsoever from the princess. Ledeen and Lewis, however, correctly understand Princess Ashraf's earlier role:

Of these three, the Shah was perhaps closest to his sister, Princess Ashraf. She was subtle of thought, unflinching where challenges confronted them, quick-witted and tough minded, a confidant with spirit, wisdom and confidence well beyond her years. Without Ashraf, the shah probably would not have survived the eternal crises of his first twenty years on the throne. (P. 24)

42. Ibid. Again, Ledeen and Lewis have it partially correct. Alam was such a source of strength for the Shah. They also report, however, that he was, similarly, a source of "integrity." In the sense that Alam was wholly and single-mindedly devoted to the perpetuation of Pahlavi rule, he had integrity. But if they were referring to his morality or financial rectitude, he was sadly lacking in those qualities. Alam was widely reputed to be one of the most financially corrupt of the senior Pahlavi officials, on a par with Princess Ashraf.

43. Sir Clarmont Skrine, *World War in Iran* (London: Constable, 1962), p. 100. Skrine dedicated his book to the memory of the Showkat-ul Molk and adds about him:

One need not altogether despair about Persia so long as there are one or two men in it like the Showkat-ul-Mulk. . . . You can get a glimpse of his love of his country . . . if you get him talking of past times. He is also a specimen of that *rara avis,* a devout and deeply religious Shi'a gentleman who is not in the least bigoted. As for his public spirit, he is one of the Persians I know who, being in charge of big religious trust (*vaqf*) properties, devotes the income from them (along with much of his own) to such objects as education (his school at Birjand contains 300 boys between 6 and 18, and 80 girls), public works (he has installed a piped drinking-water supply for Birjand town from hills 6 miles away), agricultural improvement (he has distributed free to his tenants large numbers of valuable grafts of fruit-trees and of the pistachio nut, at great expense to himself), and so on. He is hospitable in a big way, especially to the poor. With all this, he is full of humor and fun and excellent company, quite free from any kind of swank either about his ancient lineage or about his doings. (P. 100)

44. F. A. C. Forbes-Leith, *Checkmate: Fighting Tradition in Central Persia* (London: George G. Harrap and Co., n.d.), pp. 51–52.

45. Donald Stuart, *The Struggle for Persia* (London: Methuen, 1902), pp. 183–84.

46. For an impressive scholarly study on the history of Sheikh Khaz'al and his "emirate," see Mostafa Ansari, "The History of Khuzistan, 1878–1925: A Study in Provincial Autonomy," Ph.D. dissertation, Department of History, University of Chicago, 1974.

47. Some sense of the staggering expansion of Tehran is offered by the fate of the general's hideout. The general hid from Mossadegh in an empty and desolate ravine, far from the political life of Tehran. In later years, his son built a magnificent home on the very spot, complete with gardens and swimming pool. By then, it was a developed, contiguous suburb of the capital.

48. Personal interview, December 28, 1981.

49. Personal interview, December 24, 1982. This interview, with one of the participants, is the source of information for this account and for the quotes from Alam and the Shah.

50. For a fuller description of the 1963 riots, see Marvin Zonis, *The Political Elite of Iran* (Princeton: Princeton University Press, 1971), pp. 62–66. This account of how the 1963 riots were squelched is supported by a little-noted quotation in a book which reported the relationship between an American and the Shah, whom he had befriended. The author reported, "The Prime Minister who held office in 1963 privately admitted his ambivalence in finally ordering the army into action against the religiously motivated rioters." E. A. Bayne, *Persian Kingship in Transition: Conversations with a Monarch Whose Office Is Traditional and Whose Goal Is Modernization* (New York: American Universities Field Staff, 1968), p. 54.

51. Personal interview with one of these observers, March 23, 1982.

52. Personal interview, November 26, 1978.

53. Thus both the Shah and his third and last wife were twenty-one years old when they took their thrones. The Shah was born on October 21, 1919, and became king following the exile of his father, in September of 1941. Farah was born on October 14, 1938, and became empress, by dint of marriage, shortly after her twenty-first birthday.

54. Farah Shahbanou Pahlavi, *My Thousand and One Days: An Autobiography,* trans. Felice Harcourt (London: W. H. Allen, 1978), p. 65.

55. Ibid., p. 70.

56. Ibid., pp. 70–71.

57. Personal interview, November 26, 1978.

58. de Villiers, *Imperial Shah,* pp. 274–75.

59. For a fuller account of the struggle for an independent Kurdistan, see Gerard Chaliand, ed., *People without a Country: The Kurds and Kurdistan* (London: Zed Press, 1980).

60. For a fuller account of the Iran-Iraq border dispute, see Shirin Tahir-Kheli and Shaheen Ayubi, eds., *The Iran-Iraq War: New Weapons, Old Conflicts* (New York: Praeger, 1983), and M. S. El Azhary, ed., *The Iran-Iraq War* (New York: St. Martin's Press, 1984).

61. Personal interview, June 6, 1983.

62. Personal interview, December 27, 1981.

63. Ashraf Pahlavi, *Faces in a Mirror,* p. 195. Also see Mohammad Pahlavi, *Answer to History,* p. 64.

64. Personal interview, November 19, 1979.

65. Pahlavi, *Answer to History,* p. 165. Another study of the revolution explained the Shah's lack of trust in Zahedi differently: "the shah did not greatly admire Zahedi nor completely trust his advice. Mohammad Reza had removed Zahedi's father from the premiership, and feared that Ardeshir might try to vindicate his father by striking at the shah. Thus the shah discounted much of what Zahedi told him" (Ledeen and Lewis, *Debacle,* p. 175).

It is difficult to evaluate the Shah's judgment in discounting Zahedi. Certainly if the Shah would not trust his wife, it is not surprising he would not trust Zahedi. But it is doubtful that this explanation for the Shah's distrust is adequate. The

Shah's fear of Ardeshir Zahedi seeking retribution for the Shah's earlier ouster of his father seems far-fetched, especially after the closeness which had existed between the Shah and Ardeshir. In many ways, the Shah treated him as a son, even after he was no longer the monarch's son-in-law.

66. William Sullivan, *Mission to Iran* (New York: W. W. Norton, 1981), p. 27.

67. Stempel, *Inside the Iranian Revolution,* p. 156.

68. Sullivan, *Mission to Iran,* p. 158.

69. Pahlavi, *Answer to History,* p. 165.

70. Mohammad Reza Shah Pahlavi, *Mission for My Country* (New York: McGraw-Hill, 1961), pp. 321–22.

71. Heikal reports this account which he heard from Princess Ashraf's husband. *Return of the Ayatollah,* p. 59.

72. The Shah, in his last writings, recounts this tragic fate in an offhand manner.

On one occasion I flew to Panama City for a secret meeting with the American Ambassador who said he had a message from President Carter. My advisor, Robert Armao, planned to come with me to the capital, but Panamanian officials refused to let him attend. The U.S. was probably as eager as Panama not to let me be seen with my advisors—because they were American. (Pahlavi, *Answer to History,* pp. 29–30)

Chapter 6. Cancer

1. Oriana Fallaci, "The Mystically Divine Shah of Iran" (interview), *Chicago Tribune,* December 30, 1973, sec. 2, p. 1.

2. Mohammad Reza Shah Pahlavi, *Enghelab-e sefid* (The White Revolution), (Tehran: Kayhan Press, 1966), p. 16.

3. Queen Soraya Pahlavi, *Khaterat-e Soraya,* trans. Musa Majidi (Tehran: Saadat Printing House, n.d.), p. 66.

4. Personal interview, November 26, 1978.

5. Rustom Khurshedji Karanjia, *The Mind of a Monarch* (London: Allen and Unwin, 1977), p. 56.

6. Ibid., p. 98.

7. Fallaci, "Mystically Divine Shah," p. 1.

8. For example, the Shah told C. L. Sulzberger that his rule was eased by "mystical" and "inspirational" intuitions that generally prevented him from "making mistakes." *New York Times,* March 22, 1975.

9. Mohammad Reza Shah Pahlavi, *Mission for My Country* (New York: McGraw-Hill, 1961), p. 55.

10. Gerard de Villiers, *The Imperial Shah: An Informal Biography,* trans. June P. Wilson and Walter B. Michaels, (Boston: Little, Brown, 1976), pp. 245ff.

11. An important source of information on the Shah's medical history is Dennis L. Breo, "Shah's Physician Relates Story of Intrigue, Duplicity" *American Medical News,* August 7, 1981, pp. 3–22. Another account can be found in William Shawcross, *The Shah's Last Ride: The Fate of an Ally* (New York: Simon and Schuster, 1988).

12. E. A. Bayne, *Persian Kingship in Transition: Conversations with a Mon-*

arch Whose Office Is Traditional and Whose Goal Is Modernization (New York: American Universities Field Staff, 1968), p. 157.

13. Soraya Pahlavi, *Khaterat-e Soraya*, p. 79.

14. Karanjia, *Mind of a Monarch*, p. 192.

15. Personal interview, October 31, 1981. While "problems with the liver" is one of a number of explanations for disease in Iran, it is not as widespread an explanation as "problems of the heart." See Byron Good, "The Heart of What's the Matter: The Structure of Medical Discourse in a Provincial Iranian Town," Ph.D. dissertation, Department of Anthropology, University of Chicago, 1977.

16. Shawcross, *Shah's Last Ride*, p. 230.

17. From an interview with Dr. Benjamin H. Kean, the attending physician in New York. See Breo, "Shah's Physician."

18. Personal interview, March 23, 1982. Pierre Salinger, *America Held Hostage: The Secret Negotiations* (Garden City, N.Y.: Doubleday, 1981), p. 15, notes that the Shah's chemotherapy was controlled "with one pill a day." This is contradicted by the reports of numerous court insiders as well as by Empress Farah, who reported that "the Shah had been following chemotherapy treatment in Tehran, taking a great number of pills each day." *People Magazine,* vol. 13, no. 4, January 28, 1980, p. 18.

19. Personal interview, January 5, 1982.

20. *Time,* April 1, 1974, p. 41.

21. Ibid.

22. *Kayhan International,* March 3, 1975, p. 2.

23. Actually, the Shah had considered the formation of a single-party system before he learned of his cancer. As early as 1972, a full year before he learned of his illness and three years before the Rastakhiz was announced, he had begun to discuss the idea with a few of his key political officials. At the time, it was clear to them that the Shah saw the party not as an instrument to enhance democracy in Iran but as a means to ensure the institutionalization of the Pahlavi system. But other than a few discussions, the idea languished. The Shah returned to the idea of a single party in 1974, a year after he had learned of his cancer, and renewed his discussions in earnest. Personal interview, March 23, 1982.

24. *Kayhan International,* September 15, 1975, p. 1.

25. Ibid.

26. *Kayhan International,* March 23, 1976, p. 4.

27. Interview with the Egyptian journalist Mohamed Heikal, reprinted from *Al-Nahar* (Beirut), in *Kayhan International,* September 16, 1975, p. 3.

28. See the interview of Empress Farah in *Paris Match,* January 11, 1980, translated in *Joint Publication Research Service,* L/9807, February 6, 1980, NE/WAC, FOUB-80; and *People Magazine,* January 28, 1980, p. 18.

29. Shawcross, *Shah's Last Ride,* p. 237.

30. Barry Rubin, *Paved with Good Intentions: The American Experience and Iran* (New York: Oxford University Press, 1980), p. 204.

31. Dr. Benjamin Kean suggests that the Shah did not begin to take pred-

nisone until he had reached the Bahamas in exile. In April 1979, he reports that the Shah's French physicians began administering MOPP, "a combination of nitrogen mustard, oncovin, procarbazine, and prednisone" (Breo, "Shah's Physician Relates Story," p. 16). Assuming that Kean presents the fullest medical account of the Shah's drug regimens, it seems reasonable to conclude that, in fact, the Shah was not taking prednisone during the revolution.

32. Personal interview, March 13, 1981.

33. Foreign Broadcast Information Service, MEA-94-78, May 12, 1978, p. R1.

34. Personal interview, March 23, 1982.

35. Personal interview, March 13, 1981 (Mayidi).

36. Actually the Shah, until a few years before the revolution, had been a heavy smoker but had broken the habit at the advice of his doctors. Cynthia Helms, the wife of United States' penultimate ambassador to Iran, recounts a story of the Shah's smoking:

After our arrival in 1973, Dick met with the Shah often. At their first audience, Dick noticed that when he offered the Shah a cigarette, His Majesty carefully took one of his own. . . . The King's fear of poison was almost second nature. The Shah later gave up smoking and on several occasions told Dick how much better he felt as a result.

Cynthia Helms, *An Ambassador's Wife in Iran* (New York: Dodd, Mead, 1981), pp. 90–91.

37. John D. Stempel, *Inside the Iranian Revolution* (Bloomington: Indiana University Press, 1981), p. 115.

38. Personal interview, March 22, 1982. For the time being, there is no way to resolve this quandry.

39. Stempel, *Inside the Iranian Revolution,* p. 112.

40. Salinger, *America Held Hostage,* p. 31. While Salinger never identifies the country, it seems reasonable to conclude it was France. He was stationed in Paris as ABC bureau chief. France, unlike England, for example, has a president, and it was French doctors who were in on the secret.

41. Personal interview, April 12, 1983.

42. Salinger, *America held Hostage,* p. 30.

43. Shawcross, *Shah's Last Ride,* p. 239.

44. Robert D. McFadden, Joseph B. Treaster, and Maurice Carroll, *No Hiding Place* (New York: New York Times Book Co., 1981), p. 166.

45. It is perhaps further confirmation of the Shah's passive and dependent state during the revolution that it was sufficient for Rockefeller to have made a suggestion. The Shah seized on the suggestion, much as he did with Ambassador Sullivan's remarks on the Shah's economic plans and much as, it seems likely, he seized on the suggestions of other American men of affairs.

46. Shawcross, *Shah's Last Ride,* p. 243.

47. Quoted in Breo, "Shah's Physician Relates Story," p. 19. Kean also reported that the Shah apologized for having failed to inform him previously of his cancer. "You must understand," Kean remembers the Shah saying, "that for reasons of state I could not before tell you the nature of my illness" (p. 19). Two implications are suggested. One is that the Shah still harbored a hope that, as in 1953, the tables

would somehow be turned on his enemies and he would be able to return triumphantly to Tehran. A second implication is that the "reasons of state" were
actually personal, that is, the Shah could not admit his cancer to those then most in
need of that knowledge, his adviser Robert Armao and his new physician, Dr. Benjamin Kean, because to do so would require that he himself acknowledge the
seriousness of his medical condition. The Shah continued to deny the seriousness
of his medical problems as he had attempted, for so long, to deny the seriousness of
his political condition. These implications, of course, are not contradictory but,
rather, complementary.

48. Several studies of the embassy takeover and its consequences have now
been published. The most comprehensive, from the U.S. point of view, is Gary
Sick, *All Fall Down: America's Tragic Encounter with Iran* (New York: Random
House, 1985).

49. Breo, "Shah's Physician Relates Story," p. 21.

50. Shawcross says of De Bakey, "According to popular stereotypes, surgeons
are supposed to think of themselves as God. This is a cliche that the story of Michael
De Bakey does nothing to diminish. He is a god with especially divine hands. Dr.
De Bakey is . . . a genius with a vast and sometimes uncomfortable ego.

On De Bakey's wall there is also a copy of a mural tracing the history of medicine. It begins with Esculapio and ends with De Bakey" (Shawcross, *Shah's Last
Ride,* p. 361).

51. Mohammad Reza Shah Pahlavi, *Answer to History* (New York: Stein and
Day, 1980), p. 29.

52. Ibid., p. 30.

53. Breo, "Shah's Physician Relates Story," p. 22.

54. Ibid. He added, "As it is, the United States did more than other countries.
Britain, France, Switzerland are all former allies of the Shah and all have a history
of granting political asylum. They turned their backs on the Shah and that has not
been widely reported" (p. 22).

Chapter 7. Xenophobia

1. Henry Kissinger, *White House Years* (Boston: Little, Brown, 1979), p.
1261.

2. Pierre Salinger, *America Held Hostage: The Secret Negotiations* (Garden
City, N.Y.: Doubleday, 1981), p. 59.

3. Firuz Kazemzadeh, personal communication, February 20, 1969. Kazemzadeh went on to add, "The foreigners do not, however, create the internal
political forces."

4. Richard N. Frye, *The Heritage of Persia* (London: Weidenfeld and Nicolson, 1962), p. 239.

5. E. G. Browne, *A Literary History of Persia* (Cambridge: Cambridge University Press, 1953), 4: 130. Browne adds, "Soon afterwards, the Turks took
Erivan, Nakhjivan, Khuy, and Hamadan [from Iran], but were repulsed from
Tabriz. On July 8, 1724, an agreement for the partition of Persia was signed
between Russia and Turkey at Constantinople."

6. (For his part, His Majesty the Emperor of Persia undertakes to break off all political and commercial intercourse with England and to declare war immediately on that power.) Ali Akbar Siassi, *La Perse au contact de l'occident* (Paris: Ernest Leroux, 1931), p. 637.

7. Sir Percy Molesworth Sykes, *A History of Persia* (London: Macmillan, 1921), 2: 309.

8. Ibid.

9. S. F. Shadman, "A Review of Anglo-Persian Relations, 1798–1815," in *Proceedings of the Iran Society* (London: Iran Society, 1944), vol. 2, pt. 5. Lecture delivered before the Iran Society, September 23, 1943.

10. Sykes, *History of Persia*, 2: 314.

11. Siassi, *La Perse*, p. 639.

12. Sykes, *History of Persia*, 2: 327. Lord Curzon tells the story more succinctly and also manages to drop the Russians out of the account completely: "it was only owing to the inexhaustible energy and influence of Sir John Campbell, then British Minister and to the assistance of British officers in command of the Persian troops," that the rightful heir was able to "establish his legitimate claim." Lord George N. Curzon, *Persia and the Persian Question* (London: Longmans, Green, 1892), 1: 406.

13. Curzon, *Persia*, 1: 435. The telegraph to which Lord Curzon refers was introduced following concessions won by the British government in 1864, 1872, and 1882. Telegraph service within Iran and between Iran and Europe was an incidental benefit to Iran—many Iranians saw it not as a benefit at all, of course—of Great Britain's desire to ensure easy communication with the jewel of its empire, India. The British received permission from the Shah to install telegraph lines across Iran as part of the link with India. The result was that Iran was propelled into virtually instant communication with Europe and no longer was isolated from information of world events.

14. United Kingdom, Foreign Office, "Memorandum furnished by H.M.'s Legation at Tehran, Jan. 1907—Summary of Events for 1906," in *Correspondence Respecting the Affairs of Persia*, Persian no. 1, 1909, vol. 5, no. 3, p. 3.

15. This was certainly the view of the extreme "forward party" in Russia, whose organ, the Saint Petersburg *Birzheviya Viedomosti*, mournfully proclaimed that "it was obvious that Persia would succeed in obtaining reforms and even a constitution, thanks to the benevolent cooperation of the English, and that this would be another heavy blow to Russian prestige in Asia." E. G. Browne, *The Persian Revolution of 1905–1909* (London: Cambridge University Press, 1910), p. 123.

16. W. Morgan Shuster, *The Strangling of Persia: A Record of European Diplomacy and Oriental Intrigue* (London: T. Fisher Unwin, 1912), p. 25. This work has the complete text of the agreement as well as a map delineating the "spheres of influence."

17. Ibid.

18. Ibid., pp. 28–29.

19. To understand the British commitment to maintain neutral buffer states

between the British and Russian empires, it is necessary to understand the passionate commitment of British statesmen to India. As Novar has put it,

> To Curzon, India was the heart of the Empire, the brightest jewel of the imperial dominion. His faith in the British Empire in India was as much mystical as political. He dedicated his book, *Problems of the Far East,* "to those who believe that the British Empire is, under providence, the greatest instrument for good that the world has ever seen." And he regarded India as "the noblest achievement of the science of civil rule that mankind has yet bequeathed to man" . . . "the inalienable badge of sovereignty in the Eastern hemisphere" without which 'the British Empire could not exist."

Leon Novar, "The Great Powers and Iran, 1914–1921," Ph.D. dissertation, Committee on International Relations, University of Chicago, 1958, pp. 171–72. The first quote is from Sir Harold C. Nicolson, *Curzon: The Last Phase, 1919–1925* (Boston: Houghton Mifflin, 1934), p. 14; the second quote is from Curzon, *Persia,* 1:3.

20. Count Witte, *The Memoirs of Count Witte,* trans. Abraham Yarmolinsky (Garden City, N.Y.: Doubleday, Page, 1921), p. 433.

21. Ibid., pp. 433–34.

22. Additional confirmation of this notion can be found in official British documents.

> Minister for Foreign Affairs told me today that the following is the policy of the Russian Government. Abstention from all interference in the internal affairs of Persia; not to have recourse to military measures unless they are rendered absolutely necessary, and to keep them within the narrowest possible limits should such contingency become unavoidable; to act generally in close harmony with H.M.'s Government, and to do nothing without previous consultation with them. He expressed a hope that H.M.'s Government would reciprocally observe such an attitude, and I gave him assurances that he entertain no doubts that would be our line of conduct.

United Kingdom, Foreign Office, "Sir A. Nicolson to Sir E. Grey, St. Petersburgh, February 12, 1907—Telegraphic," in *Correspondence Respecting the Affairs of Persia,* Persian no. 1, 1909, vol. 105, no. 12, pp. 8–9.

23. The role of the British in the bombing of the Majles, the execution of the constitutionalists, and the deposition of the Shah is unclear. At the beginning of that fateful year, the British communicated to the Russians that they intended to "stand aloof" from the turmoil in Iran.

> H.M.'s Government, however, cannot but recognize that it would be more difficult for Russia to maintain this attitude as she has a frontier and settled districts which are coterminous with the most disturbed parts of Persia.
> If, therefore, the Russian Government adhere to the view that it is impossible for Russia to adopt the course which H.M.'s Government consider would be advisable, they are prepared to cooperate with the Russian Government in regard to future action.

United Kingdom, Foreign Office, "Sir E. Grey to Sir A. Nicholson, Foreign Office, February 3, 1909. Inclosure: Memorandum to be communicated by Nicholson to M. Isvolsky," in *Further Correspondence Respecting the Affairs of Persia,* Persian No. 2, 1909, vol. 5, no. 70, p. 43.

24. For Shuster's own account of his experiences, see Shuster, *Strangling of Persia.*

25. Novar, *Great Powers and Iran,* p. 59.

26. George Lenczowski, *The Middle East in World Affairs* (Ithaca, N.Y.: Cornell University Press, 1952), pp. 68–69.

27. See Christopher Sykes, *Wassmuss: The German Lawrence* (London: Longmans, Green, 1936).

28. F. A. C. Forbes-Leith, *Checkmate: Fighting Tradition in Central Persia* (London: George G. Harrap and Co., n.d.), pp. 75–76.

29. Novar, *Great Powers and Iran,* pp. 150–51, quoting from Archives, File 891.00/902, February 26, 1917.

30. Novar, *Great Powers and Iran,* p. 260.

31. Ibid., p. 151, quoting from Cox (Tehran) to Curzon (Foreign Office), August 7, 1919. United Kingdom, Foreign Office, *Documents on British Foreign Policy, 1919–1939,* eds. E. L. Woodward and Rohan Butler (London: Her Majesty's Stationery Office, 1952), 1st ser. vol. 4 (1919), n. 1, pp. 1125–26.

32. *Documents on British Foreign Policy, 1919–39,* 1st ser., vol. 4, chap. 5, p. 1120, as quoted in Sir Clarmont Skrine, *World War in Iran* (London: Constable, 1962), p. 59.

33. Vincent Sheean, *The New Persia* (New York: Century, 1927), p. 23.

34. *Documents on British Foreign Policy, 1919–39,* 1st ser., vol. 4, no. 792, E. C. to Sir Percy Cox (T), no. 503 Telegraphic [133564/150/34], Foreign Office, 9/24/19, p. 1183.

35. Skrine, *War in Iran,* p. 60.

36. Quoted in *Documents on British Foreign Policy, 1919–39,* vol. 4, no. 770, p. 1162, Sir Percy Cox (T) to E. C. (Rec. 9/11/19), no. 619 Telegraphic [127878/150/34], pp. 1161–62.
The Iranian government was extraordinarily concerned about the effects of foreign criticism on the chances for the adoption of the 1919 Agreement. "The Persian Minister for Foreign Affairs . . . asked the attention of His Majesty's Government might be called to the danger of unfortunate effect being produced in Persia if unfavorable criticism of Agreement found unbridled expression in the French and even American press and if such criticism were reproduced in Persia." Vol. 4, no. 743, p. 1147, Admiral Webb (Constantinople) to E. C. (rec. 88/30/19), no. 1746, Telegraphic [122862/150/34] Constantinople 8/29/19.
This sensitivity to the contents of the foreign press because of its consequences for internal Iranian politics is a long-standing Persian reality. Reza Shah broke relations with the United States over an incident of criticism against him in a U.S. newspaper. More recently, Ayatollah Khomeini's regime attacked the governments of both Italy and Germany for allowing parodies of the Ayatollah to be broadcast on state television.

37. Quoted in Skrine, *War in Iran,* p. 62.

38. See Lenczowski, *Middle East in World Affairs,* pp. 60–64.

39. *Documents on British Foreign Policy, 1919–39,* E. W. Birse, "Memorandum on Central Asia," no. 364 [171634/38], Foreign Office, 1/6/20, vol. 13, chap. 3, Persia, pp. 429–32.

40. *Documents on British Foreign Policy, 1919–39,* no. 485, Mr. Norman

(Tehran) to Earl Curzon (rec. 6/27/20), no. 417 Telegraphic [206097/150/34], Tehran, pp. 538–39.

41. Telegram 1393/S from Earl Curzon to Secretary of State for India, quoted as n. 3, pp. 675–76, to no. 623, vol. 13, Mr. Norman (Tehran) to Earl Curzon (rec. 1/3/21), no. 842 Telegraphic [E118/113/34], Tehran 12/31/20, pp. 675–77.

42. See no. 667, Mr. Norman (Tehran) to Earl Curzon (rec. 1/31/21), no. 66 Telegraphic [E/382/2/34] Tehran 1/28/21, vol. 13, pp. 710–11.

43. No. 670, Mr. Norman (Tehran) to Earl Curzon (rec. 2/6/21), no. 79 Telegraphic [E/1661/2/34], Tehran 2/3/21, vol. 13, pp. 715–16.

44. Ibid.

45. United Kingdom, Foreign Office, "Mr. Marling to Sir E. Grey, Tehran, January 2, 1908," in *Correspondence Respecting the Affairs of Persia,* Persian No. 1, 1909, vol. 105, no. 93, p. 96.

46. Forbes-Leith, *Checkmate,* pp. 78–79. Sir Harold Nicolson, long an intimate of some of the principals, put it somewhat differently: "the only hope was that Persia could be renovated under strong leadership from within; Sir Percy [Cox, the British ambassador in Tehran] rightly foresaw that Reza Khan was capable of such regeneration. And thus it came about that the Kajar dynasty was deposed by the Majles." Sir Harold Nicolson, *Friday Mornings, 1941–1944* (Boston: Houghton Mifflin, 1944), p. 7.

47. No. 683, Mr. Norman (Tehran) to Earl Curzon (rec. 2/25/21), no. 125 Telegraphic [E/2605/2/34] Tehran 2/25/21, vol. 13, pp. 731–32.

48. Donald N. Wilber, *Reza Shah Pahlavi: The Resurrection and Reconstruction of Iran* (New York: Exposition Press, 1975), p. 62.

49. Ibid., pp. 62–64.

50. The quote and the account of the turmoil is taken from Iran, *Proceedings of the Trial of Dr. Mohammad Mossadeq,* no. 257 (Tehran: Echo of Iran Publications), November 29, 1953, p. 4.

51. Donald Wilber, a longtime and acute observer of Iranian politics, notes, "Iran was to be saved by Persians who enjoyed British support, but who acted when and as they saw fit, not in response to British orders or direction" (*Reza Shah Pahlavi,* p. 39).

52. Maj. E. W. Pilson Newman, *The Middle East* (London: Geoffrey Bles, 1926), pp. 257–58.

53. The Persian and English texts of the treaty are reproduced in Hunter Miller, ed., *Treaties and Other International Acts of the United States of America,* vol. 7, documents 173–200: 1855–58 (Washington, D.C.: U.S. Government Printing Office, 1942), pp. 429–89. Those unfamiliar with the rhetorical extravagance with which Iranians use their language will benefit from the first paragraph of the treaty:

In the name of God, the Compassionate, the Merciful, by the Assistance of the Lord Almighty

We, the Great Independent King, the Deserving Noble Sovereign, the Adorner of the Seat of the Caliphate, the Embellisher of the Throne of Royalty and State, the Preserver of Justice and Equity, the Repressor of Signs of Injustice and Oppression, the

Bearer of the Crown and Throne of the Fortunate Darius, the Glorifier of the Crown of Iran, the Refuge of Islam and of the Muslims, the Administrator of Justice, the Royal Provender of the People, the Glory of the Kings of Kayan, and the Possessor by Inheritance of the vast Empire of Iran, inform whomever these lines may concern that on the fifteenth day of the month of Rabi' al-Thani of this year of 1273 (A.H.), in Istanbul, a Treaty of Friendship and Commerce has been concluded.

54. The full text of the treaty can be found in Arthur C. Millspaugh, *Americans in Persia* (Washington, D.C.: Brookings Institution, 1946), Appendix C, p. 276.

55. Donald N. Wilber, *Iran, Past and Present* (Princeton: Princeton University Press, 1958), p. 103.

56. Memorandum by John D. Jernegan of the Division of Near Eastern Affairs, "American Policy in Iran," Washington, D.C., January 23, 1943, in Yonah Alexander and Allan Nanes, eds., *The United States and Iran: A Documentary History* (Frederick, Md.: University Publications of America, 1980), p. 97.

57. William H. Forbis, *The Fall of the Peacock Throne: The Story of Iran* (New York: McGraw-Hill, 1981), p. 62. In August 1947, President Truman had told Princess Ashraf, "I am pretty darned tired of baby sitting those Russians. . . . We warned them when they were in Azerbaijan and now we've had to warn them again to keep their hands off Greece." Ashraf Pahlavi, *Faces in a Mirror: Memoirs from Exile* (Englewood Cliffs, N.J.: Prentice-Hall, 1980), p. 96.

58. It is an apt comment on Princess Ashraf that she had made a state visit to the United States before her brother, in the late summer of 1947. Official Washington turned out to assure her and Iran of their significance for the United States. In the journalese of *Time* magazine:

In Washington last week a slender, dark girl [she was nearly twenty-eight] saw with her own eyes that Persia had powerful friends in the U.S. Several hundred people thronged the elegant red brick Persian Embassy to shake hands with Her Imperial Highness Princess Ashraf Pahlevi [*sic*], twin sister of Persia's ruling Shah. President Truman received her in the White House, and Bess Truman was there too. This week the State Department scheduled a big, brilliant reception. (Ashraf Pahlavi, *Faces in a Mirror*, p. 97)

59. Dean Acheson, *Present at the Creation: My Years in the State Department* (New York: Norton, 1969), p. 502.

60. Qassem Ghani, *As yaddashthay-e Qassem-e Ghani* (London: Routledge and Kegan Paul, 1982), 9: 92.

61. Dwight D. Eisenhower, *Mandate for Change, 1953–1956: The White House Years* (Garden City, N.Y.: Doubleday, 1963), p. 163.

62. James Bill stresses the extent to which these twin targets—anticommunism and oil—dominated U.S. postwar policy toward Iran. See James A. Bill, *The Eagle and the Lion: The Tragedy of American-Iranian Relations* (New Haven: Yale University Press, 1988). Given the death of Stalin in March 1953 and the subsequent struggle for power, it is difficult to imagine the Soviet Union being in a position to take advantage of turmoil in Tehran.

63. "Exchange Between President Eisenhower and Prime Minister Zahedi Concerning the Need for Increased Aid to Iran, August 26, 1953," signed by Eisenhower, in Alexander and Nanes, *United States and Iran*, p. 252.

64. U.S. Senate, *United States and Operations in Iran,* 87th Cong., 1st sess., August 11, 1961, p. 15,607; Sen. Everett Dirksen commenting on the recommendations of the Hardy Committee on American aid to Peru, Iran, and Laos. More specifically, the United States presented Iran with $116.2 million in economic loans, $250.6 million in economic grants, and $133.9 million in military grants during the four-year period.

65. See, for example, *U.S. News and World Report,* March 6, 1961.

66. See *The Economist,* May 20, 1961, p. 786.

67. Andrew Tully, *CIA: The Inside Story* (New York: William Morrow, 1962), p. 88. This allegation is outrageous for many reasons. The account is too much from a Hollywood script to be plausible. The evidence is nonexistent. But even if one accepts the literal accuracy of the conversation, it is still unclear what it means. "One of our boys" could mean anything from a friend of the United States, which Amini clearly was when he believed it was in the interests of Iran (and himself) to be such a friend, to an employee of the CIA.

68. Some years before, Amini had a decidedly hostile attitude toward the United States:

One of the leaders of the opposition, Dr. Amini, said in the Majles, "The assignment of powers to advisers coming from a promiscuous race, to advisers who are descended from refugees who went to America from Europe, is against the interest of the state and the society." At this point, three friends of [the U.S. Aid] Mission interjected: "No! No! Do not insult the Americans and America!" "This is my private opinion," continued Dr. Amini, "and we are all free to express what we believe. Anyway, the customs and habits of this nation do not tally with ours. Their behavior is rough and rude." (Millspaugh, p. 135n, quoting Majles, *Proceedings,* July 17, 1944)

69. Mohamed Heikal, *The Return of the Ayatollah: The Iranian Revolution from Mossadeq to Khomeini* (London: André Deutsch, 1981), p. 72.

70. As recounted on June 26, 1961, by David Lilienthal, *The Journals of David E. Lilienthal: The Harvest Years, 1959–1963* (New York: Harper and Row, 1971), p. 234.

71. As reprinted in *Iran Almanac and Book of Facts, 1963* (Tehran: Echo of Iran, 1984), pp. 172–73.

72. Ibid., p. 173.

73. Interview with the Shah of Iran, *U.S. News and World Report,* January 27, 1969, p. 49. In a 1977 interview, the Shah confirmed that the appointment of Amini was due to U.S. pressure. Arnaud de Borchgrave asked the Shah, "Your government released a news report two weeks ago alleging that President Kennedy in 1961 used $35 million in U.S. aid to pressure you into appointing Dr. Ali Amini as Prime Minister. Is this report correct?" The Shah responded, "It's past history, but correct." *Newsweek,* November 14, 1977, p. 71.

74. Kenneth Bowling, State Department Report, February 11, 1961, quoted in Alexander and Nanes, *United States and Iran,* p. 320.

75. Ibid., p. 321. Many others reached the same opinion about dealing with the Shah. David Lilienthal, on the basis of his audiences in 1961, concluded that the Shah "must be quite reassured about present American intentions toward his country" (*Journals: Harvest Years,* p. 266).

76. Address of Shah of Iran to Joint Session of Congress, *Congressional Record,* 87th Cong., 2d sess., April 12, 1962, p. 6435.

77. Lilienthal, *Journals: Harvest Years,* pp. 265–66.

78. That popularity was intense. In a 1965 opinion survey of a national sample of Iranian secondary school students, I asked them in an open-ended question to list the political leaders they admired the most. Kennedy was listed first by more than 50 percent of the students. The Shah also ran, but far down the pack of leaders, listed by some 10 percent of the students.

79. Bill, *Eagle and the Lion,* p. 137. Bill goes on to add that "Kennedy was equally unimpressed by the shah, who he considered a corrupt and petty tyrant. It now appears that Kennedy's doubts about the shah were so strong that he even considered forcing his abdication in favor of rule by regency until his young son came of age" (p. 477, n. 17).

80. "Interview with H.I.M., the Shah of Iran," *Gente,* vol. 15, no. 39, February 1967.

81. Kissinger, *Years of Upheaval,* p. 670.

82. Ibid., p. 668.

83. Ibid., p. 670.

84. U.S. Congress, Senate, Committee on Foreign Relations, Subcommittee on Foreign Assistance, *U.S. Military Sales to Iran,* 94th Cong., 2d sess., July 1976, p. 5.

85. "Reverse leverage" is a term used by Michael Ledeen and William Lewis, *Debacle: American Failure in Iran* (New York: Alfred A. Knopf, 1981), p. 52. They cite a report by David Ronfeldt of the Rand Corporation who suggests that the Shah "could now exploit the 'geopolitical interests of the patron superpower'" (p. 52).

86. Kissinger, *White House Years,* p. 1264. Again, the point is not that Kissinger was wrong in his estimate of the usefulness of the role the Shah played. It would be difficult to imagine, for example, the Soviet invasion of Afghanistan in December of 1979 had the Shah still been on the throne. The point, rather, is the failure of U.S. decision makers to properly evaluate the effects of the new foreign policy and military capabilities on the psyche of the Shah as well as on internal Iranian economic, social, and political processes.

87. Undated (circa 1963) National Security Council report, in Alexander and Nanes, *United States and Iran,* p. 357.

88. Fereidoun Esfandiary, *The Day of Sacrifice* (London: Heinemann, 1960).

89. For more on men living in family structures dominated by authoritarian fathers, see Vincent Crapanzano, *The Hamadsha: A Study in Moroccan Ethnopsychiatry* (Berkeley: University of California Press, 1973), esp. pp. 7–9.

90. Jalal Al-e Ahmad, *Plagued by the West (Gharbzadegi),* trans. Paul Sprachman (Delmar, N.Y.: Caravan Books, 1982), pp. 67, 38.

91. Ervand Abrahamian, *Iran between Two Revolutions* (Princeton: Princeton University Press, 1982), pp. 466–67, quoting from A. Shari'ati, *Shi'i: Yek hizb-i tamam* (Shi'is: A complete Party) (n.p., 1976), pp. 27, 55; idem, *Islam shenasi* (n.p., 1978), lesson 2, p. 101; idem., *'Ali tanha ast* ('Ali is alone) (n.p., 1978), pp. 1–35.

92. Reza Baraheni, *The Crowned Cannibals: Writings on Repression in Iran* (New York: Vintage Books, 1977), p. 83.

93. Telegram from Tehran Embassy, July 8, 1976, to Department of State, "Bolster Iran's Modernizing Monarchy," in Iran, *Asnad-i lanah-i jasus-i amrika* (Documents from the nest of spies) (Tehran: Danishjuyan-i musalman-i payrwi-i khatt-i imam, 1980), 7: 171. Stempel certainly anticipated Iranian politics accurately. For example, in his inaugural speech as prime minister, Jamshid Amouzegar admitted difficulties in Iran's economic development, but laid the blame squarely at the foot of foreigners:

Rapidly accelerating progress inevitably brings about problems and difficulties, among which one may mention inflations resulting from a rapid growth in demand, the inability to increase supply in a short time, the emergence of multifarious bottlenecks and, in certain cases, an imbalance between the rate of growth in various sectors and the resultant shortcoming and inadequacies in the fields of manpower, electricity, building materials, transport and communications, urban services, and so forth.

I have just mentioned electricity. A study of the current problems indeed demonstrates extremely bitter realities, bitter facts which show the carelessness and neglect of foreign contractors. Had these contractors honored and fulfilled their undertakings, the Iranian people today would not be beset with these problems. . . . What is strange is that the foreign press, instead of criticizing the export of technology of this type and this illogical and iniquitous behavior, joyfully and gleefully gloats over the difficulties which have beset us, thanks to it. It is as if the papers' envy of our progress has made them blind and deaf.

"Inaugural Speech by Prime Minister Amouzegar on Economy. Blames Foreigners. Admits Economic Difficulties," Foreign Broadcast Information Service, MEA-77-161, August 19, 1977, pp. R1,2.

Chapter 8. Dependence on the United States

1. William H. Sullivan, *Mission to Iran* (New York: W. W. Norton, 1981), p. 70.

2. Ibid., p. 71. The ambassador immediately adds, "Knowing what I now know about his mental processes, I am sure that deep inside he was asking himself with the usual Iranian morbid suspicion just why it was that the United States was seeking to frustrate his industrial independence." The central theme of this chapter is that the Shah did have a "morbid suspicion," particularly when it came to the United States. The question which must be asked here is why the United States ambassador had to learn of this through his own sensitive awareness of others, after long interactions with the Shah? Where was the accumulated wisdom of the thirty-six years of U.S. involvement with the Shah?

3. Ibid., p. 72. The ambassador makes it clear that the Shah's steps had immediate negative consequences.

Unfortunately, much of this was done in such an abrupt way that it caused repercussive shocks in the business community. The bazaar merchants who had come to depend on easy credit terms, were particularly hard hit. Therefore, in making his economic corrections to address some of the political problems growing out of his industrialization program, the Shah succeeded only in raising new frustrations and creating a new area of dissidence among the merchants of the bazaar. (P. 72)

Many of these same merchants, of course, were already furious at the regime for its industrialization policies which had fostered development by a new social stratum at the expense of the domination of the economy formerly enjoyed by the bazaar merchants. They were to be among the most significant backers of the clerics when sides were drawn up in the Revolution of 1978. See, for example, Howard Rotblat, "Stability and Change in a Provincial Iranian Bazaar," Ph.D. dissertation, Department of Sociology, University of Chicago, 1972.

4. Sullivan, *Mission to Iran*, p. 72. This episode in which the remarks of an American official have led to action by an Iranian has occurred many times before in Iranian history. For example, Morgan Shuster, the U.S. financial adviser to Iran ousted by British and Russian pressure, told the following story:

> The chief baker in Tehran was one of the principal grafters in the "municipal bread ring" and a great trouble maker for the Treasury. He was a man of evil record, and reputed to have baked an offending subordinate to death in his own oven on more than one occasion. Speaking of him and his intrigues one day to several prominent nationalists, I remarked that he was the cause of most of the trouble with the bread supply in the capital, was feeding inferior bread to the people, and that he should "be gotten rid of." A morning or so afterwards, on entering my office rather late, I was informed by one of my assistants that "the chief baker had been killed in accordance with my wishes." I leave the reader to imagine my surprise and feelings.

W. Morgan Shuster, *The Strangling of Persia: A Record of European Diplomacy and Oriental Intrigue* (New York: Century, 1912), pp. 169–70.

5. Richard Cottam, *Nationalism in Iran* (Pittsburgh: University of Pittsburgh Press, 1979), p. 212.

6. Personal interview, December 30, 1981.

7. Ibid.

8. Donald N. Wilber, *Riza Shah Pahlavi: The Resurrection and Reconstruction of Iran, 1878–1944* (Hicksville, N.Y.: Exposition Press, 1975), p. 136.

9. This was hardly the position of the Shah alone but probably represented the modal position of Iranians, at least for the twentieth century. One of the leaders of the Constitutional Revolution was an Islamic cleric, Modarress, later to be killed by Reza Shah. He was asked how many years Iran was behind Europe—how many years would it take for Iran to catch up? "The number of years is inconsequential," he answered. "First we must get on the same path as Europe, we must begin to develop. Once we do that, the number of years will not matter." Quoted by Ehsan Naraghi, personal interview, November 9, 1965.

10. Henry Kissinger, *Years of Upheaval* (Boston: Little, Brown, 1982), p. 524. It is an important comment on Kissinger's theoretical structure for political analysis that he would refer to factors in a political relationship as "deeper . . . than personal idiosyncrasy" (p. 524). Of course the issue is not "idiosyncrasy"; it is psychological factors which are not alternatives to political and economic considerations or ideology, but underlay the processes by which those factors are translated into meaningful information for the individual and then into the bases of decision and action.

In another place, Kissinger returned to the same issue but described it slightly differently: "America's friendship with Iran reflected not individual proclivities but geopolitical realities. Iran's intrinsic importance transcended the personalities of both country's leaders" (p. 667).

11. In addition to the visits of the U.S. presidents, three vice presidents made official visits to Tehran. As mentioned previously, on August 25, 1962, Lyndon

Johnson arrived in Tehran. On December 10, 1953, Vice President Richard Nixon stopped in Tehran for discussions on U.S. aid and other issues shortly after the restoration of the Shah to the throne. On October 15, 1971, Spiro Agnew arrived as official representative of the United States at the twenty-five hundredth anniversary celebrations for the establishment of the Iranian monarchy.

12. For the record, the Shah's visits to the United States began on the following dates: November 17, 1949; December 14, 1954; July 6, 1958; April 11, 1962; June 5, 1964; May 19, 1965; September 2, 1966; August 22, 1967; June 11, 1968; September 23, 1969; July 24, 1973; May 15, 1975; and November 16, 1977. In addition to these visits made while the Shah was ruling Iran, his last and ill-fated visit to the United States began on October 22, 1979, when the Shah entered New York Hospital in New York for cancer treatment. That visit was used as an excuse by the "students in the line of the Imam" to seize the U.S. embassy in Tehran along with nearly all its diplomats.

13. Originally published in France in 1979 under the title *Reponse l'histoire* (Paris: Editions-Albin Michel), and translated into English by Teresa Waugh and published in 1980 as *The Shah's Story* (London: Michael Joseph, Ltd., 1980). A slightly different work was published under the title *Answer to History* (New York: Stein and Day, 1980). The frontispiece contains an "Author's Note" which states, "It is my intention that the American version of *Answer to History* be the definitive text. M. R. Pahlavi."

14. Cf. Amin Saikal, *The Rise and Fall of the Shah* (Princeton: Princeton University Press, 1980), p. 21.

15. Wilber, *Riza Shah Pahlavi*, p. 73. In fact, Reza Shah's foreign policy was more sophisticated than his speech indicated. He organized that policy along traditional Iranian lines. Saikal, for example, argues that Reza Shah's

power was shattered by the Allied occupation of Iran in 1941. His actions show that one of Reza Shah's main goals was to reduce Iran's dependence on Britain and the USSR, and hence insulate it from their rivalry. For this, he considered it necessary to achieve two major objectives: the consolidation of internal politics under the authority of the central government and, therefore, the initiation of certain essential socio-economic reforms in order to create internal stability and unity; and the establishment of a regional friendship and close relationship with a third power to secure a counterbalance against Anglo-Soviet intervention and rivalry. (Saikal, *Rise and Fall of the Shah*, p. 21)

The Shah's ambivalence about his own father and over the overthrow of his father by the British and the Soviets is indicated by the tone of his words in his autobiography, *Mission for My Country* (New York: McGraw-Hill, 1961). See pp. 66–75.

16. Pahlavi, *Answer to History*, pp. 51–52. Just how the Shah learned of the details of this trip is unclear since he was a student at Le Rosey at the time.

17. Ibid., p. 95.

18. Ibid., pp. 89–90.

19. Ibid., p. 141.

20. Ibid., p. 102.

21. The ambassador continued:

In view of Soviet Ambassador's strenuous efforts to prevent sending Tehran forces to Azerbaijan and his frequent declarations to Shah and Qavam that USSR would not remain indifferent if those forces proceeded, people are asking why the Soviets failed to give Azerbaijan any significant material assistance. Practically every Iranian, including notably the Shah, thinks answer lies primarily in fact that Soviets were finally convinced that US was not bluffing and would support any United Nations member threatened by aggression.

Embassy has received numerous visits from Iranian Cabinet officers and officials, including Minister of War, Minister of Finance, Governor of National Bank, President of last Majles, et cetera, to express appreciation to America for "giving back Azerbaijan to Iran.["]

At an informal social gathering last night Shah made a fulsome and even embarrassing tribute to our help. Azerbaijan was referred to by others present as the "Stalingrad of the Western democracies" and the "Turn of the tides against Soviet aggression throughout the world." I emphasized the Iranians themselves had regained Azerbaijan and that any credit for enabling Iran to accomplish this free from outside interference, was due to existence of a world organization which could mobilize opinion against such interference.

"The Ambassador in Iran (Allen) to the Secretary of State, Tehran, December 17, 1946," in Yonah Alexander and Allan Nanes, eds., *The United States and Iran: A Documentary History* (Frederick, Md.: University Publications of America, 1980), p. 188.

22. Dwight D. Eisenhower, *Mandate For Change, 1953–1956: The White House Years* (Garden City, NY: Doubleday, 1963), p. 165.

23. Saikal, *Rise and Fall of the Shah*, p. 46.

24. For a critical study of U.S. military assistance to Iran, see Thomas M. Ricks, "U.S. Military Missions to Iran, 1943–1978: The Political Economy of Military Assistance," *Iranian Studies* 12 (Summer–Autumn 1979): 163–93.

25. Saikal, *Rise and Fall of the Shah*, p. 57. Saikal continues:

Iran's socio-economic development and foreign policy objectives became closely tied to the interests of the capitalist world. This confirmed the country's formal opposition to communism, at both national and regional/international levels, at the cost of its relationship, with the Soviet Union—which, had it been improved, could have been used to some extent by Tehran as an effective lever to counter its dependence on the United States. In its relationship with Tehran, Washington acted as a "Patron power" in upholding and securing the Shah's regime and influencing the direction and substance of its policies in line with Western regional and international interests. . . . In order to justify and enforce this transformation, the Shah noted as early as December 1954 that "the potentialities of friendly and close relations between the people of Iran and the United States are immense. There is a deep and fundamental identity of national interests, which overshadows everything else. We both believe that the individual is the central figure in society, and that freedom is the supreme blessing. . . . Iran has a great deal in common, in convictions, with the Western world regarding freedom and democracy. The way of life of the Western world fits in with our scheme of Islamic values." (Pp. 57–58)

Saikal's quotation of the Shah is taken from the *New York Times*, December 15, 1954. That the Shah would argue, at least in the newspaper of record in the United States, that the values of his own society, especially the Islamic values of his society, were fundamentally consonant with the values of the West is a typical instance of the way the Shah played to the United States. It was from that kind of appeal that many in Iran came to loathe the Shah.

26. E. A. Bayne, *Persian Kingship in Transition: Conversations with a Monarch Whose Office Is Traditional and Whose Goal Is Modernization* (New York: American Universities Field Staff, 1968), p. 108.

27. Henry Kissinger, *White House Years* (Boston: Little, Brown, 1979), p. 1261.

28. John W. Bowling, "The Current Internal Political Situation in Iran: A Report by the Deputy Director of the Office of Greek, Turkish, and Iranian Affairs, United States Department of State to the President. February 11, 1961," in Alexander and Nanes, *United States and Iran*, p. 318.

29. David E. Lilienthal, *The Journals of David E. Lilienthal: The Harvest Years, 1959–1963* (New York: Harper and Row, 1971), pp. 257–58. Lilienthal reported that in an audience with the Shah in November 1961, he reassured the Shah that "these expressions about 'revolution' did not mean in America what they might mean when used in Iran" (p. 266).

30. Michael Ledeen and William Lewis, *Debacle: American Failure in Iran* (New York: Alfred A. Knopf, 1981), p. 43.

31. "His Imperial Majesty Interview with *Kayhan*," *Kayhan International*, September 17, 1977, p. 6.

32. Ledeen and Lewis, *Debacle*, pp. 57–58.

33. Farhad Kazemi, *Poverty and Revolution in Iran* (New York: New York University Press, 1980), p. 124.

34. Hugh Knatchbull-Hugesson, *A Diplomat in Peace and War* (London, 1949), p. 80, as found in Wilber, *Riza Shah Pahlavi*, p. 159, n. 6.

35. Interview with Farah Pahlavi, November 28, 1978. In her "autobiography," the Shahbanou put it slightly differently:

It was not really until 1973, thanks to what is usually known as the "oil boom," that Iran really attained her rightful place on the world scene. For us, the consequences of this event were extraordinarily far reaching: a successful end to the long struggle to defend the interests of the country and of the Iranian people and the realization of all the dreams cherished since the moment oil was nationalized.

Farah Shabanou Pahlavi, *My Thousand and One Days: An Autobiography*, trans. Felice Harcourt (London: W. H. Allen, 1978), p. 98.

36. As recounted in Mohamed Heikal, *The Return of the Ayatollah: The Iranian Revolution from Mossadeq to Khomeini* (London: André Deutsch, 1981), pp. 96–97.

37. An interview with Mohammad Reza Shah Pahlavi in *Der Spiegel*, reprinted in the *Washington Post*, February 3, 1974, pp. c1, c5.

38. See Marvin Zonis, *The Political Elite of Iran* (Princeton: Princeton University Press, 1971), p. 182.

39. Statistics on foreign tourism are taken from Kayhan Research Associates, *Iran Yearbook, 1977* (Tehran: Kayhan Newspaper Group, 1977), pp. 413–26A.

40. Foreign tourists were overwhelmingly from noncommunist countries. In 1975, approximately the same number of tourists visited Iran from the USSR as from Israel, slightly more than 4,000.

41. It is impossible to establish with precision, but Iranians appear to be far more committed to foreign travel than other peoples of the Middle East, perhaps with the exception of the Israelis. One possible explanation is the ease with which Iranians have dealt with and absorbed foreign cultures in the past. Another possibility is the importance of pilgrimage in Shi'ite Islam, which specifies, in addition to the desired once-in-a-lifetime pilgrimage to Mecca, more frequent pilgrimages to Shi'ite holy places: Najaf and Karbala in Iraq, if political conditions permit, but to

more local shrines in Iran as well, such as the tomb of the eighth Imam, Reza, in Mashhad.

42. See James Bill, *The Eagle and the Lion: The Tragedy of American-Iranian Relations* (New Haven: Yale University Press, 1988), p. 211.

43. See Ashraf Pahlavi, *Faces in a Mirror: Memoirs from Exile* (Englewood Cliffs, N.J.: Prentice-Hall, 1980), p. 48.

44. Elliot Roosevelt, ed., *F.D.R.: His Personal Letters* (New York: Duell, Sloan, and Pierce, 1947), pp. 1538–39.

45. Pahlavi, *Mission for My Country,* p. 88.

46. Ibid., p. 89.

47. Eisenhower, *Mandate for Change,* p. 165. (Of course, there is no evidence that the Shah was ever anything but "fully aware of the importance of the army to the security of his country." The Shah and his father before him were always prepared to reduce the funds available to any governmental ministry in the interest of increasing funds for the military.)

Elsewhere in his writings, President Eisenhower offered a commentary on the character of the Shah: "The position of the Shah in this British-Iranian imbroglio of the early 1950s was ambiguous, for he too was a nationalist but he was very young and thus far in his career had not shown himself to be a strong character." Robert H. Ferrell, ed., *The Eisenhower Diaries* (New York: Norton, 1981), p. 192.

At about this same period, Eisenhower's vice president, Richard M. Nixon, made a trip to Iran where he personally met the Shah. Subsequently, he too offered an evaluation of the character of the Shah: "The Shah was only 34. He had just come through a harrowing experience—an attempt had been made to assassinate him. In our meeting, he let Zahedi do most of the talking, but he listened intently and asked penetrating questions. I sensed an inner strength in him, and felt that in the years ahead he would become a strong leader." Richard M. Nixon, *The Memoirs of Richard Nixon* (New York: Grosset and Dunlap, 1978), p. 133.

There is no reference in any literature that the Shah was subject to an assassination attempt in the period immediately before the visit of the vice president. But other than that inaccuracy, it is telling that both the president and vice president sensed the Shah's diffidence, insecurity, and uncertainty but, nonetheless, insisted that his character would change over time. Eventually, they were sure, he would become a strong leader, not merely because his country would be economically enriched or because the Iranian state would be strengthened, but because, clearly, the character of the Shah would become stronger. Senior American officials, then, like most everyone else, are students of personality, however implicit or unformed their theories of character formation and change may be.

48. Heikal, *Return of the Ayatollah,* p. 165.

49. Iran, "Report, Embassy of Tehran to Department of State, by Ambassador, Subject: Military Procurement, August 16, 1966," in *Asnad-i lanah-i jasus-i amrika* (Documents from the nest of spies) (Tehran: Danishjuyan-i musalman-i payrwi-i khatt-i imam, 1980), 8: 10.

50. Given the ambivalence to the West, it would be sufficient on cultural grounds alone for the Shah to have felt diminished by his association with the West. This feeling was, in fact, typical for many Iranians. Indeed, Ayatollah Kho-

meini and his entourage believed that one of the principal purposes of the Iranian Revolution was to eliminate this humiliation. Thus, for example, Pres. Abol Hassan Bani Sadr told revolutionary air force personnel in 1981: "We value our martyrs . . . because their efforts destroyed centuries of humiliation that our country and people suffered under the hegemonists" (Foreign Broadcast Information Service, SAS-81-028, February 11, 1981, p. 1). The difference between Bani Sadr's— and Khomeini's—positions and the one argued here is that the Iranian revolutionaries are convinced only of the reality of the humiliating actions of the West toward Iran. Here in the text, the sense of humiliation experienced by the Shah and the Iranian people is stressed. The implicit point is that the actions of the West were less significant than the fact that Iranians perceived the consequences of those actions as humiliation.

51. Personal interview, March 23, 1982.

52. One of the insults experienced by the Shah was the ever-diminishing price of oil. The Shah railed at the fact that a barrel of oil brought $2.18 in 1947, $2.04 in 1957, but only $1.78 by 1969. Worse, by 1971 the value of the dollar, by which oil prices were calculated, had fallen to $.73 from its 1957 level. The Shah had these statistics at his fingertips (personal interview, June 16, 1971). Or see, for example, his interview with *Time,* April 1, 1974, in which he compains about the decreasing price of oil in the face of massive increases in the price of goods imported from the West.

53. John Stempel, *Inside the Iranian Revolution* (Bloomington: Indiana University Press, 1981), p. 310.

54. Personal interview, December 14, 1981.

55. Personal interview, March 23, 1982. The same informant offered another example of the Shah's belief that the United States called the shots in Iran. The Shah told this high Iranian official, "We cannot push the mullahs [the Iranian clerics] very hard because I have been told that they are bulwarks against communism." The Iranian official assumed that it went without saying that the Shah had been told this by the United States.

56. Personal interview, March 23, 1982.

57. Ibid.

58. See, for example, Jimmy Carter, *Keeping Faith: Memoirs of a President* (New York: Bantam Book, 1982); Zbigniew Brzezinski, *Power and Principle: Memoirs of a National Security Adviser, 1977–1981* (New York: Farrar, Straus, and Giroux 1983); Gen. Robert E. Huyser, *Mission to Tehran* (New York: Harper and Row, 1986); Hamilton Jordan, *Crisis: The Last Year of the Carter Presidency* (New York: G. P. Putnam's Sons, 1982); Jody Powell, *The Other Side of the Story* (New York: William Morrow, 1984); Gary Sick, *All Fall Down: America's Tragic Encounter with Iran* (New York: Random House, 1985); Stempel, *Inside the Iranian Revolution;* Sullivan, *Mission to Iran;* Cyrus Vance, *Hard Choices: Critical Years in American Foreign Policy* (New York: Simon and Schuster, 1983).

59. See Pahlavi, *Answer to History;* Ashraf Pahlavi, *Faces in a Mirror;* Darioush Homayoun and A. Qarabaghi, *Hagayiq dar barih-'i ingilab-i Iran* (Facts about the Iranian Revolution) (Paris: Suhayl Publications, 1984); Parviz Radji, *In the Service of the Peacock Throne: The Diaries of the Shah's Last Ambassador to London* (London:

Hamish Hamilton, 1983); Gholam R. Afkhami, *The Iranian Revolution: Thanatos on a National Scale* (Washington, D.C.: Middle East Institute, 1985); Fereydoun Hoveyda, *The Fall of the Shah* (New York: Wyndham Books, 1979).

60. Anthony Parsons, *The Pride and the Fall: Iran, 1974–1979* (London: Jonathan Cape, 1984).

61. Shahrough Akhavi, *Religion and Politics in Contemporary Iran* (Albany: State University of New York Press, 1980); Said Amir Arjomand, *The Turban for the Crown: The Islamic Revolution in Iran* (New York: Oxford University Press, 1988); Bill, *Eagle and the Lion;* Robin W. Carlsen, *The Imam and His Islamic Revolution* (Victoria, B.C.: Snow Man Press, 1982); Günther Estes and Jochem Langdau, eds., *Iran in der Kris* (Bonn: Verlag Neue Gesellschaft, 1980); Michael M. J. Fischer, *Iran: From Religious Dispute to Revolution* (Cambridge: Harvard University Press, 1980); William H. Forbis, *The Fall of The Peacock Throne: The Story of Iran* (New York: Harper and Row, 1980); Jerrold Green, *Revolution in Iran: The Politics of Countermobilization* (New York: Praeger, 1982); Mohamed Heikal, *Iran, The Untold Story: An Insider's Account of America's Iranian Adventure and Its Consequences for the Future* (New York: Pantheon Books, 1982); Ahmad Jabbari and Robert Olsen, eds., *Iran: Essays on a Revolution in the Making* (Lexington, Ky.: Mazda Publishers, 1981); Nikki Keddie and Eric Hoogland, eds., *The Iranian Revolution and the Islamic Republic* (Washington, D.C.: Middle East Institute, 1982); Ledeen and Lewis, *Debacle;* Mohsen M. Milani, *The Making of Iran's Islamic Revolution* (Boulder, Colo.: Westview Press, 1988); Barry Rubin, *Paved with Good Intentions: The American Experience and Iran* (New York: Oxford University Press, 1980); William Shawcross, *The Shaw's Last Ride: The Fate of an Ally* (New York: Simon and Schuster, 1988); Marvin Zonis, "Iran: A Theory of Revolution from Accounts of the Revolution," *World Politics* 35, no. 4 (July 1983): 586–630.

62. Martin Ennals, "Interview," *The Observer,* May 26, 1974, pp. 1ff.

63. See Marvin Zonis, "Human Rights and American Foreign Policy: The Case of Iran," in Tom J. Farer, ed., *Toward a Humanitarian Diplomacy: A Primer for Policy* (New York: New York University Press, 1980).

64. U.S. Congress, Senate, Committee on Foreign Relations, Subcommittee on Foreign Assistance, *U.S. Military Sales to Iran,* 94th Cong., 2d sess., July 1976, p. viii. The report continues:

Government to Government military sales to Iran increased over seven fold from $524 million in Fiscal Year (FY) 1972 to $3.91 billion in FY 1974, slackening off a little to $2.6 billion in FY 1975. The preliminary sales estimate for FY 1976 is $1.3 billion. Sales in the 1972–1976 period totalled $10.4 billion. The number of official and private American citizens in Iran, a large percentage of whom are involved in military programs, has also increased from approximately 15,000–16,000 in 1972 to 24,000 in 1976; it could easily reach 50,000–60,000 or higher by 1980.

It appears that the total number of U.S. citizens in Iran reached the level predicted for 1980 by the time of the Iranian Revolution.

65. Interview with Mohammad Reza Shah Pahlavi on "60 Minutes," CBS, October 24, 1976.

66. Parsons, *Pride and the Fall,* p. 47.

67. Actually, the Shah's oil decision of December 1976 was to be an important

source of the subsequent disaster which befell him, for international oil buyers moved from Iranian oil to less expensive Saudi oil wherever possible. Iranian oil revenues began to fall precipitously as a result. The wealth flowing to Iran decreased from its peak in 1974 and continued to decline in 1977, increasing the financial difficulties of the government and reducing the financial well-being of the Iranian people.

68. Iran, "Sullivan, Tehran to Department of State, Subject: Ambassador's Goals in Iran, Airgram, January 11, 1978," in *Asnad-i lanah-i jasus-i amrika* (Documents from the nest of spies), 12: 16.

69. Parsons, *Pride and the Fall,* p. 48.

70. This conclusion has also been drawn by John Stempel, author of the most sensitive published work on the Iranian Revolution. "On the surface," he said, "Washington's new human rights and arms sales policies were not significant, but the psychological impact on the monarch's self-confidence and his image of modernization was considerable" (Stempel, *Inside the Iranian Revolution,* p. 84).

71. Sick, *All Fall Down,* p. 22.

72. Radji, *In the Service of the Peacock Throne,* p. 81. The diary is a significant document for many reasons. For one thing, it indicates the extent to which Iranian officials paid attention to American politics and tried to read their implications for Iran.

73. Ibid., p. 89.

74. Sullivan adds with considerable dismay, "The debate that followed became a classic example of the role that the Congress had grown to play in the latter stages of the Indochina conflict, when its committees attempted to make decisions that had normally been reserved to the executive branch" (Sullivan, *Mission to Iran,* p. 115).

75. Ibid., p. 117. The report of this conversation is another instance of the phenomenon referred to above in the description of the meeting between the ambassador and the Shah on the subject of changes in the Shah's economic development plans. That phenomenon is the ambassador's predilection for focusing on the substantive issue at hand, rather than on the political and psychological issues which influence, if not determine, the orientation to the substantive issues. Here the ambassador lets the Shah "get it all out of his system," as if a single conversation would do that—without asking what the Shah was trying to get out of his system, why it was "in his system" and why he was trying to "get it out of his system," and what difference those factors would make to the future politics of Iran and the future relationship between Iran and the United States.

76. Iran, "Telegram from American Embassy to Secretary of State, from Lambrakis, Miklos, April 5, 1977," in *Asnadi-i lanah-i jasus-i amrika* (Documents from the nest of spies), 8: 168–69.

77. The changes are described in testimony by Charles W. Naas, Director, Office of Iranian Affairs, U.S. Department of State, before the Subcommittee on International Organizations of the House International Relations Committee on October 26, 1977, and reproduced in Alexander and Nanes, *United States and Iran,* p. 452.

78. This is a point made brilliantly by Stempel, *Inside the Iranian Revolution,* p.

82. Stempel also understood the consequences of liberalization in the absence of institutions to deal with the emerging demands. His argument is largely subscribed to in this work.

Liberalizing . . . began before any kind of institutional base was in place to shape the emerging participatory politics without either losing command of the changes or destroying the effectiveness of the participation scheme by retightening controls, or both.

Undoubtedly, the Shah thought problems could be worked out on an ad hoc basis, with the army as the final guardian of the system. When the pressure of the potential revolution increased, however, the monarch vacillated, acting much less strongly than his own political skills would have suggested. Certainly, there were extenuating circumstances, but one very important reason for this was the fact that the Shah had no real idea of how the various elements . . . would evolve into a more constitutional government. He never offered a real rationale for what he was trying to do. (P. 38)

79. *Kayhan Weekly International Edition,* vol. 10, no. 483, August 13, 1977, p. 2.

80. Sullivan, *Mission to Iran,* p. 128.

81. Sick, *All Fall Down,* p. 28.

82. Vance, *Hard Choices,* p. 323.

83. Sullivan, *Mission to Iran,* p. 131.

84. Ashraf Pahlavi, *Faces in a Mirror,* p. 198. I have taken this quote from Ashraf Pahlavi, fully cognizant that she is not a completely reliable witness to her brother's loss of his throne. In the very next sentences after this quote, she adds:

As he spoke, I looked at his pale face. I thought his smile artificial, his eyes icy—and I hoped I could trust him. But within that very year he sent several emissaries to Khomeini, sent a military envoy to Teheran to undermine my brother's army, and hedged his own political bets by abandoning my brother as Iran moved towards revolution. (Pp. 198–99)

To the best of my knowledge, none of these three accusations is valid.

85. Ayataollah Shariat'madari, the senior cleric in Qum and among the least political of the religious leaders, was moved to issue an open letter to "believers" after the shootings. He condemned the police action as "un-Islamic and inhumane" and declared that "we are certain that Almighty God shall in time punish those responsible." He also called for the government to respect Iran's constitution. Thus did the killings initiate the revolution and spark a call for enforcement of the constitution which limited the powers of the Shah. Many months were to pass before the revolutionaries called for his ouster. *Washington Post,* January 20, 1978, p. A31.

Chapter 9. Resolution and Collapse

1. William H. Sullivan, *Mission to Iran* (New York: W. W. Norton, 1981), p. 16.

2. Personal interview, April 5, 1982.

3. Airgram, January 11, 1978, as quoted in Iran, *Asnad-i lanah-i jasus-i amrika* (Documents from the nest of spies) (Tehran: Danishjuyan-i musalman-i payrwi-i khatt-i imam, 1980), 9:107.

4. John Stempel, *Inside the Iranian Revolution* (Bloomington: Indiana University Press, 1981), p. 305.

5. Pierre Salinger claims that Brzezinski succeeded in convincing President Carter of the wisdom of this policy in the waning days of the Shah's rule. The two men took a fishing trip together after the Guadeloupe Summit Meeting, in the first days of January 1979. On that trip, Brzezinski argued that "if the United States 'abandoned' the Shah, its word would be discounted in the future by every country in the world." Salinger, *America Held Hostage: The Secret Negotiations* (Garden City, N.Y.: Doubleday, 1981), p. 33.

6. Personal interview, January 5, 1982.

7. Sullivan, *Mission to Iran,* p. 193. The Shah was apparently correct about Zahedi being out of touch with Iranian reality. He had been out of the country for seven years.

8. U.S. Congress, House of Representatives, Committee on Foreign Affairs, Subcommittee on Europe and the Middle East, *General Huyser's Mission to Iran, January 1979,* 97th Cong., 1st sess., June 9, 1981, p. 7.

9. Gen. Robert E. Huyser, *Mission to Tehran* (New York: Harper and Row, 1986), p. 23.

10. Michael Ledeen and William Lewis, *Debacle: American Failure in Iran* (New York: Alfred A. Knopf, 1981), pp. 78–79.

11. Stempel, *Inside the Iranian Revolution,* p. 86.

12. Mohammad Reza Shah Pahlavi, *Answer to History* (New York: Stein and Day, 1980), p. 161. The Shah makes clear that the British were in on this as well. He concludes his observations about the U.S. ambassador's lack of instructions with the observation that "Sullivan, and the British Ambassador, Anthony Parsons, who so often accompanied him, met in a stiff diplomatic ballet that ended without resolution of any kind" (p. 161).

13. Personal interview, April 5, 1982.

14. Eqbal Ahmad, "The Iranian Revolution: A Landmark for the Future," *Race and Class* 21 (1979): 6.

15. James A. Bill, *The Eagle and the Lion: The Tragedy of American-Iranian Relations* (New Haven: Yale University Press, 1988), p. 236, n. 38.

16. Said Amir Arjomand, *The Turban for the Crown: The Islamic Revolution in Iran* (New York: Oxford University Press, 1988), p. 190.

17. Ervand Abrahamian, *Middle East Research and Information Project,* July–August 1978, p. 3. This lower casualty figure is consonant with recent Iranian history, insofar as that is relevant to the 1978 Revolution. Internal Iranian political processes in this century were characterized by relatively few casualties. The British estimated that not more than sixty or seventy persons were killed or wounded in the 1905 Revolution and subsequent internal turmoil. United Kingdom, Foreign Office, "Sir G. Barclay to Sir Edward Grey, Gulhak [Tehran], July 15, 1909," no. 123 in *Further Correspondence Respecting the Affairs of Persia,* Persia no. 2, 1909, vol. 5, no. 70, p. 60.

18. Stempel, *Inside the Iranian Revolution,* p. 117.

19. Personal interview, June 13, 1979.

20. Gary Sick, *All Fall Down: America's Tragic Encounter with Iran* (New York: Random House, 1985), p. 51.

21. Ledeen and Lewis, *Debacle,* p. 147.

22. Sullivan, *Mission to Iran*, pp. 167–68. In his memoirs, the Shah explained that same thought in a more eloquent fashion.

A sovereign may not save his throne by shedding his countrymen's blood . . . a sovereign is not a dictator. He cannot break the alliance that exits between him and his people. . . . A sovereign is given a crown and must bequeath it to the next generation. This was my intention. . . . The instructions I gave were always the same: "Do the impossible to avoid bloodshed." (Pahlavi, *Answer to History*, p. 168)

The Shah would repeat this same message from exile again and again. He told David Frost in Panama,

"A throne could not be based on the not too solid foundation of blood. From the beginning I begged my people, 'Don't kill, don't kill, don't kill'" (David Frost, *20/20*, ABC Television, January 17, 1980).

23. Sullivan, *Mission to Iran*, p. 212.

24. Salinger, *America Held Hostage*, p. 71.

25. Interview with Shah of Iran, *Washington Post*, May 27, 1980, p. 9-12-1.

26. Personal interview, April 5, 1982.

27. Arjomand, *Turban for the Crown*, p. 116.

28. Zbigniew Brzezinski, *Power and Principle: Memoirs of the National Security Adviser, 1977–1981* (New York: Farrar, Straus, and Giroux, 1983), p. 365.

29. Pahlavi, *Answer to History*, p. 165.

30. Ibid.

31. Ibid., p. 165.

32. Ibid., p. 27.

33. Both Brzezinski and Vance refer to the telephone conversation in their memoirs, but in a fashion which characteristically maintains their obvious disagreements on the correct pursuit of U.S. policy toward Iran. Brzezinski remembers, "The conversation took place between 7:56 and 8:02 a.m., on Sunday, September 10. The President said he was calling to express his friendship for the Shah and his concern about events. He wished the Shah the best in resolving these problems and in being successful in his efforts to implement reforms" (Brzezinski, *Power and Principle*, p. 361). Secretary of State Vance remembers the telephone call differently: "Carter telephoned the Shah on September 10 . . . to reaffirm our support and to find out how the Shah planned to restore order" (Cyrus Vance, *Hard Choices: Critical Years in America's Foreign Policy* [New York: Simon and Schuster, 1983], p. 326).

In effect, Brzezinski suggests here that the president took a Vance line toward the Shah, while Vance suggests the converse.

34. Sullivan, *Mission to Iran*, p. 163. The ambassador added that as a result of the September 10 telephone conversation, the Shah believed "he had obviously at last captured the President's attention, and after that occasion I never again heard complaints from him that the CIA or the United States government was in any way seeking to undermine his authority."

35. Personal interview January 5, 1982.

36. Sullivan, *Mission to Iran*, p. 156.

37. Ibid., pp. 156–57. The quotation indicates how the Shah had managed, over the years, to dismiss the role of Prime Minister Mossadegh in the oil nationalization.

38. Dr. Harry Trosman of the University of Chicago's Department of Psychiatry has suggested that the Shah's fear of a USSR-U.K.-U.S. conspiracy against him was an indication of his identification with his father, since the USSR and the United Kingdom had invaded Iran in 1941 and ousted Reza Shah. Interestingly, at about the same time the Shah's mother had ousted Reza Shah from her bedroom. The Shah, then, may have had psychic cause to fear his own wife.

39. Sick, *All Fall Down*, p. 51.

40. Ibid.

41. Anthony Parsons, *The Pride and the Fall: Iran 1974–1979* (London: Jonathan Cape, 1984), p. 71.

42. Ibid., p. 75.

43. Ibid., p. 71.

44. Ibid., p. 74.

45. Arjomand, *Turban for the Crown*, p. 117.

46. Ibid., p. 116. Arjomand adds, "Putting the receiver down, he turned to General Toufanian who was present and said, 'Now what more will the Americans say?'" The Shah's aside is noteworthy on two counts. It suggests how his concern for the opinions of the U.S. government appeared always central to him. It also suggests he expected American criticism for his new "get tough" policy.

47. Ibid., p. 115.

This is not the position taken by another acute scholar of Iran, James Bill. Bills states,

> Although a number of influential observers have argued repeatedly that the shah lost his will to control the situation and that he did so partly because he was ill and partly because he was concerned about pressure from President Carter, this position fails the test of historical fact. Surrounded by trusted hard-line military advisers such as Gens. Manuchehr Khosrowdad, Hassan Toufanian, Gholam Ali Oveissi, and Amir Hussein Rabi'i and SAVAK chief Nassiri, the shah initially gave orders à la 1963 to put down the disturbances with as much force as necessary. The bloodshed in Tabriz in February, Tehran in September, Isfahan in December, and Mashhad in early January 1979 bears witness to his forceful policy. During these bloody months, troops fired on funeral processions, invaded homes of religious leaders, and, on a number of occasions, fired directly into unarmed crowds of men, women and children. (Bill, *Eagle and the Lion*, p. 236)

But despite Bill's correct observations of the military's occasional use of deadly force, the orders from the Shah were always for restraint. On January 11, 1979, General Huyser, joined by Ambassador Sullivan, met with the Shah for what was to be their only meeting in the nearly four weeks the general spent in Tehran. General Huyser reports that he could not fathom how the regime had lost control between August 1978 and January 1979.

> I reminded the Shah of what he had said to me the previous summer: that I shouldn't be too concerned, and should continue to work on his Command Control programme, because

even if he fell from grace with our President, he did not intend to lose control. I asked him: "What happened Your Majesty?"

He turned and stared at Ambassador Sullivan for what seemed like a very long time. He scratched the back of his head several times and then started to change the subject. I said: "Your Majesty, I asked a question." He turned and looked at me with a very solid stare through his thick glasses. Finally, he said, "Well, you really don't understand." He went on, "Your Commander-in-Chief is different from me. I am a Commander-in-Chief who is actually in uniform, and as such, for me to give the orders that would have been necessary . . ." He stopped and asked: "Could you, as Commander-in-Chief, give the orders to kill your own people?" I said: "Your Majesty, we are not talking about me, we are talking about you." At this point he changed the subject, and I never received an answer. (Huyser, *Mission to Tehran*, p. 78)

48. Cynthia Helms, *An Ambassador's Wife in Iran* (New York: Dodd, Mead, 1981), p. 205.

49. Parsons, *Pride and the Fall*, p. 75.

50. Sullivan, *Mission to Iran*, p. 212.

51. For the general's own account, see Huyser, *Mission to Tehran*. Virtually every account of the revolution includes an analysis of the general's stay in Tehran; many of the accounts are at great variance from that of the general.

52. Arjomand, *Turban for the Crown*, p. 123. It has been suggested by certain court insiders that even at that hopelessly late date, the Shah believed the United States would intervene, à la 1953, to return him to the throne. Since he had no hand in the 1953 coup or countercoup, he need not have played a role in the 1979 version.

53. Personal interview, March 13, 1981.

54. *New York Times*, December 8, 1978, p. A14.

55. Pahlavi, *Answer to History*, pp. 161–62.

Chapter 10. Lessons for U.S. Foreign Policy

1. Zbigniew Brzezinski, *Power and Principle: Memoirs of the National Security Adviser, 1977–1981* (New York: Farrar, Straus, and Giroux, 1983), p. 371.

2. Ibid., p. 372.

3. Ibid., pp. 382–83.

4. Gary Sick, *All Fall Down: America's Tragic Encounter with Iran* (New York: Random House, 1985), p. 87.

5. Ibid., pp. 102–4.

6. Brzezinski, *Power and Principle*, p. 360.

7. U.S. Congress, House of Representatives, Select Committee on Intelligence, Subcommittee on Evaluation, *Iran: Evaluation of U.S. Intelligence Performance Prior to November 1978*, 96th Cong., 1st sess., p. 2.

8. Even given the limited bureaucratic attention to analysis, there are personnel problems within those bureaucracies based on budgetary constraints. During the entire year of the revolution, for example, INR did not have "a full time Iran analyst." Ibid., p. 6.

9. This was not a new position for the Shah. In John W. Bowling's 1961 State Department Report, he urged that the United States "be on the alert

for the rise of competent and creative alternative leadership, in or out of the military, which might allow a reconsideration of our alternatives [to the Shah]." Bowling continued, "This latter, along with the requirement that we do what we can to support moderate as against extremist opposition leadership, is very difficult in Iran, since Embassy contacts with important Mossadeqist opposition elements have met and will continue to meet with violent objections from the Shah. . . . all such contacts run the risk of alienating the Shah." John W. Bowling, "The Current International Political Situation in Iran," in Yonah Alexander and Allan Nanes, eds., *The United States and Iran: A Documentary History* (Frederick, Md.: University Publications of America, 1980), p. 321.

10. Miller was not, however, to disappear from the Iranian scene completely. When Jimmy Carter was searching for emissaries to despatch to Iran to discuss the seizure of the U.S. diplomats in November 1979, someone remembered Bill Miller and his credentials with the secular opposition. Miller was asked to undertake the trip to Tehran for discussions with the Iranians. He gladly consented. But neither he nor Ramsey Clark with whom he was to travel ever reached Tehran. After they arrived in Turkey, the new government which had replaced Prime Minister Bazargan refused to receive them.

11. Given the inclusion of the Iranian armed forces within the repertoire of acceptable targets of U.S. intelligence, it is difficult to understand why certain kinds of data were never collected by the United States. Apparently no systematic information was collected on the thousands of junior Iranian military personnel who underwent training programs at military bases within the United States. As a consequence, the United States has no data on the military officers now running the Iranian armed forces. The senior officer corps was largely known to American military personnel in Iran. But following the success of the revolution, many of the senior officers were retired (or executed). The junior officer corps was rapidly promoted, especially after the initiation of the war with Iraq. The result is that many of the officers of the armed forces of the Islamic Republic were trained in the United States but are largely unknown to the U.S. government.

12. U.S. Congress, *Evaluation of U.S. Intelligence*, p. 3.

13. John Stempel, *Inside the Iranian Revolution* (Bloomington: Indiana University Press, 1981), p. 307.

14. Ibid.

15. Ibid.

16. Ibid., p. 6.

17. U.S. Congress, *Evaluation of U.S. Intelligence*, p. 3.

18. Ibid.

19. No one tells this part of the Iran-U.S. story better than James A. Bill, *The Eagle and the Lion: The Tragedy of American-Iranian Relations* (New Haven: Yale University Press, 1988).

20. See, for example, Vamik D. Volkan and Norman Itzkowitz, *The Immortal Ataturk: A Psychobiography* (Chicago: University of Chicago Press, 1984), p. 200, for the striking psychological attraction of Ataturk for the Turkish people.

For group psychological processes, see Group for the Advancement of Psychiatry, *Psychiatry and Public Affairs* (Chicago: Aldine Publishing, 1966); and for sociohistorical processes treated psychoanalytically, see Fred Weinstein and Gerald M. Platt, *The Wish to Be Free: Society, Psyche, and Value Change* (Los Angeles: University of California Press, 1969).

Bibliography

Abrahamian, Ervand. *Iran between Two Revolutions*. Princeton: Princeton University Press, 1982.

Acheson, Dean. *Present at the Creation: My Years in the State Department*. New York: Norton, 1969.

Afkhami, Gholam R. *The Iranian Revolution: Thanatos on a National Scale*. Washington, D.C.: Middle East Institute, 1985.

Ahmad, Eqbal. "The Iranian Revolution: A Landmark for the Future." *Race and Class* 21 (1979): 3–13.

Ahmad, Jalal Al-e. *Plagued by the West (Gharbzadegi)*. Trans. Paul Sprachman. Delmar, N.Y.: Caravan Books, 1982.

———. *The School Principal*. Trans. John K. Newton. Minneapolis: Bibliotheca Islamica, 1974.

Akhavi, Shahrough. *Religion and Politics in Contemporary Iran*. Albany: State University of New York Press, 1980.

Alexander, Yonah, and Allan Nanes, eds. *The United States and Iran: A Documentary History*. Frederick, Md.: University Publications of America, 1980.

Ambrose, Stephen E. *Ike's Spies: Eisenhower and the Espionage Establishment*. Garden City, N.Y.: Doubleday, 1981.

Amuzegar, Jahangir. *Technical Assistance in Theory and Practice: The Case of Iran*. New York: Praeger, 1966.

Ansari, Mostafa. "The History of Khuzistan, 1878–1925: A Study in Provincial Autonomy." Ph.D. dissertation, Department of History, University of Chicago, 1974.

Arfa, Gen. Hassan. *Under Five Shahs*. New York: William Morrow, 1965.

Arjomand, Said Amir. *The Turban for the Crown: The Islamic Revolution in Iran*. New York: Oxford University Press, 1988.

Attar, Farid ud-din. *The Conference of the Birds (Mantiq ut-tair)*. Trans. Garcin de Tassy and C. S. Nott. London: Routledge and Kegan Paul, 1954.

Avery, Peter. *Modern Iran*. London: Ernest Benn, Ltd., 1965.

Azhary, M. S. El, ed. *The Iran-Iraq War*. New York: St. Martin's Press, 1984.

Baraheni, Reza. *The Crowned Cannibals: Writings on Repression in Iran*. New York: Vintage Books, 1977.

Bayne, E. A. *Persian Kingship in Transition: Conversations with a Monarch Whose Office Is Traditional and Whose Goal is Modernization.* New York: American Universities Field Staff, 1968.

Beeman, William O. *Language, Status, and Power in Iran.* Bloomington: Indiana University Press, 1986.

Bill, James A. *The Eagle and the Lion: The Tragedy of American-Iranian Relations.* New Haven: Yale University Press, 1988.

Bill, James A., and William Roger Louis, eds. *Musaddiq, Iranian Nationalism, and Oil.* Austin: University of Texas Press, 1988.

Breo, Dennis L. "Shah's Physician Relates Story of Intrigue, Duplicity." *American Medical News,* August 7, 1981, pp. 3–22.

Brown, L. Carl, and Norman Itzkowitz, eds. *Psychological Dimensions of Near Eastern Studies.* Princeton: Darwin Press, 1977.

Browne, E. G. *A Literary History of Persia.* Vol. 4. Cambridge: Cambridge University Press, 1953.

———. *The Persian Revolution of 1905–1909.* London: Cambridge University Press, 1910.

Brzezinski, Zbigniew. *Power and Principle: Memoirs of a National Security Adviser, 1977–1981.* New York: Farrar, Straus, and Giroux, 1983.

Bursten, Ben. "Some Narcissistic Personality Types." *International Journal of Psychoanalysis* 54 (1973): 287–300.

Burton, Arthur, and Robert E. Harris, eds. *Clinical Studies of Personality.* Vol. 2 of *Case Histories in Clinical and Abnormal Psychology.* New York: Harper Brothers, 1955.

Carlsen, Robin W. *The Imam and His Islamic Revolution.* Victoria, B.C.: Snow Man Press, 1982.

Carter, Jimmy. *Keeping Faith: Memoirs of a President.* New York: Bantam Books, 1982.

Chaliand, Gerard, ed. *People without a Country: The Kurds and Kurdistan.* London: Zed Press, 1980.

Chubak, Sadeq. "The Baboon Whose Buffoon Was Dead." Trans. Peter Avery. In *New World Writing,* 11:14–24. New York: Mentor Books, 1957.

Cottam, Richard. *Nationalism in Iran.* Pittsburgh: University of Pittsburgh Press, 1979.

Crapanzano, Vincent. *The Hamadsha: A Study in Moroccan Ethnopsychiatry.* Berkeley: University of California Press, 1973.

Curzon, Lord George N. *Persia and the Persian Question.* Vol. 1. London: Longmans, Green, 1892.

de Villiers, Gerard. *The Imperial Shah: An Informal Biography.* Trans. June P. Wilson and Walter B. Michaels. Boston: Little, Brown, 1976.

Edgcumbe, Rose, and Marion Burgner. "The Phallic Narcissistic Phase: A Differentiation between Preoedipal and Oedipal Aspects of Phallic Development." In *The Psychoanalytic Study of the Child,* 30:16–80. New Haven: Yale University Press, 1975.

Eisenhower, Dwight D. *Mandate for Change, 1953–1956: The White House Years.* Garden City, N.Y.: Doubleday, 1963.

Esfandiary, Fereidoun. *The Day of Sacrifice*. London: Heinemann, 1960.

Estes, Gunther, and Jochem Langdau, eds. *Iran in der Kris*. Bonn: Verlag Neue Gesellschaft, 1980.

Faramarzi, Borozou. *Towards the Great Civilization*. Tehran: Ministry of Information, 1974.

Farer, Tom J., ed. *Toward a Humanitarian Diplomacy: A Primer for Policy*. New York: New York University Press, 1980.

Farhang, Mansour. "Resisting the Pharaohs: Ali Shariati on Oppression." *Race and Class*, 21 (1979):31–40.

Federn, P. "On Dreams of Flying," in R. Fliess, ed., *The Psychoanalytic Reader*. London: Hogarth Press, 1950.

Ferrell, Robert H., ed. *The Eisenhower Diaries*. New York: Norton, 1981.

Fischer, Michael M. J. *Iran: From Religious Dispute to Revolution*. Cambridge: Harvard University Press, 1980.

Forbes-Leith, F. A. C. *Checkmate: Fighting Tradition in Central Persia*. London: George C. Harrap and Co., n.d.

Forbis, William H. *The Fall of the Peacock Throne: The Story of Iran*. New York: Harper and Row, 1980.

Forman, Max. "The Narcissistic Personality Disorder as a Regression to a Pre-Oedipal Phase of Phallic Narcissism." Paper presented to the Chicago Psychoanalytic Society, June 23, 1981.

Freud, Sigmund. *The Interpretation of Dreams*. Trans. and ed. James Strachey. In *The Standard Edition of the Complete Psychological Works of Sigmund Freud*, vols. 4 and 5. London: Hogarth Press, 1953. Originally published in 1900.

———. *Leonardo da Vinci: A Study in Psychosexuality*. New York: Random House, 1947.

———. *Moses and Monotheism*. New York: Alfred A. Knopf, 1939.

Freud, Sigmund, and William C. Bullitt. *Thomas Woodrow Wilson: A Psychological Study*. Boston: Houghton Mifflin, 1967.

Frye, Richard N. *The Heritage of Persia*. London: Weidenfeld and Nicolson, 1962.

Gasiorowski, Mark. "The 1953 Coup d'Etat in Iran." *International Journal of Middle East Studies* 19 (August 1987):261–86.

Gedo, Mary. *Picasso: Art as Autobiography*. Chicago: University of Chicago Press, 1980.

George Alexander L., and Juliette L. George. *Woodrow Wilson and Colonel House: A Personality Study*. New York: Dover, 1956.

Ghani, Qassem. *Az yaddoshthaye Qassem-e Ghani*. Vol. 9. London: Routledge and Kegan Paul, 1982.

Good, Byron. "The Heart of What's the Matter: The Structure of Medical Discourse in a Provincial Iranian Town." Ph.D. dissertation, Department of Anthropology, University of Chicago, 1977.

Goodell, Grace E. "How the Shah De-Stabilized Himself." *Policy Review* 16 (Spring 1981):55–72.

Graham, Robert. *Iran: The Illusion of Power*. New York: St. Martin's Press, 1978.

Green, Jerrold. *Revolution in Iran: The Politics of Countermobilization*. New York: Praeger, 1982.

Green, William, and John Fricker. *The Air Forces of the World: Their History, Development and Present Strength*. London: Macdonald, 1958.

Group for the Advancement of Psychiatry. *Psychiatry and Public Affairs*. Chicago: Aldine Publishing, 1966.

———. Committee on International Relations. *Self-Involvement in the Middle East Conflict*. New York, 1978.

Halliday, Fred. *Iran: Dictatorship and Development*. New York: Penguin Books, 1979.

Heikal, Mohamed Hassanein. *Iran, The Untold Story: An Insider's Account of America's Iranian Adventure and Its Consequences for the Future*. New York: Pantheon Books, 1982.

———. *The Return of the Ayatollah: The Iranian Revolution from Mossadeq to Khomeini*. London: André Deutsch, 1981.

Helms, Cynthia. *An Ambassador's Wife in Iran*. New York: Dodd, Mead, 1981.

Homayoun, Darioush, and A. Qarabaghi. *Hagayig dar barih-'i ingilab-i Iran* (Facts about the Iranian Revolution). Paris: Suhayl Publications, 1984.

Hoveyda, Fereydoun. *The Fall of the Shah*. New York: Wyndham Books, 1979.

Huyser, Gen. Robert E. *Mission to Tehran*. New York: Harper and Row, 1986.

Iran. *Asnad-i lanah-i jasus-i amrika* (Documents from the nest of spies). Tehran: Danishjuyan-i musalman-i payrwi-i khatt-i imam, 1980.

———. *Proceedings of the Mossadegh-Riahi Trial*. No. 257. November 23, 1963. Tehran: Echo of Iran Publications.

———. *Proceedings of the Trial of Dr. Mohammad Mossadeq*. No. 257. November 29, 1953. Tehran: Echo of Iran Publications.

———. Ministry of Power. *A Survey of Nuclear Power Stations in Iran*. Tehran, 1969.

Jabbari, Ahmad, and Robert Olsen, eds. *Iran: Essays on a Revolution in the Making*. Lexington, Ky.: Mazda Publishers, 1981.

Jordan, Hamilton. *Crisis: The Last Year of the Carter Presidency*. New York: G. P. Putnam's Sons, 1982.

Kakar, Sudhir. *The Inner World: A Psychoanalytic Study of Childhood and Society in India*. Dehli: Oxford University Press, 1981.

Karanjia, Rustom Khurshedji. *The Mind of a Monarch*. London: Allen and Unwin, 1977.

Katouzian, Homa. *The Political Economy of Modern Iran: Despotism and Pseudo-Modernism, 1926–1979*. New York: New York University Press, 1981.

Kavka, Jerome. "The Analysis of Phallic Narcissism." *International Review of Psycho-Analysis* no. 3 (1976): 277–282.

Kayhan Research Associates. "Tourism." In *Iran Yearbook, 1977,* 413–26A. Tehran: Kayhan Newspaper Group, 1977.

Kazemi, Farhad. *Poverty and Revolution in Iran*. New York: New York University Press, 1980.

Kazemzadeh, Firuz. "The Origin and Early Development of the Persian Cossack Brigade." *American Slavic and East European Review* 15 (1956): 351–63.

Keddie, Nikki, and Eric Hoogland, eds. *The Iranian Revolution and the Islamic Republic*. Washington, D.C.: Middle East Institute, 1982.

Khalilzad, Zalmay. "The Political, Economic, and Military Implications of Nuclear

Electricity: The Case of the Northern Tier." Ph.D. dissertation, Department of Political Science, University of Chicago, 1978.

Kissinger, Henry. *White House Years*. Boston: Little, Brown, 1979.

———. *Years of Upheaval*. Boston: Little, Brown, 1982.

Kohut, Heinz. *The Analysis of the Self: A Systematic Approach to the Psychoanalytic Treatment of Narcissistic Personality Disorders*. New York: International Universities Press, 1971.

———. "Forms and Transformations of Narcissism." *Journal of the American Psychoanalytic Association* 14:243–72.

———. *How Does Analysis Cure?* Ed. Arnold Goldberg with the collaboration of Paul Stepansky. Chicago: University of Chicago Press, 1984.

Kramer, Martin, ed. *Shi'ism, Resistance, and Revolution*. Boulder, Colo.: Westview Press, 1987.

Kwitny, Jonathan. *Endless Enemies: The Making of an Unfriendly World*. New York: Congden and Weed, 1984.

Laing, Margaret. *The Shah*. London: Sidgwick and Jackson, 1977.

Ledeen, Michael, and William Lewis. *Debacle: American Failure in Iran*. New York: Alfred A. Knopf, 1981.

Lenczowski, George. *The Middle East in World Affairs*. Ithaca, N.Y.: Cornell University Press, 1952.

———. *Russia and the West in Iran, 1918–1947: A Study in Big Power Rivalry*. Ithaca, N.Y.: Cornell University Press, 1949.

———, ed. *Iran under the Pahlavis*. Stanford: Hoover Institution Press, 1978.

LeVine, Robert A. *Culture, Behavior, and Personality*. Chicago: Aldine Press, 1973.

Lilienthal, David. *The Journals of David E. Lilienthal: The Harvest Years, 1959–1963*. New York: Harper and Row, 1971.

McFadden, Robert D., Joseph B. Treaster, and Maurice Carroll. *No Hiding Place*. New York: New York Times Book Co., 1981.

Makki, Hossein. *Tarikh-i bist salah-yi Iran* (The twenty-year history of Iran). Tehran: n.p., 1944–45.

Mazlish, Bruce. *In Search of Nixon: A Psychohistorical Inquiry*. Baltimore: Penguin Books, 1973.

———, ed. *Psychoanalysis and History*. Englewood Cliffs, N.J.: Prentice Hall, 1963.

Meissner, W. W. "Narcissistic Personalities and Borderline Conditions: A Differential Diagnosis." In Chicago Institute for Psychoanalysis, *The Annual of Psychoanalysis*, 7:171–201. New York: International Universities Press, 1979.

Milani, Mohsen M. *The Making of Iran's Islamic Revolution*. Boulder, Colo.: Westview Press, 1988.

Miller, Hunter, ed. *Treaties and Other International Acts of the United States of America*. Washington, D.C.: U.S. Government Printing Office, 1942.

Millspaugh, Arthur C. *Americans in Persia*. Washington, D.C.: Brookings Institution, 1946.

Mosca, Gaetano. *The Ruling Class*. Trans. Hannah D. Kahn. New York: McGraw-Hill, 1939.

Newman, Maj. E. W. Pilson. *The Middle East*. London: Geoffrey Bles, 1926.

Nicolson, Sir Harold C. *Curzon: The Last Phase, 1919–1925*. Boston: Houghton Mifflin, 1934.

———. *Friday Mornings, 1941–1944*. Boston: Houghton Mifflin, 1944.

Nixon, Richard M. *The Memoirs of Richard Nixon*. New York: Grosset and Dunlap, 1978.

Novar, Leon. "The Great Powers and Iran, 1914–1921." Ph.D. dissertation, Committee on International Relations, University of Chicago, 1958.

Pahlavi, Princess Ashraf. *Faces in a Mirror: Memoirs from Exile*. Englewood Cliffs, N.J.: Prentice-Hall, 1980.

Pahlavi, Farah Shahbanou. *My Thousand and One Days: An Autobiography*. Trans. Felice Harcourt. London: W. H. Allen, 1978.

Pahlavi, Mohammad Reza Shah. *Answer to History*. New York: Stein and Day, 1980.

———. *Enghelab-e sefid* (The White Revolution). Tehran: Kayhan Press, 1966.

———. *Mission for My Country*. New York: McGraw-Hill, 1961.

———. *The Shah's Story*. Trans. from the French by Teresa Waugh. London: Michael Joseph, Ltd., 1980.

———. *The White Revolution*. Tehran: Ministry of the Imperial Court, 1966; Tehran: Imperial Pahlavi Library, 1967.

Pahlavi, Queen Soraya. *Khaterat-e Soraya* (Remembrances of Soraya). Trans. from the German by Musa Mahjidi. Tehran: Saadat Printing House, n.d.

Parsons, Anthony. *The Pride and the Fall: Iran 1974–1979*. London: Jonathan Cape, 1984.

Post, Jerrold. "Narcissism and the Charismatic Leader-Follower Relationship." *Political Psychology* 7, no. 4 (1986):675–88.

Pourkian, Mohammad. *Ernest Perron, Showhar-e Shahanshah-e Iran*. Berlin: Druck und Werbung Ghamgosar, 1979.

Powell, Jody. *The Other Side of the Story*. New York: William Morrow, 1984.

Radji, Parviz. *In the Service of the Peacock Throne: The Diaries of the Shah's Last Ambassador to London*. London: Hamish Hamilton, 1983.

Ramazani, Ruhollah K. *Iran's Foreign Policy, 1941–1973: A Study of Foreign Policy in Modernizing Nations*. Charlottesville: University Press of Virginia, 1975.

Reich, W. *Character-Analysis*. New York: Noonday Press, 1933.

Ricks, Thomas M. "U.S. Military Missions to Iran, 1943–1978: The Political Economy of Military Assistance." *Iranian Studies* 12 (Summer-Autumn 1979): 163–93.

Roosevelt, Elliot, ed. *F.D.R.: His Personal Letters*. New York: Duell, Sloan, and Pierce, 1947.

Roosevelt, Kermit. *Countercoup: The Struggle for the Control of Iran*. New York: McGraw-Hill, 1979.

Rotblat, Howard. "Stability and Change in a Provincial Iranian Bazaar." Ph.D. dissertation, Department of Sociology, University of Chicago, 1972.

Rubin, Barry. *Paved with Good Intentions: The American Experience and Iran*. New York: Oxford University Press, 1980.

Runyan, William. *Life Histories and Psychobiography: Explorations in Theory and Method*. New York: Oxford University Press, 1982.

Sahebjam, Freidoune. *Mohamad Reza Pahlavi, Shah d'Iran: Sa vie trente ans de règne (1941–1971)*. Paris: Editions Berger-Levrault, 1971.

Saikal, Amin. *The Rise and Fall of the Shah*. Princeton: Princeton University Press, 1980.

Salinger, Pierre. *America Held Hostage: The Secret Negotiations*. Garden City, N.Y.: Doubleday, 1981.

Sanghvi, Ramesh. *Aryamehr, the Shah of Iran*. London: Transorient Press, 1968.

Shadman, S. F. "A Review of Anglo-Persian Relations, 1798–1815." In *Proceedings of the Iran Society*, vol. 2, pt. 5. London: Iran Society, 1944.

Shari'ati, A. *'Ali tanha ast* ('Ali is alone). N.p., 1978.

———. *Shi'i: Yek hizb-i tamam* (Shi'is: A complete party). N.p., 1976.

Shawcross, William. *The Shah's Last Ride: The Fate of an Ally*. New York: Simon and Schuster, 1988.

Sheean, Vincent. *The New Persia*. New York: Century Co., 1927.

Shuster, W. Morgan. *The Strangling of Persia: A Record of European Diplomacy and Oriental Intrigue*. New York: Century, 1912.

Siassi, Ali Akbar. *La Perse au contact de l'occident*. Paris: Ernest Leroux, 1931.

Sick, Gary. *All Fall Down: America's Tragic Encounter with Iran*. New York: Random House, 1985.

Skrine, Sir Clarmont. *World War in Iran*. London: Constable, 1962.

Stempel, John. *Inside the Iranian Revolution*. Bloomington: Indiana University Press, 1981.

Stuart, Donald. *The Struggle for Persia*. London: Methuen, 1902.

Sullivan, William H. *Mission to Iran*. New York: W. W. Norton, 1981.

Sykes, Christopher. *Wassmuss: The German Lawrence*. London: Longmans, Green, 1936.

Sykes, Sir Percy Molesworth. *A History of Persia*. Vol. 2. London: Macmillan, 1921.

Tahir-Kheli, Shirin, and Shaheen Ayubi, eds. *The Iran-Iraq War: New Weapons, Old Conflicts*. New York: Praeger, 1983.

Tully, Andrew. *CIA: The Inside Story*. New York: William Morrow, 1962.

United Kingdom. Foreign Office. *Correspondence Respecting the Affairs of Persia*. Persian no. 1. 1909.

———. *Documents on British Foreign Policy, 1919–1939*. Eds. E. L. Woodward and Rohan Butler. London: Her Majesty's Stationery Office, 1952.

———. *Further Correspondence Respecting the Affairs of Persia*. Persian No. 2. 1909.

U.S. Congress. House. Committee on Foreign Affairs. Subcommittee on Europe and the Middle East. *General Huyser's Mission to Iran, January 1979*. 97th Cong., 1st sess. June 9, 1981.

———. Subcommittees on International Organizations and Movements and on the Near East and South Asia. *U.S. Foreign Policy and the Export of Nuclear Technology to the Middle East*. 93rd Cong., 2d sess.

———. Committee on International Relations. *Reports on Human Rights and U.S. Policy: Argentina, Haiti, Indonesia, Iran, Peru, and the Philippines*. 94th Cong., 2d sess. Submitted by the Department of State. December 31, 1976.

———. Select Committee on Intelligence. Subcommittee on Evaluation. *Iran:*

Evaluation of U.S. Intelligence Performance Prior to November 1978. 96th Cong., 1st sess.

―――. Senate. *United States and Operations in Iran.* 87th Cong., 1st sess., August 11, 1961.

―――. Committee on Foreign Relations. Subcommittee on Foreign Assistance. *U.S. Military Sales to Iran.* 94th Cong., 2d sess., July 1976.

Vance, Cyrus. *Hard Choices: Critical Years in America's Foreign Policy.* New York: Simon and Schuster, 1983.

Volkan, Vamik D., and Norman Itzkowitz. *The Immortal Ataturk: A Psychobiography.* Chicago: University of Chicago Press, 1984.

Weinberger, Jerome L., and James Muller. "The American Icarus Revisited: Phallic Narcissism and Boredom." *International Journal of Psycho-Analysis* 55 (1975).

Weinstein, Fred, and Gerald M. Platt. *The Wish to Be Free: Society, Psyche, and Value Change.* Berkeley: University of California Press, 1969.

Wilber, Donald N. *Iran, Past and Present.* Princeton: Princeton University Press, 1958.

―――. *Riza Shah Pahlavi: The Resurrection and Reconstruction of Iran, 1878–1944.* Hicksville, N.Y.: Exposition Press, 1975.

Williams, Alan. *A Bullet for the Shah.* New York: Popular Library, 1976.

Witte, Count. *The Memoirs of Count Witte.* Trans. Abraham Yarmolinsky. Garden City, N.Y.: Doubleday, Page, 1921.

Zabih, Sepehr. *The Mossadegh Era: Roots of the Iranian Revolution.* Chicago: Lake View Press, 1982.

Zonis, Marvin. "Iran: A Theory of Revolution from Accounts of the Revolution." *World Politics* 35, no. 4 (July 1983):586–630.

―――. *The Political Elite of Iran.* Princeton: Princeton University Press, 1971.

Zonis, Marvin, and Daniel Brumberg. "Interpreting Islam: Human Rights in the Islamic Republic of Iran." In *Proceedings of the Symposium on the Relationship of the Baha'i Faith and Islam.* Forthcoming.

―――. *Khomeini, the Islamic Republic of Iran, and the Arab World.* Cambridge: Harvard University Middle East Papers, 1987.

Index

Acheson, Dean, 194

Admiration of Iranian people for Shah: as
one pillar of Shah's psychic strength, 20,
21, 60, 240, 255; four sets of acts
undermining, 84

Afghani, Seyyed Jamal ed din al-, 174

Afghanistan: as buffer between U.K. and
Russia, 175–76

Agnew, Spiro, 67

"Agreement between the governments of
Great Britain and Persia" (1919), 181;
failure to be submitted to Majles, 182–
83; struck down by Moshir ud-Dowleh,
184

Ahmad, Jalal al-e, 204, 205

Air Force, Iranian: assessment by U.S.
Senate of, 7–8; under Reza Khan, 8

Ala, Hussein, 194

Alam, Assadolah, 5, 95, 125, 131–37;
appointed prime minister, 197; forms
Mardom party, 217

Alborz College, 190–91

Algiers accords, 70

Ali, Shah Ahmad: installed as Shah, 177;
loses control, 186

Ali, Shah Muhammad: attempted
assassination of, 176–77; ousted by
constitutionalists, 177

Allies: concern over Iranian-German
relations, 26; U.K. and Soviet Union
oust Reza Khan, 26, 53, 189

Ambivalence, Iranian: toward foreign
powers, 170–71; broken by Khomeini,
170

Amini, Ali: Shah's mistrust of, 295 n.35;

appointed prime minister, 95, 108;
initiates reforms, 94, 197; restores
authority of Pahlavi system, 147–48;
resigns, 135; appointed ambassador to
U.S., 195; dismissal of, 195–96

Amnesty International: Shah's human
rights record assessed by, 231

Amouzegar, Jamshid: appointed prime
minister, 125, 237; withdraws from day-
to-day duties, 91–92

Anglo-Iranian Oil Company, 104, 188, 217

Anglo-Russian Convention (1907), 174–
75, 176, 186

Ansary, Hushang: role in Antiprofiteering
Campaign, 77; as chair of Iran-U.S.
Commission, 79; advocates Iranian self-
criticism, 111

Anti-Land Speculation Bill, 74

Antiprofiteering Campaign, 76–79;
discrimination against Baha'is and Jews
during, 77–78; as precursor of
Revolution, 78

Armao, Robert, 149, 161, 162

Arrogance: Shah's narcissistic, 19, 20, 219,
221

Arsanjani, Hassan, 94, 197

Ascensionism, 15, 16

Atomic Power: in Iran, 79–80

AWACS: Shah's attempts to purchase,
235–36

Azerbaijan, 183, 184; Soviets withdraw
from, 193, 209; Democratic party of, 193

Azhari, Gen. Ghulam Reza, 126, 251

Baghdad Pact, 217

Bakhtiar, Shapour, 1, 58

Bakhtiar, Gen. Teymour: exiled, 152–53; assassinated, 153

Baku: captured by Ottomans, 180; captured by U.K., 180; oil fields of, 184, 188

Baraheni, Reza, 205

Baskerville, Howard C., 190

Bast. See Shrines, Iranian

Bayne, E. A., 52

Bazargan, Mehdi, 2, 163

Behbehani, Seyyed Abdullah, 174

Bernard, Jean, 154

Bill, James: AT&T data collected by, 223; estimate of Revolution-related deaths, 248

Black Friday (September 8, 1978), 131, 248–49, 253–54; Shah's regression and, 254–55

Bolshevik Revolution, 179

Bowling, Kenneth, 197

Brzezinski, Zbigniew, 144; meets with Bazargan, 163; divides U.S. response to Revolution, 244, 264; advocates U.S. loyalty to Shah during Revolution, 244; encourages Shah to halt Revolution, 250, 251–52

Byrd, Sen. Robert C., 250

Calendar: alteration of Iranian, 63, 81–82, 289 n.49

Carter, Jimmy (James Earl): becomes presidential candidate, 230; position on human rights and arms sales, 109, 231; damages Shah's self-esteem, 169–70, 198, 233–35, 257; as threat to Pahlavi system, 231; authorizes weapons sales to Iran, 199; attempts to sell AWACS to Iran, 235–36; receives Shah at White house, 237–38; supports Shah after Black Friday, 253, 254; encourages Shah to avoid using violence to halt Revolution, 249–50

Central-Caspian Dictatorship, 180

Central Treaty Organization (CENTO), 217

Chosroes II, 171

Chubak, Sadeq, 85

Churchill, Winston, 17, 183–84

CIA: barred from collecting intelligence on Iran, 267

Coleman, Morton, 163

Communism, Iranian, 194

Constantinople Agreement (1915, among Russia, Great Britain, and France), 179

Constitutionalists, 174; oust Shah Muhammad Ali, 177

Constitution, Iranian, 174

Cossack Brigade, Persian, 23, 24; ordered to eliminate constitutionalists, 177, 178–79; bombards the Majles, 177

Countercoup (1953 ouster of Mossadegh), 45, 52, 100–104, 128; role of U.S. and U.K. in, 100; U.S. goals for, 194

Cox, Sir Percy, 181

Cult of Mithra, 81

Curzon, Lord, 173–74, 181, 185

"Cynosural narcism," 15, 16

Day of Sacrifice (Esfandiary), 203–4

De Bakey, Michael, 164, 165

"Democrats," Persian, 178

Discrimination, Iranian: against Baha'is and Jews, 78–79

Divine protection: as one pillar of Shah's psychic strength, 21, 60; visions and Shah's, 38–40, 55, 281 n.49; Shah describes his, 150, 152; as factor in ousting Mossadegh, 151

Dowleh, Mashir ud-: installed as prime minister, 184; refuses to submit 1919 Agreement to Majles, 184

Dowleh, Vossugh ud-: kept in power by U.K., 181, 182; ousted, 184

Dulles brothers, 194

Dunsterville, Maj. Gen. L. C., 179–80, 183

Eisenhower, Dwight D., 195; visits Tehran, 214; praises Shah, 215; assesses Shah, 226

Elite, Iranian, 222

Ennals, Martin, 231

Eqbal, Manouchehr: founds Melliyun party, 217

Erdman, Paul, 61

Esfandiary, Fereidoun, 203

Ettala'at, 122; attacks Khomeini, 243

Exhibitionism, 17, 18, 19

Extraterritoriality, Russian, 172

Fahd ibn-Aziz, King, 202

Fallaci, Oriana: interview with Shah concerning women, 34–35; concerning his reforms, 64–65; concerning his divine protection, 150

Family Protection Act, 73

Fardoust, Hussein, 46, 140–43, 295 n.36; linked to Khomeini, 143; fate after the Revolution, 143

Farma, Farman, 173

Farmandehi ("commandership"), 83, 290 n.54

Flandrin, Georges, 154, 161

Flying fantasies: application of psychoanalysis to, 16; Murray's theories on, 14–16; Kohut's theories on, 16, 17, 18; and Shah's psychic strength, 9, 10

Foroughi, Mohammad Ali, 147

Free Officer's Coup, 127

Freud, Sigmund, 14

Gharbzadegi ("Weststruckedness"), 205

Ghavam, Ali, 147

Grandiosity. *See* Psychic strength

"Great Civilization," 62, 285 n.3

Gromyko, Andrei, 193

"Grope", 14, 15, 16

Groseclose, Elgin, 190

Hajir, Abdul Hossein, 123

Hamid, 220–21

Harriman, Averell, 104

Height, Shah's fascination with, 13, 14

Heikal, Mohamed, 196; visits Khomeini in Paris, 263

Helms, Richard, 229

High Council of Women's Organizations, 128

Holmes, Julius, 218

Homayoun, Darioush, 125

Home, Sir Douglas, 160

Hormuz, Strait of: Iran seizes three islands near, 69

Hoveyda, Amir Abbas, 5, 81; increasing powers of, 89; and Princess Ashraf, 130; advocates Iranian self-criticism, 111; dismissed, 237; arrested, 124

Human rights: Shah's record on, 108–10, 111, 112, 113, 231; Carter's position on, 109, 110, 231

Hua, Kuo-feng, 6

Huyser, Gen. Robert: sent to Iran to help Shah during Revolution, 246–47, 263; and Brzezinski, 247

Icarus complex, 14, 15, 16

Idealization, Shah's: of Reza Pahlavi, 36, 42, 45, 55–56, 59; of U.S. and U.S. presidents, 167, 198, 210, 215, 220, 233. *See also* Carter, Jimmy: damages Shah's self-esteem

Identifications, Shah's: with father, 21, 36, 42, 45, 55–56, 59; with masculinity, 21, 40, 59–60; with mother, 21, 33, 36, 37, 40, 55, 56, 60; with femininity, 33, 37, 55, 57, 59, 60; with the Prophet, 101–2; with the U.S. and U.S. presidents, 21, 210; competition among, 40, 54

IGAT-1, 79–80

Imperial Organization for Social Services, 128

Industrialization: Shah's programs of, 207–9

Inferiority: narcissistic sense of, 19

Institutionalization of Pahlavi system: attempts at, 96–97, 107–8, 153, 242; Reza Khan as means of, 42–43, 50–51; oil and, 70–72; male heir and, 93; Shah's mortality and, 157; Shah's son and, 157; psychic strength and, 95

Iran: Constitutional Revolution (1905–7), 174; divided into three spheres of influence, 174–75

Iran-Iraq War, 259

Iran Nuclear Energy Commission, 80

Iranian people: offended by the Shah, 61–62, 66, 67, 68, 72, 73, 76–78; contact with West increases, 222–23, 322 n.41; detest Shah for his ties to U.S., 212, 241–42, 279 n.31, 280 n.41, 321 n.25; feelings toward Americans, 190–91; shame and humiliation of, 220; ambivalence of, 188, 191, 202–6, 212, 221–22; Khomeini breaks ambivalence of, 213; as decisive factor in Revolution, 5–6; effects of Revolution on, 258–60; as immigrants to U.S., 258

Iranian Plan Organization, 194

Iraq: breaks diplomatic relations with Iran, 69; signs treaty with USSR, 69–70; signs Algiers accord with Iran, 70; anger over Iranian borders, 141–42; pro-Axis sympathies, 188

Jam, Fereidoun, 49, 50

Javadi, Haj Seyyed, 111

Jhaleh Massacre. *See* Black Friday

Johnson, Lyndon B.: warns Shah, 196; visits Iran, 214; praises Shah, 215

Jordan, Samuel Martin, 190–91

Kashani, Ayatollah, 123–24

Kayhan International, 63, 237, 286 n.6

Kazemi, Farhad, 220

Kazemzadeh, Firuz, 170

Kean, Benjamin, 161, 162, 164, 165

Kelardasht, 45, 51–52, 102

Kennedy, John F., 107; election of, 195; Shah's hostility toward, 195, 196, 197, 198, 218; applies pressure to Shah, 196; praises Shah, 215; assassination of, 198

Khajenouri, Ibrahim, 110

Khan, Abbas Ali, 27

Khan, Kuchik, 180

Khiaban, Sheikh Muhammad: proclaims Azerbaijan an independent state, 184; feared by Iranians, 185

Khomeini, Ayatollah Rouhollah al-Mousavi al-: in 1963 riots, 134, 136, 152; revolutionary activities, 5; exile of, 219; returns to Iran, 1; establishes new government, 2; as ideal Iranian leader, 84–85; breaks Iranians' ambivalence, 203, 205, 170; fosters sense of Iranian independence, 234; exploits Iranians' ambivalence, 204, 205; provides Iranians with effective selfobjects, 212–13

Khomeini Regime, 258–60

Khrushchev, Prime Minister, 107

Kissinger, Henry: as chair of U.S.-Iran Commission, 79; accompanies Nixon to Iran, 69, 199, 210; assesses Shah, 166, 218; comments upon U.S. arms offer to Iran, 199–200

Kohut, Heinz: on flying fantasies, 161; on narcissistic grandiosity, 16–18; on selfobjects, 115–16

Kurds: U.S. and Israel support for, 70; anger toward Iran, 142

Land reform, 94, 196–97

Leadership: Iranian conception of, 85, 86, 87

League of Nations, 24

LeRosey, 46–48, 116–17

Liakhoff, Colonel, 177

Liberalization: Shah's programs of, 107–14, 236–38, 301 n.77

Lilienthal, David, 198

Majles: bombarded by Cossack Brigade, 177; Shuster and, 178; U.K. and Persian government fail to submit 1919 Agreement to, 182

Mansur, Hassan Ali, 125; assassinated, 152

Mardom party, 217

Marja-e taqlid ("source of imitation"), 65, 86

Melliyun party, 217

Mexico: refuses to allow Shah to re-enter, 164

Miller, William G., 266

Millspaugh, Arthur C., 190

Mirroring. *See* Psychic Strength; Transferences; Admiration of Iranian People for Shah

Mirza, Abbas, 172

Mirza, Prince Akbar, 182

Mirza, Prince Firuz, 182

Mirza, Muhammad, 173

Modernization: of Iran, 62, 64–65, 285 n.3

Mossadegh, Mohammad: appointed prime minister, 124; ousts Ashraf, 124; gains political power and attempts to usurp Shah, 100–106; nationalizes oil industry, 104, 123, 127, 226; criticizes Reza Khan, 187–88; adherents after his ouster, 5, 45, 52. *See also* Countercoup

Muhammad the Prophet, 86, 101

Mujtahids, 86

Muller, James, 15

Murray, Henry, 14–16

Murrow, Edward R., 196

Napoleon I, 122, 171

Narcissism: characteristic of Shah, 19, 20, 23; splitting and projection in Shah's, 58–59. *See also* Psychic strength; Exhibitionism

Narcissistic depletion. *See* Psychic strength: collapse of Shah's

Narcissistic imbalance: of Shah, 53–54. *See also* Psychic strength

Nasser, Gamal Abdul, 127

Nassiri, Gen. Nematollah, 102; arrested, 125

National Front, 226; as political opposition to Shah, 245

National Iranian Oil Company (NIOC), 217

Natural Gas, Iranian, 80

Nazis: invade USSR, 188

Nazism, in Iran, 26

Newspapers, Iranian: as mirrors for Shah's grandiosity, 62–64, 286 n.5; *Ettela'at*, 122, 243

1919 Agreement. *See* "Agreement between the governments of Great Britain and Persia"

1921 Agreement (between Iran and USSR), 185

1963 riots, 134–36, 152

NIOC, 217

Nixon, Richard: offers any U.S. non-nuclear weapons system to Shah, 7, 69–70, 199–200, 210

Nixon Doctrine. *See* Nixon, Richard; Kissinger, Henry

Nuclear energy: Shah's plans to develop, 79–80

Oil, Iranian: U.K. dependence on, 26; industry is nationalized, 104, 123, 226; countercoup and, 194; increased Iranian revenues from, 5, 13, 17, 61, 62, 66, 70–71, 76–77, 219, 232; Shah buys U.S. arms with revenue from, 70–71; NIOC, 217; Western companies drilling, 217; as a weapon against the West, 71, 221, 227–28; White Revolution and, 72; is piped to Azerbaijan, 79–80; monopolizes attention of Pahlavi system, 90–91, 92, 194; plummet in revenues from, 243

OPEC: 1973 price hike by, 71–72, 199, 201–2; role of Libya in, 199; role of Shah in price hike by, 7, 71, 72, 199, 201–2; Shah does not participate in oil embargo of, 228

Operation Ajax. *See* Countercoup

Ottomans: agree to withdraw from Iran, 179; capture Baku, 180

Oveisi, Gen. Gholam Ali, 251

Pahlavi, Ali Reza, 23; exiled, 53

Pahlavi, Princess Ashraf, 4–5, 23, 121–31; marriage, 49–50; visits father in exile, 53; love for Houshang Teymourtash, 119, 121; as selfobject, 121; meets with Stalin, 123; meets with Truman, 123; is exiled by Mossadegh, 124; women's rights and, 128; public policy and, 128; role in the United Nations, 128; attempted assassination of, 129; Hoveyda and, 130; leaves Iran permanently, 130–31

Pahlavi, Empress Farah, 4, 62; marries Shah, 94; gives birth to son, 94; arrogance of, 72–73; bitterness toward Europeans, 221

Pahlavi, Shah Mohammad Reza: mother of, 31, 35; idealization of Reza Khan, 27–28; fear of Reza Khan, 29–31; insulted by Reza Khan, 51–52; adult assessment of Reza Khan, 43–45, 116–17, 278 n.12; childhood illnesses of, 37–38, 55; designated Crown Prince, 25, 36; education, 25, 46–48, 116–17; marriage to Fawzia, 25, 49; becomes Shah, 26, 189; feelings about 1941 invasion, 224; earns pilot's license, 8; reasserts control of Azerbaijan, 9, 193; crashes airplane, 9–10; divorces Fawzia, 11; travels to England, 11; assassination attempt upon, 98, 123, 152; meets Soraya, 12; flees from Mossadegh, 45, 52; creates two-party system, 217–18; birth of son, 94; *Mission for My Country,* 27; addresses Congress, 197–98; negotiates arms purchase with U.S., 226–27; *The White Revolution,* 52; coronation of, 95; as ultimate focus for studying the Revolution, 2, 3, 6; creates single-party system (Rastakhiz party), 75; ambivalence toward U.S., 209–10, 220, 222, 224; forms his emotional and political ties to U.S., 210, 279 n.31, 280 n.41, 321 n.25; becomes dependent upon the U.S., 228–29; invited to Washington, 237; failing mental capacities of, 253–55, 256; avoids using violence to halt Revolution, 249–50, 255–56; blames U.S. for Revolution, 228; medical history of, 96, 153–65; settles in Mexico, 161; receives treatment in New York, 162; expelled from U.S., 163–64; enters Panama, 164; enters Egypt, 164–65

Pahlvai, Reza: personality of, 27, 52–53, 221; Cossack Brigade and, 23; seizes power, 24, 25, 186, 187, 277 n.8; denies role of U.K. in coup, 186–87; leaves his wife and children, 33; removes Mohammad Reza from mother's house, 36–37; instructs Mohammad in kingship, 49–54, 283 n.79; lacks confidence in Mohammad, 51, 52–53; reaction to Perron, 117; attempts to establish Iranian autonomy, 188, 214–15; signs Saadabad Pact, 26; signs Treaty of Trade and Commerce, 26; ousted by British and Soviets, 26, 53, 189

Pahlavi, Princess Shahnaz, 11; marries Ardeshir Zahedi, 135

Pahlavi, Princess Shams, 23; introduces Soraya to the Shah, 12; marriage of, 49–50; exile of, 53; conflict with Ashraf, 123

Pahlavi, Queen Soraya: introduced to Shah, 12; contracts typhoid, 154

Pahlavi System: as reflection of Shah's personality, 61, 62, 72–73, 90; administrative failure of, 90–93; attempts to liberalize, 107–14, 236–38, 301 n.77; as abuser of human rights, 108–10, 111, 112, 113

Panama: allows Shah to enter, 164

Parsons, Sir Anthony, 250, 254

Passivity: Shah's, 19, 20. See also Regression, Shah's

Perron, Ernest, 48, 116–20; as selfobject, 116, 117–18, 120

Persepolis, celebration at, 66–68

Persian Gulf Command, 191

Prospection of falling, 15, 16

Psychic Strength, Shah's: narcissism and, 16, 17, 18, 54; Reza Khan and, 50–52; four pillars of, 20–22, 61, 84; U.S. contributions to Shah's, 167, 169, 198, 210, 215, 220, 233; collapse of, 22, 27, 53, 169–70, 198, 224–27, 233–35, 257; institutionalization and, 95; oil and, 18, 20, 70, 96, 153, 156, 169, 210, 219 (see also under United States; Admiration of Iranian people for Shah; Twinship relations; Divine protection). See also Regression

Psychoanalysis: as a useful tool for foreign policy, 270–71

Psychohistory, 3; of Iranian Revolution, 4; of Shah, 26–27

Qaddhafi, Colonel, 199, 270–71

Qajar coffee, 119

Qarani, General, 195

Qavam, Ahmad, 100, 193

Qavam, Ali, 49, 50

Quran, 86

Radjii, Ambassador, 234–35

Rafsanjani, Hojjat ul-Islam Ali Akbar Hashemi-, 249

Rastakhiz party: 75, 110, 113

Razmara, Ali, 104, 149

Reed, Joseph V., 161

Regression: Shah's, 22, 227, 253, 257; Black Friday and, 255

Reporter, Shahpour, 160

Reverse Leverage, 201, 212, 225, 240; Iranians doubt the power of, 241–42

Revolution, Iranian: alternatives to, 2; guerrilla youth organizations and, 5; roots in Antiprofiteering Campaign, 78; beginnings of, 111–14, 125–26; effects on Shah, 240, 241–43; U.S. divided in response to, 244; estimates on number of deaths during, 248; effects on Iranians, 258–60; U.S. responsibility for, 200, 228, 231, 233–35, 242–53, 257, 269–71

Roosevelt, Franklin Delano: meets Stalin and Churchill in Tehran, 168, 192–93, 213–14; letter to the Shah by, 224–25

Roosevelt, Kermit (Kim): role in ousting Mossadegh, 100–101, 102, 103, 128

Russia: wars with Iran, 172; negotiates its "sphere of influence" within Iran, 175; rivalry with U.K. for dominance in Iran, 173–81; installs Shah Ali Ahmad, 177; demands ouster of Shuster, 178

Russo-Japanese War, 176

Saadabad Pact, 26

Sadat, Anwar, 164–65

Sadat, Jihan, 165

Saikal, Amin, 217

SAVAK (State Security and Intelligence Agency): importance to Shah, 5; role in media, 62; failure to collect intelligence,

90; pervasiveness of, 107; efforts to quell domestic opposition, 240, 293 n.22; becomes source of U.S. intelligence on Iran, 266–67
SAVAMA (National Security and Intelligence Service), 143
Selfobjects, 115–16, 118; U.S. and U.S. presidents as, 167, 170, 198, 210–12, 214, 215, 220, 223. *See also* Twinship relations
Shah. *See* Pahlavi, Shah Mohammad Reza
Shah, Ahmad: British influence upon, 23–24; ouster from power, 25
Shah, Fath Ali, 172
Shari'ati, Ali, 66, 204, 205
Shari'at-madari, Ayatollah Kazem, 5
Shi'at Ali, 85–86
Shi'ite shrines. *See* Shrines, Iranian
Showkat-ul Molk, Amir, 132–33
Shrines, Iranian, 141–42; as site of *bast*, 174; bombed by Russians, 178
Shuster, Morgan, 177–78, 190
Sick, Gary, 238, 249; comments on failing mental capacities of Shah, 254
Skrine, Sir Clarmont, 182
Soviet Union: occupation of Azerbaijan by, 9; reaction to 1919 accord, 24; guarantees Iran self-determination, 181, 183; captures Enzeli and Caspian region, 184; withdrawal from Azerbaijan, 193
Spring-Rice, Sir Cecil, 175
Stalin, Josef, 180
Stempel, John, 206, 244
Sullivan, William H., 146; appointed U.S. ambassador to Iran, 234; Shah's reaction to, 208–9; advises Shah on industrialization, 207–8; describes Shah's dual personality, 40–41; responsibility for Revolution, 209, 245; becomes mistrusted by Department of Defense and Executive branch, 245, 247; receives mixed signals from Washington, 247
Sultan, Zill ul-, 173
Sunnis, 86
Sykes, Sir Percy: on the Treaty of Gulistan, 172; on the succession struggle after Fath Ali Shah's death, 173

Tabataba'i, Seyyed Zia ed Din: role in 1921

coup, 24, 25, 186; ousted from power, 25, 187
Tahmasp II, 171
Taj ol-Moluk, 23, 32; exiled, 53
Taleghani, Ayatollah Mahmoud, 111, 237
Tamaddon-e bozorg, 62
Terrorism: directed against Iran, 153
Teymourtash, Gen. Abdul, 119
Teymourtash, Houshang, 119
Teymourtash, Mehrpour, 46, 119
Torrijos, Gen. Omar: allows Shah to enter Panama, 164
Toufanian, Gen. Hassan, 232
Transferences: mirroring, idealizing, and twinship, 115–16, 198, 210–12, 215, 220, 233. *See also* Twinship relations
Transference objects: U.S. and U.S. presidents as, 167, 170, 198, 210–12, 214, 215, 218, 220, 223–24, 233
Trans-Iranian Railroad, 189, 191
Treaty: of Finkenstein (1807, between Iran and France), 171; of 1809, 1812, and 1814 (between Iran and U.K.), 171; of Gulistan (1813, between Iran and Russia), 172; of Brest-Litovsk (1918), 179; of Turkmanchai (1828, between Iran and Russia), 172; of Friendship and commerce (1856, between Iran and U.S.), 189; Tripartite, of Alliance (1942, among Iran, U.K., and USSR), 191
Tripartite Agreement, 123
Truman, Harry S.: warns USSR to withdraw from Azerbaijan, 193, 209; Shah's perception of, 225
Twelver Shi'ism, 86
Twinship relations, 115; as one pillar of Shah's psychic strength, 20–21, 60; with Ernest Perron, 20, 116–20; with Assadollah Alam, 21, 132–37; with Princess Ashraf, 21, 121–32; with U.S. and U.S. presidents, 167, 198, 210–12, 220, 233; failure of, 116, 137, 240. *See also* Selfobjects

United Nations Security Council: settlement of Azerbaijan dispute by, 9, 193; Mossadegh pleads Iran's case before, 104
United Kingdom: 1919 accords with Iran, 24; role in 1921 coup, 24, 186–88,

United Kingdom (*continued*)
277 n.8; withdraws from Gulf, 69; disputes nationalization of Iranian oil industry, 104; negotiates "sphere of influence" in Iran, 175; rivalry with Russia for dominance in Iran, 173–81; installs Shah Ali Ahmad, 177; withdraws most troops from Iran, 183; implements 1919 Agreement without consent of Majles, 182–83; withdraws entirely from Iran, 185; abandons Suez, 199

United States: role in Iranian affairs before 1970s, 3–4, 190–202; as one pillar of Shah's psychic strength, 21, 60, 166–70, 257; fails as a pillar of Shah's psychic strength, 257; Shah's visits to, 194, 214, 320 n.12; learns of Shah's cancer, 160; Iranians' view of, 190–91; becomes dominant foreign power in Iran, 191–92; greatly increases assistance to Iran, 195, 216, 225; role in Iranian Revolution, 200, 228, 231, 233–35, 242–53, 257, 260–71; fails to collect Iranian intelligence, 229, 265–68; assessment of Shah in 1970s, 240–41; divided in response to Iranian Revolution, 244–45, 264; encourages Shah to avoid using violence to halt Revolution, 249–50; effects of Iranian Revolution on, 260

Valian, Abdul Azim, 92; arrested, 125
Vance, Cyrus, 235; ties to Sullivan, 245, 247; divides U.S. response to Revolution, 244, 264
Velayat-e faqih, 86, 290 n.54
Vietnam War, 199, 201
Visions. *See* Divine Protection

Waldheim, Kurt, 112
Watergate, 229
Weinburger, Jerome, 14
White Revolution, 72, 95, 107–8; effects on women, 34; factors leading to, 218, 219; oil and, 72
Witte, Count, 176
Women: Shah and, 12, 34–35, 55, 58–59, 73, 285 n.108
Women's Organization of Iran, 128

Yamani, Sheikh Ahmad Zaki, 202
Yom Kippur/Ramadan War, 228
Youth, Iranian: guerrilla organizations of, 5; in Pahlavi system, 5; in private sector, 5; in Antiprofiteering Campaign, 77; first protest Pahlavi system, 111; demand the return of Khomeini, 112, 243; capture U.S. embassy in Tehran, 163

Zahedi, Ardeshir, 144–45; efforts to halt Revolution, 246; Shah's distrust of, 306 n.65
Zahedi, Fazlollah, 100, 133–34; meets with Eisenhower, 194–95

DATE DUE

DEMCO 38-296

Please remember that this is a library book, and that it belongs only temporarily to each person who uses it. Be considerate. Do not write in this, or any, library book.